GEOGRAPHIES OF IDENTITY

DISPLACEMENT, DIASPORA, AND GEOGRAPHIES OF IDENTITY

EDITED BY SMADAR LAVIE & TED SWEDENBURG

DUKE UNIVERSITY PRESS DURHAM & LONDON 1996

Printed in the United States of America on acid-free paper ♾
Typeset in Galliard by Tseng Information Systems, Inc.
Library of Congress Cataloging-in-Publication Data
Displacement, diaspora, and geographies of identity /
edited by Smadar Lavie and Ted Swedenburg.
Includes bibliographical references and index.
ISBN 0-8223-1710-9 (cloth : alk. paper). —
ISBN 0-8223-1720-6 (pbk. : alk. paper)
1. Culture—Case studies. 2. Ethnology.
I. Lavie, Smadar. II. Swedenburg, Ted.
GN357.D57 1996 306—dc20 95-39399 CIP

CONTENTS

DISPLACEMENT, DIASPORA, AND GEOGRAPHIES OF IDENTITY

INTRODUCTION: DISPLACEMENT, DIASPORA, AND GEOGRAPHIES OF IDENTITY

SMADAR LAVIE AND TED SWEDENBURG

Old certainties—never certainties for everyone in any case—are increasingly wearing thin. The essays in this volume are concerned with the undoing of one particular old certainty—the notion that there is an immutable link between cultures, peoples, or identities and specific places. The confidence in this permanent join between a particular culture and a stable terrain has served to ground our modern governing concepts of nations and cultures. In these still powerful conceptual frameworks, there is a homology between a culture, a people, or a nation and its particular terrain, and both the culture and its associated place are regarded as homogeneous in relation to other cultures/places (even if those are characterized by internal differentiation). A series of related spatially conceived hierarchical dualities have flowed from and depended upon this mode of conceiving culture and nation. Such binaries radically distinguished as well as hierarchized "home" and "abroad," the West and the Orient, the center and the margin, and the subject of study and the disciplinary object of study.[1]

The discipline of anthropology played a significant role in the extraordinarily complex historical process by which the world came to be seen as divided into the world "Here" (the West) and the world "Out There" (the non-West), as well as in the process whereby the dominant U.S.-Eurocenter (henceforth, for convenience, to be termed simply "Eurocenter") was homogenized. Anthropology's unique function as an official discipline was to differentiate between self and other (Kearney 1991:64). The discipline therefore consistently denied the "coevalness" of the "native," whom it conceptualized as the inhabitant of a space (the "field") that was at once spatially and temporally distant and distinct (see Fabian 1983). Anthropology's own self-conception depended on a notion that "they" were supposed to be "there" and "we" were supposed to be "here"—except, of course, when "we" showed up "there" as ethnographers, tourists, missionaries, or development experts. As those others were subjugated by colonial institutions, anthropology performed the additional mission of humanizing the Others while differentiating them (Kearney 1991:65).

Underpinning all this was the assumption of a homology between the modernist space of the nation-state Here and linear time that progresses toward enlightenment. It was also assumed that if one is positioned in the modernist linear time-space, one is then able to compare and contrast homogeneities of timeless Out There cultures. This relativistic notion of culture, based on the inseparability of identity from place, was not peculiar to anthropology, but reigned throughout the humanities and the social sciences as well as in the political institutions of the nation-state that shape public discourse.

A varied set of forces has increasingly called into question the set of assumptions outlined above. These include national liberation movements in the colonies and neocolonies, the new social movements in the West, and the waves of migration from the former colonized territories. Such movements have called into question the Eurocenter's self-conception as the pinnacle of disinterested, absolute, uncontaminated truth (Balibar 1991:21–22). As the Eurocenter has been relativized, its assumed homogeneity and inherent superiority have been fractured, both by forces from without—Third World nationalisms and revolutionary movements—and by forces within—movements of civil rights, women, immigrants, gays and lesbians. The notion of culture based on the transmutation of race into cultural relativism, a notion that immutably ties a culture to a fixed terrain, has become increasingly problematic. Massive migrations by racialized non-white subjects into the heart of the Eurocenter, for instance, and these subjects' refusal of fixity have called into question the humanistic anthropological notion of culture. The "savage" is no longer out "there" but has invaded the "home" Here and has fissured it in the process. (What would Margaret Mead have made of Samoan gangs in Los Angeles, or of the L.A.-Samoan gangsta rap group the Boo-Yah Tribe, named after the Samoan term "boo-yah!," for a shotgun blast in a drive-by shooting?) The presence of the "savage" not only dehomogenizes and racializes "home's" whiteness, but also reveals its homogeneity to be a mythology sustainable only through control over the global political economy, which is thereby seemingly fissured as well (Appadurai 1990; Harvey 1991). Thus the First World is beginning to be "Third-Worlded" (Koptiuch 1991).

The fact that these categories, these spatial-cultural habits of mind, have seemed so natural and permanent has meant that recent changes in the cultural organization of space have caused rather severe surprise and shock among those accustomed to thinking according to such dualities. The forces of order and discipline have responded with a wide variety of strategies to contain these disruptions and manage the implosion into the Eurocenter. Koptiuch shows in this volume how, in the name of a benevolent and relativist "cultural sensitivity," emergent legal strategies in the United States are unwittingly reincarcerating people of Third World origins within their timeless, unchanging primitive cultures. The repressive style of response is exemplified in the hysterical talk in Western Europe about the "invasion" and the "flood" of immigrants, refugees, Muslims, and foreigners, and the concerted and ever escalating official efforts to stem the flow, to erect the ramparts of "Fortress Europe," to refuse residence to asylum seekers, to deny full citizenship rights to second- and third-generation resident "others," and to marginalize, criminalize, and exploit the labor of undocumented Third World residents.[2]

These "within" and "without" processes have also led to a kind of postmodernist celebration of fragmentation, in which identity becomes an infinite interplay of possibilities and flavors of the month. In this version, culture becomes a multicolored, free-floating mosaic,[3] its pieces constantly in flux, its boundaries infinitely porous. This postmodernist reading of new, emergent time-spaces and the dizzying array of fragments did deconstruct the spatially and temporally conceived hierarchical dualities of center/margin, but at the same time it ignored power relations, the continued hegemony of the center over the margins. Everyone became equally "different," despite specific histories of oppressing or being oppressed. "Gathering and re-using" (Tawadros 1989:121), a historical tactic of the margins, was appropriated by the postmodernist avant-garde from Here, brought to the center, and translated into a tool to construct literary and philosophical theories of otherness. "Gathering and re-using" Here became dehistoricized and thereby universalized.

Many minorities, exiles, diasporas, and other marginal groups, however, understood not only what historical difference is but also how difference operates, and protested this *vive la différence* ability of the privileged "to exoticize themselves selectively" (Lubiano 1991:155–56). The margins appropriated such fragmentation to facilitate their theorization of racialized difference, to "prevent [it] from cohering into essentials" (Lubiano 1991:158). Theorists from the margins also insisted that some po-mo (postmodernist) theorists failed to comprehend that positions and temporalities of the margins were not only multiple and constantly shifting, but also historically anchored to specific locations that allowed for politicized interventions (Alarcón 1990a). While the center appropriated the space that opened up as "post"/modern and "post"/colonial,[4] some at the margins called for the reperiodization of modernity and colonialism (Gilroy 1992a; Tawadros 1989).

In this volume, for instance, Frankenberg and Mani interrupt the emergent universalization of the concept of the postcolonial by proposing a complementary, but more local and situated, concept of "post-civil rights," and by arguing for a rigorously conjuncturalist approach to the "posts." And not everyone, Narayan argues, is moving in the "fast lane of transnational postmodernity." Displacement, we learn, is not experienced in precisely the same way across time and space, and does not unfold in a uniform fashion. Rather, there is a range of positionings of Others in relation to the forces of domination and vis-à-vis other Others. Nor, we learn from several essays, are postmodern critiques of modernity entirely "new," for as Wahneema Lubiano has reminded us, "at least three hundred and fifty years ago some of us [African Americans] were already in training to be both cynical about the Enlightenment and less than optimistic about modernism" (1991:156). Chandler's essay argues that W.E.B. Du Bois, whose theorization of the subject in terms of the spacing of a system of distinctions, was already innovating, early in the twentieth century, in a domain subsequently believed to be the exclusive property of "post" theorists like Foucault, Althusser, and Derrida.

Several essays also show that as the margins resisted and decentered the center, they also transformed themselves. Unable to sustain a seamless, autonomous selfhood of Otherness, some margins embarked on internal critiques of their own homogenization (Rutherford 1990:23–24). The center/margin dichotomy was undermined, and spaces opened up between center and margins. Due to the multiplicity of specific histories of oppression, several processes of center/margin dissolution could occur in various combinations. Some margins moved into the center. Some margins began to communicate with each other, without the center as interlocutor between them (Mohanty 1991:11).

There are, therefore, many geographies of identity. One of the most significant ways in which marginal/minority identity has historically been articulated is through "differential consciousness." (Here we acknowledge our heavy debt to the theoretical work by feminists of color that has enabled these observations.) Chela Sandoval, writing of Third World women in the United States, explains that "differential consciousness" involves weaving "between and among" four types of oppositional consciousness, which she labels "equal rights" consciousness, "revolutionary" consciousness, "supremacist" consciousness, and "separatist" consciousness. Mobilizing this oppositional strategy involves the refusal to privilege any one of these four tactics but, rather, opting situationally for the most effective strategy at any particular moment. This "differential" or "tactical subjectivity" possesses "the capacity of recentering depending upon the kinds of oppression to be confronted" (Sandoval 1991:12–14). Such strategies for coping with and articulating the historicity of experience, working with and against postmodernist fragmentation, fracture not only the binaristic linear narrative of the relation between Third World Self and First World Other, but also the linearity of the Eurocenter's Self and Other as well.

"POST"-FORDISM AND THE NEW WORLD ORDER

We wish here to underscore the importance of this paradigm shift from self/other to historically grounded multiple subject positions. As the articulation of such positions wedges open the self/other time-spaces within and between First and Third Worlds, it deterritorializes the loci and foci of these dualisms. Still, it should be underscored that these dualisms are not finally dislodged. Although racialized and gendered subjects may act out a multiplicity of fractal identities (Gilroy 1990/91), the dominant forces still police the boundaries of binary opposition. Because the Eurocenter constantly consolidates itself against the margins' assaults, it continually redeploys these binarisms in an effort to contain the margins by reasserting their identity in the form of the Other. Hence the continuing purchase of colonialist discourses in U.S. legal practices like "cultural defense" (discussed by Koptiuch in this volume) and during the 1991 Gulf War (discussed by Frankenberg and Mani in this volume).

The Eurocenter most successfully controls the marginal and subaltern through the global political economy. We have been ushered, so we are told, into a new era of capitalist restructuring, known variously as post-Fordism, flexible specialization, and just-in-time production. This new era is characterized by the demise of the old Fordist social pact between capital and labor, in which high productivity was rewarded with relatively high wages—and by a shift to new "information technologies." Some would have us celebrate this internationalization of financial markets and the reorganization of the geographic division of labor and dispersal of production across the globe (see Appadurai 1990; Curry 1993). The Eurocenter's multinational and transnational corporations take advantage of their global organization of production to increase their hegemony, even as they substantially increase their autonomy from local or nation-state control. The economies of both First and Third World nations, therefore, are now increasingly subordinate to global forces. The multinationals and transnationals constantly deploy the threat that they can relocate production elsewhere as a weapon to discipline labor, depress wages, and pressure local governments to ease taxation rates and lift environmental and safety regulations. In the interests of "flexible specialization," the processes of manufacturing and even of final assembly have sprawled across the globe—a production process enhanced by a reduction of institutional barriers to capitalist mobility. Central to this globalization of production processes has been the multinationals' exploitation of female labor. Key industries (electronics and garment) now depend principally on the labor of Third World women, which can be purchased at extremely low rates due to their subordination by patriarchal structures. At the same time, we witness the rapid rise of part-time work, casual work, and homework, under Third World, low-paying sweatshop conditions, performed chiefly by women (especially undocumented migrants) in the First World (Mitter 1986; Ong 1987; Fuentes and Ehrenreich 1983; Chang 1994).

In the arena of the social, meanwhile, the boundaries between Margins and Center are gradually dissolving—but not peacefully. In part, this is because economic and political power is increasingly centralized by the Eurocenter's decentralizing tactics. Power is firmly lodged in the hands of multinational and transnational firms whose permanence has become detached from place, and whose loyalties now appear to transcend community or even national boundaries (Harvey 1991:73; see also Harvey 1989). This mobility of multinational capital is the key force generating the disorienting sense that "the truth of . . . experience no longer coincides with the place in which it takes place" (Jameson 1988:349).

The economic horizon of capitalist internationalization remains crucial to any understanding of how sensibilities of identity are dislocated between cultures and territories. Michael Kearney argues that Western immigration policies, for instance, aim "to separate labor from the jural person within which it is embodied, that is, to disembody the labor from the migrant worker" (1991:58). Capital requires migrant labor but rejects the person and the culture within which abstracted labor is contained. These dynamics are constitutive of struggles of *maquiladora* women of *la frontera* (Alarcón in this volume) and Franco-Maghrebis who desire to change their status from temporary migrant laborers to permanent resident citizens (Gross et al. in this volume). Global capital-labor relations are also intrinsic to an understanding of the forces that have attracted and continue to suck Asian labor into the United States (Koptiuch and Kondo in this volume), and of trends that pull labor out of highland Indian communities and leave behind marooned marginals (Narayan in this volume).

This deceptive decentralization is what makes the wrenching of marginal identity from place such a painful process. The multinationals detach themselves from place without having to rework their Eurocentric identity. The Eurocentered mode of production, however, now forces marginalized workers all over the globe to hybridize their collectivities-that-were, not only with the atomized and hierarchized production relations that they have to enact in order barely to make a living, but also with the deceptively egalitarian hyped-up consumerism that keeps the Eurocenter's wheels turning (Miyoshi 1993).[5]

A form of resistance that engages with this deceptive decentralization only by reacting to the Eurocenter, and narrating itself linearly in imitation of the model provided by the Eurocenter's autonarration, will fail, as it has in the past, when it crashes tangentially against the large political-economic wall surrounding the Eurocenter. Nevertheless, some concepts and tactics of reactive resistance can be effective if combined with new and more creative modes of resistance. Creative resistance could capitalize on the multiplicity of in-between time-spaces situated around the wall's margins by linking them to encircle the wall, and Wall Street, until the latter implodes upon itself.

We now turn to an exploration of these modes of creative resistance, as well as how to combine reactive and creative resistances through the construction of hybridities, on the one hand, and the construction of essences, on the other.

HYBRIDITY—THE EMPIRE STRIKES BACK

When anthropology started coming to terms with the failure of its humanistic project of modernizing the primitive, modernist ethnographic theory focused on suturing together the primitive and the modern. This joining took place in distant time-spaces through a deployment of such concepts as syncretism and bricolage.[6] But at least by the 1980s such suturing became impossible. Alleged primitivities and modernities were colliding at the heart of the Eurocenter. The movements, flows, and interpenetrations of populations and cultural practices frequently produced startling and creative juxtapositions and cultural fusions—phenomena that Guillermo Gómez-Peña, speaking of the Mexican-United States encounter, has dubbed the hi-tech Aztec and the heavy metal Nahuatl (Fusco 1989:68). The products and processes of fusion and intermingling have been endowed with various names: hybridity, syncretism, cyborgs, interculturation, transculturation, and—in Chandler's essay in this volume—intermixture. Recently there has arisen a tendency to turn such vibrant hybrid and syncretic practices into prescriptive models or to celebrate them as the only true forms of resistance and oppositionality. The frequent justification is that they replicate the familiar formal characteristics of the Western po-mo avant-garde—fragmentation, loss of subjecthood, self-conscious significations, and the blending of popular culture with high artistic forms. Such celebrations, usually based on literary or cinematic translations of lived experience and on theoretical readings of such cultural artifacts, tend to dismiss practices that are not so familiarly postmodern and discount them as simply realist, traditionalist, passé, and essentialist. A new hierarchy of cultural practices seems to be in the making, in which the hybrid replaces the old category of the exotic, and the Other, now hybrid, is once again reinscribed by the Eurocenter. Hybridized cultural productions appear outlandish and weirdly funny to white Western consumers due to the persistence of their primordial notions of culture as forever fixed and impermeable. Such visual/textual images, also currently mobilized in many new ethnographies, are elements of a new discourse of the alien. And, at least in the ways they are presented and read, these images frequently deny Third World agencies, impose a passive mimicry (Bhabha 1984, 1985), and continue to lock Third World subjects within the panopticon of the First World (JanMohamed 1985).

But the hybrid articulations that white Western consumers might perceive as bizarre juxtapositions have long been matters of routinized, everyday life for members of the margins in First and Third Worlds (hooks 1990; Lowe 1991; Lubiano 1991). For in some sense, the Third-Worldization and hybridization in the First World merely follow upon the prior flows of population, armies, goods, and capital that in the colonial era mainly moved "outward" from the center to the periphery, where displacements and disruptions of people's relation to place were felt, endured, or suffered most acutely, and which was therefore the chief site of syncretisms and hybridities. It seems that hybridizations and dislocations are simply more noticeable in the center these days, particularly in those global cities (like New York, London, Tokyo, Los Angeles) which Sassen suggests are now as fully internationalized as were the capitals of the colonies in the colonial era (Sassen 1993; see also King 1990). It should be recalled, too, that Asian immigrants (see Kondo and Koptiuch in this volume) started arriving in California in the nineteenth century, that Native Americans have experienced dislodgings, confinements, and erasures/genocide for half a millennium (see Sarris in this volume), and that African Americans have been refining what W.E.B. Du Bois called their "double consciousness" or "second sight" (see Chandler in this volume) for over 350 years. The hybridizations we now encounter therefore are not just the product of entirely "new," epochal postmodern conditions, for as Judith Butler reminds us, "if anything, the postmodern casts doubt upon the possibility of a 'new' that is not in some way already implicated in the 'old'" (Butler 1992:3).

Hybrid products are thus results of a long history of confrontations between unequal cultures and forces, in which the stronger culture struggles to control, remake, or eliminate the subordinate partner. But even in the case of extremely imbalanced encounters, subordinates have frequently managed to divert the cultural elements they were forced to adopt and have rearranged them for their own sly purposes within a new ensemble—as in the case of the Native American Kashaya Pomo of California, who took on the trappings of an austere Victorian Christianity in order to protect themselves against decimation (see Sarris in this volume). Hybrids often subversively appropriate and creolize master codes, decentering, destabilizing, and carnivalizing dominant forms through "strategic inflections" and "reaccentuations" (Mercer 1988:57). Chandler (in this volume) demonstrates how in W.E.B. Du Bois's discourse, the strenuously denied and suppressed fact of racial intermixture questions the very logic of the global colonial system founded on racial distinctions. Other syncretizations and hybridizations undermine the oppositional logic undergirding ideologies of nations and cultures. The performances of Cheb Khaled (Gross et al. in this volume), the East/West Players (Kondo in this volume), Gómez-Peña, Marga Gómez, and the Po-Mo Afro Homos all represent distillations of quotidian experiences that occur when the center penetrates the margins, when the margins relocate into the center and force it to implode, and even when the margins stay put. The essays of this volume bear testimony to the fact that the hybridities which result from the interminglings of disparate cultures necessarily implicate cultures that themselves are already syncretized, always in the process of transformation. All cultures turn out to be, in various ways, hybrid. Intercultural creations and miscegenations expose as a hoax the modernist and colonialist discourse concerning the homogeneity of cultures—a myth sustained chiefly by the center's stranglehold on the global political economy.

Some of the essays in this volume (Narayan, Gross, et al.) emphasize the varieties of hybridity and intermixture, the different degrees and forms of interculturation, and they contend that syncretic practices and identities are differentially gendered, raced, and classed as well.[7] There are no pregiven or singular models of hybridity guaranteed to be "politically correct." These creolized articulations mark an emergent shift from the discourse of ethnicity, an inwardly directed discourse of difference, to the discourse of minority, a discourse of coalition politics confronting dominant state formations (Lloyd 1992). From heterogeneous ethnic enclaves, the minority strikes back, resisting the center's violent attempts to assimilate or destroy it. Such processes occur both in the urbanscapes of the Eurocenter, where formerly colonized subjects have relocated, and in "peripheral" geographical zones (Narayan in this volume; Lavie 1990), where minorities not only reinscribe the Third World nation-state in their fight against becoming homogenized citizenry, but also recast the history of the Eurocenter that "worlded" the Third World (Spivak 1985:143).

Hybridity is a construct with the hegemonic power relation built into its process of constant fragmented articulation. One minority can form alliances with another, based on experiences its heterogeneous membership partially shares, each in his or her fragmented identity, without trying to force all fragments to cohere into a seamless narrative before approaching another minority. Having recognized that insisting on an all-or-nothing approach is counterproductive, many minorities are building bridges among themselves based on such overlapping fragments. They strategically suspend their unshared historical specificities, at a price, for the moment. Yet one of the most intractable problems for creating such bridges is the white Left, which often misperceives the minorities' strategic syncretized articulations as a business-as-usual, avant-garde, free-floating fragmentation (or, in other cases, condemns minorities for their essentialist politics). Although the humanistic enterprise in theory has collapsed in the wake of poststructuralism, in practice the white Left still wants to arrogate to itself the humanistic role of interlocutor between the various minorities (Lavie in this volume; Mohanty 1991:11). Such attempts to act as gatekeeper hinder the free flow of dialogue that minorities need in order to sort out their historical commonalities and differences. The white Left could best contribute to the interminority dialogue by clearing out of the way and becoming an active listener rather than a patronizing participant.[8]

RETHINKING ESSENCE

We live in human bodies that embody difference because they refuse homogenization; because they are not allowed to assimilate into the compulsory heterosexual, legally married, middle-class white citizenry; or because they define the "normal" (white) against which difference is measured. Such differences, however, are culturally learned and then naturalized as essence. We use the word "nature" here in the sense of the Frankfurt School's distinction between "First Nature" and "Second Nature." First Nature is mute, obvious, and meaningless (Lukacs, in Buck-Morss 1989:422)—pure objects outside the realm of production relations. Learning about First Nature depends on the cultural process of knowing. This is complicated by the fact that the learned First Nature is as fragmentary and transitory as history, and history reads as "a process of relentless disintegration" (Benjamin, in Buck-Morss 1989:161, 422). Second Nature is the mimetic conjuring up of First Nature. Second Nature is thus always being produced and reproduced from an oscillatory movement between an imagined pure form of First Nature and its process of construction and decomposition (Taussig 1993).

Second Nature is comprised of reproductions that can be endlessly replicated. But because they seemingly flow from First Nature, they inspire or provoke a search for an uncontaminated and unruptured original. For minorities and Third World nationalities, this involves a process of selecting one of many possible sets of experiences from their history, in order to narrativize it linearly and frame it as the "authentic representation." Tradition, folklore, and realism are authenticity's preferred modes of enframing. Yet we wish to stress not only that such modes conceal hybridity but also that hybridity is equally "authentic."

Here we take "the 'risk' of essence" (Fuss 1989:1; 65). "Essence" has been defined as a natural property of a given entity, a property that through a process of transcendence becomes a pure form (Fuss 1989). Our discussion of Nature, however, highlights it as a dialectical process of historical composition and decay, endlessly reproduced. Since such Nature can be transcended only in thought, even essence is a social construction. Just as we argue that essence is a social construction, so we argue that a social construction can become an essence—become essentialized. Texts produced by classical anthropology provide vivid examples of this process. "Too often, constructivists presume that the category of the social automatically escapes essentialism" (Fuss 1989:6).[9] Anthropologists' model of the eternal tribe—their assumption of the naturalized fixity of social structure and organization Out There, unless impinged upon by forces of modernity from Here—demonstrates that even their construction of the social was often indeed an essence.

Minorities and national liberation movements often appropriate ethnographic essentialism as a strategy to authenticate their own experience, as a form of reactive resistance to the Eurocenter (Spivak, in McRobbie 1985:7). A safe "home," argues Kondo, is "something we cannot not want." If "we" are racial minorities, immigrants, women, refugees, colonized peoples, or queers, we cannot not desire the basic privileges that accompany membership and citizenship in a community, group, or nation. Often such essentialism is a political necessity, particularly when the group or culture is threatened with radical effacement. Hybridity therefore does not appear to be a viable strategy in the struggle for Palestine—a case of an exilic identity demanding to return to its historic territory. Such is also frequently the case for Native Americans fighting ethnocide and forced relocation (Sarris in this volume). Similarly, in Kondo's essay in this volume, we find Asian Americans yearning for authenticity and self-mirroring in theatric representations—in literary terms, a desire for "realism." Narayan advocates—almost apologetically—a kind of salvage ethnography, as a means of saving "old" and marginalized "folk" songs of older women in India from obliteration.

In many contexts, therefore, essentialism is a process of appropriating the concept of fixity of form and content from the Eurocenter for the margin's recovery and healing. This is frequently a guerrilla war or a war of maneuver rather than a war of position, a fight against the Eurocenter's domination, not its hegemony (Gramsci 1971:52–57). Strategic acts of appropriation and re-creation must often be concealed and denied in the heat of such battles even though these non-Eurocentric cultures are themselves essentially hybrid. These processes of essentialization/naturalization (Taussig 1993) are twofold. Minority national movements want to establish their own cohesive grand narratives as countercanons to that of the Eurocenter. They appropriate the ethnographic method of cross-cultural comparison, hoping that the overlap in their essentialized narratives of resistance and oppositionality will be sufficient for these groups, threatened with effacement, to communicate with each other in order to build coalitions.

Taking the risk of essence, constructed, calls for remapping the terrain between identity-as-essence and identity-as-conjuncture. This undertaking allows us to reconceptualize the hybrid space, not devoided of its situated hegemonic construction. Social analysis can thus move beyond the boundaries of the concept of culture that is based on the interplay of alterities that clash only around the essence pole or the conjuncture pole. Thus many of the essays in this volume demonstrate a constant shuttling between reversal and displacement; they track resistances that are both or at once arboreal and rhizomic, sometimes nomadic and sometimes sedentary (see Deleuze and Guattari 1987; Malkki 1992). This is demonstrated by the Asian Americans discussed by Kondo (in this volume), whose nostalgia for authentic community is unabashedly hybrid: they hanker after "avocado cha-shu burgers and teryaki burritos . . . Hawaiian-Japanese favorites like Spam fried rice and Portuguese sausage and eggs."

BETWEEN AND AMONG—DIASPORAS, BORDERS, AND THE THIRD TIME-SPACE[10]

Much work on the issue of resistance to the Eurocenter has been response-oriented, occupying either the essence pole or the conjuncture pole. We wish to stake out a terrain that calls for, yet paradoxically refuses, boundaries, a borderzone between identity-as-essence and identity-as-conjuncture, whose practices challenge the ludic play with essence and conjuncture as yet another set of postmodernist binarisms. This terrain is old in experience and memory but new in theory: a third time-space.[11] This volume in part represents a call for further ethnographic and theoretical examination of third time-spaces. In this terrain opposition is not only reactive but also creative and affirmative. It involves a guerrilla warfare of the interstices, where minorities rupture categories of race, gender, sexuality, class, nation, and empire in the center as well as on the margins. The third time-space goes beyond the old model of culture without establishing another fixity.

Yet while the third time-space designates phenomena too heterogeneous, mobile, and discontinuous for fixity, it remains anchored in the politics of history/location (Mohanty 1987; M. B. Pratt 1984).

Diaspora is one attempt to name this hodgepodge of everyday "out-of-country, . . . even out-of-language" experience (Rushdie 1991:2) and its textual representations. Challenging our received notions of place, disrupting those normative spatial-temporal units of analysis like nation and culture, it accounts for one type of displacement. "Diaspora" refers to the doubled relationship or dual loyalty that migrants, exiles, and refugees have to places—their connections to the space they currently occupy and their continuing involvement with "back home." Diasporic populations frequently occupy no singular cultural space but are enmeshed in circuits of social, economic, and cultural ties encompassing both the mother country and the country of settlement (Rouse 1991). The phenomenon of diasporas calls for reimagining the "areas" of area studies and developing units of analysis that enable us to understand the dynamics of transnational cultural and economic processes, as well as to challenge the conceptual limits imposed by national and ethnic/racial boundaries (Gilroy 1992b; Rafael 1993).[12] Yet we wish to emphasize that diaspora is understood here "beyond its symbolic status as the fragmentary opposite of an imported racial essence" (Gilroy 1990/91:15). Diaspora theories are derived principally from the historically specific experience of "the Black Atlantic," a transnational unit of analysis that addresses the complex socioeconomic and cultural interconnections between the Caribbean, Europe, Africa, and Afro-America (Gilroy 1992b, 1993; Hall 1989:75–79; 1990). In this volume, Gross et al. examine the complex and intricate interconnections between *rai* music's uses in the Franco-Maghrebi diaspora and in the Algerian homeland, and they suggest the Mediterranean as another transnational site of analysis.

"Borders" is another name for this jumble of daily practices and its textual representations. Like diaspora theory, border theory emerges from the everyday; in this instance, as articulated by Chicana and Chicano cultural workers situated in the practices of the boundary region between the United States and Mexico. Norma Alarcón in this volume examines the path-breaking book of Gloria Anzaldúa, a Chicana lesbian poet from a working-class South Texas background, who writes an ethnography of her community devoid of the voyeuristic gaze of some anthropologists trained Here to do fieldwork Out There. For Anzaldúa, the border is an "open wound . . . where the Third World grates against the First and bleeds. And before a scab forms it hemorrhages again, the lifeblood of two worlds merging to form a third country . . . a border culture" (Anzaldúa 1987:2–3). Yet this culture moves beyond the reification of space, for "a borderland is a vague and undetermined place created by the emotional residue of an unnatural boundary. It is in a constant state of transition" (Anzaldúa 1987:3).

Borderzones are sites of creative cultural creolization, places where crisscrossed identities are forged out of the debris of corroded, formerly (would-be) homogeneous identities, zones where the residents often refuse the geopolitical univocality of the lines (Alarcón, this volume). Both an "intellectual laboratory and . . . conceptual territory," the border "deconstruct[s] binary opposition" (Fusco 1989:53, 61). As such, the border is a process of deterritorialization that occurs both to and between the delimited political realities of the First World and the Third World. Yet borders, like diasporas, are not just places of imaginative interminglings and happy hybridities for us to celebrate. They are equally minefields, mobile territories of constant clashes with the Eurocenter's imposition of cultural fixity (Fusco 1989:58). Borders are zones of loss, alienation, pain, death—spaces where "formations of violence are continuously in the making" (Alarcón, this volume).[13] Living in the border is frequently to experience the feeling of being trapped in an impossible in-between, like cosmopolitan Franco-Maghrebis who are denied the option of identifying with either France or Algeria and are harassed both by white racist extremists and Islamist xenophobes (Gross et al. in this volume). Lavie's investigations of intercultural life in Israel-Palestine shows the varieties of borderzones. The racialized Mizrahi-Ashkenazi border is relatively "wide" and offers considerably more "free space" than the border separating Israeli Jews and Palestinian-Arab citizens of Israel, which is more like a razor-edged line, the site of exploding villages.[14]

Borders and diasporas offer new frames of analysis that resist and transcend national boundaries through their creative articulations of practices that demonstrate possible modes of corroding the Eurocenter by actively Third-Worlding it. Such Third-Worldings shove a mirror in the unwilling face of the Eurocenter, forcing it to examine its now miscegenated self (Chandler in this volume). Yet many studies of borders and diasporas tend to focus on the processual shuttling of peoples and capital between two distinct territorial entities, as if these cultures were not both already hybridized. Such concepts, moreover, are used mainly in analyses of artistic representations of the shuttle, and so miss the fact that, in practice, not all margins can ride it. At times, imperialist capitalism writes off marginal time-spaces, letting them die a slow death or self-destruct. In other times and places, displacement does not require that people get on the shuttle, because the Eurocenter will reach out to grab them right where they are (Narayan in this volume; Lavie 1990). And even for those shuttling back and forth, the reasons for travel are as heterogeneous as the vehicles (Cohen 1987). Furthermore, literary theorists sometimes conceive migrants' experiences as if the poetic ruminations of writers like Salman Rushdie "represent" the vagaries of the daily lives of Asian settlers in England. But Rushdie's diasporic novels fissure the Eurocenter in ways very different from the practices of the mass of the immigrant population. Before Ayatollah Khomeini called for his execution and forced him into hiding, Rushdie could indulge in the postcolonial bohemian privileges of the borderzone, whereas the working-class Muslims of Bradford lived on a much more dangerous, racially charged borderline.[15]

Borders and diasporas are phenomena that blow up—both enlarge and explode—the hyphen: Arab-Jew, African-American, Franco-Maghrebi, Black-British. Avoiding the dual axes of migration between the distinct territorial entities, the hyphen becomes the third time-space. A sense of time is created in the interstices between "nonsynchronic fragments and essentialist nostalgia" (Hicks 1991:6). A space is charted in the interstices between the displacement of "the histories that constitute it" (Bhabha 1990b:211) and the rootedness of these histories in the politics of location. The third time-space is thus an imaginary homeland (Rushdie 1991:9) where "the fragmentation of identity" is conceived not "as a kind of pure anarchic liberalism or voluntarism, but . . . as a recognition of the importance of the alienation of the Self in the construction of forms of solidarity." The fragmentation of identity "articulat[es] minority constituencies across disjunctive and differential social positions [so that] political subjectivity as a multi-dimensional, conflictual form of identification" is mobilized and able to build coalitions (Bhabha 1990b:213, 220–21).[16] This is a time-space of the "lives of those who dare to mix while differing . . . [in] the realm in-between, where predetermined rules cannot fully apply" (Trinh 1991:157). It is the realm of "subjects-in-the-making" (Trinh 1989:102). The third time-space is one of creativity and affirmation and community, despite political skepticism. In it, subjects who are fragments of collectivities-that-were "return to a derived identity and cultural heritage" (Trinh 1991:187).

Yet the hyphenated time-space is a process not of becoming a something but one that remains active and intransitive (Trinh 1991:161). This process "does not limit itself to a duality between two cultural heritages. It leads, on the one hand, to an active 'search of our mother's garden' . . . —the consciousness of 'root values' . . . ; and on the other hand, to a heightened awareness of the other 'minority' sensitivities, hence of a Third World solidarity, and by extension, of the necessity for new alliances" (Trinh 1991:159).

The Eurocenter also seems to crave borders and diasporas as new frontiers to civilize (Anzaldúa 1987:11).[17] To prevent border crossings from being "both the 'self' and 'other'" that they are, the Eurocenter operates its "border-machine, with its border patrol agents, secondary inspection, helicopters, shifts in policy" (Hicks 1991:xxv). Third time-spaces, however, attempt to frustrate frontierization and to throw the Eurocenter's policing energy back upon itself, to make the fissures between identity and place unmendable.

Both essences and conjunctures have created counterinstitutions to challenge the institutions of the Eurocenter. But the third time-space, the borderzone between identity-as-essence and identity-as-conjuncture, seems to resist institutionalization. Third time-spaces refuse closure and are fluid, constantly shifting practices that create fault lines in both institutions and counterinstitutions. The essays in this volume therefore resist the new dualisms of a certain brand of postmodernism, a neo-orthodoxy that would privilege identity as constructed, hybrid, fragmented, conjunctural, and would reject any notion of identity as essence, fixed, rooted. But at the same time third time-spaces paradoxically do practice their own arbitrary provisional closures, in order to enact agency toward dismantling the Eurocenter, or to enable identity politics beyond the reactive mode (Hall 1988a:45; Trinh 1991:158). They deploy a "differential" mode of resistance that situationally opts for the most effective strategy of the moment (Sandoval 1991:12–14).

Because of its fleeting, shifting, and emergent character, it is difficult to provide a vivid, fixed image of third time-space. Perhaps we are really speaking of some utopian space whose future outlines we can only vaguely begin to make out. But a few examples, even if evanescent, may offer hopeful images for action in the future.[18] We propose, for instance, the interracial dancers at a rave, or the weekend gatherings of the families of Mizrahi Jews and Palestinians from the Gaza Strip who used to work together at job sites inside Israel (such meetings virtually stopped during the *intifada*), or the multi-ethnic youth gangs of the Paris *banlieues* (Gross et al. in this volume).

The interdisciplinary field of minority discourse also deploys the concepts of third spaces, third texts, and third scenarios, usually using cultural studies methodologies. The cultural materials analyzed through the modalities of "the third," however, have tended to be highly stylized domains of knowledge, framed as dramatic, literary, cinematic, artistic, and musical texts. Bridging ethnography, cultural studies, and minority discourse will be possible if we incorporate the primary daily realities from which such textual representations emerge. Many essays in this volume implicitly call for a reconceptualization, from the standpoint of lived identities and physical places as well as the texts of expressive culture, of the multiplicities of identity and place. As identity and place are forced into constantly shifting configurations of partial overlap, their ragged edges cannot be smoothed out. Identity and place perpetually create both new outer borders, where no imbrication has occurred, and inner borders, between the areas of overlay and the vestigial spaces of nonoverlay. The grating that results from their forced combination sparks inchoate energies that mobilize and activate the agency of coalition politics.

THIRD TEXTS/THIRD PRACTICES—METHODOLOGICAL BRIDGES

In order to develop an understanding of the interstices that constitute third time-spaces, it will be necessary to revise the ethnographic method so as to displace the anthropological notion of culture. A decolonized notion of culture might help mediate between studies of expressive cultural texts in minority discourse and cultural studies, and studies of lived experience by ethnographers.

Based on a simulated relation between theory and experience, and between identity and place, anthropology in the past played a pivotal role in establishing the concept of culture. Although according to the anthropological definition, culture always happened in the empire's outback, this notion of culture also infiltrated the Eurocenter's discourse about itself by being extended to encompass and buttress the imagined nation. Today, curiously, as the field of cultural studies mushrooms in the U.S. academy, its practitioners tend to view the texts of expressive culture as the privileged arenas of practice. Anthropology, decolonized or not, is rarely involved in this discussion. Moreover, despite cultural studies' powerful interventions on issues of race, gender, and difference, its inquiries tend to concentrate on Western geohistorical periods and Western expressive culture (minority or majority, high or popular) (see Rooney 1990:23–24). The time zones of cultural studies are usually North American or European. Even when culture à la cultural studies deigns to travel, the caravan has its preferred Anglophile vacation spots. India definitely wins out over Syria. Papua New Guinea is beyond the pale, unless encountered through deconstructions of the Banana Republic catalog.[19] Ghettos and barrios are almost always discussed in the context of the Western metropole, not of Cairo or Bangkok. Multiculturalism is a concept that seems to apply only to the minorities of the Eurocenter and to ignore minorities elsewhere.

Culture, we want to argue, is not just a cut 'n' mix of films, sound tracks, New Age advertisements, or great counterhegemonic novels; it also includes everyday lived experience. Cultural studies scholars might argue that when they enter libraries, archives, movie theaters, art galleries, or even New Age Trekkie conferences, from a subaltern, racialized position of oppositionality, they go through the ethnographic experience.[20] But such ethnographic experiences rarely appear explicitly in their own texts, though traces may be discernible between the lines. Furthermore, theories derived from such experience take a shorter time to produce and publish, because the text to be analyzed is already there, usually in no more than a couple of languages, and embedded in its political/cultural fabric, which is analyzed as well. Such research does not require a long-term immersion in minute, everyday actions that cannot be theorized unless they make sense in retrospect (see Bruner 1986), after the data has been translated into English—the imperialistic language required for being quoted and promoted. Thus experience-rooted analysis, especially in the Third World, finds itself lagging behind in its participation in the move to dismantle the phallogocentric theories of culture.[21]

Anthropologists working in third time-spaces are nonetheless deeply indebted to cultural studies, which has helped them to problematize their concepts of lived experience and to begin to deconstruct the process of fieldwork itself. Still, anthropology has an important contribution to make to these burgeoning discourses and institutions of criticism and resistance. Perhaps intervention by anthropologists (and others) could help prevent cultural studies' threatened institutionalization in English literature departments. We are not expecting that those trained in literary and archival methods will immediately undertake fieldwork in the Kalahari Desert or south-central L.A. We do propose, though, that analysis of the quotidian be integrated into this interdisciplinary venture as a crucial method of enunciating the multivalent critique of culture. Such a critique will not be limited to the reactive mode, but will provide necessary tools to allow cultural studies-cum-anthropology to chart new geographies and histories of identity, particularly through Sandoval's groundbreaking notion of differential oppositional consciousness (Sandoval 1991:12–14).

This strategy of oppositional consciousness, the method of daily living and surviving in the third time-space, also calls for radical revisions of the ethnographic method. Such a revision demands, among other things, the rethinking of "field" sites and "home" sites. These days, some of us from Out There live Here, perhaps next door, and read and protest our neighbors' depiction of us. A few have Ph.D.'s in anthropology, having survived the monochromatic elitist boot camp of graduate school. Some of us from Out There even sit in decision-making rooms with those who used to rely on our silence in order to ethnograph us. Many of our colleagues are still irritated by our ability to talk back, in multiple tongues: the languages of Here, the languages of Out There, and the languages of the third time-space. For us, field and home blur, and sites of research (what used to be roughing it in the field Out There) and sites of writing (what used to be the detached contemplation at home, Here) intermingle. Out There is still home.

Studying third time-spaces requires an ongoing negotiation and renegotiation of positionalities, rather than a one-time journey into a faraway wilderness. Kamala Viswesvaran terms this method "homework." Viswesvaran connects the moment when the practice of anthropology at home became acceptable to the effort to decolonize anthropology and the moment when it began to be assumed that "a critical eye would necessarily be cast upon a whole range of practices at 'home' which authorized American interventions in the 'Third World'" (Viswesvaran 1994). She distinguishes, however, between anthropology "at home," which is still mainly practiced by white fieldworkers, and "homework," which involves the dehegemonization of the white West and the study of it as a field site itself. The process of decolonizing fieldwork and turning it into homework destabilizes home. Home therefore can no longer remain "an illusion of coherence and safety based on the exclusion of specific histories of oppression and resistance, the repression of differences even within oneself" (Martin and Mohanty 1986:196). The shift from "field"work to "home"work responds to the Eurocenter's failure to unlearn its own epistemologies, whether essentialist or conjuncturalist.

Doing homework, as a consequence, breaks down the difference between ethnographer and subject of study. The ethnographer becomes engaged in blowing up, both enlarging and exploding, the oxymoronic hyphenated identity of participant-observer by taking an active role in shaping his or her home, as "ethnography [and other disciplinary writing] becomes another way of writing our own identities and communities" (Kondo in this volume). This is no longer the safe Eurocentric home, rooted in whiteness from time immemorial, but the diasporic-at-home, whose geographies and identities are multiply positioned and in flux. In this volume, Sarris describes his mixed (Jewish-Indian) natal heritage and his mixed (Indian practitioner of the Bole Maru cult-academic) adult positioning. This dislocation, this boundary and multiple positioning, gives him a location from which to "start talking interculturally and interpersonally about that which is in fact intercultural and interpersonal." Like Anzaldúa, the ethnographer becomes the chronicler of third time-spaces by involving himself or herself in making culture, both by producing ethnographic texts and by engaging in political activism (Fusco 1989:70). Yet even such acts of creating, constructing, and defending the home turf, Sarris reminds us, necessarily engage one in an "intercultural" conversation.

Such movements within and between various positionalities call for dismantling the method of detached narration through naturalized observation. Capturing the fragmented, rapidly shifting registers and modalities of the forces that shape everyday life in third time-spaces requires writing that mixes and juxtaposes genres.[22] The ethnographer needs to be a multicultural "smuggler . . . choos[ing] a strategy of translation rather than representations . . . [in order to] ultimately undermine the distinction between original and alien culture" (Hicks 1991:xxi, xxiii; see also Bhabha 1990b:209). He or she needs to acknowledge his or her presence in the construction of the text and adopt the polyphonic montage technique developed by DuBois in *The Souls of Black Folk* (DuBois 1986b; Gilroy 1990/91:14). But the polyphonies should not succumb to the writer's authority. Writing about third time-spaces, he or she ought to "gather and reuse" (Tawadros 1989) theories as tactics of his or her guerrilla tool kit, to create organic connections between such theories and the quotidian flows of experience that led to their articulation.

Many essays in this volume advocate and exemplify this blurring of disciplines and genres of writing, an intermingling that in some cases reflects disciplinary displacements already at work within the wider social field.

Koptiuch shows how the legal strategy of "cultural defense" redeploys classical anthropological discourses of cultural relativism in the name of cultural sensitivity, and thereby unwittingly buttresses monogenous and patriarchal constructions of East Asian cultures. Bruner demonstrates that ethnographic discourse can bleed into tourism, as tourists seek out the integrated, holistic visions of "native" culture that the "new" ethnography thought it had successfully banished from the field. As academic-cum-tour guide, Bruner finds himself in the uncomfortable position of "authenticating" tourists' encounters with Balinese culture even as he tries to deconstruct them.

Other versions of border crossings in this volume are more oppositional. Lavie does fieldwork with "natives" who happen to be intellectuals and who theorize their own condition. Sarris juxtaposes several contradictory discourses on the history of the Kashaya Pomo—official, ethnographic, indigenous, autobiographical. And many essays blur the boundaries that are expected to distinguish authors from their subjects of research, turning authors into subjects or semi-subjects of study. Such insertions of the author as subject are not just pretexts to occupy center stage in narcissistic self-displays or as omniscient text controllers. Chandler eloquently underscores the methodological importance of attending to the particular, the autobiographical, the concrete, in order to grasp its general implications, the broader historicity: "The staging of the autobiographical example, the responsibility it demands as a demonstration, seems to resolutely insist that any recognition of a meaning of history in general can be articulated only by the risky and unavoidable passage by way of the micrological." In many instances, the interjection of the autobiographical is also connected with the authors' own engagement and/or belonging or partial belonging to the community under study, which produces a kind of lovingness toward the embattled groups, as in Narayan's wistful defense of the residual knowledges of elderly peasant women, seemingly abandoned by fast-track pomo theory, and Sarris' poignant account of the Pomo, whose experiences threaten to be erased by theoretical concerns for "postcoloniality and California."

The shift from "field" to "home" can open up more third time-spaces in the interstices between the raw experiences of the everyday and the texts about them. Just as identity and place grate against each other, and are forced into constantly shifting configurations of partial overlap, so the locations of home and of field, and those of text and experience, scrape against each other, only partially overlapping, creating methodological borders along their contiguities. These realignments of the formerly hierarchical arrangement of the power/knowledge binarism are redefining not only our work but also the academic disciplines (and especially anthropology) themselves.

NOTES

This essay has gone through numerous drafts, composed variously in Irvine, Berkeley, Tel Aviv, Seattle, Cairo, Palo Alto, and Washington, D.C. As it traced its circuitous path to completion, many friends offered invaluable suggestions, proddings, and criticisms. Ruth Frankenberg in particular deserves an enormous acknowledgment for her massive contribution, which took the form of critiques, suggestions, and copious notes and comments on the essays in this volume. Many of her observations and formulations were incorporated into this essay. We also wish to thank all the contributors to this volume for their engagements with this introduction, particularly Dorinne Kondo, Kristin Koptiuch, Lata Mani, Kirin Narayan, and Greg Sarris. We also are grateful to Anna Tsing, whose long letter helped us to bring forward the main themes of the essay, and to Vilashini Copan, John Gonzalez, and Martina Rieker for their critical suggestions. Thanks to Abdul R. JanMohamed, in May 1992 we presented a sketchy draft of the essay to the Minority Discourse Collaborative Seminar at the Humanities Research Institute of the University of California-Irvine, where we benefited from the careful readings of Norma Alarcón, Abdul JanMohamed, and Cedric Robinson. We also were helped and encouraged by discussions with audiences to whom we presented earlier drafts of this paper: at the Unit for Criticism and Interpretive Theory of the University of Illinois at Champaign-Urbana, the Department of Anthropology at the University of California-Davis, the Department of Anthropology at the London School of Oriental and African Studies, the Center for Critical and Cultural Theory at the University of Wales, College of Cardiff, and the American Anthropological Association meetings of November 1993 in Washington, D.C. Finally, we would like to acknowledge the support and enthusiasm of our editor at Duke, Ken Wissoker.

This essay is based in part on an article that originally was published in *Cultural Studies* 10, no. 3 (1996).

1 For a related discussion of these issues, see Gupta and Ferguson (1992).

2 See *Europe: Variations on a Theme of Racism,* a special issue of *Race & Class* 32, no. 3 (1991).

3 The mosaic image was attributed to culture in the 1950s (see Coon 1951), but in those days its pieces were assumed to be distinctive and impermeable.

4 Appiah (1991) provides a somewhat cynical discussion of the relationship between postmodernity and postcoloniality. Frankenberg and Mani (this volume), Shohat

(1992), Coombes (1992), and McClintock (1992) provide eloquent analyses of the problematic temporality of the "post" in "postcolonial" and its lack of a situated political edge.

5 Miyoshi's (1993) bold critique of the institutionalization of postcoloniality as the cutting edge in English literature departments charts the relationships between postcoloniality's emergence and the erasure of multinational corporate economics from the agenda of liberal/progressive academe.

6 Concepts of syncretism and bricolage arose in Western Europe in opposition to U.S. theories of acculturation (see Lévi-Strauss 1966:17–33; Worsley 1968). Narayan (1993:498, 503) suggests the need for further investigation of U.S. anthropologists' earlier theories of "cultural contact," like diffusionism and acculturation, despite their assumptions of a culture/space homogeneity and their ignoring of power inequalities.

7 It should be noted, however, that much of the work on "hybridities" is gender-neutral (for instance, Paul Gilroy's). Perhaps a concerted move should be made to adopt Haraway's notion of the "cyborg," a concept of syncretization that is intensely gendered (Haraway 1985).

8 The genealogy of the white Left's attempts to dismantle "the master's house" with "the master's tools" can be traced to Audre Lorde (1984). Diana Jeater (1992) suggests that considerable work, both academic and activist, is required in order for progressive whites to participate in the dismantling project. Whiteness as a category needs to be interrogated so that the hybridity built into the category is brought to the surface of social relations and the analytical discourse about those relations. Rather than borrowing/exploring/putting on/exoticizing the trappings of other ethnicities, progressive whites need simultaneously to radicalize and deprivilege their own (see also Frankenberg 1993).

9 See the groundbreaking article by Epstein (1987), which we assume permitted Fuss (1989) to take "the risk of essence."

10 For this discussion, we trace the anthropological genealogy of our thinking to the formative work of Gupta and Ferguson (1992), to whom we are gratefully indebted.

11 Bhabha (1990b) has suggested a third space, without the temporal component, as an area for theoretical exploration. Whereas Bhabha's third space lacks the feminist-of-color concept of the politics of location, Trinh (1991:155–236), writing as a woman of color, theorizes the time element of this space and anchors this third space/time grid in the politics of location. Bhabha theorizes the space from texts. We call for examination of the everydayness of this space and time.

12 In a presentation Rafael (1993) characterized area studies as reproductions of the Orientalism that underwrites the discourse of pluralist liberalism. Taking Southeast Asian studies as an example, he calls for the radical revision of area studies by putting what he terms "immigrant imaginary" at its crux. Such a move would relocate the bits and pieces of a so-called area so that it could no longer be visible as the seamless Out There.

13 Both Lavie (1992) and Torstrick (1993) discover through ethnographic examina-

tion that contra Said (1983b), who finds that theory tends to mellow as it travels, Chicana/Chicano border theory gets radicalized on its journey to the Arab/Israeli borderlands.

14 A different historically specific example of a diasporic circuit is the Levant. The founding of the European, Zionist settler state of Israel in Palestine displaced both Arabs and Jews who were historically situated in the Levant. This is examined in the pioneering work of Alcalay (1993) and Shohat (1989). Other Middle Eastern conceptualizations of diasporic circuits include the Iran/Los Angeles axis (Naficy 1991).

15 See Asad (1990).

16 Although we have reservations about Bhabha's path-breaking early work on colonial mimicry, due to its underemphasis on the possibility of subaltern agency, we find this deficiency somewhat remedied in his current work, from which we quote here.

17 The articulation of the history of the Eurocenter's voracious appetite for frontiers can be traced to the turn of the twentieth century, in the work of Frederick Jackson Turner (1963 [1893]).

18 See Alcalay (1993), Gilroy (1993), and Mercer (1987) for examples of studies of the type of intercultural zones that we are calling third time-spaces.

19 This, despite the fact that Papua New Guinea has enjoyed a celebrated status in U.S. anthropology similar to that of India in British anthropology.

20 It should be noted that before the boom, cultural studies in its Birmingham origins was often based on ethnography, particularly when it came to the study of subcultures. See, for instance, Willis (1977) and Hall and Jefferson (1976).

21 At the same time we must acknowledge the inherent limitations of a sociohistorical understanding based solely on experience conceived of as methodological fetish, given that many historical structures and movements are inaccessible to fieldwork-based experience. Appadurai, for instance, while asserting that it is necessary to study the "finanscape," notes that "the disposition of global capital is now a more mysterious, rapid and difficult landscape to follow than ever before" (1990:8). He does not propose how we might overcome the impossible obstacles of doing an ethnography of the finanscape, that is, fieldwork on the secret decisions made by immensely powerful transnational corporations and international banks. Such cautions are usefully discussed in Asad (in press).

22 Examples of such juxtapositions are the pioneering feminist-of-color anthologies Moraga and Anzaldúa (1981), Hull et al. (1982), and Anzaldúa (1990), published in the United States; and Grewal et al. (1988), published in England. An anthropological anthology with similar aims (Behar and Gordon 1995) also mixes genres of writing and traces their historical trajectory.

LIVING WITH MIRACLES: THE POLITICS AND POETICS OF WRITING AMERICAN INDIAN RESISTANCE AND IDENTITY

GREG SARRIS

Anthropologists and others interested in California Indian culture and history have long wondered about the Bole Maru (Dream Dance) cult, the latter-nineteenth-century nationalistic and revivalistic movement among the Pomo Indians and their neighbors. Scholars such as Cora DuBois have wondered about its origins, its purposes, its decline. I know much about this movement. I know how it started, and about its purposes and its persistence in a certain Pomo community today. I know about the Bole Maru because I am a member of that Pomo community and participate in ceremonies associated with the cult. Yet my particular position as a writer is awkward. As writer or ethnographer, I am also insider, subject and object at the same time. Consequently, I am positioned so that in talking about the Bole Maru to outsiders, I may be jeopardizing my people's resistance to cultural and political domination. What am I doing talking or writing about the Bole Maru to an unknown reader? What can be accomplished for me, for the reader, or for my Indian community?

In this essay, I want to explore these questions and demonstrate the ways that writing about the Bole Maru can at once illuminate the complex intercultural topic and the identity of the writer, and serve to interrogate and ultimately replace a single dominant (colonial) discourse with a multi-voiced discourse that more accurately represents the life of the writer and the topic at hand.[1]

California Indian peoples' participation in the Bole Maru varies. Just as I have been taught by my elders, I am writing only about my own tribes, my own Indian family, my own experiences and history. My voice, my authority as speaker, is shaped by my experiences and history. My father, Emilio Hilario, was a descendant of the Kashaya Pomo and Coast Miwok tribes. Coast Miwok territory extends from what many people now call San Francisco Bay north to the Russian River in Sonoma County, California.

The Russian River is the acknowledged boundary between the Miwok and the Kashaya Pomo. Kashaya territory extends north from the Russian River for about forty miles along the coast and inland for about twenty-five miles.

"Miracles" is the Kashaya Pomo term for white people—first the Spanish, then the Russians, then other Euroamericans. At one point, during the Mexican occupation of the surrounding Pomo (i.e., southern Pomo) and Coast Miwok territories, the term applied to Mexicans also. In Kashaya Pomo it is *ph alá? cay?*. As one Kashaya Pomo elder told me, "The invaders are miracles, miraculous. They think they can kill and plunder and get away with it." The word reminds us of who they are, and of course of who we are. We read certain behaviors seemingly characteristic of whites as *ph alá? cay?*. A glance across the room at one another when in the presence of whites signals *ph alá? cay?*. We know then what to say and what not to say. We shift and adjust our behavior, our responses. We remember that the miracles don't see things as we do, that they will take our words and use them in inappropriate ways, ways that to us are miraculous, unbelievable, dangerous for everyone in the long run. The same elder who talked about the invaders (miracles) plundering and killing, laughed and said, "But the miracles ain't really miracles or special. Look around, it has all come back on them, on everything. Look at the world, the pollution, the sick people. Still, they act like miracles. Watch them."

Ph alá? cay?. The word has always been a way of dealing with the invaders. So has the Bole Maru.

It's history.

It's a long story, and it's many stories.

HISTORY (RECORDED)

1579 Drake sails into a bay in southern Coast Miwok territory. Drake and his men land, and from June to July of that year trade with the native people for food and artwork—baskets, beads, costumes.

The Spanish ship *Cermeño* sinks in Drake's Bay before its crew is able to land.

1603 Spanish explorer Vizcaino sails into Coast Miwok territory, looking for the *Cermeño*'s wreck.

1769 The Bucareli party, arriving by land, discovers the site of

San Francisco and sets its sights on land to the north, across the bay.

1770 Ayala, on the *San Carlos,* lands off the Coast Miwok territory and trades beads and trinkets for pinole.

1775 Bodega y Cuadra discovers Bodega Bay in north Coast Miwok territory.

1794 Spanish padres establish a mission in San Francisco.

1800–10 Large numbers of Natives—Valley and Delta Yokuts, Miwok (Coast and Inland), and Wintun—appear at the San Francisco mission.

1809 Russian explorer Kuskof spends the spring and summer in the Bodega Bay area.

1810 The Spanish officer Gálvez marches his company of armored soldiers from the Presidio in San Francisco north through Coast Miwok territory, into southern and central Pomo territories.

1811–12 Kuskof returns to Coast Miwok/Kashaya Pomo territory and establishes a Russian colony at the site of the Kashaya central coastal village called Metini. Ninety-five Russians and probably eighty Aleuts, brought by the Russians from the Russian colony of Alaska, build Fort Ross.

1817 Spanish padres and military establish Mission San Rafael in central Coast Miwok territory.

1835 Mission San Rafael is secularized, and Mexicans continue settling Coast Miwok and Pomo territories. They establish an elaborate slave raiding and trading system, forcing Pomo and Miwok people into slavery and taking them as far away as Mexico. The Russians, in a territorial dispute with the Mexicans, arm the Kashaya Pomo against the Mexicans. Fort Ross and surrounding Russian-occupied territory is considered a sanctuary for Indians.

1838 Smallpox epidemic kills over 90 percent of the remaining Miwok and over 80 percent of the Pomo.

1842 Russians abandon Fort Ross after depleting the coast from San Francisco to Oregon of sea otters.

1850 California, now a state, passes the first official piece of legislation: the Act for the Government and Protection of Indians, which legalizes Indian slavery, stipulating that

	Indians are the rightful property of the owners of the land on which they reside.
1865	Large-scale logging operations begin in Coast Miwok and coastal Pomo territories. By the turn of the century, 99 percent of original redwood forests are gone.
1868	Act for the Government and Protection of Indians is repealed.
1870–1900	Small land plots are established by priests and others for homeless Indians. Plots are locally known as *rancherías.*
1914	Kashaya Pomo are federally recognized as an Indian tribe and are given thirty-nine acres on top of a mountain in Kashaya territory, the site of the present-day Kashaya Pomo reservation.
1928	The Coast Miwok are for the third time denied federal recognition as an Indian tribe as well as their requests for a land base.
1975	Park rangers at Point Reyes State Park, in Coast Miwok territory, note, as part of their tour routine, that there are no more Coast Miwok Indians.

HISTORY (TRIBAL/FAMILY)

Mrs. Juanita Carrio, late Coast Miwok elder and granddaughter of Maria Copa, Isabel Kelley's informant for the Coast Miwok tribe: "It flew into the Roundhouse at Nicasias. The white owl. My grandmother told me this. The people were dancing. Some kind of ceremony. And they looked up. It was on the rafters, the white owl. It said to all the people: 'Prepare to die. Ghost people are coming, a strange people. They are coming and gonna kill everything, kill the earth. They gonna kill people with all kinds of sickness.'

"After that the people started crying. It watched them, that white owl, and I suppose it cried, too, because how would it live if it couldn't talk to people?

"Well, when that first white man came, what you call Drake, the people, they ran into the hills. They waited some time. Then they put ashes all over their bodies, painted themselves like they were dead. They cried out loud, wailed. That way they went back down to meet that man.

"He left after a while. He didn't kill the people. I heard a couple of those white men stayed. I don't know. Anyway, the people thought it would be

O.K. But the White people came back. That was just the start. The owl was true."

Juanita Carrio: "The old people say their parents used to hide them anytime Mexicans or whites came around. Those Mexicans and whites, they took the children and sold them. The mothers had to hide their children. Hardly no men around because the Mexicans got them all. This my grandmother told me, too."

David Carrio (son of Juanita Carrio): "My Mom told me that her grandmother's [Maria Copa's] uncle was a medicine man. He had a power spirit. He could hide from the whites and watch over his people. But he couldn't kill. That was the rule. Then one day he found two soldiers raped and killed his wife. He tracked them down and killed them. Then the whites sent a posse after him. They caught him. They lynched him in San Rafael. I hear it was in the newspapers."

A family story: My great-great-grandfather's mother was named Tsupu. She was Coast Miwok. She was captured by General Vallejo's Mexican soldiers and taken to his fort in Petaluma. She was about twelve or thirteen. Vallejo's soldiers molested the young Indian girls they captured. People say they tortured them, raped them. Most of them died. Tsupu escaped. At the time she was the last living member of her Miwok band. She walked over fifty miles to Kashaya Pomo territory, to Fort Ross. There she married a Kashaya Pomo man. His name was Komtechal. People say it was a Russian name. I don't know.

Juanita Carrio: "I think about a lot of things I don't want to think about. But they come up. Like mean, twisted flowers. I think of Crawling Woman, my grandmother's grandmother. That wasn't her name, Crawling Woman. We just remember her that way. I think the mission [in San Rafael] has her down as Juana Maria. That isn't her name either.

"She was a grown woman when the first Spanish came and set up the mission. They say she ran away [from the mission] once and they found her in the creek. She was face down, stiff as a board. Like she was dead. They brought her back that way. On a wagon bed. She was stiff as a board.

"She lived a long time after that. She lived up to this century. She saw everything right up to this time. But she was senile. Last years of her life she was like a child. She didn't know anybody. She couldn't take care of herself. And she crawled. She crawled everywhere, out of the house, up the road. She went fast. Lots of times my grandmother couldn't find her. Then lots of times she wouldn't come back. They used to have an old Mexican general's coat in the house. It had shiny brass buttons down the front. They used to put that on and go out after the old lady. The kids did that. She would see that coat and the buttons, those brass buttons, and she would screech, scream like murder, and crawl back to the house and get under the bed."

Violet Chappell, Kashaya Pomo historian: "Those Russians worked us like slaves. I don't care what the history books say. Grandma Rosie told me. Then when they was going, those Russians roped six of our women. They caught them, tied them up like cattle, and took them on their boat. We never seen those women again. I suppose we got cousins in Russia. I don't know. But now those Russians, they come back to see their history. They go to the Fort [Ross]. One of them asked to meet the Indians."

David Carrio: "Yeah, one day I took my kids to Point Reyes. We was in a group of people taking the tour and this park ranger says all the Miwok is dead. I looked at my kids and started crying. Then I looked at the ranger and shouted out: 'Do I look dead?' "

THE BOLE MARU (RESISTANCE AND REORGANIZATION)

In the winter of 1871–72 a Pomo medicine man called all the Pomo and neighboring tribes to the eastern shores of Clear Lake in Lake County, where his followers had constructed seven semi-subterranean earth lodges to protect the Indians against the flood that this man claimed would cleanse the world of white people and restore the earth. Over a thousand people gathered under the seven earth lodges. It rained steadily for four days and four nights, and then stopped. When the faithful emerged from the earth lodges, they found themselves face to face with the U.S. Cavalry, who had been called in to handle "an Indian uprising." The U.S. military dispersed the Pomo, Miwok, Wappo, and Wintun who had gathered to witness the old medicine man's dream of restoration and rebirth.

Of course the people were disappointed when Taylor's Dream proved untrue. But what they carried home with them, what they had heard during their stay in the lodges, was the spirit of revitalization. Each tribe of Pomo,

Miwok, Wappo, and Wintun subsequently produced its own prophets, locally known as Dreamers, who carried on and developed what came to be known as the Bole Maru (Dream Dance) cult in specific ways, with specific dances and rituals.

Although the influence of these Bole Maru dreamers was different from tribe to tribe, and each tribe had its own Dreamer and individual dances, songs, and costumes associated with that Dreamer, certain features new to native religion and social organization emerged throughout the territory. Where once there had been many private or secret cults within a tribe, now the entire tribe was united under one cult, the Bole Maru. The Dreamers stressed the afterlife and preached the Protestant work ethic and Puritan principles of cleanliness and abstinence. They forbade gambling and drinking. They insisted that women keep their bodies covered at all times, particularly during ceremonial activities, in high-necked, long dresses that covered the legs and upper arms. The dreamers were predominantly women, and although they were not called chiefs, they assumed the role of the tribal leaders, organizing their respective tribes' social and political activities around the doctrine of their Dreams.

Cora DuBois, the Harvard anthropologist who studied the Bole Maru in the 1930s, saw the movement as a significant revivalist effort. Yet she seemed to imply that in the long run it generally opened the door to further Christianization and the decline of Indian religion and ideology. In 1939 she wrote: "At the moment it represents one of the terminal points in a progressively Christian ideology, for which [like the Plains] Ghost Dance and its subsequent cults were the transitional factors" (1971:499). By the winter of 1871–72, massacres, disease, and slave raiding reduced most of the tribes (i.e., Pomo, Coast Miwok) to well under 10 percent of their precontact population. They had lost virtually all of the land they once called home and lived on the land of local ranchers, only with the approval of the ranchers, whom they served as a source of cheap labor (Bean and Theodoratus 1978:299). Christian groups moved in, Catholic and Protestant, and agreed to protect and help those Indians who converted. Given these conditions and the general domination and oppression that has followed the Natives to the present, it is no wonder that what DuBois saw, like the settlers and missionaries before her, were the ways in which the Natives, in a surviving religious cult or otherwise, integrated the Christian religion and Victorian ideology at the expense of their own identities and beliefs. Clearly, the Natives could not afford to show how a blending of different religious and cultural ideas laid the foundation for a fierce Indian resistance that exists in many places to this day.

While Indian people donned Victorian clothing and lived seemingly Christian lives, their Bole Maru leaders inculcated an impassioned Indian nationalism in the homes and roundhouses. They deemed everything associated with the white world taboo; they forbade interactions with whites except for necessary work-related situations. They prohibited intermarriage with the foreigners or miracles. They taught that the invaders had no place in the afterlife, and that unnecessary association with them could cost a person the reward of everlasting life. Some Pomo tribes practiced the infanticide of mixed-blood children. Seen from an Indian nationalist perspective, the assimilation of Victorian ideology looks very different. The ban on drinking, gambling, and adultery assured the continuance not only of individual tribes but also of given family lines within the tribes. And while the Bole Maru united each tribe around a particular cult, it influenced the revival of other ancient cults and secret societies. Families associated with certain secret cults again had sons and daughters who could learn and carry on special traditions. So while the Bole Maru was emergent in terms of its doctrine and social and religious structure, it simultaneously enhanced the resurgence and fortification of many precontact structures integral to Native life and ideology. In sum, it seems, from this perspective, that the Native people adopted what was useful in Victorian ideology and biblical religion.

Of course an understanding of the dynamics of any resistance movement and its success or lack of success depends on who is examining it, what the circumstances are, and the methods being employed. Any perspective will have its limitations. Representatives from the dominant culture exploring the resistance of a subjugated people are likely to see little more than what the people choose, or can afford, to show them, as with Cora DuBois and her study of the Bole Maru. In turn, a subjugated people may not see the ways their resistance may further their alienation from the dominant culture, weaken their resistance, and hasten their demise as a result. Some Pomo groups isolated themselves to the extent they would not make any land deals with the whites and U.S. Government, even when they could have gained a land base as a result. Thus, these tribes were never federally recognized, and have had to marry into other Pomo tribes to obtain food and government benefits for their children. These isolated Pomo tribes usually fell apart. And it must also be remembered that the method and narrative format, written or otherwise, used by either side in reporting what it sees or chooses to tell will compromise the experience of the movement in given ways. The story is not the experience, whether it is DuBois' story or my story, as I will point out. Ultimately, the possibility of open cross-cultural communication productive for both cultures usually will be strained, even in the sometimes safer, sometimes more comfortable neocolonial contexts, by the history of domination and subjugation, and persistent behavioral and cultural patterns of intercultural communication associated with that history.

What I have said about the Bole Maru from a Native perspective—that is, about its impassioned nationalism and use of Victorian ideology and biblical religion—comes from my own experiences and what I have learned from my family. I know much else. Cora DuBois and other outsiders who have studied the Bole Maru have been puzzled about its origins. It started, as I mentioned, in the winter of 1871–72, nearly two decades before the Ghost Dance cult, which shows some similarities, spread through the Plains tribes.[2] DuBois notes that she could not get any information that would clearly state the origins of the cult. She says it may have started with a Hill Patwin (or Eastern Pomo) called Lame Bill. How he got the religion is anyone's guess. One day, while I was driving along Cache Creek with Pomo Dreamer Mabel McKay, I learned what happened. In a rather casual conversation about something else, Mabel told me that her grandmother's brother was the first Dreamer. His name was Richard Taylor, and he had been taken as a slave and sold to ranchers in southern California, over four hundred miles from his Lake County home. There he had contact with a few of the Paiute disciples of Wovoka, the Paiute prophet who dreamed that the earth would be cleansed of white people and restored for the Natives. Richard Taylor was freed from slavery in 1868, and it took him over a year to get home to Lake County, where he began preaching the Dream. "Was he the same one they called Lame Bill?" I asked Mabel. She laughed. "That's just the name we gave the white people."

The Pomo and Coast Miwok always have been generally private, averse to open exchange with persons outside their respective tribal communities. The Bole Maru, with its emphasis on local individual dreamers, reinforced the stringent localism of the precontact cultures. Secrecy as an aspect of precontact culture became an asset for the resistance and reorganization.

THE AUTHOR

So what am I doing writing about the Bole Maru?

What am I doing telling this story?

In creating narratives for others about our narratives, religious or otherwise, in what ways am I not only compromising those narratives but at the same time compromising my tribes' resistance and identity, which are largely dependent upon these narratives? How might my particular discussion of the Bole Maru from an insider's perspective be appropriated by outsiders for their purposes, political or otherwise? The fact that I am writing, or even speaking, about the Bole Maru in this essay requires that my presentation utilize certain narrative forms, alone or together, that are accessible and intelligible to those of you who are not Kashaya Pomo or Coast Miwok. The ways I hear about and experience the Bole Maru religion are generally not similar in form to my narrative form of presentation and explanation, which is, at least in the middle part of this essay, "hypothetical-deductive" (R. Rosaldo 1989:132). I present an event or narrative, say about the Bole Maru, and deductively prove or disprove given hypotheses regarding the event or narrative. If you are an outsider to Bole Maru tradition, your sense and understanding of the tradition are based largely on this narrative model. The model affords little regarding my Kashaya/Coast Miwok sense of the Bole Maru in terms of its relationship to other facets of Pomo or Miwok culture and individual identity. Is the fact that for you I must distort and reinvent my Bole Maru stories and experience of them assurance that they are safe, at least in their previous forms? Will significant content leak out and be appropriated regardless? What can possibly be achieved here for both you and me?

So far I have mentioned only features of the Bole Maru that are generally known or that, if known, would be of no particular threat to Kashaya Pomo and Coast Miwok people. I have spoken of the movement in the past tense. You do not know, for example, the ways in which a meaningful retention of Pomo and Miwok values is maintained or the ways in which retention constitutes resistance. Specifically, what I have not talked about is the present state of affairs. What of my family's current activities associated with the Bole Maru tradition? We do not and, according to my Auntie Violet Chappell, we never have, referred to that tradition as Bole Maru. "Those are white men's words," Violet says. According to DuBois, "This is a compound term consisting respectively of the Patwin and Pomo words for the cult" (1971:497). What Pomo tribe was she referring to? Pomo and Patwin are also "white men's words," terms ethnographers used to categorize us by language families that they invented with linguists to order to make sense of the cultural diversity they encountered among Native peoples in the area.

We are Pomo, Kashaya Pomo, or whatever Pomo because we must be such for the purposes of the Bureau of Indian Affairs (B.I.A.) and other U.S. government agencies. It is something we don, like the Victorian clothes of the old. The Kashaya Pomo, or southwestern Pomo, are, and have been since time immemorial, ***wina•má•bakě ya'***, "people who belong to the land."

Enough already.

I have talked about this before.

Back again to the questions I must ask: What am I doing telling this story? Who am I as a writer?

The problem isn't just that I am an Indian working in the academy and writing this paper. The problem is compounded by the fact that I am a mixed-blood Indian. My mother, Bunny Hartman, was Jewish. I was adopted early on by a white family and later ended up with my paternal grandmother's people. Race relations between whites and Indians are tense to this day, given their histories. I often find myself in an uncomfortable borderlands existence. "Don't let the white come out in you," Indian relatives admonish. "Don't sell out your Indian self in the schools. Remember who you are."

Because I am a mixed-blood I often feel self-conscious around Indian relatives. I want to be true to my Indian family. And they seem to tell me so much. I think of the warm summer nights Mrs. Carrio took time off from her large family to talk to me. I see her face, kind eyes, and earnest expression, hear the soft sounds of her high, clear voice, as she sat with me in her kitchen. "This happened to my grandmother," she would say. And my Auntie Violet up at Kashaya Reservation. The smell of wood smoke from her wood-burning stove, the smell of fresh-baked huckleberry pies. I see all the family pictures on her walls. I see her taking down her shell-adorned tribal cross before a prayer ceremony. I hear her songs. I hear her talking. "This is what Mom said. About the creation, how beautiful it is, who we are."

I see, too, the poverty, the sadness. My father died of a massive heart attack at age fifty-two. He was a chronic alcoholic. He seemed to hate whites, as did his mother, my grandmother. Yet he married three white women. He beat those women.

Who I am as a writer, as a person, is someone containing the conflict, the coming together, of histories, cultures. My education and training as an academic and writer only add voices, inner disputants, to a world of multiple voices. The chorus of intermingling, often conflicting, voices grows, produces new sounds. What I do, then, as a writer, is convey as much as possible the multiple voices that constitute not only me but also what I think and write about. The politics, personae, and different points of view (and narrative styles associated with the different points of view) about a given topic, say the Bole Maru, begin to shine through the writing. What I hope to have done is provide a way for us to start talking interculturally and interpersonally about what is in fact intercultural and interpersonal. As a so-called minority person I have within me from my experiences multiple discourses that illuminate the intercultural topic and the politics associated with writing about the topic. I must use that voice which is personal as well as critical, showing ultimately the arbitrariness of the terms. Each voice informs the other. My writing, or poetics, then, is in form my politics. By reducing or conflating the different voices and narratives into a single and dominant discourse, I would replicate in the poetics and politics of writing the colonial history of cultural domination. I would silence many voices. I would silence the opportunity for all of us to talk with and hear one another.

Of course any silencing of the multiple voices ultimately works to fix my identity and sense of self in given ways. As I write and present the politics, personae, and different points of view about a given intercultural topic, I am calling forth the multiple voices and points of view that not only inform me but also constitute my identity. The multivoiced self as such becomes, in Lavie and Swedenburg's words, "constantly mobile contiguities whose rugged edges cannot be smoothed out. . . . [This identity] goes beyond boundaries, frustrating frontierization and throwing its negative energy back at the Eurocenter, thereby making the fissures unmendable" (1992). I am an American Indian, but not an isolated subject in the bush to be studied by others. I, too, study. I am a scholar, but one informed by activity, cultural and otherwise, that can interrogate and inform the activity of the academy. I do not stay put. Dorinne Kondo (in this volume) notes that "Asian American playwrights, writers, artists are creating identities that defy binary categorization into Asian or American, or into some third mediating term. They are articulating for Asian Americans something new, something that exceeds previous categories."

If I silence any of the voices that constitute my identity, I not only fix the self in given ways, say as a certain type of scholar or American Indian, but I also become containable and fixed by others. My writing then expresses and opens up the self. And, as important, my writing, my various styles of narrative presentation, the various voices, do not allow my subject to be containable, fixed by others. The Bole Maru cannot be torn apart here; its power and the agency of our people cannot be invaded, diminished, appropriated. Instead, the Bole Maru and my writing about it make for new possibilities of understanding in a history that shapes not only my self but also that of the reader.

So much of the Pomo and Coast Miwok history with miracles continues today. The Bole Maru continues today. It was and is a Native response to colonialism. Richard Taylor's Dream and much of the early Bole Maru doctrine were essentialist, separatist. Taylor dreamed of an "uncontaminated and unruptured past" that would return. That didn't happen, and much of the early doctrine only furthered our problems with the white world, as I noted. An important feature of the Bole Maru, aside from its emphasis on individual Dreamers for each tribe, is the stipulation that with each new Dreamer a new set of costumes, dances, and ceremonies must be brought forth. When a Dreamer dies, most of her particular ceremonies are stopped and her costumes are destroyed. Hence, the Bole Maru is continually reinvented and suited to the changing (historic) times. Essie Parrish, the last Bole Maru Dreamer among the Kashaya Pomo, favored more open relations with the outside world and felt formal schooling could help our people communicate with others. She allowed non-Indians to witness many of our ceremonies. The Bole Maru, then, at least under the Dream of Essie Parrish, moved away from an essentializing, separatist cult. Yet open communication between Indians and non-Indians remains strained. Mrs. Parrish admonished us to keep our secrets, remember the Dream rules, and sing our songs in a world where we have lost everything else.

Perhaps in talking about the problems of talking about the Bole Maru, we can continue to open the doors, slowly and respectfully: whites, Indians, mixed-bloods.

HISTORY (RECORDED)

1992 Many museums display Pomo and Coast Miwok artifacts.

— Eighty percent of California Indian schoolchildren drop out of school by ninth grade. Less than 8 percent graduate from high school.

— Life expectancy for a California Indian male is forty-eight years. The teenage California Indian male suicide rate is eight times the state average for the same age group. Kashaya Pomo and Coast Miwok statistics are consistent with California stats.

— Early this year the Kashaya Pomo were without running water for three months.

— The Coast Miwok continue to fight for federal recognition (as an Indian tribe) and a land base. Descendants of Tom Smith, Bill Smith, and Maria Copa lead the battle, pointing to anthropologists Alfred Kroeber and Isabel Kelly's use of Tom Smith and Maria Copa as Coast Miwok informants for the Coast Miwok tribes.[3]

HISTORY (TRIBAL/FAMILY)

Violet Chappell: "What changes? Remember, we are living with miracles."

NOTES

1 I wrote about the Bole Maru and some of these same problems in an earlier paper. See "Telling Dreams and Keeping Secrets: The Bole Maru as American Indian Religious Resistance," *American Indian Culture and Research Journal* 16, no. 1 (Spring 1992):71–85.

2 For interesting discussions of the Plains Ghost Dance religion, see James Mooney, *The Ghost Dance Religion and the Sioux Outbreak of 1890* (1965). Also, readers might be interested in A. F. C. Wallace's "revitalization" model and his *The Death and Rebirth of the Seneca* (1970). Wallace provides a description and analysis of American Indian revitalization.

3 On my birth certificate the race of my father is listed as "unknown non-white." With clearly documented lineage to Tom Smith, such identification of my father tells part of the larger story of our struggles with a U.S. government that works to systematically destroy our identity and sovereignty as a people and at the same time cast us as non-white, distinct and separate from the Euroamerican center. Of course, as a people the Coast Miwok continue to name the "unknown non-white," for ourselves and for others.

ANZALDÚA'S *FRONTERA*: INSCRIBING GYNETICS

NORMA ALARCÓN

THE INSCRIPTION OF THE SUBJECT

In our time the very categorical and/or conceptual frameworks, through which we explicitly or implicitly perceive our sociopolitical realities and our own contextual subject insertion, are very much in question. Theoretically infused writing practices, like those found in anthologies such as *This Bridge Called My Back; All the Women Are White, All Blacks Are Men, but Some of Us Are Brave;* and *Making Face/Making Soul: Haciendo Caras,* call attention to that insertion. The self that writes combines a polyvalent consciousness of "the writer as historical subject (who writes? and in what context?), but also writing itself as located at the intersection of subject and history—a literary practice that involves the possible knowledge (linguistical and ideological) of itself as such" (Trinh 1990b:245). Self-inscriptions, as "focal point of cultural consciousness and social change . . . weave into language the complex relations of a subject caught between the contradictory dilemmas of race, gender, ethnicity, sexualities, and class; transition between orality and literacy"; and the "practice of literature as the very place where social alienation is thwarted differently according to each specific context" (Trinh 1990b:245).

Self-inscription as "focal point of cultural consciousness and social change" is as vexed a practice for the more "organic/specific" intellectual as it is for the "academic/specific" intellectual trained in institutions whose business is often to continue to reproduce his hegemonic hold on cognitive charting and its (political) distribution in the academy itself. As a result, it should be no surprise that critics of color, in a different context than that of *Bridge* and thus differently articulated, nevertheless critique through their exclusion, their absence, or their displacement from the theoretical production and positions taken by Euroamerican feminists and African Americanists: "The black woman as critic," says Valerie Smith, "and more broadly as the locus where gender-, class-, and race-based oppression intersect, is often invoked when Anglo-American feminists and male Afro-Americanists begin to rematerialize their discourse" (Valerie Smith 1989:44). Thus cultural/national dislocations also produce cognitive ones as the models that assume dominance increasingly reify their discourse through the use of nonrevised theories, thus resembling more and more so-called androcentric criticisms. In other words, Smith says, "when historical specificity is denied or remains implicit, all the women are presumed white, all the blacks male. The move to include black women as historical presences and as speaking subjects in critical discourse may well then be used as a defense against charges of racial hegemony on the part of white women and sexist hegemony on the part of black males" (Valerie Smith 1989:44–45).

Thus the "black woman" appears as "historicizing presence," which is to say that as the critical gaze becomes more distanced from itself as speaker, it looks to "black women" as the objective difference that historicizes the text in the present, signaling the degree to which such theorists have ambiguously assumed the position of Same/I. In this circuitous manner the critical eye/I claims Same/not Same, an inescapability that itself is in need of elaboration. I would suggest at this time that it is not so much that, as it is the possibility that the writing practices we are compelled to work with, and their concomitant demands for certain kinds of linear rationality, demand that self/other duality. Consequently, the difference within, as such, cannot be grasped; rather, one is forced to discover it in a specular manner in *her*. She is the "objective" difference that serves to mediate the discourse produced oppositionally to the "Name of the Father and the Place of the Law," which in my view currently accounts for the demand in the academy for the texts of "women of color," who may soon be supplanted. Smith goes on to affirm that as Black feminist theorists emerge, they challenge "the conceptualizations of literary study and concern themselves increasingly with the effect of race, class, and gender on the practice of literary criticism" (Valerie Smith 1989:46–47).

My intention here is not so much to produce a "literary criticism" for Chicanas, nor do I want to be limited by the reach of what are perceived as "literary texts." I want to be able to hybridize the textual field so that what is at stake is not so much our inclusion or exclusion in literary/textual genealogies and the modes of their production—which have a limited, though important critical reach—as it is coming to terms with the formation and displacement of subjects, as writers/critics/chroniclers of the nation, and with the possibility that we have continued to recodify a family romance, an oedipal drama in which the woman of color in the Americas has no "designated" place. She is simultaneously presence/absence in the configurations of the nation-state and textual representation. Moreover, the moment she emerges as a "speaking subject in process," the heretofore triadic manner in which the modern world has largely taken shape becomes endlessly heterogeneous and ruptures the "oedipal family romance." That is, the underlying structure of the social and cultural forms of the organization of modern Western societies, which have been superimposed through systems of domination—political, cultural, and theoretical—and which subsequent oppositional nation-making narratives have adapted, is, in the Americas, disrupted by the work of writers/critics of color such as Chicanas, so that we must "make *familia* from scratch."

In an earlier essay, "Chicana Feminisms: In the Track of the Native Woman" (1990b), I appropriated, as metonym and metaphor for the referent/figure of the Chicana, Lyotard's notion of the "differend," which he defines as "a case of conflict, between (at least) two parties that cannot be equitably resolved for lack of rule of judgment applicable to both arguments. One side's legitimacy does not imply the other's lack of legitimacy" (Lyotard 1988:xi). In part her conflictive and conflicted position emerges, as Smith affirms, when the oppositional discourses of "White" women and "Black" men vie for her "difference" as historical materialization and/or a shifting deconstructive maneuver of patriarchy, "The Name of the Father and the Place of the Law." Yet one must keep in mind that Lyotard's disquisition on the term doesn't negotiate well the transitions between textual representation and political/juridical representation. As Fraser has noted, "There is no place in Lyotard's universe for critique of pervasive axes of stratification, for critique of broad-based relations of dominance and subordination along lines like gender, race and class" (Fraser and Nicholson 1990:23). Relations of dominance and subordination arise out of the political economy and the ways in which the nation has generated its self-representation in order to harness its population toward its own self-projection on behalf of the elite—as such the formation of political economies, in tandem with the making of nations—provide the locations from which historical material specificity arises, generating its own discourses that philosophically may or may not coincide with theories of textual representation.

The shift from theories of symbolic self-representation to juridical and phenomenological theories is not seamless; indeed, the interstice, the discontinuity, the gap is precisely a site of textual production: the historical and ideological moment in which the subject inscribes herself. In other words, the historical writing subject emerges into conflictive discourses generated by theories of representation, whether juridical or textual/symbolic. Each is rule-governed by different presuppositions, and a Chicana may have better fortunes at representing herself or being represented textually than legally as a Chicana. That is, the juridical text is generated by the ruling elite, who have access to the state apparatuses through which the political economy is shaped and jurisprudence is engendered, whereas representation in the cultural text may include representations generated by herself. However, insofar as the latter are, as it were, "marginalia," they not only exist in the interstices; they are produced from the interstices. She, akin to Anzaldúa's "Shadow Beast," sends us as "stand-ins," reinforcing and insuring the interstitiality of a differend as the nonsite from which critique is possible. Her migratory status, which deprives her of the protection of "home," whether it be a stable town or a nation-state, generates a historical discourse of displacements that it is our task to rearticulate.

The "Shadow Beast," ultimately, undermines a monological self-representation and "threatens the sovereignty" of such a consciousness, because it kicks out the constraints and "bolts" "at the least hint of limitations" (Anzaldúa, 1990:16).

INSCRIBING GYNETICS

Gloria Anzaldúa is a self-named Chicana from Hargill, Texas, a rural town in what is known as El Valle, "the Valley." It is an agricultural area notorious for its mistreatment of people of Mexican descent. Indeed, many of the narratives that emerge from that area tell of the conflictive and violent relations in the forging of an anglicized Texas out of the Texas-Coahuila territory of New Spain, as well as of the eventual production of the geopolitical border between Mexico and the United States. These borderlands are spaces where, as a result of expansionary wars, colonization, juridico-immigratory policing, *coyote* exploitation of émigrés and group vigilantes, formations of violence are continuously in the making. As racialized confrontations, these have been taking place at least since the Spanish began to settle Mexico's (New Spain) "northern" frontier, what is now the Anglo-Americanized Southwest. Subsequently, and especially after the end of the

Mexican-American War in 1848, these formations of violence have been often dichotomized into Mexican/American, which actually has the effect of muting the presence of indigenous peoples yet setting "the context for the formation of 'races'" (Montejano 1987:309).

Consequently, the modes of autohistoricization in and of the borderlands often emphasize or begin with accounts of violent racialized collisions. It is not surprising, then, that Anzaldúa should refer to the current U.S./Mexican border as an "open wound" from Brownsville to San Diego, from Tijuana to Matamoros, where the former are considerably richer than the latter, and the geopolitical line itself artificially divides into a two-class/culture system; that is, the configuration of the political economy has the "third" world rub against the "first." Though the linguistic and culture systems on the border are highly fluid in their dispersal, the geopolitical lines tend to become univocal, that is, "Mexican" and "Anglo."

Of Hargill, Texas, and Hidalgo County and environs, Gloria Anzaldúa says: "This land has survived possession and ill-use by five powers: Spain, Mexico, the Republic of Texas, the United States, the Confederacy, and the U.S. again. It has survived Anglo-Mexican blood feuds, lynchings, burnings, rapes, pillage" (Anzaldúa 1987:90). Hidalgo is the "most poverty stricken county in the nation as well as the largest home base (along with the Imperial Valley in California) for migrant farmworkers." She continues, "It was here that I was born and raised. I am amazed that both it and I have survived" (Anzaldúa 1987:98).

Through this geographic space, then, people displaced by a territorialized political economy, whose juridical centers of power are elsewhere—in this case Mexico, D.F., and Washington, D.C.—attempt to reduce the level of material dispossession through the production of both counter- and disidentificatory discourses. That is, the land is repossessed in imaginary terms, in both the Lacanian and the Althusserian senses. I shall return below to a more elaborate discussion of this proposition, in which I will further characterize the senses as dialogically paradigmatic and syntagmatic, respectively, yielding a highly creative heteroglossia.

However, before turning to Anzaldúa's attempt to repossess the borderlands, let's quickly review one area of counteridentificatory or oppositional discursive productions. Américo Paredes, and now his follower José E. Limón, claim El Valle as the site where the *corrido* originated. That is, in the Americas, in the Valley of a landmass now named Texas, a completely "new" genre emerged, the *corrido*. As such, Limón strategically moves the emergence toward a disengagement from claims of the *corrido*'s origins in the Spanish *romance*—Spain's own border ballads. The Paredes-Limón move could be contextualized as racialized, class- and culture-based. The trans(form)ation and trans(figure)ation in raced class-crossing remains unexplored (Limón 1992:chap. 1). That is, the metamorphoses of the Spanish ballad form are induced by the emergence of an oppositional hero in the U.S.-Mexico border whose raced class position is substantially different. Limón's strategy is in contradiction to that of María Herrera-Sobek in her book *The Mexican Corrido: A Feminist Analysis,* where she aligns the *corrido* with the Peninsular origins theory in which border ballads also emerged in the making of Spain. Herrera-Sobek's lack of desire to disengage the formal origins from Spain and relocalize them in Texas could be a function of an implicit feminist position: the representation of women, be it in the *romance* or in the *corrido,* reenacts a specularly Manichaean scenario in the patriarchal tableau.

The point of my analysis, however, is to call attention to the need to "repossess" the land, especially in cultural nationalist narratives, through scenarios of "origins" that emerge in the selfsame territory, be it at the literary, legendary, historical, ideological, critical, or theoretical level—producing in material and imaginary terms "authentic" and "inauthentic," "legal" and "illegal" subjects. That is, the drive to territorialize/authenticate/legalize and deterritorialize/deauthenticate/delegalize is ever present, thus constantly producing "(il)legal"/(non)citizen subjects in both political and symbolic representations, in a geographical area where looks and dress have become increasingly telling of one's (un)documented status (Nathan 1991). It should be no surprise, then, that the *corrido* makes a paradigmatic oppositional hero of the persecuted in the figuration of the unjustly outlaw(ed), the unjustly (un)documented: in Gloria's terms, Queers. Thus, also, in Anzaldúa's terms, the convergence of claims to proper ownership of the land "has created a shock culture, a border culture, a third country, a closed country" (Anzaldúa 1987:11) where the "detribalized" population not only is comprised of "females . . . homosexuals of all races, the darkskinned, the outcast, the persecuted, the marginalized, the foreign" (Anzaldúa 1990:38) but also is possessed of the "faculty," a "sensing." In short, a different consciousness, which, as we shall see, is represented by the formulation of the consciousness of the "new mestiza," a reconceptualized feminine/feminist.

If, however, Gregorio Cortés becomes a paradigmatic oppositional *corrido* figure of Texas-Mexican ethnonationalism, given new energy after the

1958 publication of Paredes' *With His Pistol in His Hand* (1971), Gloria Anzaldúa crosscuts masculine-coded "Tex-Mex" nationalism through a configuration of a borderland "Third Country" as a polyvocal rather than univocal Imaginary. She says, "If going home is denied me then I will have to stand and claim my space, making a new culture—*una cultura mestiza*—with my own lumber, my own bricks and mortar and my own feminist architecture" (Anzaldúa 1987:22). To the extent that she wavers in her desire for reterritorialization à la Gregorio Cortés' oppositional paradigm, the "third country" becomes a "closed country," bounded; to the extent that she wants to undercut the "Man of Reason," the unified sovereign subject of philosophy, she constructs a "crossroads of the self," a mestiza consciousness. Anzaldúa's conceptualization of the mestiza as a produced vector of multiple culture transfers and transitions corresponds simultaneously to Jameson's version of the Lacanian preindividualistic "structural crossroads." That is, "in frequent shifts of the subject from one fixed position to another, in a kind of optional multiplicity of insertions of the subject into a relatively fixed Symbolic Order" (Jameson 1991:354). It has resonance with Cornelius Castoriadis' version as well: "The subject in question is . . . not the abstract moment of philosophical subjectivity; it is the actual subject traversed through and through by the world and by others. . . . It is the active and lucid agency that constantly reorganizes its contents, through the help of these same contents, that produces by means of a material and in relation to needs and ideas, all of which are themselves mixtures of what it has already found there before it and what it has produced itself" (Castoriadis 1987:106).

Notwithstanding the different locations of each theorist—Anzaldúa, Jameson, and Castoriadis—the resonance is inescapable. That transversal simultaneity is the one where the speaking subject-in-process is both traversed "by the world and by others" and takes hold so as to exercise the "lucid agency that constantly reorganizes . . . contents." Now, the relatively fixed symbolic order that Anzaldúa's text crosscuts is differently reorganized as Anzaldúa shifts the targets of engagement. It is now cutting across Eurohegemonic representations of Woman, now Freudian/Lacanian psychoanalysis ("I know things older than Freud" [Anzaldúa 1987:26]), through Jungian psychoanthropology, and the rationality of the sovereign subject as she, in nonlinear and nondevelopmental ways, shifts the "names" of her resistant subject positions—Snake Woman, La Chingada, Tlazolteotl, Coatlicue, Cihuacoatl, Tonantsi, Guadalupe, La Llorona . . . . The polyvalent name insertions in *Borderlands* are a rewriting of the feminine, a reinscription of gynetics. Of such revisionary tactics, Drucilla Cornell says, in another context, "in affirmation, as a positioning, as a performance, rather than of Woman as a description of reality" (Cornell, 1992). Since the category of Woman, in the case of Chicanas/Latinas and other women of color, has not been fully mapped, nor rewritten across culture classes, the multiple-writing, multiple-naming gesture must be carried out, given the absence of any shared textualization. Thus, a text such as Anzaldúa's is the "ethnic" performance of an implicitly tangential Derridean deconstructive gesture that "must, by means of a double gesture, a double science, a double writing, practice an *overturning* [*sic*] of the classical opposition *and* [*sic*] a general *displacement* [*sic*] of the system" (Derrida 1982a:329). That is, through the textual production of, and the speaking position of, a "mestiza consciousness," and the recuperation and recodification of the multiple names of "Woman," Anzaldúa deconstructs ethnonational oppositional consciousness and its doublet, "the Man of Reason."

Insofar as Anzaldúa implicitly recognizes the power of the nation-state to produce "political subjects" who are now legal, now illegal, deprived of citizenship, she opts for "ethnonationalism" and reterritorialization in the guise of a "closed/third country." Although she rejects a masculinist ethnonationalism that would exclude the Queer, she does not totally discard a "neonationalism" (i.e., the "closed/third" country) for the reappropriated borderlands, Aztlán. However, it is now open to all of the excluded, not just Chicanos but all Queers. That is, the formation of a utopian imaginary community in Aztlán would displace the ideology of the "holy family"/"family romance" still prevalent in El Valle and elsewhere in the Southwest, which makes it possible for many to turn away from confronting other social formations of violence.

The imaginary utopian community reconfirms from a different angle Liisa Malkki's claim that our confrontation with displacement and the desire for "home" brings into the field of vision "the sedentarist metaphysic embedded in the national order of things" (1992:31). That is, the counter-discursive construction of an alternative utopian imagined community reproduces the "sedentarist metaphysic" in (re)territorialization. Malkki continues, "Sedentarist assumptions about attachment to place lead us to define displacement not as a fact about sociopolitical content, but rather as an inner, pathological condition of the displaced" (1992:32–33). Anzaldúa has clear recognition of this in the concept of a "mestiza consciousness," as well as in her privileging of the notion of migratoriness, the multiplicity of our names, and the reclamation of the borderlands in feminist terms that risk the "pathological condition" by representing the nonlinearity and the break with a developmental view of self-inscription: "We can no longer blame you nor disown the white parts, the male parts, the pathological parts, the queer parts, the vulnerable parts. Here we are weaponless with open arms, with only our magic. Let's try it our way, the mestiza way, the Chicana way, the woman way" (Anzaldúa 1987:88). Indeed, the hunger for wholeness—*el sentirse completa*—guides the chronicles, and that hunger is the same desire that brings into view both the migratoriness of the population and the reappropriation of "Home." That is, in the Americas today, the processes of sociopolitical empire and nation-making displacements over a five-hundred-year history are such that the notion of "Home" is as mobile as the populations, a "home" without juridically nationalized geopolitical territory.

THE "SHADOW BEAST" MOVES US ON

The trope of the "Shadow Beast" in the work of Gloria Anzaldúa functions simultaneously as a trope of a recodified Lacanian unconscious, "as the discourse of the Other," and as an Althusserian Imaginary through which the real is grasped and represented (Lacan 1977; Althusser, 1971). That is, the "Shadow Beast" functions as the "native" women of the Americas, as a sign of savagery—the feminine as a sign of chaos. The speaking subject as stand-in for the "native" woman is already spoken for through the multiple discourses of the Other, as both an unconscious and an ideology. Thus, the question becomes what happens if the subject speaks through both simultaneously and, implicitly grasping her deconstruction of such discursive structures, proposes the New Consciousness: "This almost finished product seems an assemblage, a montage, a beaded work with several leitmotifs and with a central core, now appearing, now disappearing in a crazy dance" (Anzaldúa 1990:66). "It is this learning to live with *la coatlicue* that transforms living in the borderlands from a nightmare into a numinous experience. It is always a path/state to something else" (Anzaldúa 1987:73).

The Lacanian linguistic unconscious sets in motion a triangulated, paradigmatic tale of mother/daughter/lesbian lover. The Althusserian Imaginary, on the other hand, sets in motion syntagmatic conjunctions of experience, language, folklore, history, Jungian psychoanthropology, and political economy. Some of these are authorized by "academic" footnotes that go so far as to appeal to the reader for the authorizing sources that will "legitimate" the statement. Some of these conjunctions in effect link multiple ideologies of racist misogyny as it pertains to Indians/mestizas. Simultaneously the Shadow Beast is metonymically articulated with Snake Woman, Coatlicue, Guadalupe, La Chingada, et al., and concatenated into a symbolic metaphor through which more figures are generated to produce the axial paradigm—the totalizing repression of the lesboerotic in the fabulation of the modern nation-state. The chronicle effect, however, is primarily produced through the syntagmatic movement of a collective text one may call "pan-Mexican," yet relocated to the borderlands, thus making the whole of it a Chicano narrative. The indigenous terms and figurations have filtered through the Spanish-language cultural text; the code switching reveals the fissures and hybridity of the various incomplete imperialist/neocolonial projects. The terms and figurations preserved through the oral traditions and/or folk talk/street talk coexist uneasily with "straight talk," that is, Standard Spanish and Standard English, all of which coexist uneasily with scholarly citations. The very "symbolic order" that "unifies" in Anzaldúa's text—the production, organization, and inscription of mestiza consciousness—is granted the task of deconstruction in order to reconstruct, to recenter elsewhere.

In short, then, Coatlicue (or almost any of her metonymically related sisters) represents the non(pre)-oedipal (in this case non[pre]-Columbian) mother, who displaces and/or coexists in perennial interrogation of the "Phallic Mother," the one complicitous in the Freudian "family romance." Coatlicue is released as non(pre)-oedipal and non-Phallic Mother: "And someone in me takes matters into our own hands, and eventually, takes dominion over serpents—over my own body, my sexual activity, my soul, my mind, my weaknesses and strength. Mine. Ours. Not the heterosexual white man's or the colored man's or the state's or the culture's or the religion's or the parents'—just ours, mine. . . . And suddenly I feel everything rushing to a center, a nucleus. All the lost pieces of myself coming flying from the deserts and the mountains and the valleys, magnetized toward that center. Completa" (Anzaldúa 1987:51). Anzaldúa resituates Coatlicue through the process of the dreamwork, conjures her from nonconscious memory, through the serpentine folklore of her youth. The desire to center, to originate, to fuse with the feminine/maternal/lover in the safety of an imaginary "third country," the borderlands disidentified from the actual site where the nation-state draws the juridical line, where formations of violence play themselves throughout miles on either side of the line: "she leaves the familiar and safe homeground to venture into the unknown and possibly dangerous terrain. This is her home/this thin edge of/barbwire" (Anzaldúa 1987:13).

The sojourner is as undocumented as some *maquila* workers in southern California. In this fashion the syntagmatic narratives, as an effect in profound structural complicity with ideologies of the nonrational "Shadow Beast," contribute to the discursive structuration of the speaking subject who links them to figures (like Coatlicue) of paradigmatic symbolicity recodified for ethical and political intent in our time, engaged in the search, in Anzaldúa's vocabulary, for the "third space." Anzaldúa destabilizes our reading practices as autobiographical anecdotes, anthropology, linguistic forms, legend, history, and "Freud" are woven together and fused for the recuperation that will not go unrecognized this time around. Anzaldúa's work is what Caren Kaplan calls a resistance to modernist autobiography (Kaplan 1992).

When Gloria says she knows "things older than Freud," notwithstanding the whispering effect of such a brief phrase, she is, I think, announcing her plan to re(dis)cover what his system, and in Lacanian terms the "patronymic legal system," displaces. This is so especially with reference to the oedipal/family romance drama. The Freudian/Lacanian systems are contiguous to rationality, the "Man of Reason," the subject-conscious-of-itself-as-subject, insofar as such a subject is the point of their departure (Lacan 1977). Thus the system that displaces the Maternal Law replaces it with the concept of the "unconscious" where the "primal repression" is stored, so that consciousness and rationality may be privileged especially as the constituted point of departure for the discovery of the "unconscious." Further, it constitutes itself as the science-making project displacing what will thereafter be known as mythological systems, that is, the multiple systems of signification of the "unconscious-as-the-discourse-of-the-Other," to which the maternal/feminine is also imperfectly banished.

In a sense Anzaldúa's eccentricity—effected through non-Western folk/myth tropes and practices as recent as yesterday in historical terms, through the testimonies textually conserved after the conquest, and, more recently, through icons excavated in 1968 by workmen repairing Mexico City's metro—constructs a tale that is feminist in intent. It is feminist insofar as through the tropic displacement of another system, she re(dis)covers the mother and gives birth to herself as inscriber/speaker of/for mestiza consciousness. In Julia Kristeva's words, "Such an excursion to the limits of primal regression can be phanthasmatically experienced as a 'woman-mother'." However, it is not as a "woman-mother" that Anzaldúa's narrator actualizes the lesboerotic "visitation" of Coatlicue but as daughter and "queer." Kristeva gives us a sanitized "homosexual facet of motherhood" as woman becomes a mother to recollect her own union with her mother. Though in her early work Kristeva posited the semiotic "as the disruptive power of the feminine that could not be known and thus fully captured by the masculine symbolic," she has "turned away from any attempt to write the repressed maternal or the maternal body as a counterforce to the Law of the Father" (Cornell 1992:7). We are left instead with a theorization of the "maternal function" in the established hierarchy of the masculine symbolic (Cornell, 1991:7). Gloria's narrator, however, represents the fusion without the mediation of the maternal facet. In Kristeva's text the "sanitization" takes place on the plane of preserving rather than disrupting the Freudian/Lacanian oedipal/family romance systems, not to mention the triadic Christian configuration (Kristeva 1980:239).

Anzaldúa's rewriting of the feminine through the polyvalent Shadow Beast is an attempt, on the one hand, to reinscribe what has been lost through colonization—she says, "Let's root ourselves in the mythological soil and soul of this continent" (1987:68), and on the other hand, to reinscribe it as the contemporaneous codification of a "primary metaphorization" as Irigaray has posited it—the repressed feminine in the symbolic order of the Name of the Father, as expressed in the Lacanian rearticulation of Freud and the Western metaphysic (Butler 1990). According to Irigaray, the psychic organization for women under patriarchy is fragmented and scattered, so that this is also experienced as dismemberment of the body, that is, "the nonsymbolization" of her desire for origin, of her relationship to her mother, and of her libido, and acts as a constant to polymorphic regressions due to "too few figurations, images of representations by which to represent herself" (Irigaray 1985:71). I am not citing Irigaray so that her work can be used as a medium for diagnostic exercises of Anzaldúa's work as "polymorphic regressions." Anzaldúa's work is simultaneously a complicity with, a resistance to, and a disruption of Western psychoanalysis through systems of signification drastically different from those of Irigaray, for example. Yet the simultaneity of conjunctures is constitutive of Anzaldúa's text. Indeed, what Irigaray schematizes as description is the multiple ways in which the "oedipal/family romance," whatever language form it takes, makes women sick even as it tries to inscribe their resistance as illness.

The struggle for representation is not an inversion per se; rather, the struggle to heal through rewriting and retextualization yields a borrowing of signifiers from diverse monological discourses, as Anzaldúa does, in an effort to push toward the production of another signifying system that not only heals through re-membering the paradigmatic narratives that recover memory and history, but also rewrites the heterogeneity of the present. The desire is not so much for a counterdiscourse as for a disidentificatory one that swerves away and begins the laborious construction of a new lexicon and grammars. Anzaldúa weaves self-inscriptions of mother/daughter/lover that, if unsymbolized as "primary metaphorization" of desire, will hinder "women from having an identity in the symbolic order that is distinct from the maternal function and thus prevents them [us] from constituting any real threat to the order of Western metaphysics" (Irigaray 1985:71)—or, if you will, the national/ethnonational "family romance." Anzaldúa is engaged in the recuperation and rewriting of that feminine/ist "origin" not only in the interfacing sites of various symbolizations but also on the geopolitical border itself—El Valle (Saldívar-Hull 1991).

Anzaldúa's "Shadow Beast," intratextually recodified as Snake Woman, La Llorona, and other figurations, sends her stand-in forth as an Outlaw, a Queer, a *mita y mita,* a fluid sexuality deployed through a fluid cultural space, the borderlands, which stands within sight of the patronymic Law, and where many (except those who possess it) are Outlaws, endlessly represented as alterities by D.C. and D.F. *Borderlands/La Frontera* is an "instinctive urge to communicate, to speak, to write about life on the borders, life in the shadows," the preoccupations with the inner life of the Self, and with the struggle of that Self amid adversity and violation with the "unique positionings consciousness takes at these confluent streams" of inner/outer. An outer that is presented by the Texas-U.S., Southwest/Mexican border . . . and the psychological borderlands, "the sexual and spiritual borderlands" (Anzaldúa 1990:preface). A self that becomes a crossroads, a collision course, a clearinghouse, an endless alterity who, once she emerges into language and self-inscription so belatedly, appears as a tireless peregrine collecting all the parts that will never make her whole. Such a hunger forces her to recollect in excess, to remember in excess, to labor to excess, and to produce a text layered with inversions and disproportions, which are functions of experienced dislocations, vis-à-vis the text of the Name of the Father and the Place of the Law.

BLOWUPS IN THE BORDERZONES: THIRD WORLD ISRAELI AUTHORS' GROPINGS FOR HOME

SMADAR LAVIE

"I don't feel grounded anywhere. I've come back to the village, but it feels like a hotel, not home."

We were sitting on Naʿim ʿAraidi's balcony as he spoke into my tape recorder. ʿAraidi is a Druze writer who uses Hebrew as his language of poetic expression. From his book *Back to the Village*,[1] the words of the title poem flashed through my mind.

Back to the village
Where I found how to cry my first cry
Back to the mountain
Where nature's so full
The walls bear no art
Back in my home, of stones
My fathers hacked from rock
Back to myself—
And that was why I came. . . .

The verse describes the stunning Galilean scene below the balcony. ʿAraidi's cool house, built as a second story over the roof of his parents' house, crowns the mountain ridge above the rest of the village, Meghar, which clusters down the steep slope. Beyond lie fields, rolling squares of green and yellow shimmering in the July heat.

As in the poem, the solid walls bear no framed pictures nor photographs. Instead, someone has meticulously painted the brown outlines of large stones, forming several rounded arches. Inside these skeletons is the plain cream-colored wall. They are dream arches that lead nowhere, to a blank. Against this rose the apparition of the Western-trained anthropologist I was trying to be, the promise of whose Baltic heritage from her father was disrupted by her mother's Yemeni family, Arab-Jews in Palestine for several generations.[2] The anthropologist's nostalgia for the essentialized rebellious peasant, that dominant trope of "salvage ethnography" (Clifford 1986:112–118), was rudely interrupted by mundane cinder blocks, typical of Israeli construction, peeking out from the unfinished stone facade. As the heat wavered up the valley, we drank hot, bitter coffee spiced with cardamom, cyclically alternating with icy orange Coke from nonrecyclable plastic bottles.

"I could have felt grounded here at home," ʿAraidi continued. "I could be king here and make my own rules like an Arab tribal patriarch. But no. This is where I live, but it is not the home of my symbolic geography. I don't know what I would consider my symbolic home. Not this house. Here everyone lives on 'village time,' and I don't like it. When I lived in Haifa, I lived on Western time. I didn't like that either. Now, back in the village, in a paradoxical conflict, I try to live in both times. But even so, my dubious freedom in Israel's mutation of a Western democracy is better for me than my own stagnant village."

The following summer I sat in a smoky Jerusalem café announcing itself as The Wooden Horse—A Restau-Pub. In this favorite watering hole of left-wing intellectuals, up an alley in the Soho of West Jerusalem, one of our group, who happened to be from ʿAraidi's village, informed me that "back to the village" had become the current catch phrase of Arab intellectuals in the Zionist state. It was what he, for one, wished to avoid, by a career change from an aspiring Hebrew writer and journalist to a liability attorney.

"So why don't I move back to Haifa?" asked ʿAraidi, meeting the eyes of his wife and two teenage children. "Well, I can't. I owe my children their mother culture. Their mother tongue. When they grow up, they can choose. I can't force a new culture on them. I have no right. I owe them a home. But as for myself, I'm living on a fence—one foot here, one foot there, always trying to close my legs, sometimes with the literary establishment's help, sometimes despite their protest. I know I can never become a real Hebrew author. Never. It's a matter of pride. They won't let me be that, but I won't let myself be that, either."

As ʿAraidi spoke, I recalled more of his key poem (1985:7–8):

O, my dream number 32
Here, the paths no longer here
And houses layered up like the tower of Babel
O, this heavy dream of mine—
No sprout from your root will bear! . . .

O little village, you're a
Township. Tamed. . . .
All those peasants I wanted to sing with—
Stanzas of hay to the nightingale's song—
Laborers, throats thick with smoke.
Where are they all, who were, and are gone?

O, my heavy dream
I came back to the village
To flee the city and all its ways
But arrived
As if coming from one exile
To another.

Naʿim ʿAraidi, born in Palestine, is a non-Jew, a Druze who is a citizen of Israel, the homeland of the Jews. His first exile was that he had to leave his native village in order to get a good education in Haifa, a major Israeli city. This education forced him into spatial and cultural exile in the schools of the privileged Jewish elite. After that, he perceives his return home to his village as an exile from exile.

The Israeli home is also an exilic Arab home for the majority of Israeli Jews—the *Mizrahim,* who immigrated to Israel from Third World countries. Albert Swissa, for example, moved to Israel as a child from Casablanca, Morocco, and has published a momentous novel, *The Bound* (Swissa 1990). In it he describes the disintegration of the Moroccan communities after they arrived in Israel:

> The elders roused Mr. Pazuello's bitterness. He saw them as plucked fowl, desecrated. He knew most of them . . . "from there" [Morocco], by the names of their clans. . . . Shocked, still not digesting a rule without a king, innocent to the point of stupefaction. Reversible world. Some are even beaten up by their own sons, who at this very [mid-morning] hour are lying around on their beds? . . . A disappearing generation, followed by one destroying itself. Exile! there is no other way, exile in the holy land itself. (Swissa 1990:19)

For Swissa and his Moroccan Jewish protagonists living in the cinder-block housing projects on the outskirts of Jerusalem, very near its dangerous 1967 border, Israel is not home but their diaspora's diaspora (see Rogoff 1994).[3]

NEGOTIATING HOME AND BORDER

The modern state of Israel declares itself to be the homeland of a citizenry consisting of three major social groups. Of the 4.3 million Israeli citizens, about 20 percent belong to the group that the government and popular culture term "Arab citizens of Israel" or "Israeli Arabs," thus avoiding mention of their Palestinian identity. Throughout this essay I will refer to them by the name they prefer, "Palestinian citizens of Israel" or "Palestinian-Israelis." These various non-Jewish Palestinians indigenous to the region are the remnants of a much larger population of Muslim, Christian, Druze, and bedouin Palestinians dispersed by the founding of the state of Israel in 1948 (see Sayigh 1979).

The second group is the *Mizrahim* (literally, "Orientals" in Hebrew), who constitute 68 percent of the Jewish population and 54 percent of the total population of Israel. They immigrated to Israel, mainly in the 1950s, from Arabic-speaking countries like Morocco, Tunisia, Algeria, Egypt, Yemen, Syria, Lebanon, and Iraq, or from Iran, Turkey, Ethiopia, or India. The official government term for them is "descendants from Asia–Africa" (*Yotzei Asia–Africa*), or *'Edot Hamizrah,* "bands of the Orient." Below even these, Ethiopian Jews are termed the primordial "tribes of Africa." The second group's apolitical term for themselves is Sephardim ("Jews originating in Sepharad" [Spain], in Hebrew), but Mizrahim and "Arab-Jews" are the terms they use when advocating their rights before the ruling minority, the 28 percent of Israeli Jewry called Ashkenazim. This third group originated in Central and Eastern Europe and spoke Yiddish. Some started arriving in Palestine at the turn of the twentieth century, though most came after the Holocaust. After 1948, some trickled in from Western Europe, North or South America, or South Africa. Official Israeli terminology endowed them with the appellation *Kehilot Ashkenaz,* "the communities of Central/Eastern Europe."

Throughout this essay I will follow Ella Shohat's (1989) groundbreaking analysis of Israeli society. Traditional analysis of Israeli society uses the dichotomy of Jew/non-Jew. Shohat, however, collapses this distinction, which ultimately is based on religious differences. Instead, she uses the categories "Third World" and "First World," which derive from the Middle East's history of colonization. Thus, Third World Israelis are the first and second groups above, the non-Jewish Palestinians and the Jewish Mizrahim, who together comprise about 70 percent of the population of

Israel. The First World component of Israeli society is the third group, the Ashkenazim, the demographic minority that constitutes the Eurocenter of Israeli culture and politics.

Because Israelis have one of the highest rates in the world for readership of literature, literature plays a key role in forming Israeli national identity and culture. Hebrew literature, in the revived biblical language, has been central to imagining the new Israeli national identity. Since the beginning of Eastern European Jewish immigration to Palestine in the late nineteenth century, Zionism has been the ideology of Jewish nationalists colonizing the area. To write in Hebrew, instead of Yiddish, German, Russian, or Polish, was for them a powerful act of anti-diaspora defiance in the epic struggle to return to a utopian biblical homeland. Writers and poets are therefore honored among the pantheon of Zionist pioneers. The epic hero these writers imagined was a new Israeli-born Jew, the *Sabra*. In Arabic, a *sabra* is the fruit of the prickly pear cactus, and like the fruit, Sabras are said to be prickly on the outside but sweet on the inside. In defiance of the meekness attributed to diaspora Jews, Sabras are to be frank and direct, even impolite and rude, if necessary. Ironically, the *sabra* cactus is not native to the region—it was imported from Mexico by the Spaniards. In a further irony of displacement, if you drive around Israel and see rows of these cacti, you know they are traces left by pre-1948 Palestinian peasants, to separate fields belonging to different clans.

Sabra national identity includes several main tropes. First, in order to redeem the persecuted Eastern European Jews, the Zionists imported European cultural technology, and to reinforce its superiority, they primitivized the native Palestinians.[4] Second was the bold social experiment of pure communalism in the kibbutz. Third was the David-and-Goliath myth to bolster military heroism: the image of the tiny new Jewish state confronting, like David with his slingshot, the Goliath of the combined military might of "fanatic" Arab states that had sworn a holy war to drive Israel into the sea. A fourth main trope was the Holocaust—the epitome of diasporic suffering—redeemable only by reimagining Jewish identity on the model of Masada, a fortress where Jewish rebels chose to kill themselves with honor rather than suffer capture and death at the hands of the Romans. Zionists consider Masada preferable to standing in line to be gassed and cremated, but they are determined not to let even a Masada happen again to the nation of Israel (see Shohat 1989:40–41). All these tropes appear in canonical, that is, Ashkenazi, Israeli literature. These books are a crucial emphasis of the school curriculum, as well as a hot commodity in the consumer market.

Many literary authors have daily or weekly opinion columns in Israel's newspapers. Their literary debates transcend intellectual circles as well, permeating Israeli public culture through newspaper and magazine articles or television programs. Authors appear among the celebrities in daily newspaper gossip columns, where their personal trials and tribulations are reported in exquisite detail. The canonical literature is catalytic in transforming Israel's national ideology into practice—some prime ministers and Knesset members have been known to discuss with journalists what novels and poems they have been reading lately, and even quote them on the Knesset floor.

In the mid-1960s, when I was in the sixth grade in a Tel Aviv suburb, we studied four hours of Hebrew literature and poetry per week. One of our favorite pastimes was to take a bus to Dizengoff Street to watch a celebrity spectacle: the canonical authors we studied in school arguing over a beer, a cognac, or a steamy cup of strong Slavic tea with lemon. Dizengoff Street is now Tel Aviv's garish version of Fifth Avenue, where you can eat a MacDavid's kosher hamburger (but not cheeseburger) while gazing at a poster of an F16 bearing the Star of David. But then, in the golden age of French-Israeli cooperation, Dizengoff Street was dotted with small, smoke-filled cafés where Edith Piaf and Georges Brassens lamented from the radio and Mirage jets occasionally streaked overhead.

Almost all these café habitués—authors, publishers, and critics—were of Eastern European descent. As part of the Zionist utopian project, many of them had changed their last names to Sabra Hebrew ones—names of biblical rebels, or biblical flowers, bushes, and trees, or biblical manly virtues like courage and defiance. To the average Israeli, it is amazing to see people with non-Sabra, Arabic names like Swissa or ʿAraidi being published and widely reviewed in the Israeli literary press. In the Israel of the mid-1960s, Swissa might have been a housemaid for the literati, and ʿAraidi, given his peasant background, might have trimmed the garden hedge. But these days, ʿAraidi and Swissa are two of the twenty-five or so recently recognized literary figures in Israel whose native tongue is Arabic but who write in Hebrew. These figures are an influential intellectual minority that has emerged from the marginalized majority, the lower- and lower-middle-class Middle Eastern social groups.

Despite religious differences, Mizrahi and Palestinian-Israeli authors share an Arab culture and a subaltern historical experience under colonialism.[5] Ironically, they grew up in a more cosmopolitan setting than many authors, critics, and publishers of Ashkenazi descent did. The Eastern European Jews, most of whom were confined to ghettos, had only irregular and indirect contact with Western European high culture prior to their immigration to Israel. In contrast, Palestinians, and Jews who immigrated to Israel from the Arab world, had regular, direct contact with Western European culture by being raised and educated in the urban centers of British colonies such as Palestine, Iraq, and Egypt, or French colonies such as Lebanon, Syria, Morocco, Tunisia, and Algeria.[6] Does the writing of the Third World Israeli authors follow in the epic Sabra tradition, or does their non-European origin mean that their Hebrew literature will have a positionality other than Sabra?

History of Home as Exile

Palestinian citizens of Israel now live as exiles in their own homeland. A long history of land expropriations has transformed them from peasants to the cheapest of blue-collar laborers, living under military rule and curfews until 1964 (see Rosenfeld 1964; Segev 1984). They are still the weakest sector of Israeli society, discriminated against in all aspects of their lives, particularly employment, simply because they are not Jewish. Currently, only 12,000 Palestinian-Israelis are university graduates, and 42 percent of them work at occupations that do not utilize their education (*Ha'aretz,* August 12, 1990). Since many of the better-paying jobs are related to military industries, Palestinian-Israelis, because they are denied security clearance, cannot compete with Jewish university graduates (see *Ha'aretz,* July 8, 1990).

The fact that around 20 percent of Israel's citizens are Palestinians should translate into voting power, but their seven Knesset members control only 6 percent of the Israeli legislative authority. Even this disproportionate representation is now under threat from the massive immigration of Soviet Jews. Their relative electoral power will shrink at this crucial historical moment, just when their political and religious leaders, grassroots activists, and intellectuals are arguing for equality and are bringing a genuine Palestinian-Israeli consciousness to bear in an effort to redefine Israel (see Lavie 1991).

Palestinian-Israeli villages have been transformed from homes into a diaspora at home. Thus 'Araidi's ancestral stone home feels like a hotel to him. At an even greater degree of dislocation, the Mizrahim—Arab-Jews like

Swissa, who thought they were at last moving out of their Jewish diaspora in the Arab world, and returning to the mythic homeland of Israel—in fact became another Arab diaspora in the Eurocentric Jewish state. Some came because, after the collapse of British colonialism, the Arab nationalist regimes were hostile toward the Zionism that had gathered momentum in urban Arab-Jewish communities. Others came because the Mossad (Israel's foreign intelligence agency) and the immigration authorities managed to present Zionism as a millennarian movement, using Mizrahi Jewish messianism to persuade them to resettle in the sovereign Jewish state. In addition, the Mossad activated rings of Iraqi and Egyptian Zionist saboteurs, who bombed both Jewish and Arab institutions to create panic in the Jewish communities and spur a mass exodus. When the saboteurs were caught, mobs attacked Jewish neighborhoods. If necessary, the Israeli government paid ransom to get Jews out.[7]

When these Arab-Jews arrived in Israel, the socialist Labor Party was in power. Based on the advice Ben-Gurion received from leading Israeli sociologists about how to use European cultural technologies to Westernize (Eastern Europeanize?) the Arab-Jews, the government deliberately fractured their extended family structures that affiliate them into larger communities. This was done in order to facilitate their rapid transition to a nuclear-family-based contractual relation with the centralized socialist nation-state. The government trucked small remnants of these families to different border towns, where they would serve Israel as human shields. Many of these urban petty traders in commodities ended up on agricultural cooperatives, where they were instructed how to cope with chickens running around outside the pot. Since the government provided no long-term employment options, they eventually became blue-collar laborers for their idealistic kibbutznik neighbors, who contradicted their own egalitarian ideology by degrading Mizrahi Arab culture. Whereas Ashkenazim went to universities for professional training, the Mizrahim received only government-sponsored training programs for production-line jobs. Like the Palestinian-Israelis, the Mizrahi majority has only a small minority of representation in all national political and cultural institutions (see Lavie 1991; Shohat 1988, 1989).

Since the early 1970s, the Palestinians of the Occupied Territories have been doing the blue-collar jobs for even lower wages, so some Palestinian-Israelis and Mizrahim have found themselves unemployed and without the means to train for better jobs. Many others, however, managed to penetrate the Ashkenazi middle class of professionals during the economic boom of the early 1970s. For Mizrahim to do this smoothly, they would "forget" their Arabic, change their last name, "de-Semitize" their Hebrew accent (see Shohat 1989:54), and avoid the summer sun. Since Palestinian-Israelis in theory are welcome to reside anywhere they want, but no one would be likely to rent them an apartment in a Jewish neighborhood except in a few mixed Israeli cities,[8] they did not even have the Mizrahi option of "passing."

Reparations payments by Germany to survivors of the Holocaust have skewed the class structure of Israeli society by giving Ashkenazim as a group a momentous financial advantage in hard currency. The Mizrahim and the Palestinian-Israelis had no resource to compare with this, so they became the cheap labor that enabled this Ashkenazi capital to be invested quickly (Segev 1984; Shohat 1988; Swirski 1981). While fully acknowledging the suffering for which these payments are a mere token, one must nevertheless note that this money enabled the Ashkenazim to establish their hegemony in Israel and to appropriate Western Europe's high culture. Western-educated Mizrahim and Palestinian-Israelis were therefore forced into the lower class only after the founding of Israel in 1948, when they ran up against the institutionalized Ashkenazi discrimination against them that permeates Israeli society. The dominant culture Arabized and primitivized Palestinians and Mizrahim far beyond their actual hybrid colonial Arab identity (Kahanov 1978:13–67), accusing them of sharing the "primitive" culture of the dangerous enemy, and systematically prevented them from accomplishing much that would prove otherwise (Kahanov 1978).

In 1977 a great political paradigm shift occurred when the underdog Menachem Begin and his right-wing Likud Party were swept into power on the votes of the underdog Mizrahi majority. The Mizrahim voted for the Right in order to protest the patronizing Ashkenazi oligarchy of the Labor Left, even though most Likud leaders are Ashkenazim.[9] Paradoxically, the Mizrahi Likud voters could sympathize with Begin's anti-Arab ideology because the Labor Party, in the process of socializing Mizrahim into the Jewish nation-state, had taught them to hate themselves for originating in the "primitive" Arab world. The Begin government was so frankly anti-Arab in policy, however, that the Palestinian citizens of Israel seized the rights of civil recourse previously available only to Jews: assembly, demonstrations, marches, strikes, lobbying groups, and the publication of privately owned newspapers. All these tools now have been brought to bear on the problem of creating an Israeli national identity separable not only from Zionism but also from Judaism. Ironically, it was in the Begin-Shamir era, one bright

August day in 1991, that the Communist mayor of Majd al-Kurum, a Galilean village most of whose lands were expropriated by the military and the exclusively Jewish city of Karmiel, said to American alternative media and leftist activists, "When the Palestinian state is created, I want the same relationship with it that American Jews have with Israel. That means I want to be a full citizen of Israel, even though I am not Jewish."[10]

A corresponding cultural shift did not soon follow the political one. From 1977 on, however, Ashkenazim have gradually begun to lose their status as the sole arbiters of Israel's fate. Representatives of the Third World Israeli majority are infiltrating the Ashkenazi elite. Given the demographics, if the Mizrahim would combine forces with the Palestinian citizens of Israel, then together, as around 70 percent of the population, they could force the Eurocenter to implode. But the Mizrahim are politically fractured. Most of them buy into the Zionist state ideology based on the religious distinction between Jew and non-Jew. They vote for the Likud not just to oppose the Labor Party and its anti-Mizrahi racism, but also because they identify themselves as Jewish (thus setting themselves apart from the Arab enemy) rather than as a Third World culture colonized by a First World Eurocenter.

The Palestinian-Israelis, in contrast, have managed to mend some seams in the ruins of their culture, because their Self/Other dualism is as clear to them as it is to other Israelis. They are an almost ultimate Other: they are not Jewish, nor have they immigrated to Israel from anywhere. They are articulating a linear narrative of their oppression vis-à-vis the Zionist nation-state. The citizenship they hold in that state, however, fractures their narrative's linearity, and collapses the Self/Other dualism into multiple subject positions. This fracturing happens when their discourse is juxtaposed to the discourse of other Palestinians even more alienated from and victimized by Israel, such as those of the Occupied Territories, or the Palestinian diaspora in the Arab world or in the West.[11]

The Mizrahim are situated in the gap between their subjective experience of their unruptured preimmigration communities and the objectified history of Jewish persecution, a main Sabra trope.[12] The Mizrahim find it difficult to mend any seams in the ruins of their preimmigrant cultures because, being both Jewish and immigrants, like the Ashkenazim, they feel, as a group, obligated to consent to the state ideology. They therefore cannot establish a clear Self/Other dichotomy, as the Palestinian-Israelis have. The ambivalence immanent in their multiple subjectivities interferes with their attempt to establish their own linear narrative of oppression vis-à-vis the state—a narrative that could draw them into coalition politics with

Palestinian-Israelis to create a Third World opposition. Thus both Mizrahi and Palestinian-Israeli intellectuals are left with only the alternative of infiltrating the Ashkenazi elite one by one.

This process is occurring gingerly, in spite of the elite's reluctance to accept Mizrahim and Palestinians, just as the rest of the Western World has had to tolerate Third World infiltration into its hegemonic structures. Most of Israel's subaltern authors started to write and publish during the years that the Labor Party was decaying and the Likud was emerging. Furthermore, some of them spent these crucial years in Western Europe or the United States, observing the power shift from afar. Only outside of Israel did they allow themselves to begin to explore their fractured Arab selves and articulate them in literary forms.

Given the trope of the Sabra (the prototypical literary protagonist is Elik, the Sabra who emerged from the sea, i.e., who had no diasporic genealogy—see Shohat 1990:253), canonical Israeli literature has a taboo against nostalgia for anything predating Zionism. But the Third World authors, being non-Sabra, need not observe this taboo, and therefore are called by the establishment to produce nostalgic literature, ethnic yet indigenous to the region—a literature that might include absorbing the Zionists into the precolonial history of the Middle East. This is not what they are doing. In fact, they are resisting doing it. In terms of the national canon, their literature is generally dismissed as mere folklore. Only one Israeli literary critic, far Left but inside the Zionist establishment (Hever 1989),[13] recognizes the work of Palestinian-Israelis as even "minor literature" (JanMohamed and Lloyd 1987). Yet he mentions neither the Mizrahi authors nor the volatile connections between the two Third World groups.

In this essay I argue that the Third World Israeli authors' writings, as well as their private and public lives, are presenting a new literature, counter-hegemonic to the Sabra tropology. I will show how these authors have been trying to negotiate the "deterritorialization" (Deleuze and Guattari 1986:16–20) of their home in the borderzone—to articulate the locus and the process of the intersections where Arab and European, Palestinian and Israeli, Mizrahi and Ashkenazi, clash and merge.

Minority/Majority Discourse and Nation/Empire

Almost all Israeli sociologists and anthropologists are Ashkenazim, and some have built world-class careers studying Palestinians and the various Arab-Jewish diasporas in Israel as ethnicities.[14] David Lloyd, however, distinguishes between ethnicity and minority as follows: "An ethnic culture is transformed into a minority culture only along the lines of its confrontation with a dominant state formation which threatens to destroy it by direct violence or by assimilation" (Lloyd 1992). Zionism has attempted to destroy Palestinian culture by direct violence, and also has violently assimilated the Mizrahim as more Jewish bodies against the Arab threat. Lloyd argues that minority discourse is shaped by its necessity of responding to state oppression through a critique of the dominant culture. The Third World authors under consideration here do produce such discourse, though they go beyond such response-oriented articulation. In fact, they represent the lived experience of the Israeli majority.

Yet Israel itself is the creation of minority nationalism—the Zionist ideology that emerged in Europe, where Jews had been a minority persecuted by anti-Semites for generations. Even though Britain supported the establishment of a Jewish state in Palestine as early as 1917, with the Balfour Declaration, Palestine was a British colony until 1948, and Jewish nationalists resisted British imperialism there.[15] The frontier of the new nation of Israel, however, is the Arab world, and that had to be tamed in the manner of all empires. So the distinction between Nation and Empire blurred, as did that between the Nation's borders and the Empire's frontier.

Is this dominant minority Ashkenazi culture Israel the Jewish Nation, the imagined safe space, the bold last resort for Jewish minorities, European or other, fleeing persecution? Or is it Israel the Empire, the state apparatus bringing European technologized civilization into the heart of the Arab world, aiming to de-Arabize the Jewish Mizrahim by assimilation, and to primitivize its non-Jewish Arab citizenry—thus transforming its elusive borders with the Arab world into the Empire's frontier?[16]

Benedict Anderson has argued that there is an "inner incompatibility" between Nation and Empire (Anderson 1983:88; see also Bhabha 1984:128). Israel, however, purposely blurs the boundaries between its cultural nationalism, stemming from the European persecution of the Jews, and the Israeli state's coercive practices against its own Mizrahi and Palestinian-Israeli populations.[17] Even though the Ashkenazim are themselves of hybrid ethnicities, from many different Eastern European communities, they can overlook their hybridity thanks to their political and economic power, which translates into influence on both popular and high literary culture in the form of the evoked image of the Sabra, an artificially created essence. The Sabra trope, attractive on the outside but hollow on the inside, enables the Ashkenazim to collude in the blurring of the boundaries between Nation and Empire. Thus their Jewish nationalism becomes co-opted as part of the oppressive machinery of the Israeli Empire.[18]

The Third World Israeli writers recognize the oppressive consequences of thinking of Israel as simultaneously Nation and Empire, and they recognize that Ashkenazim do think that way. They note that many Ashkenazim deny their own hybridity by invoking the mythical Sabra, the tall, blond, blue-eyed, square-jawed, broad-shouldered neo-Adam, who rose unengendered, unbegotten, from the sea (Shohat 1990). The fact that this Sabra trope already exists as an essence opens up a space for the Third World writers to make conjunctures. Because they can contrast themselves to the trope, they can acknowledge their own complex hybridity: raised in British or French colonies and then becoming the subaltern citizenry of Israel, they are already hybridized conjunctures between Arab simulations of the West and Israeli ones. So they can use this sense of hybridity with powerful agency to create new works of Israeli literature. They set their task as one of deterritorializing the boundaries of the Sabra Hebrew language, culture, and place.

Decades before Israel was founded as a nation, the Zionists not only had staked out a European turf in the heart of the Arab world but also had accomplished the seemingly impossible project of reviving ancient written Hebrew as the national spoken language. They created a Sabra Hebrew by "de-Semitizing" (Shohat 1989) the old language in accent and rhythm. The Third World Israeli authors write so as to make Hebrew a Semitic language again, like Arabic. This deterritorializes the language by removing it from Zionist claims.

In terms of the content of their writing, the Third World Israeli authors not only reject their Zionist assignment to produce nostalgic folklore that would legitimize Sabra Israel as a presence in the region, but also deterritorialize Zionist claims to be the only legitimate Israeli culture. By writing their own lived experience in new literary forms, they articulate alternative worldviews. To do this, they write using a flowing narration based on traditional Arab storytelling, but starkly juxtaposed with a spare narration revealing their alienation from the Eurocentric project of Israeli nation-building. Some of the authors syncretize these two narrative worlds. Others let them mirror off each other until they illuminate each other in the blinding flash of specular literature.[19] The continual juxtapositions create borders along the contiguities, where images and ideas intersect explosively in the text—deterritorializing the Sabra culture. Because these authors are blowing up both the Sabra language and its culture, they are reinserting Israel, that Eurocentric island, into the Arab world.

Border Models

Gloria Anzaldúa and Homi Bhabha present two models, polar opposites, concerning the textualization of the hybrid's lived experience that occurs in the interstitial borderzones between Nation and Empire (Anzaldúa 1987; Bhabha 1983, 1984, 1990a). Both models assert that the hybrid's ambivalence toward both Nation and Empire catalyzes remappings of the blurred borderzones between them (Anzaldúa 1987:79; Bhabha 1983). Bhabha argues that the difficulty hybrids face in attempting to authenticate a precolonial dignified past insulted by European representations is the dangerous ease of slipping into essentialized nostalgia.[20] Thus he constructs hybridity as mimicry in the form of hegemonized rewriting of the Eurocenter. This is a response-oriented model of hybridity. It lacks agency by not empowering the hybrid. The result is a fragmented Otherness in the hybrid. The fragments of the Other, however, can be mended together, forming seams, so that they can be narrated in a Cartesian linear manner.

Anzaldúa argues that when hybrids delve into their past, it need not be either essentialized nostalgia or salvaging an "uncontaminated" precolonial past. On the contrary, reworking the past exposes its hybridity, and to recognize and acknowledge this hybrid past in terms of the present empowers the community and gives it agency. Her emphasis on community contrasts sharply with Bhabha's assumption of the hybrid as a fragmented individual Other. In her model, hybridity is a Self that fractures into multiple subjectivities[21] that are unable to mend by forming seams, so the hybrids refuse a Cartesian linear narration. The hybrids' refusal of individuation empowers them to agency as a group, to resist the hegemony of the Eurocenter, not only by reacting to it but also by opening a new creative space in the borderzone. The group's creative action can implode the Euro-USA center. Therefore the borderzone is not just a dangerous space but a festive one, because of the energy liberated by the common struggle of resistance.

Even though Bhabha's and Anzaldúa's models of hybridity are the two poles of the theory of hybridity, both can easily distinguish between Nation and Empire. The Nation is the Third World construct, either "postcolonial" or minority, and the Empire is Euro-USA. In addition, the cultural movements they describe are comparable. People from Third World nations colonized by Euro-USA cross over to enter their colonizer, take up residence there, and implode the center of the Empire from within. For these migrants the border is a space of creativity, and the "crossover" (Anzaldúa 1987:49) itself moves the borderzone between Nation and Empire into the center of the empire.

But in the case of Israel, neither of these models works adequately. As in Bhabha's model, Third World Israeli authors currently do not act as a cohesive group to challenge the Hebrew literary canon—in fact, some of them started talking to each other for the first time through my fieldwork. But they face a difficult problem not present in the other two models: the Israeli center keeps usurping, as its own frontier, the borderzones between European and Arab, Israeli and Palestinian, and Ashkenazi and Mizrahi. Not only is it difficult to distinguish the Israeli Nation from the Israeli Empire, but their overlap is not exact and is constantly in flux. Some vestiges of one or the other are always left over. The inner borders where these vestiges meet the larger central area, where Nation and Empire are fused, may be the only zones remaining for exploration by the Third World Israeli writers. Thus, as I will demonstrate, the case of Israel presents an alternative model of border hybridity.

This essay on the problematics of Third World authors writing in a First World context also involves an inversion of the traditional power relationship in anthropology, in which the privileged ethnographer, situated in the West, primitivizes Third or Fourth World "informants." Because some of my "field informants" have transcended their anthropologist's authority by publishing widely in prestigious literary journals, I felt obliged to phone Ann Arbor to talk to Anton Shammas, author of *Arabesques* (1986) and perhaps the most internationally known Palestinian who writes in Hebrew. How does he negotiate his home on the border? With these lines Shammas ends his collection of poems, *No-Man's Land* (1979):

> My childhood home gropes around in me.
> I grope around the empty house,
> and keep telling myself I'm a grown-up now. . . .
>
> I, for one, do not understand:
> a language on the one hand
> a language on the other hand
> I imagine things in no-man's land.
> (Shammas 1979:44–46)

I shared with Shammas my scholarly ruminations. He said: "So, what you're actually arguing is that these writers' only means of getting into the center is through their writing. From the sociopolitical point of view, they—well, why am I saying 'they,' it's 'we.' . . ."

He stopped, then continued hesitantly. "So we have been constantly pushed from the center, and therefore we try to penetrate into the center by means of literary forms. We think that the moment we conquer the canonical critics, we conquer the Israeli sociopolitical center. We, and here I will use the 'they,' do not notice that there are two different processes here. Even if any one of us wrote the masterpiece of Israeli literature, he still would be on the periphery socially and culturally. We get pushed back into the margins, now along with our texts. But the problem is, how wide are the margins? How porous is the border?"

AMBIVALENCES

The Israeli political Left, composed of yuppies who can afford to be progressive, seems to be almost exclusively Ashkenazi. "They haven't even discovered cultural relativism or pluralism yet. They say, 'What can we do when we have a bunch of monkey idiots here who came from Africa and Asia? We live here with Third World barbarians.'" So said Ben-Dror Yemini, writer and editor for *The Hammer,* "The Newspaper That Will Crack Your Head Open."[22] This Mizrahi leftist weekly, distributed free nationally among the Mizrahi working class in inner cities and development towns, is, ironically, wholly funded by the mainstream Labor Party, to win back their votes from the Likud.

"The morality of the Left begins where that of the Right leaves off—that is, the Right is concerned with the Jews, and the Left with the Palestianians, mainly in the Occupied Territories." Yemini stopped, and then sighed. "Because the West has decided to care about the Palestinians, and the Israeli leftist yuppies see themselves and the state of Israel as part of the West, they worry about the Palestinians as well. No one cares about the Mizrahim."

Yemini's office was piled high with fluttering papers and photos. An old floor fan struggled against the humid heat, and a decrepit air conditioner coughed in a corner. The noisy alley out front was just off the main drag, General Allenby Street—named after the British commander who had "liberated" Palestine from the Ottoman Turks—a border separating the marketplace slums from the newly gentrified yuppie center of Old Tel Aviv. Its stylish Sheinkin Street is where the po-mo crowd like to be seen. Dizengoff is for the old modernists now, I was informed. For those who haven't guessed, as I didn't, "po-mo" is Tel Aviv avant-garde slang for "postmodernist."

Most authors I interviewed see Yemini—with his John Lennon wire-frame glasses, so typical of the Ashkenazi intellectual elite—as the epitome of Third World co-optation. But he says, "I live in a no-man's land. It's painful for me to realize now, and tell you, that I've become the fig leaf, representing the Southside slums at all those lavishly catered North Tel Aviv parties I travel to. . . . I know I'll always be on their leash. But then they say, 'See? There *is* freedom of speech. Even Ben-Dror Yemini writes for us.'"

Ashkenazi leftists such as those who leash Yemini live surrounded by objects Palestinians and Mizrahim would use every day. In the spring of 1988, in the wake of the *intifada,* I attended a meeting of Peace Now activists in Jerusalem's Bak'a neighborhood, whose mansions housed the Palestinian aristocracy until 1948, and now many of the intellectual upper middle class of Israel. I was probably invited to participate because I now came from Berkeley, one of the largest donors to the liberal Israeli Peace Camp—not because they needed a Mizrahi fig leaf.

I entered a living room exhibiting colorful Bedouin weavings on the wall and floor. Old Palestinian copper cooking pots and clay water jars held flowers or dry wild thorns. Intricate embroidery pieces from the fronts of Palestinian dresses were framed and hung near realistic paintings of Israeli landscapes by local artists. Throw pillows on the sofas were made of slightly less exquisite embroidery. A traditional wooden rake that a Palestinian peasant would use to cultivate narrow mountain terraces was leaning into the curve of a small concert piano. Three rusty sickles lay carefully arranged in a Jericho-style wicker basket. All this stuff, I thought, is available in West Bank tourist shops. The living room table was a large, round copper platter standing on crossed wooden legs. Neatly displayed on it were the latest copy of *Ha'aretz,* Israel's equivalent of the *New York Times,* and the glossy monthly *Politika,* Israel's cross between *The New Republic* and *Mother Jones.*

From the Palestinian living room, my eyes wandered into the adjacent dining space. There a heavy European buffet crowned with glass doors displayed Sephardi Judaica: large leather and silver amulets inscribed with Judeo-Arabic or biblical Hebrew; Yemeni Shabbat candle holders, intricately worked pieces of silver artisanry; elaborate Moroccan silver Torah crowns with tiny bells, for decorating Torah scroll handles; and a thin-necked Persian pitcher for pouring rose water during the *havdala* ritual, when the Shabbat is ending.

But scrutiny of the bookshelves revealed nothing much that had to do with the Arab world. Most of the living room books (the study might be different) were in Hebrew, about half canonical Hebrew literature and half Hebrew translations of Western literature from Tolstoy to Toni Morrison. This living room reminded me of James Clifford's museums: "Collecting and displaying are crucial processes of Western identity formation. Because the objects salvaged are given, not produced, the historical relations of power are occulted" (Clifford 1988a:220). The Bang and Olufsen stereo was softly playing the perennial 1970s hit "A Horse with No Name," by America. I felt I was just inside the frontier that both nation and empire were creating ever anew, by usurping the slippery borderzones.

In Old Tel Aviv, across the street from Ben-Dror Yemini's office, lives Shimʿon Ballas. Born in Baghdad, he immigrated to Israel as a young adult in the early 1950s, and is now a professor of Arabic literature at Haifa University, an author of many novels and scholarly articles, and a political activist on Palestinian human rights issues. The current aspiration of the Israeli avant-garde is to live in a flat like the one he has lived in for many years—a rooftop apartment just a block from Sheinkin Street, right across from the bustling souk. Entering Ballas' living room, I noted with interest the Danish Modern furniture, the many abstract expressionist paintings (his Ashkenazi wife is an art professor), and the sleek bookcases with titles in Hebrew, Arabic, French, and English. On my second visit a year later, I felt secure enough to ask him to explain the discrepancy between where he chose to live and how he chose to furnish his living space.

"My father was a petty commodity trader," Ballas said. "I'd rather keep him as a memory, and not clutter my living space with Oriental artifacts. All these Oriental living rooms arrived here via the European Left. They have a sort of ambiance. You sit on the floor . . . ."

He then announced firmly, "I do *not* like to sit on the floor!"

We both burst out laughing.

"And all that living room Orientalia—who can afford a housekeeper to dust it all? Frankly, if I had more space in my study, I wouldn't even have books in here."

Speaking further of his avoidance of nostalgia, Ballas said, "When my first writing appeared, I was interviewed on the radio by someone who told me, 'These are beautiful stories, but it is hard to tell that a Jew wrote them.' It's not just the issue of my communism." Ballas was an active member of the Iraqi and then the Israeli Communist Party until 1961. "It's that certain things are expected of a Jewish author who comes from the diaspora. Well, they want him to write on the ghetto, but the ghetto experience ended with the Holocaust—the trope most antithetical to the bold Sabra—it's shameful for a Sabra writer to nostalgize about that. But the Mizrahi author can write about the Mizrahi ghetto—that's safer nostalgia. He can write on—I don't really know—on food, or holidays. But you see, that's not me. My nostalgic Judaism and diaspora are different. I don't feel like I have to write on Iraq."[23]

In Ballas' novel *And He's an Other* (1990), the protagonist is an unnamed Iraqi Jew who, instead of immigrating to Israel, chooses to stay in Iraq. He has become a high-powered figure in Saddam Hussein's regime, but now, old and retired, he contemplates converting to Islam on the eve of the Iran-Iraq war. Through his protagonist, Ballas critiques the way Arab intellectuals in the modern Middle East, when they long for the golden age of medieval Islam, mimic the Western nostalgia for the Orient. He writes about such nostalgia, which his protagonist, educated in the United States, does not want to feel toward his Arab origins. The protagonist recalls his youth, soon after he returned to Iraq in the 1930s:

> I wrote a letter to the *London Times,* saying that under the flag of Islam a great culture blossomed while Europe was sunk in medieval darkness. . . . I added that the opportunity to shake off the backwardness in which the people of the East live will not be found in denying Islam, or in mimicking the West, but rather in keeping their identity as having a different culture. . . . But the *Times,* supposedly an advocate of freedom of expression, omitted this last main part of my letter, I suppose because it saw in it a deviance from what the native can say! I was 28 when I wrote these things. I wrote them as a Jew. (Ballas 1990:66)

Unlike his protagonist, Ballas did immigrate to Israel. He said, "My biggest crisis was not the move from Iraq to Israel, though this was disappointing—the place I wanted to live was France, because the Iraq of my childhood was so British. My biggest crisis was the transition from Arabic to Hebrew. I felt that if I had moved from Iraq straight to France, I would have moved from one language to another but maintained my fractured identity. Moving from Arabic to Hebrew, though, I felt forced to unlearn my Arabic and refracture my identity."

He lifted his thin arms and clasped his hands together behind his bald head, then leaned forward, and rested his elbows on his knees.

"The evening before my first novel in Hebrew came out, I was working as a typesetter for a newspaper, late at night. And I happened to pick up a book by Taha Hussein.[24] I started reading, just like that, I don't know why. And it felt surreal. I turned off the light. I want to sleep. I can't sleep. Words. Sentences. Poems I had learned. Attacking me. Buzzing in my head. Arabic. I tried so hard to sleep. I couldn't. Until morning. Everything came. All at once. Resurrected from the dead. During the years of my move to Hebrew, I imprisoned them in some hidden place. But it all blew up in my face when I read Taha Hussein. From then on, I figured I'd better hybridize. Arabic and Hebrew. Now I write Hebrew. Sometimes when I write Arabic, I enjoy it. As if meeting your first love in the city where you were born."

The epitome of Ballas' border ambivalence came when he accompanied me to the door.

"Do you want a ride to your office at Tel Aviv University?" he asked. "I'm going to the Ramat Aviv supermarket to do some shopping for the Sabbath."

"Why do you shop in North Tel Aviv? You live right here by the market." I recalled snatches of conversation from the Sheinkin cafe crowd about their adventures in the souk.

"It's air-conditioned, I suppose."

Throughout his life and career, Ballas has managed to find, as the space where he could live and create, the inner borderzones between the vestigial spaces of Nation or Empire and the central area where they had fused. But the centripetal force of the Eurocenter sucked in other writers (see, e.g., Mansour 1966; Shamosh 1974, 1989), who tried to become Sabra and discovered only later that even after they had done everything the center required of them, they were still not allowed to become an integral part of it. That was when their journey back to the margins, and their writing in the borderzones, began.

By experiencing firsthand the Sabra Eurocenter's power to require, but prevent, their entry into itself, the Third World Israeli authors become acutely aware of how the political and economic power of the state is constituted in their hybridity. In order to maintain their creative force, they continually have to remap their borderzones, so that they can maintain their exilic home in the homeland of the Jews. Their creative force and their agency now arise out of their sense that their home is in exile and their exile is their home. The remapping is intended to separate out an independent space in a borderzone, one that cannot be usurped as a frontier by Israel's

Eurocenter. The borderzone thus emerges "as the locus of re-definition and re-signification . . . of the conflicting pressures toward both exclusion and forced incorporation" (Flores and Yúdice 1991:60).

The conflict of these pressures has two outcomes. First, it calls for displacement of nostalgia for a nonborderland home that was.

"I am lucky I can't visit Baghdad," said Sami Michael, an Iraqi Jewish author of many best-selling novels,[25] "and I'll tell you why. I took a strange trip with Yitzhak Gormejano-Goren, to his childhood home in Alexandria. You know that home from his writing—the dance-hall living room and the chandeliers and all that.[26] It was supposed to be a journey to wealth and happiness. But after suffering and searching, we found only a dirty shack, about to collapse. When the home became real, there was no more room for nostalgia. So I'm displacing my nostalgia now, so I don't crash later. For a Palestinian like Shammas, it's even worse. Gormejano can visit Alexandria, but Shammas can't visit the Palestine that was before Israel."[27]

The second outcome of the conflicting pressures—forced incorporation and forced exclusion—is that these authors realize how they must define their main "burden of representation" (Hall 1988b:27): to authenticate their past and envision their future without resorting to nostalgia, which must therefore be kept displaced (see Joseph 1991a, 1991b). But when the authors try to enact their agency, and really represent the subordinated majority of Israel from which they made their climb to the middle class, they become acutely aware that the Eurocenter has racialized them, and that the discourse on race has so narrowed their borderzone that they are not able to have a home. They feel they have either to compromise with the center or to go on to yet another exile.

BORDER AND RACE: THE RACE TO THE VANISHING BORDERZONE

In the spring of 1991, Erez Biton was appointed president of the Hebrew Authors' Association. Given his Mizrahi background, he would not have been elected, but the former president had just been deposed for mismanaging both funds and literary politicking. Biton, who immigrated to Israel from Morocco as a child, is a poet and the editor of *Apiryon,* a literary journal.[28] Its stated aims are to express Mediterranean trends in Israeli culture and to offer an expressive outlet for Middle Eastern intellectuals (*Apiryon* 1989). *Apiryon* is funded by the Center for Culture and Education of the

Histadrut, Israel's labor union founded and still controlled by the Labor Party. Biton also has a weekly column in the mass-circulation right-wing daily newspaper *Maʿariv,* started by founders of the Begin-Shamir Irgun,[29] owned until recently by the Robert Maxwell consortium.[30] Perhaps because of this contradiction, when Biton came to work on Sukkoth of 1987 he was shocked to find his office door covered with insulting graffiti: "Mizrahi sellout, ass-licker of Ashkenazim—your day will come, maniac, traitor" (*Maʿariv,* October 11, 1987). This probably was reported not because Biton works for that paper but because at that time Mizrahi militancy was so rare.

Despite these sociopolitical contradictions, Biton struggles to displace his nostalgia in his attempt to represent the development town of Lod, from which he rose to the middle class and where his brothers' families still live. Though he enjoys a warm and mutually supportive relationship with his extended family, he feels some ambivalence toward his past home. In a poem he describes his nomadism, both actual and symbolic, between Lod's cinder-block housing projects and Tel Aviv's literary milieu, typified by the Café Roval on Dizengoff Street, which is frequented by authors, actors, media personalities, models, and socialites. He deliberately misspells the street name as one would pronounce it in Moroccan-accented Hebrew.

Shopping on Dizengov Street

I purchased a shop on Dizengov
to strike a root
to buy a root
to find a spot at the Roval
but
that Roval crowd
I ask myself
who is this Roval crowd
what's with this Roval crowd
what goes for the Roval crowd
I don't approach the Roval crowd
when they turn toward me
I fast-draw language
cleaned-up speech
yes sir
please sir
the latest Hebrew

and the flats tall over me here
loom over me here
and the openings here
closed to me here
at the darkish hour
in the shop on Dizengov
I pack stuff
to head back to the slums
to the Other Hebrew.
(Biton 1990:38)

Sitting in his large *Apiryon* editorial office in Tel Aviv's satellite city of Ramat Gan (he did not want to be interviewed at his home), Biton spoke of his search for home.

> I am so lonely. I can't combine habitus and family. When I started looking for a home, I searched and searched, day after day, unable to decide. Should I live in Tel Aviv? What do I have in Tel Aviv? Perhaps Ramat Gan nearby. But Ramat Gan isn't near the sea, and I have a love affair with the sea. Then I caught myself developing relationships with objects, like apartment buildings and the sea, though I was raised to have relationships with people, with neighbors, a community. So I said, "I'll live in Lod, near my brothers." But then I said to myself, "What?! My children grow up in a run-down place like that, a development town?" And living near my brothers, I'd have to give up any intellectual dialogue, like we are having, or I have with my wife. And then it hit me. I've lost my brothers. It's not exactly that I lost them—we still drink ouzo and have a good time, and try to have some kind of authentic experience together. But it doesn't work.

He paused. With his good hand, he touched his prosthesis, a replacement for the arm he lost above the elbow when, as a child, he played with a hand grenade he found in the abandoned fields around Lod (formerly Lydda, a thriving Palestinian town). His voice broke as he groped for words.

> I don't think I still have any authentic, concrete cultural expression I can call my own. I always felt that lullabies might be one of the more genuine expressions of a seamless culture. But then when my son was born, I had no lullaby to sing to him, because I've lost the memory of my mother's lullabies, and the Israeli culture didn't offer me any to re-

place them. There are some synthetic Israeli lullabies, but at the tender moment when I put my son to bed, I longed for something organic, and there was nothing. So I read him Lorca instead. By the way, I'm saying all this for the first time, to you. Maybe because you're from abroad, it's easier to tell you embarrassing things. If I told any of this to an Ashkenazi here, it could be curtains.

Biton and his family live in Ramat-Hasharon, an upper-middle- to upper-class Tel Aviv suburb, home to many Tel Aviv University faculty members.

"My daughter, she's five-and-a-half years old, came home one day from kindergarten and said, 'Daddy! They told me I'm a *koushit* [Negro].' In the kindergarten! I said, 'But my God, Shlomit, who's telling you you're a Negro? You're so beautiful!' She *is* beautiful, everyone says so. So I ask my wife, 'Tell me, is she . . . really dark?' "

Biton is blind. The same hand grenade that took his arm took his eyes.

"My wife said, 'I don't know, I don't feel she's black. She's a bit . . . uh . . . darker than those Ashkenazi kids, but . . . , But probably in the day-care place, it was the parents' values speaking through the children's mouths. I'm a blind man. I have vague memories of real colors. For me, race is a cultural construction."

After three and a half hours of intense conversation, I apologized and told Biton I had to leave, because it was past nursing time for my baby, and my breasts were hurting. As I spoke, the anthropologist again felt the awkwardness of this kind of ethnographic fieldwork, "studying up" (Nader 1969). I was rushing to pack my tape recorder when Biton hastily added that he might have been too harsh on both his brothers and the Ashkenazim.

When he opened the door for me, he grasped my wrist and said, "When I talked to you on the phone and when you first came in and started talking, I pictured you as very tall, thin, and light-skinned—a well-coiffed blonde. But the more we talked, the more you became short, full-figured, and olive-skinned, with a long black braid."

I was stunned by the accuracy of his intuition.

"I hope I didn't hurt your feelings by saying this. Next time, we'll have you over to our home."

Biton brought to the surface the fact that there is a struggle on the border between the Eurocenter's notion of the frontier and the noncanonical minority's notion of the border as a refuge. In this struggle both the Eurocenter and the Third World Israelis are "racializing" the border (Omi and

Winant 1986:64; Gilroy 1987:23). The Israeli Eurocenter, simulating the heritage of all Eurocenters, does it in the stereotypical way, using the idea that race is biologically determined, as when Biton's daughter was called a Negro. They use the dominant group's tropes of race/class formation (Gilroy 1987) to explain the subordinate political economy of Mizrahim and Palestinians. But for the subordinate group, race is not a matter of biology. Race is situated in the gap between identity as an essence and identity as a cultural construction.[31] The idea of racial identity as essence is well understood by Mizrahim who look like Palestinians, and are mistaken for them and beaten by angry mobs whenever a homemade bomb blows up in a local Jewish trash can. But the subordinate group is also acutely aware of racial identity as a cultural construction because they know that some Ashkenazim are darker than some North African Jews, who, despite their light skin color, will never be mistaken for Ashkenazim because of their non-European past.

Can the Third World Israeli authors use the categorization of race/class attributed to them as a means to mobilize against the Eurocenter? From their middle-class positionality, can they separate race from the lower class and use race not only to represent the subordinated groups but also to protect their shrinking borderzone? This urgent problem impels them to race toward the edges of their borderzones.

The Burden of the Represented

After a long, hot bus ride that Friday afternoon from Ballas' home to my mother's, I settled down in her air-conditioned living room and started to chip away at the thick stack of Sabbath newspapers. A large ad in the classified section of *Ha'ir,* the Tel Aviv simulation of *The Village Voice,* caught my eye. "Put your shoulder to the 'Aliya effort!" it exhorted homeowners. "Rental apartments of all sizes needed for the Jewish Agency. What's in it for you? (a) rent in advance every three months in U.S. dollars; (b) cultured, university-educated tenants; (c) guaranteed tax-free rental income. For details, call," and here were three Tel Aviv area code phone numbers. "Closed on the Sabbath" (*Ha'ir,* July 13, 1990).

When the Sabbath was over, I told my mom that the next morning, I was going to do some fieldwork in the Jesse Cohen neighborhood of my home town, Holon. This neighborhood, named after a rich Los Angeles Jew, was called in my middle-class childhood "Jesse Congo," for its wildness, its otherness. "I'm going to visit these newly homeless Mizrahim who have been living in tents for the past couple of weeks because their landlords raised the rent to what they could get from the government for housing the cultured tenants—Soviet Jews. I'm going to take Shaheen with me. In grad school we learned that babies help a lot for entry into the 'field.'"

"Are you out of your mind?!" shrieked my mom. "He'll bring lice and diseases back here!"

Meanwhile, the anthropologist had been anticipating the relief she would feel when she got back to normal power relations between the Western-trained fieldworker and his drumming and dancing informants in "the heart of darkness." Lost in amazement at this regression on my part, I overheard my mother's tirade.

"They're lazy! If they wanted to, they could do the same jobs as the West Bankers, especially now that there are *intifada* curfews. Look at these hands!" she demanded, holding them up as if shaking down the whole Mizrahi burden. "With these hands I pulled myself and six brothers and sisters out of those Yemeni slums in Jerusalem! I worked hard, day and night, even cleaning the houses of my grammar school classmates who felt sorry for me and got their parents to give me work."

"But what about Dad?" I asked meekly.

"It's true your dad was Ashkenazi, and well-connected. But I put him through school! You know that a third of the Jewish marriages in Israel now are mixed—it's a good road to upward mobility."

She paused, then asked, baffled, "But why tents? The best thing we've got left is the family—why didn't they go live with their families?"

"Mom," I said gently. "Don't you think it's resistance?"

"Okay. . . . But don't take the car."

So I took the bus to California Avenue, a short ride to the Other Israel, the Second Israel—and the tents. I got off, schlepping just one heavy stroller, one diaper bag, some rattle toys, and a baby boy. The anthropologist was too embarrassed to show up there with her ethnographer gear—notebook, camera, and tape recorder. I figured I would write it all down when I got home.

"Hey! Here's a lady from Peace Now!" yelled an excited nine-year-old boy to the families gathered around portable picnic tables in front of their cheerfully colored tents—orange, red, blue, green, and white. "She's probably here to help plan the demonstration tomorrow. She doesn't look like a journalist."

"No, Rami,"[32] a woman shouted back. "Peace Now ladies don't bring babies."

I was so confused by being mistaken for an Ashkenazi that I wasn't sure what to do next. So I just stopped right where I was and set up camp on the bus stop bench. I put my prop in the stroller and started cooing and rattling toys at him. Four children came wandering over, and another woman called to them, "Am I hearing that right? Didn't she call her kid Shaheen? That's Arabic!"

"Traditional" fieldwork started flowing when Shaheen got hungry. As soon as I held him to the breast, several women dressed in fashionable outfits strolled over, some holding their own babies. An older woman, gap-toothed, said to a young mother, "You see? That's how I nursed your mother when we came here from Tunisia. But a lady from the kibbutz came and told us we didn't know how to raise children. She made us learn weird ways of diapering and clothing kids, and said that only primitives nurse ten-month-old babies. So your mom nursed you only three months, like they said in that class we had to take on Ashkenazi mothering."

Then she turned to me and said, "What are you? American? We saw on TV that they are into long nursing. Or are you one of us?"

So we clicked.

During the next few days, I learned from personal stories how these people had been abused by the Israeli state system. They could not afford the luxury of the ambivalence I saw in the authors I was studying. They had no choice but to take a stand with the only thing they had—themselves. Yet one of their favorite tapes was by *Habreira Hativ'it* (The Natural Choice), an East-meets-West Mizrahi rock group whose songs included lyrics by Erez Biton—early poems reminiscing about the Morocco he had invented.

"A home is a home is a home," Moshe, one of the compound's leaders, told me. "By living in a tent here, I'm going to force them to give me a home in my hometown, Holon. They say they have plenty of empty apartments on the West Bank, but I don't want to go there. I'm even willing to set myself on fire, and my family, too, like that guy from Haifa almost did[33]—it was on the radio—if they don't give me a home here, like they gave the Russians."

In my air-conditioned office, I word-processed a diary entry:

> Perhaps the hegemonized relationship between Ashkenazim and Mizrahim cannot be analyzed in terms of ethnicity. Maybe the analogy between the Ashkenazi and the Mizrahi immigrations to Israel effaced the Third World specificities of the Mizrahim. The tragedy of their up-

> rootedness from the Arab world was trivialized because they did not experience the Holocaust. Such trivialization assumed that the Mizrahi ethnic groups could be incorporated into Israel's Eurocenter the same way as the Ashkenazi ones were [cf. Omi and Winant 1986: 12, 17].[34] The racialization of Israel's Palestinians is much more clear-cut. If "race is a pre-eminently *socio-historical* concept . . . [and] racial categories and the meanings of race are given concrete expression by the specific social relations and historical context in which they are embedded . . . [then] racial formation[s] refer to the process by which social, economic and political forces determine the content and importance of racial categories, and . . . in turn shape racial meanings." (Omi and Winant 1986:60–61)

The racialization of the borderzone forces some Third World Israeli authors to enact their agency, but such individual acts further contract their political and economic borderzones. The contraction forces each of them individually to leave his or her hybrid space and effaces the borderzone until only the border itself remains, with its barbed wire, lookout towers, and minefields.

In November 1990 I received a letter from Moshe. It was postmarked from Ariel, the fastest-growing town on the West Bank, or even in Israel.

> Ariel, that's where we live, among all these right-wing fanatics and all these Other Israelis who couldn't afford a home in Israel proper. So they used the government incentives to start a decent life here. Winter rains came and the media were distracted by the coming war with Iraq. So we had to fold up our tents and take what we could get. This is *intifada* land. This is a war zone. The whole town is surrounded with barbed wire and soldiers in towers. This is not home, it's just a roof over our heads. How's your baby?

Whereas some Mizrahi homes become tents and then disappear, others, belonging to Palestinian-Israelis, do not even officially exist, but are dynamited by the state. Such were the homes of Ras al-Nabiᶜ (the Spring on the Cliff Top, in Arabic), an officially nonexistent Palestinian village in the Galilee. Like about forty other villages, it was built in the early 1950s by Palestinians who became internal refugees when their original villages were uprooted so that kibbutzim could be built. The government declared the new settlements illegal and omitted them from the maps (*Haʿaretz,* June 17, 1990).

On August 13, 1991, I visited the Khouri family of Ras al-Nabiʿ.[35] I had heard about them at the Cafe Tamar, the po-mo mecca on Sheinkin Street. When I parked my rented car near the ruins of their house, I was loaded down with cameras and tape recorders, but childfree, so a bit worried about my "entrance" into the "field."

"Some woman is here," called a little girl to her family in Arabic. She had two thick pony tails, one on each side of her head. "Maybe her car broke down."

From the remaining half of another house emerged a youngish man in jeans and a traditional white headdress.

"No, she's a tourist," he said, noting the cameras.

"They're wrecking our homes because of this little spring here on the cliff," he told me later over an orange Coke, "so they can declare this place a nature reserve."

His father, the man whose house was blown up, was wearing the traditional headdress and peasant baggy pants, and a bright yellow T-shirt with "Peace Now" written on it in Hebrew. "Since they started dynamiting homes here, the spring has dried up," he said. "But the Interior Ministry's Gray Patrol keeps blowing up more of them. We have nowhere to go."

I was baffled that though I had spoken to them in fluent colloquial Arabic, and had told them I was an Israeli who had lived in the U.S. for over a decade, they kept addressing me in Hebrew.

"Come on, let's go visit the ruins," said the old man's wrinkled wife matter-of-factly. She was garbed in a traditional long dress. "You must have come to see them like all the other leftist tourists."

I suddenly realized where the Peace Now T-shirt had come from.

"I'll show you where we lived until last week. Take pictures of us, and when you look at them back home, try to imagine how it was with us."

So we climbed over the rubble of cinder blocks and Galilean stones, glass shards, and fragments of furniture and toys. A doll's arm poked out between stones—a mute appeal for help.

It was too much.

"Don't cry—it's all politics," the old woman comforted me, as she broke down, too. Her husband, grown children, grandchildren, and assorted neighbors were all sniffling and biting their lips.

"Here was the living room wall," she said, rebuilding it with both hands in mime. Walking further, she said, "And here was the kitchen, and here the bedroom." She walked and wept and rebuilt the whole house.

This is far beyond Benjamin's allegorical ruins, the anthropologist was thinking, a material culture decaying into stories connecting stones (Benjamin 1985; see also Lavie 1990). This was a real explosion.

Finally, when the house stood again in imagination, she lined up the whole family according to age in front of the ruins, and ordered me to take a picture.

"Wait," said the old man. "Before you take the picture and go, I want to tell you something I just thought of. After all our talk about borders and homes, I have to tell you that until this home was blown up, I had lived here all these years mourning my ancestral home, the one they blew up in 1949. I never felt at home in this house. But now that it's gone, I realize it was home. I don't know where to go now. When the whole village is blown up, where will we all go? We have no place, even though this is our land—because I'm not from Europe and I'm not a Jew."

Click.

"Don't forget to send us the picture," said the son in jeans. "If there's anywhere to send it to. . . ."

Some homes become borderzone tents and then disappear. Other homes do not exist in the first place, as far as the dominant group is concerned. It is precisely because such homes do not exist that the Eurocenter dynamites them. Proof that the racialized physical homes do in fact exist comes only when the dominant group blows them up. For the Third World Israeli authors, this act also blows up (magnifies) the dilemma of locating a home on the border, and even the question of the borderzone's very existence, into a major issue, one they cannot avoid confronting in their works. The contracting borderzone denies them room to breathe, until they race toward the edges of it, looking for a way out. Either they race toward the inner edge, until they have to compromise with the Eurocenter while still striving to maintain their own Third World positionality, or they race toward the outer edge and move on to yet another exile. If they can do neither of these, they fall into silence.

BORDER RACE-D AND ERASED

Lavie: You know, the whole concept of the border, what Renato Rosaldo calls the zone of difference within and between cultures, where people can maintain "cultural citizenship" instead of national citizenship,[36] has emerged from the "hyphenized" ethnic studies—like Asian-American or Latin-American.[37] The lived experience of the borderzone sparks authorial creativity. It allows people to travel between the Eurocenter and the margins, and from one margin to another. It allows people to redefine the literal and lived canon, through redefining what Rosaldo calls "culture as a busy intersection of multiple borderzones."[38] There is an assumption here of the ability to travel between cultures as linguistic forms. Such travel allows the border to be a site of creativity.[39]

Shammas: Zionism gave the Jews a territory in the form of language. Hebrew is the only real victory of Zionism. The whole business of the nation-state that came later failed along the way. So the Hebrew is the homeland. It's a paradox. Israel doesn't have internationally agreed-upon official borders—it's a blob of color floating around without defined edges. The Hebrew that was resurrected was not the Mizrahi Hebrew. And that was the tragedy. For the non-Jewish Arab writer, Ashkenazi Hebrew is not only the homeland of the Jews—it's the language of threat. The biggest achievement—in quotes—of the state of Israel is that it took the most wondrous thing that Jews have created on earth, one of the most beautiful languages, and turned it into a language of destruction. . . .

I can't write literature in Arabic anymore. I don't want to. The exile you create inside the language is a home. An exile is a home, and Jews are the best proof of this. If my diaspora is the Jewish home, for me writing in Hebrew is like blowing it up from within. . . .

We are talking here not only about matters between Arabs and Jews, Mizrahim and Ashkenazim—we are talking about the problematics of existence in the postcolonial world. All of us write Ashkenazi Hebrew, even though in *Arabesques,* I tried to re-Semitize it. Every other Hebrew that authors have tried as an alternative has failed. . . . I tried . . . to bring about a new version of Israeli identity, but I couldn't make it happen outside the text. I wrote in the language of the territory. I approached the territory and told her, Territory, come on—is your language Hebrew? Great! I'll write in it. Are you going to give me part of yourself? . . .

I was born in the Galilee and my earth talks to me in Arabic and I talk to her in Arabic, but I have to negotiate my Israeli territory in Hebrew. At bottom, what I do is, I'm trying, as the man of the margins who writes in the language of the majority, I am—it's as if I blow up the language of the majority from the inside.

As I am writing this now, I suddenly wonder whether the Khouri family had kept addressing me in Hebrew just because, for them, I represented the Israeli center, both nation and empire—or was it because, after the center had blown up their home, they were using Hebrew in order to blow it up from the inside?

Shammas and I were sitting in a sleek, metallic gray and mauve cafe in Ann Arbor, Michigan. In his book *Arabesques,* the narrator permitted himself to evoke his Galilean childhood in the village of Fassouta only after he had traveled to Paris or the Iowa Writers' Workshop (Hever 1987).

> *Lavie:* So what are you permitting yourself to narrate from your Michigan exile?
> *Shammas:* I . . . I don't stick to anything here. I slide right off the American Teflon. [*Laughter*] I have no foothold at all, and I feel it. I can't enter the English language. They close it before I make my way in.

In his search for a less constrictive creative space, Shammas raced to the United States to protect his shrinking Israeli borderzone. Muhammad Hamza Ghanayim, on the other hand, did not have that option. "I used to work in East Jerusalem," Ghanayim said as we were sitting on the floor of his home's central space after dinner. Ghanayim's woefully thin arms hugged his bony knees, and his eyes looked through me into the distance, as if he were posing to have his picture taken.

"Come off it, Muhammad," said his modestly garbed wife, Haniyya, reclining comfortably on her elbow into a large cushion. "She won't get your picture in the paper. She's just an anthropologist."

He went on, ignoring her.

> I translated from the Hebrew press for the Palestinian media. But I couldn't be one of them—most of them come from the pre-1948 landowning class. The hip aristocracy. They're rich. I'm the son of a peasant, and they treated me like one, too. So that was End Number One of my dream of entering the pantheon of Palestinian national authors. I went back to the village, just like in the poem. I felt I was feminized. I felt like, not just a woman but a dark one, unable to support myself financially using my own language, or to contribute to

> the struggle of Palestinian nationalism. I joined the Israeli Communist Party and wrote for them in Arabic. But they had too many restrictions on what and how I should write. I was constantly edited, so I quit. Then came the End Number Two. I took a cab from Bakka [his village in Israel proper] to Tul-Karm [on the West Bank]. There were cab drivers there who were yelling out, "To Amman! To Amman!" So I thought, maybe I, too, can go to Amman and from there join the PLO and become a national Palestinian author. And then it hit me—I couldn't go there with an Israeli passport. So I took a special cab and thought, he'll drop me off on the border near the Dead Sea, and I'll just sneak in. Halfway there, it was raining, it was flooding. The skies wept, and I shared my plan with the cabbie. When he heard that, he slammed on the brakes and told me, "Kid, I'm not going to drive you to your death. They'll just shoot you. Go home and write in Hebrew."

As Ghanayim said this, Haniyya was weeping. "I teach Hebrew here in the village school," she said, trying to hold back tears. "But I'm not like Muhammad. Because there is no borderzone between Hebrew and Arabic, he is always on the front lines, getting hurt or hurting himself. I decided that work is work and life is life. So I've become a penitent Muslim. That gives meaning to my Palestinian life."

In the wake of the *intifada,* the prestigious *Koteret Rashit,* precursor to *Politika,* sent Ghanayim to write about life in Gaza (Ghanayim 1988), a poetic journey in the style of David Grossman's "Yellow Wind" (1987).[40] It was the very first time an Israeli publication had given most of its pages to a Palestinian author who writes in Hebrew. Best of all, it was the big, festive Passover issue.

> I thought this was my big break. They had given me plenty of power. After all, *Koteret Rashit* was *the* publication of the liberal Israeli Left. I hoped it would be reissued as a book, and would be translated into English. But I guess I was closer to the Gaza Palestinian refugees than Grossman was to the West Bank ones. Grossman could play anthropologist, but I couldn't. And a Muhammad is not a David. "The Land of Fire" wasn't even reviewed, even though they had given me the whole issue. I crashed. I had a heavy episode with hard drugs. Sometimes I feel like suicide. My wife and children keep me going. But I don't live in a home. It's a house, a cinder-block house my father built me.

Haniyya looked shocked. In a choked yet distant voice, she reflected, "Several years ago, Muhammad built this study downstairs. He divided the walls—one for books in Arabic, the other for Hebrew. I felt happy. I said, 'No more journeys to Jordan. He's starting to live with it.' But that bubble burst as the study got messier."

"If you want to write Hebrew literature," Ghanayim concluded, "there comes a point where you have to aim at the center, or quit. I don't write in Hebrew anymore."

> *Shammas* [*in my rented car en route from the sleek cafe to the University of Michigan campus*]: This border business. The margins. Traveling inside the borderzone—what a luxury! But the price! The more you expand the margins, the more room you have for traveling in the borderzones—but the more diluted everything becomes. The intensity dissipates and disappears. You know, you can spread one pat of butter on one slice of a baguette, or over a whole big pita bread and feed the whole family breakfast. With the baguette you get plenty of butter taste, but are still hungry. The pita feeds everyone but not with much butter each. I'm afraid the minority authors in Israel have precious little bread—but the butter taste is intense. That's why I'm going back. It's better to be on the margins there than nowhere here. But I'm afraid that the Israeli [authors of the] margins have caved in to playing their marginal role. And justifiably so, so they won't go crazy. It's out of exhaustion, like the fatigue after a constant state of war. Under the steamroller of canonical Israeli literature, you have to be a national hero just to survive. That's how the center shrank the borderzone into nothing but a line. . . .
> *Lavie:* So that the borderline can then be tamed as the center's frontier. Border raced, borderzone erased—right?

How regrettable it is, the anthropologist mused on the plane back to Berkeley, that all these writers, who have so much in common, have been trying only individually to break into the Eurocenter. Politically, and in literary politics, they exist as fragments, each orbiting the center. They have not accelerated into an alternative center of their own, a school, a movement—a clique like any other Israeli literary clique. If they could all get beyond thinking Jew/non-Jew, as some of them have, and instead think in terms of Third World/First World, their combined mass could not only deterritorialize but also implode the center's colonial constructions of language, culture, and place.

In spite of this, however, the agency of these writers is transforming the West in Israel from within, as their Eastern, Arab voices rise, speaking and writing in Hebrew. Because they are positioned as interlocutors between Arab and Jew, and East and West, as well as between literature and popular culture, they are forming bridges even as they break boundaries. Through the relationships between the lives of these authors, their literary works, and the hegemonic social structures they rupture, Israel's Middle Eastern majority is reclaiming its centrality to a genuine Israeli identity.

Border Crossings

"Thursday night's the real action at the Wooden Horse," said Irit, my ultra-Sabra old pal. "Everyone who's anyone is there. All our radical college chums. The men are married and this is their night out—the wives stay home with the kids. But most of the women there are like me—single or divorced. Don't let this shit offend you. Remember, it's all fieldwork."

So I walked the half block from my rented apartment to the Restau-Pub. The lights were dim and the smoke heavy. Through the haze I found Irit, and she identified for me at least five different fringe political cliques, each at its own table. The women were stylish and the men slobs. I became aware that my Macy's outfit was not up to snuff for this scene. Not only that, but as more and more people crowded their chairs around our table, I realized I was the only Mizrahi in sight. Nevertheless, none of them introduced themselves or anyone else, including me. Wow, thought the anthropologist, the ultimate in instant entrée.

"You've got to order the goose-liver pate in cognac and ʿEin-Gedi date sauce," a bearded man I had never seen before advised me, peering through his wire-rim glasses.

"Remember him?" asked Irit. "He used to hang out at our table in the campus cafeteria. Now he writes for *Yediʿot Aharonot* [Israel's largest-circulation newspaper]."

"Remember her?" Irit turned to the beard. "It's Smadar-the-Bedouin, who researched the Sinai. She's back from Berkeley."

The main topic of conversation around the table was U.S. Secretary of State James Baker's imminent visit to town. Some at the table wanted to compose a petition requesting negotiations on Jerusalem, arguing that if this issue could be solved first, everything else would be solved. They wanted to take it to East Jerusalem the next day, to get signatures from Palestinian political leaders and intellectuals, and then buy space to publish it in a large-circulation daily Hebrew newspaper. Only a few voices objected that this was a waste of money, because the right-wing government wouldn't give an inch on anything, and certainly not on Jerusalem.

Though the anthropologist was reluctant to interrupt the process of documenting this fascinating flow of data, as an Israeli frustrated by the perpetual logjam of Israeli politics, I felt moved to say, "Why walk even ten minutes to talk to the East Jerusalem Palestinians, when they don't vote?[41] If you really want to change the government, you need to get the Mizrahim to stop voting for the Likud. They *are* the majority, after all. You need to go into their neighborhoods and do serious grassroots politics."

The table erupted.

"They'll just throw us out!" somebody yelled.

"They're barbarians! You can't talk to them rationally. They're too emotional about this nationalism business."

A deep baritone boomed over all the other voices. "I don't know what your Berkeley Left has been doing," he said, "but around here, we're still into class struggle. All this ethnic stuff is just a distraction."

Transfixed by his self-assured Sabra gestures, I realized only slowly that his accent had traces of North Africa.

"What do you mean, 'class struggle'?" snapped a woman. "All our energy is in this Israeli-Palestinian thing."

A massive argument ensued on whether/how to get Mizrahi activists to support the Left by inviting them to planning meetings.

"Not in *my* living room," announced a black-clad coquette with an asymmetrical bright red hairdo, and one enormous copper earring dangling over her shoulder.

Through the noisy babble, the anthropologist was able to overhear some alternative scenarios. One included giving up on the Mizrahim and instead courting the new Soviet population, even though they had just managed to leave their own Left.

Then suddenly everything fell silent. Looking up, I followed everyone else's gaze toward the door. There stood a darkish man of medium height, wearing a white shirt with long, puffy sleeves and a carefully buttoned-up neckline. His black bushy eyebrows met over his piercing brown eyes. Our eyes momentarily clicked, as if to ask each other, "What are *you* doing here?" then immediately averted.

He pulled a chair up to our table. I was amazed to see the conversation resume sedately on James Baker and the petition. After another half-hour of this, I had to get home to rescue the baby-sitter.

Two weeks later, on a Friday, I saw the man's photo in *Kol Haʿir,* Jerusalem's version of *Haʿir,* Tel Aviv's *Village Voice.* This was Albert Swissa, author of *The Bound.* Due to his fame for that work, the editor had sent him on assignment to cover the West Bank town of Hebron, and he wrote an article "Bound to Each Other," asserting that the Palestinians and the extreme right-wing nationalist settlers there were now tragically interlinked (Swissa 1991).

Here they go again, the anthropologist thought to herself. First goes David Grossman to the Occupied Territories, to contemplate his Ashkenazi Left guilt. Then they send Ghanayim there, to find his roots, but they won't review or reprint it. And now they send Swissa—is this co-optation, or what? And the only Jew on a crowded Palestinian bus!

Then it clicked. That was the only patch of the article where a gap was discernible, where Swissa's subaltern positionality had escaped the editor's scissors. His fear for his life had subsided, he wrote, when he looked around and saw that no one was particularly watching him—he looked like everybody else (Swissa 1991:50).

The next day, I was invited to a theater performance in East Jerusalem. An actor of my acquaintance, a Palestinian citizen of Israel who has done most of his acting in Hebrew, told me he was going to act for a change in Arabic. I could have walked the ten minutes to get there, but being from California and in a hurry, I drove my rented car. I greatly enjoyed the totally surreal performance. Emerging from the theater, I found my car firebombed—a charred skeleton of buckled metal and soot.

Sympathetic theatergoers gathered around and tried to comfort me. From a lit-up window across the dark street, a man poked his head out and called, in English, "Yeah, they firebombed your car. They knew from the car that you were the only Israeli here—and if you came to this play, you must be OK. But you crossed the border."

NOTES

This essay is based on fieldwork carried out in 1990 (June–September, December) and 1991 (April, June–September). The fieldwork was sponsored by three Junior Faculty Research Fellowships from the University of California at Davis. Since this is the first textualization of the many interviews I conducted with Third World Israeli authors, only a few of them appear here, though all will be included in the book I am developing. Although this essay focuses on some of the men, my next writing project will be on the women. Given my space limitations and the complexity of the intersection of race and gender, I could not address their issues here. I wish to express to all these authors my heartfelt gratitude for sharing with me their lives and words.

This work was conceived during my fellowship at the Humanities Research Institute of the University of California at Irvine. I participated in the collaborative research project titled "Dependency and Autonomy: The Relation of Minority Discourse to Dominant Culture." Lillian Manzor-Coates carefully summarized and analyzed my paper for our stormy weekly seminar discussion and helped me revise it. For incisive and helpful discussion, I wish to thank all the members of the group, particularly Norma Alarcón, Vincent Cheng, Kimberle Crenshaw, Abdul JanMohamed, May Joseph, and Clarence Walker. For their helpful suggestions for revisions and further reading, I wish to thank Angelika Bammer, Lisa Bloom, Jonathan Boyarin, Nahum Chandler, Virginia Dominguez, Michael Fischer, Suad Joseph, Lata Mani, Larry Michalak, Anton Shammas, Ella Shohat, Carol Smith, Paul Stoller, Ted Swedenburg, Becky Torstrick, and Yael Zerubavel. I also wish to thank Helene Knox for her able assistance in translating the authors' prose and poetry.

A shorter version of this essay originally appeared in *New Formations* 18 (1992).

1 *Back to the Village* was published at Tel Aviv in 1985 by ʿAm ʿOved (literally, "Working People"), Israel's most prestigious press. Berl Katzenelson, one of the Labor Party's leading intellectuals, founded the press in 1941.

2 I discuss in detail my textual method of writing in the split authorial voice, "the anthropologist" and "I", in Lavie 1990:37–38.

3 In his careful reading of an earlier version of this essay, Jonathan Boyarin writes: "The trope of exile at home is also found among Ashkenazi writers, e.g., Dan Pagis." Although this is true, the power of the Ashkenazim, as the demographic minority that rules Israel, makes this comparison insensitive to the historical/cultural specificities Third World Israelis must endure.

4 Taussig (1987) offers a useful model of the process by which colonialism in Colombia (and elsewhere) primitivizes the indigenous populations in order to justify using methods of terror against them.

5 I am using the term "subaltern" here in accordance with Gramsci's theory of class (Gramsci 1971:54–55). Lisa Lowe's fine reading of subalternity makes it applicable to the study of racial and ethnic minorities:

> The subaltern classes are, in Gramsci's definition, prehegemonic, not unified groups, whose histories are fragmented, episodic and identifiable only from a point of historical hindsight. They may go through different phases when they are subject to the activity of ruling groups, may articulate their demands through existing parties, and then may themselves produce new parties. . . . The definition of the subaltern groups includes some noteworthy observations for our understanding of the roles of racial and ethnic immigrant groups. . . . The assertion that the significant practices of the subaltern groups may not be understood as hegemonic until they are viewed with historical hindsight is interesting, for it suggests that some of the most powerful practices may not always be the explicitly oppositional ones, may not be understood by contemporaries, and may be less overt and

recognizable than others. Provocative, too, is the idea that the subaltern classes are by definition "not unified"; that is, the subaltern is not a fixed, unified force of a single character. Rather, [Gramsci's] assertion of "integral autonomy" by not unified classes suggests a coordination of distinct, yet allied, positions, practices, and movements—class-identified and not class-identified, in parties and not, ethnic-based and gender-based—each in its own not necessarily equivalent manner transforming and disrupting the apparatuses of a specific hegemony. The independent forms and locations of cultural challenge—ideological, as well as economic and political—constitute what Gramsci calls a "new historical bloc," a new set of relationships that together embody a different hegemony and a different balance of power. (Lowe 1991:29–30)

6 See Kahanov 1978; Segev 1984; Shohat 1988, 1989, 1990.

7 Among the many authors and scholars who discuss these events are Aharoni 1985:92–98,108–117; Beinin 1990:12,171,262; Kahanov 1978; Segev 1984:155–87; Shiblak 1986; Shohat 1988:12.

8 Some Israeli cities, like Jaffa, Akko, Haifa, Ramla, and Lod, are "mixed cities," with both Jewish and Palestinian populations. Before 1948, they were either completely Palestinian or segregated into Jewish and Arab neighborhoods. After 1948 only a few Palestinians remained. Due to demographics and lack of government support for Palestinian housing, Palestinians have recently started renting homes from Jews, who use the rent money to finance their own upward mobility out of the mixed cities.

9 For example, in the early 1950s Begin strongly opposed the Knesset's approval of accepting West German reparation payments—not because they would skew the Israeli class structure, as they have, but because he wanted Israel to have nothing to do with Germany—thus he was known for a long track record of standing up to the Labor Party.

10 I wish to thank Jonathan Boyarin, a fellow fieldworker, who put me in contact with The Challenge—Forum for Action for Freedom of the Press, who kindly invited me to join their tour.

11 In a rigorous yet poetic essay, Gabriel (1989) brilliantly juxtaposes the relationship between the seamless Western Self and its linear narration, and the relationship between the colonized (and thus ruptured) non-Western Self and its nonlinear, fragmented narration.

12 For theoretical elaboration of the fertile gap between subjective minority experience and objective dominant history, see Alarcón (1992) and Chandler (1991).

13 Even this exploratory (and, to my mind, timid) move got immediate response from the establishment left of center but right of Hever, sparking a debate with those left of Hever. It started in the same literary periodical where Hever's piece appeared, but immediately spilled over into the popular media (Hever 1989, 1990; Shai 1990; Shammas 1990; Snir 1990a, 1990b, 1990c).

14 See, for example, Ben-David 1970; Ben-Rafael 1982; Deshen 1970; Deshen and Shokeid 1974; Eisenstadt 1953, 1967; Goldberg 1972; Marx 1976; Peres 1977; Shokeid 1971; and Weigrod 1965. An exception to the rule is the work of Shlomo Swir-

ski. Though trained in the venerable patron–client scholarly relations of the Eisenstadt tradition—doing "objective" scholarship from a Zionist positionality—his two books (Swirski 1981, 1982) discuss intra-Jewish racism in Israel from a Mizrahi positionality (Swirski is Ashkenazi and Argentine). Perhaps this explains why he was denied tenure and forced out of academia.

15 Atran (1989) problematizes this Zionist resistance, given that it also was a surrogate colonization of Palestine.

16 The pre-1967 borders of Israel were not internationally recognized as borders, but only as the cease-fire lines of Israel's 1948 War for Independence. Since 1967, Israel has occupied territories from Egypt, Syria, Jordan, and Lebanon, and once again the cease-fire lines serve as the state borders, though they are not internationally recognized. Since 1982 Israel has had one internationally recognized border—between it and Egypt, due to the Camp David Accords.

17 Julien and Mercer find an odd parallel between the institution of British Thatcherism and the "re-articulation of the category 'black' as a political term of identification among diverse minority communities" in Britain (Julien and Mercer 1988:3). Britain and Israel are interesting to compare because most of the authors under scrutiny here started to write and publish during the years of the right-wing Likud. Yet in the case of Britain, the distinction between Nation and Empire is more easily discernible than in Israel. Through the implosion of minority discourse in the British center, stemming from the fact that British postcolonial subjects have migrated in large numbers to live in England, minority subjects can no longer be framed or contained by the monologic terms of majority discourse (Julien and Mercer 1988:5). Reading Joseph's (1991a, 1991b) incisive analysis of Black British theater made me further aware of the parallels between the British and the Israeli situations. Joseph's work in remapping the spatial visualization of Nation and Empire calls into question the idea that postcolonial Nation and Empire are separate and collide along a border (Bhabha 1983, 1984, 1990a). Discussing the migration of formerly colonized subjects into the belly of the former colonizer, she shows how, in that case, nation and empire overlap and fuse in a series of clashes.

18 Israeli nationalism is a weird cross between the models of First and Third World nationalisms discussed in Chatterjee (1986). Shohat provides an alternative model to my empire/nation, which she terms "anomalies of the national" (Shohat 1990:252–58).

19 Placing Edward Said as a specular border intellectual, JanMohamed (1992) offers the innovative and useful distinction between two kinds of Third World intellectuals writing in the West: syncretic and specular.

20 Criticizing Bhabha's crusade against authentication of the precolonial past, JanMohamed (1983, 1985) argues that such authenticating anchors the colonized into agency. Parry (1987) brilliantly criticizes both scholars, but offers no solution to the essentialism/antiessentialism dilemma. I hope that this essay is a step forward in the debate.

21 Reading Renato Rosaldo's (1989) analysis of Anzaldúa (1987) made me aware of her powerful use of the concept of multiple subjectivities.

22 See also Yemini 1986.

23 One of Ballas' novels, *The Last Winter* (1984), was voted among the books of the year by the highbrow literary supplement of *Ha'aretz*. The novel describes the final few years in the life of Henri Curiel, the legendary founder of the Egyptian Movement for National Liberation, "a Jew from the wealthy family and originally an Italian citizen, who exercised a profound charismatic influence over many indigenous Egyptians, despite his French education and broken Arabic, and shaped the political debate in the communist movement of the 1940s" (Beinin 1990:58). Curiel was exiled to France during Egypt's era of Pan-Arab nationalism, because he was Jewish and therefore suspected of being a Zionist. He was murdered in Paris in April 1978, probably by Abu Nidal, because he had facilitated a dialogue in Paris between the non-Zionist Israeli Left and PLO intellectuals (Beinin 1990).

24 Taha Hussein was a prolific and famous Egyptian author. One of his books, *The Future of Culture in Egypt* (1975), banned for quite a while, asserted that in addition to being Muslim and Arab, Egypt should not overlook its Hellenic and Mediterranean origins.

25 See, for example, Michael 1977, 1987.

26 Gormezano-Goren 1978, 1986.

27 Gabriel suggests that imaginary nomadism from the site of displacement might in some cases be preferable to an actual visit to the longed-for site of origins, because the actual journey "might rupture the umbilical cord forever" (Gabriel 1989:135).

28 For a discussion and analysis of the founding of *Apiryon,* see Dominguez 1989:102–12.

29 Irgun is short for *Irgun Tzva'i Le'umi,* Hebrew for "National Military Organization," which was a pre-1948 terrorist group founded by, among others, Menachem Begin and Yitzhak Shamir, to resist British colonialism and smash Palestinian nationalism.

30 Robert Maxwell was the right-wing British publishing mogul who died in 1991 (*San Francisco Chronicle,* 25 October 1991).

31 Taussig (1993) defines this gap as "second nature." For him nature is the cultural process of knowing, and mimesis is the process culture uses to create second nature. Mimesis is becoming, and in the context of the late twentieth century, becoming articulates an Other who oscillates wildly between essentialism and construction. This oscillation is the cause of both racialization and racism (cf. also Alarcón 1992).

32 Names of the tent dwellers have been changed, at their request.

33 *Ha'aretz,* July 17, 1990 (see Lavie 1991).

34 A rare example is Virginia Dominguez's work (1989). Even though she does use ethnicity as her general theoretical framework, she discusses and analyzes the great rift between Ashkenazi and Mizrahi ethnicities.

35 The family's name has been changed at their request.

36 See R. Rosaldo 1989.

37 See Manzor-Coates in press.

38 R. Rosaldo 1989:20, 166.

39 As in the case of Spanish and English (Anzaldúa 1987; Flores and Yúdice 1991), or Japanese or Chinese and English (Gong 1980; Lowe 1991).

40 On the eve of the twentieth anniversary of Israel's 1967 occupation of the West Bank and Gaza, *Koteret Rashit*'s editor sent David Grossman, then a young, talented, but not internationally known author, to write a journalistic essay about the volatile intersections between Israeli and Palestinian lives. The essay, which appeared as the Independence Day issue of *Koteret Rashit* (Grossman 1987), immediately sold out and became a collector's item. Within a year it was reissued as a book in Hebrew, and a year later, translated into English, was serialized in *The New Yorker* and published as a book by Farrar, Straus and Giroux. After this, American publishers expressed interest in translating Grossman's two novels into English, because the success of "*Yellow Wind*" had created a market for them.

41 Because Israel has officially annexed East Jerusalem, its Palestinian residents are entitled to vote. They refuse to vote, however, because doing so would acknowledge the fact of the annexation.

THE NARRATIVE PRODUCTION OF "HOME," COMMUNITY, AND POLITICAL IDENTITY IN ASIAN AMERICAN THEATER

DORINNE KONDO

> Community, then, is the product of work, of struggle; it is inherently unstable, contextual; it has to be constantly reevaluated in relation to critical political priorities; and it is the product of interpretation, interpretation based on an attention to history. (Martin and Mohanty 1986:210)

"Home," for many people on the margins, is, to paraphrase Gayatri Chakravorty Spivak, that which we cannot not want. It stands for a safe place, where there is no need to explain oneself to outsiders; it stands for community; more problematically, it can elicit a nostalgia for a past golden age that never was, a nostalgia that elides exclusion, power relations, and difference. Motifs of "home" animate works by peoples in diaspora, often peoples of color, who may have no permanent home; people on the margins, such as gays and lesbians, for whom home was rarely, if ever, safe; and women and children, for whom the "haven" of home can be a site of violence and oppression. Martin and Mohanty concentrate on the narrative production of home and identity by white Southern lesbian writer Minnie Bruce Pratt. Their problematic recognizes the desire for safety and the construction of an identity while it problematizes that construction, interrogating its suppression of differences within, highlighting its always provisional nature, and examining its enmeshment in networks of power. What the Martin-Mohanty article and the essay by Pratt (1984) highlight is the necessity and inevitability of a desire for a "home" in an inhospitable world, the accompanying dangers of that desire, and the continuing need to create "homes" for ourselves.

I take up the problematic of "home" and "community" as racial and ethnic identities, produced and created through narrative, discourse, and performance. The site is Asian American theater in Los Angeles, more specifically, a play called *Doughball,* the January 1991 production at East/West

Players, the oldest existing Asian American theater company in the country. Perry Miyake, a Sansei (third-generation Japanese American) from Venice, California, wrote the play, and the production starred Steve Park, the Korean grocer in *Do the Right Thing* and formerly a regular on *In Living Color.* I examine the narrative and performative production of "home" as a work of collective memory and as a safe place, focusing on the discursive creation of home in the text, in the production itself, and in the specific site of East/West Players and of Asian American theater in Los Angeles. The essay ends with the implications of productions like *Doughball* for a cultural politics, addressing particularly the question of the political weight of "realist" representation.

"HOME" IN ASIAN AMERICAN LITERATURE

The narrative and performative production of home, community, and identity is a particularly urgent issue in the case of Asian Americans. The term "Asian American" itself bears the marks of the civil rights and student struggles of the 1960s. It was created to displace the term "Oriental," a word eschewed for its stereotypical associations with exoticism, despotism, and inscrutability, and for its reinscription of the East/West binary defining the East in terms of the West. Minimally, Asia names a continent, not some imaginary phantasmic landscape. Asian American, then, is a historically specific, constructed political identity, a specific response to a particular social, cultural, economic, political, and historical situation in North America, where people of Asian descent tend to be lumped together regardless of national origin, and where violence, racism, or prejudice against any Asian American becomes an act of violence against all Asian Americans. Asian American, then, is a coalitional identity par excellence. The historically constructed, emergent nature of this identity is further highlighted in the term now gaining increasing approbation: Asian Pacific American, adding people from the many societies of the Pacific Islands to the coalition.

Given this particular sedimented history, Asian Americans have a specific relation to the notion of "home." For mainland Asian Americans, surely one of the most insistent features of our particular oppression is our ineradicable foreignness. The fiftieth anniversary of the forced imprisonment of Japanese Americans was commemorated in 1992. Certainly the incarceration of Japanese Americans was attributable at least in part to this elision of Japanese Americans with Japanese nationals, a savagely ironic situation, given that exclusion laws prevented Issei, the foreign-born immigrants, from becoming citizens until the passage of the McCarran-Walter Act in 1952. No matter how many generations Asian Americans are resident here, no matter how "articulate" we seem, inevitably we will attract the comment "Oh, you speak English so well," or its equivalent, "Where are you from?"—which somehow never seems to be adequately answered by Oregon or Illinois or New Jersey, for the question "Where are you *really* from?" is sure to follow.

We are seeing, and will continue to see, this elision of Asian and Asian American in the present climate of inflammatory Japan-bashing. In the *Los Angeles Times,* an article appeared with the headline "Japanese-Americans Stung by Vandalism at Center":

> Members of a judo class were shocked when they arrived recently at a Japanese-American community center in Norwalk and discovered "Go Back to Asia" and other epithets smeared on the walls in white paint. It was the third time in a week that the center had been vandalized. . . . it was the racial graffiti that stirred painful memories for some of the older members of the Southeast Japanese Community Center who recall being taken from their homes during World War II. (November 17, 1991)

Nor is it only Japanese Americans who suffer from the confusion of Asian with Asian American. The emblematic case, a "mournful reference point"[1] (Commission on Wartime Relocation and Internment of Civilians 1982: 301) among Asian Americans, is that of Vincent Chin, the Chinese American engineer beaten to death with baseball bats by two unemployed "all American" white autoworkers, who blamed Japan for their plight.

Given the continuing confusion of Asians with Asian Americans, perhaps it is not surprising that one of the most insistent themes in Asian American literature and Asian American theater is a preoccupation with the claiming of America as "home." This motif animates works by Asian Americans: Maxine Hong Kingston, Shawn Wong, and Jessica Hagedorn, among others.[2] Perhaps it is most eloquently encapsulated in a poem from Mitsuye Yamada's book of poetry, *Camp Notes* (1976). Yamada is a Nisei, a second-generation Japanese American, and the volume, as the title suggests, deals mostly with experiences in the concentration camps where Japanese Americans were imprisoned during World War II. She ends the volume with a poem called "Mirror Mirror," a dialogue with her son Doug.

> People keep asking me where I come from
> says my son.

Trouble is   I'm american on the inside
                  and oriental on the outside
          No Doug
          Turn that outside in
          THIS is what American looks like.

As a resonant postlude to this book thematizing the dislocation of the camps, the poem functions as a testimony to the ongoing legacy of the camps: the continuing racism defining America as white, and the internalization of that definition by young people of color. Equally, it stands as an affirmation of an Asian American identity. Yamada thus refigures America, recognizing that one need not be Euro to be American.

Even more fundamentally, Asian American playwrights problematize notions of a singular home and of a singular identity. Dislocation, contradiction, unforeseen cultural possibilities, multiple geographies of identity exceeding the boundaries of nation-states emerge as motifs. Jessica Hagedorn, Pilipina American musician, performer, and writer, states in her introduction to her play *Tenement Lover:*

> In all my writing there are always these characters who have a sense of displacement, a sense of being in self-exile, belonging nowhere—or anywhere. I think these themes are the human story. When it comes down to it it's all about finding shelter, finding your identity. I don't care whether you're an immigrant or native-born, you're discovering who and what and where you are all the time. When I think of home now I mean three places. The San Francisco Bay area really colored my work. New York is where I live. But Manila will always have a hold on me. What is the threshold of my dreams? I really don't think of myself as a citizen of one country but as a citizen of the world. (Hagedorn 1990:79)

For Hagedorn, multiple, site-specific identities enable her to transcend the boundaries of nation-states, yet also create contradiction and dislocation. The notion of belonging to the world subverts and refigures any singular notion of identity and rootedness in only one place, where stable geography reproduces the stability of the bounded monad, the singular self. Rey Chow says it this way: "The question, 'When are you going home?' can be responded to in the following manner: home is here, in my migranthood" (Chow 1990:48).

David Henry Hwang captures the traces of history in Asian American identities in his one-act play *As the Crow Flies.* Mrs. Chan, a Chinese American grandmother, narrates her complex geography of identity:

> The day I arrive in America, I do not feel sorry. I do not miss the Phillipine. I do not look forward live in America. Just like, I do not miss China, when I leave it many years ago—go live in Philippine. Just like, I do not miss Manila, when Japanese take our home during wartime, and we are all have to move to Baguio, and live in haunted house. It is all same to me. Go, one home to the next, one city to another, nation to nation, across ocean big and small. We are born traveling. We travel—all our lives. I am not looking for a home. I know there is none. (Hwang 1990:104)

This relentlessly anti-nostalgic passage arises from a realism born of having "no options," in Hwang's words. Geopolitical upheaval, dislocation, and migration have been a way of life for Mrs. Chan, even if she is now comfortably ensconced in her upper-middle-class suburb.

Hwang treats the cleavages of class, race, and different sedimented histories as they operate in the lives of Mrs. Chan and her African American housekeeper, Hannah. Both have no "home," but whereas for Mrs. Chan "home" is an impossibility because of constant dislocation, migration, and endless travel, Hannah's situation stands at the opposite extreme. This passage is narrated by Hannah's alter ego/ghost, Sandra Smith:

> She spends most of her life wanderin' from one beautiful house to the next, knowing intimately every detail, but never layin' down her head in any of 'em. She's what they call a good woman. Men know it, rich folks know it. Everyplace is beautiful, 'cept the place where she lives. Home is a dark room, she knows it well, knows its limits. She knows she can't travel nowhere without returnin' to that room once the sun goes down. Home is fixed, it does not move, even as the rest of the world circles 'round and 'round, picking up speed. (Hwang 1990:105–6)

Home here spells confinement, loss, and the relentless fixity of the intersections of gender, racial, and class oppression that secure and maintain Hannah's position as a domestic. The endless and relentless migration of Mrs. Chan's life is counterpointed to the relentless fixity and closure of Hannah's, articulating the differences of race, class, and history that separate the women. Yet neither woman has options, and each asserts her triumph over the need for a home. Their shared bleak realism, their cauterization of nostalgic desire, are belied by the yearning Mrs. Chan and Hannah both feel for "home"—one that, according to Hwang, can only be "metaphysical." Lured—indeed, impelled—by the promise of home, they pursue the crow, the bringer of disaster:

> They run on faith now, passing through territories uncharted, following the sound of their suffering. And it is in this way that they pass through their lives. Hardly noticing that they've entered. Without stopping to note its passing. Just following a crow, with single dedication, forgetting how they started, or why they're chasing, or even what may happen if they catch it. Running without pause or pleasure, past the point of their beginning. (Hwang 1990:107)

Having no other options in life, having neither home nor the luxury to indulge in the desire for home, they cannot erase their longing. For them, home is attainable only in death.

DOUGHBALL AND THE NARRATIVE PRODUCTION OF "HOME"

Perry Miyake's *Doughball* was produced at East/West Players during January and February 1991. The review in the *Los Angeles Times* (December 21, 1990) characterized the production as "uneven." Though some of the acting was favorably reviewed, the closing sentence reveals the reviewer's ambivalence: "The title refers to a game of chance played at the annual Venice carnivals fondly rekindled here, but with only random, not tight focus." Although this is not precisely a pan of the play, and though the reviewer does much to credit the acting of several of the key members of the cast, the impression is of yet another earnest, well-intentioned, but not fully realized production.

Postponing the inevitable, I attended the closing performance more out of a sense of duty than out of desire. The lead actor, Steve Park, had been among a group of Asian American actors who had spoken at our teach-in protesting the performance of Gilbert and Sullivan's *The Mikado* at the Claremont Colleges. I should further preface my reactions by saying that the playwright and I are exactly the same age, and that I went to the performance with a friend of Basque descent, from my hometown in Oregon, who graduated from high school a year after I did. ("The Bascos and the Buddhaheads used to run together," as he so eloquently put it.) Expecting clumsy earnestness, my friend and I found instead a production of incredible intensity, "authenticity," and luminosity. As the play began, my skepticism ebbed as I felt transported into the space and time of my high school. My friend and I kept looking at each other in amazement: "My God, that's Mrs. Yamaguchi!" "And they're like Bob Maeda and Russell Murata!" We could rename all the characters, because we knew them all. And I laughed at that production the way I have never laughed before or since. I laughed the laughter of recognition. As the play continued, I was even more startled by the two young women in the play, uncanny refractions of my own high school self: one, the bookish valedictorian with a crush on the protagonist, David; the other, the protagonist's dream girl, who herself dreams of leaving her confining world for Stanford and for France. Emerging from the theater, I felt slightly drunk, as though the intensity of the experience had been too much for my body to assimilate. Then it struck me forcibly: Asian Americans never laugh the laughter of recognition because we are systematically erased from view. We never see ourselves portrayed the way *we* see ourselves. Small wonder I experienced this play with almost physical force, in my whole being. Small wonder I spent the subsequent week in a fog, musing about the place of Stanford and of France as utopian landscapes for Sansei girls. And small wonder that mainstream critics were unable to understand the play fully. Instead of exoticism, they were exposed to the less spectacular, but infinitely more resonant, small truths of everyday life: the truths of "home." As with *M. Butterfly,* I was consumed by urgency to write about this play, to document its resonance, for never in my life have I seen anything so "true" to "my experience."

Now, what might such a reaction mean? Rather than simply taking that "experience" as transparent, the poststructuralist suspicion of notions like "truth," "authenticity," and "experience," requires a critical interrogation of those terms. What writing or performative practices created the effects of authenticity or verisimilitude? How can we account for the discursive production of a culturally essentialist Japanese American identity? In other words, just what was so "homey" about this play?

First, and most important, there was no exoticism, an incredible rarity when Asian Americans are depicted in mainstream venues. In *Doughball,* there were no fake "Oriental" accents, no Asian women as wilting flowers, no quasi-Japanese music, no "Oriental" splendor. Steve Park said it this way: "Just from my experience with Pan Asian and East West . . . I think Asian American theater tries to pander to the white audience too much. And that's what I liked about *Doughball,* there was no sense of that in

Doughball." I think this may be a critical factor in the lukewarm mainstream reception of the play. For Japanese Americans, the absence of Japonaiserie means we can see ourselves represented "authentically," not as whites with an exotic veneer but as normal, everyday Japanese Americans.

A key feature producing authenticity effects is the sensuousness of language: its textures, its familiarity, its evocative power. Especially resonant for Sansei, who as a rule do not grow up speaking Japanese, is what one might call "family Japanese": phrases for food, words about the body and bodily functions, epithets signaling intense feeling, phrases that bring a start of recognition and stir memory. Take this example, from David's irrepressible mother:

> *Yuki:* I was over there, but Frank had to go *benjo,* so I'm here now! Oh, Wayne, did you get some *udon?* They're probably running out so you better get some if you want some! (Miyake 1991a:57)

Yuki uses the word *benjo,* a very rough slang word for bathroom, one that would raise eyebrows in contemporary Japan for its crudity. It is, however, a word that most JAs know. In Japan, it would be particularly horrifying to hear an urban woman saying this; for me, it elicits childhood memories. The energetic "eat, eat," admonition, with *udon* (noodles) as the lure, eloquently captures the verbal and interactional styles of many tough Nisei women. To the credit of Miyake and of Alice Kushida, who gave a compelling, vibrant, and unerringly "authentic" performance, Yuki embodied this energetic toughness.

Another exchange enacts a particularly Sansei identity:

> *Eric:* Ooh, negative vibes, man. Bad *bachi.*
> *David:* Okay, we'll hang out here and if she shows, cool.
> (Miyake 1991a:24)

This is quintessential West Coast Sansei language: the California slang combined with a reference to Japanese American family talk: *bachi* as divine retribution—*bachi ga ataru, bachi* will strike, you'll be punished, for some misdeed. It can also be used as a disciplinary admonition, especially for young children, as in "Don't touch that—it's dirty, it's *bachi.*"

Derogatory epithets are another linguistic practice spurring memory; these Japanese phrases occur only in situations involving friends, family, and the Japanese American community—after all, these are the only people who can understand the insult. Two fathers speak:

Mits: Who's crying? I don't cry. I complain a lot, but I don't cry.
Frank: Yes, you, *monku-tare.*

(Miyake 1991a:24)

The *tare* here is a particularly rough and countrified suffix. *Monku* means "complaint," so *monkutare* is a complainer, a kvetch. *Tare* is combined with other words to create salty, direct epithets associated with family and friends in the JA community: *unkotare,* "shithead," a term appearing in the play, and *bakatare,* "stupid idiot." These expressions are extremely crude and regional, and have a rustic air; middle-class Tokyo residents would laugh at their provincial quaintness. Accordingly, these expressions define for Japanese Americans a particularly familial world that is neither Euro-American nor Japanese, but JA.

Small epiphanies and moments of recognition like these demonstrate how linguistic practices can define a community.[3] These languages in Japanese American plays enable the creation of a Japanese American identity transcending a particular family's idiosyncrasies. As an Asian American, often one does not know what is peculiar to one's family and what is common to a larger community. Or, if you believe that you are engaging in practices that are "typical" of your ethnic group, you still may not be sure "what is Chinese tradition and what is the movies" (Kingston 1977:6). What these linguistic practices accomplish is to create the sense of recognition and "authenticity," asserting and affirming one's belonging to a family and to a "culture."

The play discursively produces "home" and "community" just as forcefully through its embeddedness in a very specific geography: Venice, California. When the play went into production, Perry Miyake took the actors on a tour of the part of Venice where he grew up; he took me on the same tour when I interviewed him. This is not the Venice of rollerblading and Muscle Beach and Dennis Hopper, but the Japanese American and Chicano Venice on Centinela Avenue, the Venice of Mago's, the fast food joint where you can still get avocado cha-shu burgers and teriyaki burritos; of the funky 1950s pharmacy where the boys used to stand for hours reading comics; of Kenny's Cafe, where you can enjoy Hawaiian Japanese favorites like Spam fried rice and Portuguese sausage and eggs. The play itself occurs during a summer carnival at the Japanese American Community Center in Venice, still a lively hub of community activity. This Venice has a funky, lived-in feeling of families and communities that have existed for at least a generation; artsy glitz has little purchase here. *Doughball* attempts to write this Venice into collective memory.

A fourth element in the discursive production of "home" arises from the resonance of sensory memory and, through its deployment, a Proustian evocation of a world. In particular, foods, sounds, and smells serve as symbolic vehicles of ethnic identity. One eloquent example is a monologue delivered by Wayne, the protagonist's cousin, a Vietnam vet who is mostly mute until David decides he wants to join the army and go fight in Vietnam. To discourage David, Wayne speaks, uttering this soliloquy on home:

> I love the smell of rice cooking in the evening. It don't smell like death no more.
>
> I sit in our kitchen, on the same old chair I sat on since I was a kid. Mom's at the sink chopping vegetables, wearing that same old apron she always wears. Dad comes in the back door and stomps off his boots in the back porch.
>
> There's hamburger *okazu* on the stove. Hamburger *okazu*. Poor man's sukiyaki. Same ol' shit I was so sick of eating six days a week before and now I can't wait. Hamburger, onions, green onion, string beans, eggplant, sugar-shoyu, tofu, and that wiggy shit that looks like worms. All cooking in that big ol' black cast-iron frying pan.
>
> I smell the rice cooking. I hear the lid rattling on the rice cooker. Sun's going down outside the kitchen window. And I can't believe I'm back. Mom puts a big bowl of *okazu* in front of me, raw egg on the side, *chawan* full of hot rice in my left hand, *hashi* in my right. Dad says, "*Itadakimasu,*" and nothing ever tasted better.
>
> So I eat. I savor. I enjoy. And I don't look up 'cause there's tears in my eyes.
>
> I'm home. Goddammit, I'm home. (Miyake 1991a:94, 95)

Just as a world emerged from Proust's teacup and his tisane-drenched madeleine, so an entire landscape of memory arises from the cast-iron pan full of hamburger *okazu,* memories that go beyond the Venice JA community certainly to "mine" in Oregon and, I suspect, to others as well.[4] Sounds—the rattling of the rice cooker, the stomping of the boots—the smells of rice, the cast iron pan and the description of the food in it, the phrases of fragmentary Japanese most Sansei know—*hashi* (chopsticks), *chawan* (rice bowl), *okazu* (a meat- and-vegetable main dish), as well as the hot rice and raw egg, indispensable accoutrements to sukiyaki—create family and home from memory, inscribing a larger set of practices that define "Japanese American culture."

Through the erasure of exoticism, through linguistic practices, and through exploring the evocative power of sensory memory, Perry Miyake and *Doughball* created a Japanese American community and culture. As he put it:

> *David:* I miss this. Being somewhere where you don't have to explain yourself, and what you are.
> *Andrea:* Home. (Miyake 1991a:101)

HOME, IDENTITY, AND POLITICAL CHANGE

Given this, what more does one say about this discursive production of "home" in a naturalistic play such as this? What kind of political weight can it sustain?

Recent work by poststructuralist feminist critics attempts to assess the political consequences of deploying certain kinds of narrative strategies. Some have argued for the subversive potential of particular strategies, tending to privilege particular tactics in advance. For example, Catherine Belsey argues that expressive realism is associated with the constitution of both author and reader as autonomous, whole subjects, with certain Aristotelian notions of art as mimesis, and with a particular moment in the development of capitalism. Contradiction is minimized in realist representation. The conventional narrative structure introduces disruptions in the social order, and then through plot and character development—a development that elicits audience identification—the play or text arrives at a narrative closure that reestablishes order, thus, in Belsey's estimation, foreclosing political possibilities and leaving codes of representation intact (Belsey 1980). Jill Dolan, a feminist critic of theater, also tropes realism as politically conservative and inadequate to the kind of materialist feminist theatrical practice she envisions as subversive. Her argument is given particular weight by her analysis of several plays that deal with lesbian issues, in which the realist narrative inevitably leads to a closure in which the lesbian, and in particular the butch lesbian, ends up dead, vilified, recuperated to the heterosexual norm, or some combination of the above (Dolan 1988, 1990). Both she and Belsey would call for a text that problematizes the process of representation, foregrounding contradiction and disrupting easy identification. One way of doing so would be through Brechtian alienation effects, calling attention to the theatricality of theatrical production: for example, having the actors address the audience "out of their roles," or undercutting psychological realism by staging a series of seemingly unrelated vignettes that cannot be recuperated into a smoothly flowing narrative line. Certainly such critiques of realist representation are incisive and well taken. Realism can lull the spectator into an overly easy identification that reinscribes the whole subject who freely chooses to give her/his labor and to exercise "free choice" in consuming the products of capitalism. As Belsey eloquently argues:

> The ideology of liberal humanism assumes a world of non-contradictory (and therefore fundamentally unalterable) individuals whose unfettered consciousness is the origin of meaning, knowledge, and action. It is in the interest of this ideology above all to suppress the role of language in the construction of the subject, and its own role in the interpellation of the subject, and to present the individual as a free, unified, autonomous subjectivity. Classic realism, still the dominant popular mode in literature, film and television drama, roughly coincides chronologically with the epoch of industrial capitalism. It performs . . . the work of ideology, not only in its representation of a world of consistent subjects who are the origin of meaning, knowledge and action, but also in offering the reader, as the position from which the text is most readily intelligible, the position of subject as the origin both of understanding and of action in accordance with that understanding. (Belsey 1980:67)

Given what can be described only as cogent and incisive critiques, one must then ask whether a play like *Doughball* is indeed simply a fond rekindling of memories. Is it merely nostalgic? Does it inscribe a golden age, a mythical community, that fails to see its own exclusions and never "really" existed? Does it rely on a realism that privileges narrative closure and an insidious reinscription of the whole subject? And must that realism be transcended and disrupted in order to be politically subversive?

First of all, there is inevitably a sense in which *Doughball* and other realist narratives can be read as having this "conservative" political weight. *Doughball* relies on psychological realism and on the production of the familiar; without a doubt it elicits the "identification" of the spectator. Any narrative is exclusionary in some ways, and this is most definitely a Sansei *man's* text, privileging a male point of view of that historical period, and in its warm nostalgia it idealizes to some extent this very problematic moment in history and in the life of the protagonist. Critics indeed focused on the play's nostalgia, finding it aesthetically and politically retrograde. Miyake countered with the following: "The reviewers are all intellect, no heart. I write from the heart. They see that and they say, 'Oh that's just sentimental . . . nostalgic. Ping [Wu, an Asian American actor who has been active in the *Miss Saigon* protests] was saying, 'So what if it's nostalgic; its OUR nostalgia.' They expect us to be satisfied with THEIR nostalgia."

I think Miyake and Ping Wu are onto something here, and that the issue is considerably more complex. We must ask who is creating this nostalgic "home," for whom, and for what purpose. Morley and Robins point out the politically insidious construction of a European homeland, a home that would enshrine Eurocentrism and defensively shore up boundaries against threats from "non-Europeans" in what they call "a fortress identity" (Morley and Robins 1990:3). How different this seems, for example, from Black lesbian feminist Barbara Smith's invocation of "home," the house in Cleveland on 132nd Street off Kinsman, a home where she learned about "feminism" from the women in her household. Hers is a home that stands for claiming one's Blackness, a claim that one does not leave "the race" when one is a feminist or a lesbian (Smith 1983:xxii). The questions of "who" and "for whom" are crucial in these examples. The *Heimat* is part of a fortress identity addressing (white, Northern) Europeans, an attempt by the center to retain its power. Differently positioned, Barbara Smith's "home" is a safe place for other African Americans and lesbians. And Perry Miyake's *Doughball* implicitly addresses Asian American, and specifically Japanese American, viewers, without explaining and without exoticizing for a mainstream audience. To reiterate Steve Park's comment, there was no "pandering to a white audience" in this instance. Perhaps at this particular historical moment one kind of political intervention would subvert precisely in its verisimilitude, in its "authentic" representation of a "reality" of marginal peoples in ways not captured in dominant cultural representations. Perhaps, in these instances, it is precisely the realism of the narrative that is politically effective.[5]

Further, perhaps the term "realism" itself must be problematized and opened to the play of historically and culturally specific power relations.[6] The speaker's position, the intended audience, the stakes, and the larger discursive fields of history and power through which meanings are constituted are not mere "contexts" that nuance an essentialized meaning; rather, these are essential in determining the political weight of any narrative strategy.

Indeed, I would argue that the authenticity effects and conventional narrative line of *Doughball* support a politically urgent project: a Sansei's attempt to write Sansei identity into existence. My own experience of drunkenness from the laughter of recognition was followed by anger that Asian Americans in general, Japanese Americans, Sansei, as we get more and more ethnically and generationally specific, are systematically erased from representation in mainstream media. In very real ways, we do not exist. Either we are absent entirely or, what is often worse, when we are depicted, it is only in the most stereotyped way, thus subjecting us to psychological violence rather than offering affirmation or recognition. Miyake himself said this, in a statement both apocalyptic and poignant:

> . . . for once, we got to present ourselves as we are onstage. I believe we haven't yet defined ourselves onstage and I really do fear that a whole generation of Asian Americans, us Sanseis, will be ignored not only by the mainstream media, but by ourselves, meaning Asian American theatre groups, simply because we are too far removed from the immigrant experience, and we will become extinct without a trace of our art, our self-expression, to be remembered by. (Miyake, personal communication, January 30, 1991)

For me this statement captured the urgent necessity for Asian Americans to write ourselves into existence, and it is the urgency I feel in the need to document this struggle in my work with Asian American theater, a sense that somehow my own life, and the lives of others, are at stake. Miyake writes for himself and for other Japanese Americans first; his implied spectator is not from the dominant culture. The question of realism, then, must be a question of realisms in the plural, realisms deployed by positioned subjects with different stakes, who constitute themselves within shifting fields of power and history.

The realist impulse in *Doughball* is equally linked to a sense of urgency arising from the specificity of geography and place, and the historical circumstances in which Miyake writes. He desires to write a moment into history, for his play is an act of collective memory, a nostalgic remembrance of the time when there was "a community." Miyake was born and grew up in Venice, left it for a number of years, then returned. He commented on the changes: "It just got to be a less friendly place, and it was strange to be living at home and feeling sort of out of place. I wanted to capture that time again in high school, because no one else was . . . writing about that period, our generation . . ." (Miyake 1991b). With preservation and historical memory as goals, Miyake actually creates a history and a community by paying his respects to his lived experience of community as it lives in memory. His Venice is poised between relocation and redevelopment, a moment of seeming calm and safety before other forces disrupt it anew. It is also the midst of the Vietnam War, and the everyday concerns of the boys in high school—girls, mostly—are shadowed by the specter of the draft. David, the protagonist, and Mits, his father, talk about changes in the community:

> *Mits:* Boy, I'm getting too old for this. Maybe next year they'll just have some kinda high-tone, ***kanemochi,***[7] black-tie dinner and skip the carnival.
> *David:* Skip the carnival?
> *Mits:* They gotta raise big bucks to build a new community center. Pave this parking lot over.
> *David:* They gotta have a carnival. Where are all the junior high kids gonna hang out?
> *Mits:* The way they're talking about getting rid of all the old stuff. Japan's getting rich, starting to whaddayacallit?—redevelop Little Tokyo, just move all the Issei out. They don't give a damn about us.
> *David:* Yeah, but this is Venice.
> *Mits:* Maybe we're too small for them to get their paws on. We still gotta rebuild this place. Judo dojo's falling apart. This place is old. (*looks around*) We stayed here when we got outa camp and finally came back.
> *David:* Where?
> *Mits:* Here. (*points to porch*) Dojo was the mess hall. (*points USL*) Kitchen was in the same place. (*points USC*) All the families stayed in the rooms where the offices are until they found a place to live. (*looks around*) They even had to put up tents in the parking lot. No room for everybody coming back out here. That's how old this place is. Falling apart.
> *David:* I could do without the dirt.
> *Mits:* Nah, when this place is all cement, it's gonna be too cold. Too clean. Lose touch. (Miyake 1991a:83, 84)

Relocation and impending dislocation are themes here, and in an interesting way this passage enacts the contradictions of Japanese American identity. The site of the community center holds memories of dislocation from imprisonment and of "coming home" from that imprisonment. At the moment of the play, it provides the funky, down-home space for the creation of "Japanese American community" in events like the summer carnivals or Obon festivals. But it is disintegrating, as the memories fade and the community disperses. And the new threat is symbolized by Japan. Accordingly, Japanese Americans find themselves "caught between," if you will.[8] The grounds of the Venice Japanese Community Center have in fact been paved over, as Miyake showed me, and he views part of his mission as preserving in memory the time when the Community Center was exactly that, a provisional safety zone amid past and impending dislocation.

Assessing these moves to write history and identity, and assessing the political weight of plays like *Doughball*, for the production of home and community does not stop with the text. The actual production mirrored this creation of a provisional home for the cast, crew, and playwright. At first plagued by various illnesses (for example, the lead, Steve Park, had debilitating arthritis), injuries, car accidents, deaths in families (Miyake lost a close relative) and by an initially tense relationship between actors and the director, Patricia Yasutake, the cast built solidarity through the production. Lissa Ling Lee, who played Andrea, the class valedictorian, described the atmosphere:

> . . . this experience was really unique, everyone here was very supportive of each other, which is really usually not the case in Hollywood. . . . I think because of the fact that we were Asian American actors, we had more of a need to see this project come together, rather than just ourselves shine. So we tried to help each other. So it was very different. I can't really compare it to anything else. (Lee 1991)

In fact, the cast actually had occasional reunions and, in Steve Park's words, "after the show we'd do *Doughball* things, like *Doughball* went to see *Hedda Gabler*, and we were to try to go see *Canton* together, but it was overbooked. . . . That's rare, that after the show we'll be like, 'Oh let's do this together'" (Park 1991). Both the themes of the play and the actual production, in which initial strife led to solidarity among cast, crew, and writer, created a shared, provisional home that writes Asian American identity.

The "home" of *Doughball* can be further placed in the context of sites such as East/West Players, the oldest Asian American theater troupe in the country. Over the years the company has sponsored workshops and classes in various aspects of theatrical production, including acting, and now playwriting, a way of producing producers of Asian American identity. In April

1992 the first David Henry Hwang Writers' Institute presented staged readings of the first plays, all one-acts or portions of one-acts, from the Institute; among the fledging playwrights was this author. Originally, I enrolled in the Writers' Institute largely as a "participant observation" technique, so that I might learn about the craft of playwriting and make contacts in the Asian American theater world. However, inspired by the work of artists such as Perry Miyake and by the vibrancy of Asian American cultural production in Los Angeles, many people like myself can feel empowered to venture into the arts themselves, to enter realms we had heretofore assumed to be closed to us, thus proliferating the possibilities for constructing Asian American identities.

Doughball's geography of identity and creation of home must also be located within the specific site of Los Angeles, easily the center for the production of Asian American art and culture at this historical moment. Smaller centers of Asian American theater exist in San Francisco, New York, and Seattle, but the relative stability and continuity of an organization like East/West Players, as well as the relative receptiveness to Asian American theater in mainstream venues such as the Mark Taper Forum (as well as in smaller theaters like the Fountain and the Odyssey, and alternative spaces like Highways), make Los Angeles an incredibly exciting place to be for a person of color and an Asian American at the end of the twentieth century. California generally should continue to be a key locale for cultural production by peoples of color, as whites in the state rapidly become a plurality rather than a majority, and as diasporic communities and communities of color are creating, narrating, and performing themselves.

Given these multiple layerings of home, community, and identity, and the vibrancy of this particular historical moment on the West Coast, I want to argue for the political weight of plays like *Doughball*. Three points must be underlined here. One has to do with the question of audience reception and realist representation. Seeing theater and performance of, by, and about Asian Americans—whether the narrative strategy is realist, nonrealist, avant-garde, or some combination of strategies—has among its effects the empowering of other Asian Americans. The question of realist representation, then, must take into account not only narrative strategy but also effects on actual audience members, mindful of a historical context in which there is a general subversiveness in simply being able to see progressive plays by and about peoples of color. Second, I wanted to gesture toward the implications of such moves for anthropological ethnography. As more of us anthropologists from the borderlands go "home" to study "our own communities," we will probably see increasing elisions of boundaries between ethnography and "minority discourse," in which writing ethnography becomes another way of writing our own identities and communities. And writing that identity in the context of writing one's scholarly work creates a narrative space in the dominant discourse, a space that could refigure the disciplines as "home" for us. Certainly, "going home"—not only to study one's own community, with all the asymmetries of power that term implies, but also to help create it, gives one a wholly different relationship to the usual anthropological project of distanced observation and "studying down." For the first time in my life, I feel myself as a totally engaged participant in a common struggle of incredible emotional, intellectual, and political urgency, a struggle to which—for a change—I can contribute as much as I receive.

Finally, the debate about the political effects of realist representation must move beyond the familiar positions based on binarized and dehistoricized notions of realism and avant-gardism. The lulling of the spectator into the transparency of reality, the reinscription of the whole subject, and the elicitation of nostalgia that masks oppression and difference, are all recognizable effects of realism. Other approaches that call attention to the representational frame itself also draw predictable charges: elitism and lack of accessibility to large audiences. Usually the counterattack is to argue that realism is just as constructed as other forms of representation, and that to consider avant-garde representation beyond mainstream audiences is itself an elitist presupposition. (Trinh 1991:87, 88)

Perhaps these questions cannot be answered in the terms in which they are posed. Perhaps they must be answered specifically, and in reference to particular productions, texts, audiences, venues. For though I think the work of feminist poststructuralist literary critics like Belsey and Dolan is on the mark in many ways, I also think the prescriptive nature of those readings is unwarranted, given their purely formal and textual basis and their essentialized reading of realism. That is, the literary critic, through her analysis of formal properties of the text, can trace out the political weight of certain textual strategies for an idealized conventional audience. But doing so elides the question of realisms in the plural, received and interpreted by diverse, multiply positioned audiences, in all their complex and contradictory messiness. I cannot call myself a typical viewer of *Doughball*, but I do want to highlight the fact that seeing *Doughball* led, in my case, not (only) to an idealization of a Japanese American community that never was, but also to rage and anger that Asian Americans generally, and Japanese Americans specifically, are never depicted in the media. That is, precisely the realist moves in *Doughball* spurred me to action: provoking a problematizing of representation of Asian Americans by the dominant culture, motivating the writing of this essay, and, in part, my decision to take the playwriting class. The realism of *Doughball* heightened the felt necessity to create "homes" for ourselves, however problematic and provisional, figuring home not as an essentialized space of identity but as a historically and culturally specific construct inseparable from power relations. Rather than privileging certain representational strategies in advance, I am arguing for a more complex view of the relationship between aesthetics and politics, and for more thoroughgoing studies of reception that would go beyond the positing of the idealized author and the idealized audience, positioning sites, venues, productions, and audiences within larger matrices of power, history, and culture.

Though *Doughball* makes no attempt to subvert codes of realist representation, I think one must seek its political and aesthetic value elsewhere . . . or precisely in its deployment of reality effects. It underlines the salience of Chela Sandoval's incisive analysis of what she calls "oppositional consciousness" in U.S. Third World feminism. She describes the contextually specific tactics in which Third World feminists engage, arguing that one cannot necessarily privilege in advance and for all time the utility of any particular tactic. "Differential consciousness" is a mode of "weaving 'between and among' oppositional ideologies," and it mobilizes a "tactical subjectivity with the capacity of recentering depending upon the kinds of oppression to be confronted" (Sandoval 1991:14). Biddy Martin and Chandra Mohanty, in their discussion of the construction of home, community, and identity in lesbian autobiography, make a similar point.

> Basic to the (at least implicit) disavowal of conventionally realist and autobiographical narrative by deconstructionist critics is the assumption that difference can emerge only through self-referential language, i.e., through certain relatively specific formal operations present in the text or performed upon it. Our reading of Pratt's narrative contends that a so-called conventional narrative such as Pratt's is not only useful but essential in addressing the politically and theoretically urgent questions surrounding identity politics. (Martin and Mohanty 1986:194)

I want to concur with Sandoval and with Martin and Mohanty, and end by saying that Perry Miyake's *Doughball* draws our attention to the constructedness of "home," identity, and culture, underlining the necessity for people on the margins to create, produce, and assert our identities. Its specific locations in Venice, East/West Players, and Los Angeles, its framing by a particular history of dislocation, of the Vietnam War, and of urban redevelopment, underscores the historically and politically constructed nature of those identities. Indeed, as I stated at the outset, the term "Asian American" itself is inextricable from history and politics, as an identity forged through the student struggles of the 1960s—before, after all, we were merely Orientals. Asian American theater, including productions like *Doughball,* and sites like East/West Players, Highways, Pan Asian Repertory in New York, and Asian American Theater Company in San Francisco, continue to explore the aesthetic and political possibilities of such identities. However problematic the notion of home, whatever differences within are effaced, and however provisional that home may be, *Doughball,* East/West, L.A., and my ongoing experiences as documentor and perhaps producer of Asian American theater highlight for me the continued urgency for us to create our homes and our identities for ourselves. As Elaine Kim has argued, "claiming America for Asian Americans means inventing a new identity" (Kim 1990:147). I would suggest that such an identity would be neither Asian nor American if the latter means Euro, nor does it mean hyphenated Asian-American, if that means riding on the hyphen "between two worlds." Rather, I think Asian American playwrights, writers, artists are creating identities that defy binary categorization into Asian or American, or into some mediating third term. They are articulating for Asian Americans something new, something that exceeds previous categories. I would suggest that despite the human suffering incurred through dislocation, incarceration, and diaspora, the historical experiences of Asian Americans can become a source of strength, the openness of identity a field of possibility. For as performance artist Dan Kwong urged us, we must continue to "tell our stories" (1991); we must continue to write ourselves into existence.

NOTES

1 A phrase describing the effect of "relocation" on the Japanese American community.

2 Elaine Kim (1990) provides a cogent analysis of the oppositional quality of the Asian American claim on "America" as "home."

3 The winter production at East/West Players in 1992 was R. A. Shiomi's *Uncle Tadao,* a play thematizing the lingering memories and pain of relocation, brought alive by the redress campaign of the 1980s. Again, the small details of language created au-

thenticity effects, particularly through Sab Shimono's brilliant portrayal of a Nisei man. Small expressions, inflections, and intonations reminded me of "home": the use of the term "high tone" to mean "classy" or "elegant," and the particular way Nisei pronounce that word; Shimono's pronunciation of "goddamn," which many Nisei men pronounce "gotdamn," and so on. A Hawaiian-born and -raised Sansei colleague commented on the word "yakking," and its familiarity to him; to that point, he had thought that it was strictly a Hawaiian JA term, but Shiomi is a Japanese Canadian playwright from Toronto.

4 I invoke Proust both to deflate the kind of elevated world of the mundane allowed "great French literature" and to elevate the work of Asian American theater, to argue that the same attention can be paid the evocative power of sensory memory in both settings.

5 Of course naturalistic representation may not be the only mode of "capturing reality."

6 See Emily Apter's work on "colonial realism."

7 Rich person.

8 As an analyst, this strikes me as problematic. Japanese capital has sometimes been behind redevelopment—for example, in Japantown in San Francisco, where the building of the Japanese mall displaced many Japanese American residents—but never without the key intervention of white developers. In one sense this passage inevitably feeds the current Japan-bashing discourse that is dangerous and life-threatening for Japanese Americans; on the other hand, it does the work of distinguishing Japanese Americans from Japanese, and demonstrates the ways that Japanese Americans' lives are shaped by larger forces of war, racism, and global capitalism.

ARAB NOISE AND RAMADAN NIGHTS: RAI, RAP, AND FRANCO-MAGHREBI IDENTITIES

JOAN GROSS, DAVID MCMURRAY, AND TED SWEDENBURG

CAN'T TAKE NO MOOR

> For two thousand years, essentially the same people have posed the same dangers to us. Aren't the Iranian *mujahidin* the descendants of the Persians who were defeated at Marathon; isn't the Islamic World, now striking at Europe's frontiers and slowly penetrating her, composed of the sons of the Ottoman Turks who reached Vienna, and the Arabs whom Charles Martel routed at Poitiers?—Jean-Marie Le Pen[1]

In the aftermath of the Berlin Wall's collapse, Western Europe has been forced to rethink its identity. If in the recent past its conception of itself as a haven of democracy and civilization depended—in part—on a contrast to the evils of the Communist Empire, today an idea is being revived of Europe as Christendom, in contradistinction to Islam. Only this time around, the Islam in question is not being held back at Europe's Spanish or Balkan frontiers but has penetrated its very core, in the shape of new "minority" populations of Muslim background. Questions about the nature of Europe's identity and the place of Muslim immigrants within it are now among the most contentious on the Continent (Morley and Robins 1990). So acute is the anxiety about the ten to twelve million "immigrants" that many white Western Europeans feel they are living under cultural and economic siege (Miller 1991:33).

The Spanish novelist Juan Goytisolo brilliantly lampoons this European hysteria about "foreigners" in his hilariously provocative *Landscapes After the Battle*. It opens with the inexplicable appearance of unintelligible scrawls on the walls of the Parisian neighborhood of Le Sentier. At first the natives assume the marks are the secret language of a gang of kids, but then someone spots a man with "kinky black hair" inscribing the mysterious messages. The natives conclude that the scrawls are written in a real alphabet

—but backward—and are the handiwork of "those foreigners who, in ever-increasing numbers, were stealthily invading the decrepit buildings abandoned by their former tenants and offering their labor to the well-heeled merchants of Le Sentier" (1987a:3). Then one morning, a working-class native of Le Sentier drops in at his local bar for a pick-me-up of calvados, to discover that the sign identifying his tavern has been replaced by one written in that incomprehensible script. Wandering through the neighborhood, he is horrified to find that every marker—the Rex Cinema's marquee, McDonald's, street signs, the placard on the district mayor's office—has been transformed. Even the sign outside the office of the newspaper of "the glorious Party of the working class," *L'Humanité,* now reads الإنسانية. A catastrophic, cacophonous traffic jam has broken out, for drivers cannot decipher the street signs, and the traffic police are no help. "Trying to hide his laughter, a swarthy-skinned youngster with kinky hair purveyed his services as guide to whichever helpless soul bid the highest" (1987a:7). "Colonized by those barbarians!" the unnerved Le Sentier native thinks to himself (1987a:5).

Goytisolo's send-up of the French nightmare about *immigrés* seems remarkably prescient today, more than a decade after its publication. For French antipathy is especially virulent toward those "foreigners" who have been coming from North Africa for decades and who utilize that "backward" script, Arabic. French society has never come to terms with the legacy of colonization or its bloody war against the Algerian national liberation movement, which cost one million Arab and ten thousand French lives.[2] Instead, one might imagine, from the frenzied reactions of so many white French men and women to all things "Arab" and "Islamic," that colonialism had been a magnanimous and bloodless project, and that Arabs in France live in the lap of luxury and have nothing to complain about.[3]

So severe are apprehensions about the *immigré* "problem" that during the "*hijab* affair" of 1989, when nine female Franco-Maghrebi students in state-run lycées demanded the right to wear Islamic headscarves, the media fused the signifiers "immigrant," "Muslim fundamentalist," and "invasion" together into a specter of an eventual Islamic France—a vision that horrified a good portion of the French population, on both the Left and the Right (Koulberg 1991).[4] Even President François Mitterrand, who postured as an anti-racist, was prompted to assert that the country had gone beyond "the threshold of tolerance" (Riding 1990:I-16). Jacques Chirac, former prime minister, mayor of Paris, and leader of the right-wing Rally for the Republic (RPR), complained about the "overdose of immigrants"—a code word for "Arabs"—while former president Valéry Giscard d'Estaing warned of a foreign "invasion" (Gorce 1991:30; Singer 1991:814). These elite opinions lent legitimacy to widespread popular sentiments. Two 1991 surveys indicated that 71 percent of the populace thought there were too many Arabs in France and that over 30 percent of the electorate supported the platform of Jean-Marie Le Pen's far-right National Front, which calls for the expulsion of *immigrés* (*Le Monde,* March 22, 1991; Riding 1991).[5] And Chirac, in a now-infamous statement, expressed his sympathy for the decent French working people who are being driven "understandably crazy" by the "noise and smell" of foreigners (Drozdiak 1991; Hall 1991b:18).[6] (Chirac's RPR is the leading force in the center-Right French government that was brought to power in the March 1993 elections.)

"Noise and smell"—music and cuisine—are crucial cultural forms of expression, essential vehicles through which North Africans assert, sustain, and reconfigure their identities in France. And probably the best-known "Arab noise" blasting out of the boomboxes in Maghrebi neighborhoods of Paris and Marseilles is *rai,* a musical genre that arrived in the United States as part of the "World Music" wave in the late 1980s.

This essay tracks the complex trajectory of *rai,* from its origins and evolution in Algeria, to the transformations in its uses and meanings as migrant workers brought it to France, and as it has moved back and forth across the Mediterranean and into the World Music scene. We assess *rai*'s role in the construction of Franco-Maghrebi identities, particularly with regard to gender, tradition, and religion, seeing it as an exemplar of the various hybrid cultural practices that typify Maghrebi integration into French life. We compare the "defensive" cultural identities associated with *rai* against the assertive and multiethnic sensibilities affiliated with rap, the music now favored by young Franco-Maghrebis. Finally, we argue that, despite their marginality, Franco-Maghrebis and their expressive culture are integral to an understanding of contemporary French identity. France is being "Third-Worldized," for assimilation of Maghrebis into French life results not in their "acculturation" but in "cultural syncretism" (Gilroy 1987:155). Against its will the country is shedding its Europeanness and becoming "mestizo, bastard, [and] fecundated" by formerly victimized civilizations (Goytisolo 1987b:37–38; see Koptiuch 1991). Franco-Maghrebi expressive culture, in its most utopian moments, serves as a model of decentralized plurality and multiple affiliations, a means of recasting contemporary French identity and undermining French national exclusivism.

ALGERIAN RAI: FROM COUNTRY TO POP, BORDELLO TO PATRIMOINE NATIONAL

Modern *rai* emerged during the 1920s, when rural migrants brought their native musical styles into the growing urban centers of northwestern Algeria, particularly the port town of Oran (Wahran in Arabic), Algeria's second largest city. In the new urban settings, *rai* developed as a hybrid blend of rural and cabaret musical genres, played by and for distillery workers, peasants dispossessed by European settlers, shepherds, prostitutes, and other members of the poor classes (Virolle-Souibès 1989:51–52). Oran's permissive atmosphere proved congenial for *rai* artists, who found spaces to perform in its extensive network of nightclubs, taverns, and brothels, as well as in more "respectable" settings like wedding celebrations and festivals. Women singers were prominent from the genre's beginnings, and the performance of *rai,* unique among Algerian musical genres, was associated with dancing, often in mixed-gender settings (Benkheira 1986:174).

Oran's proximity to Morocco and Spain and its port economy meant that its culture was permeated by multifarious influences. *Rai* musicians therefore absorbed an array of musical styles: flamenco from Spain, *gnawa* (a musical genre performed by Sufis of West African origin) from nearby Morocco, French cabaret, the sounds of Berber Kabylia, the rapid rhythms of Arab nomads. *Rai* artists sang in Orani, an Arabic dialect rich with French and Spanish borrowings and liberally seasoned with Berber.

As early as the 1930s, *rai* musicians reportedly were harassed by the colonial police for singing about social issues of concern to Algeria's indigenous inhabitants, such as typhus, imprisonment, poverty, and colonial oppression. Likewise, during the independence struggle, *rai* artists composed songs that expressed nationalist sentiments (Virolle-Souibès 1988b:184–86). But throughout this period, *rai*'s main themes were wine, love, and the problems and pleasures of life on the margins. One of *rai*'s most renowned, and bawdy, singers was Cheikha Rimitti,[7] one of whose songs went:

> Oh my love, to gaze upon you is a sin,
> It's you who makes me break my fast.
> Oh lover, to gaze upon you is a sin,
> It's you who makes me "eat" during Ramadan.[8]
> (Virolle-Souibès 1988a:208)

Another of Rimitti's songs went: "When he embraces me, he pricks me like a snake," and "People adore God, I adore beer" (Virolle-Souibès 1988a:211, 214).

After Algeria won national independence in 1962, a state-sponsored Islamic reformist chill descended over all manifestations of popular culture until the late 1970s. In the wake of official puritanism, drastic restrictions were imposed on public performances by women singers (Virolle-Souibès 1989:54). But the genre flourished on the fringes, at sex-segregated events like wedding parties and in the demimonde. Meanwhile, adolescent boys with high-pitched voices replaced female *rai* vocalists in the public arena. At the same time, musicians were supplementing and sometimes replacing the *gasba* (reed flute), the *rbaba* (single-stringed instrument played with a bow), the *gellal* and *derbouka* (Maghrebi drums)—the instruments that had typified the genre for decades—with the more "modern"-sounding *'ud* (Oriental lute), violin, and accordion.

In 1979, *rai* reemerged from the shadows, following President Chadhli Benjedid's loosening of social and economic restraints. By now, *rai* artists had incorporated additional musical influences—including the pop musics of Egypt, India, the Americas, Europe, and sub-Saharan Africa—and were performing and recording with trumpets and electric guitars, synthesizers and drum machines. A new sound known as "pop *rai*" was inaugurated, its stars a generation of young singers known as *chebs* (young men) and *chaba*s (young women). In its "pop" incarnation, *rai* shed its regional status, and massive cassette sales quickly made it the national music for Algerian youth. Its popularity derived from its lively, contemporary sound and its raciness. Pop *rai* lyrics, just like "traditional" *rai,* dealt frankly and openly with subjects like sex and alcohol while at the same time challenging both official puritanism and patriarchal authority within the family. The "modernity" of its musical texture and the insubordinate spirit of its messages earned pop *rai* a substantial audience among a generation of disaffected and frequently unemployed youth, chafing at traditional social constraints and the lack of economic opportunities.

As cassette sales soared, producers tried to boost profits by insisting on more risqué lyrics (Virolle-Souibès 1989:59). The pop *rai* star Chaba Zahouania, whose ruggedly sensual voice earned her the sobriquet "the Billie Holiday of Oran" (Virolle-Souibès 1988b:197), sang: "I'm going with him, Mamma, I'm climbing in next to him," and "Call Malik so he'll bring the beer" (Virolle-Souibès 1988a:211, 213). Chaba Fadela, another major pop *rai* star, similarly spiced up her lyrics: "I want to sleep with him, I want him to open up his shirts" (Virolle-Souibès 1988a:210).

These racy lyrics not only spurred sales; they incurred government wrath in the early 1980s. The association of *rai* with dancing, particularly in mixed-gender company, also provoked the hostility of state officials who adhered to orthodox Islamic views that dancing is obscene (Benkheira 1986:174–76). But more important, the government felt compelled to suppress an increasingly influential cultural practice that seemed to articulate the sentiments of insubordinate youth claiming new sexual and cultural freedoms—the "*rai* generation." Police rounded up single women patronizing nightclubs featuring *rai,* while the government denounced *rai* as "illiterate" and lacking in "artistic merit," banned it from the state-run airwaves, and prohibited the import of blank cassettes in an attempt to halt distribution (McMurray and Swedenburg 1991; Bizot 1988:89).

But in mid-1985 the government abruptly reversed its position. One reason for the volte-face was the lobbying of a former liberation army officer-turned-pop music impresario, Colonel Snoussi, who hoped to profit if *rai* could be mainstreamed. Another factor in officialdom's shift was the music's growing popularity in France, where the diasporic Maghrebi community provided an expanding market for the music, as well as facilities for production and a distribution network (via the massive to-and-fro movement of immigrants who smuggled cassettes). Pressure was also brought to bear by French Minister of Culture Jack Lang, who urged Algerian officials to grant exit visas to *rai* stars wishing to perform in France. Some sectors of the Algerian *nomenklatura,* moreover, argued that *rai* should be promoted as a counterweight to the growing militant Islamist trend among youth (Benkheira 1986:177).

So the government relaxed its opposition, *rai* festivals were duly organized in Oran and Algiers, and the music began to receive radio and television exposure. But at the same time that officialdom brought *rai* in from the periphery and claimed it as part of the national patrimony, it attempted to tame, contain, and mainstream the music. A line originally sung by several *chebs* as "we made love in a broken-down shack" was broadcast on Algerian radio as "we did our military service in a broken-down shack" (Bizot and Dimerdji 1988:133). The police tried to prevent audience members from dancing at the first Oran festival in 1985 (Benkheira 1986:176). Such pressures prompted the music industry to practice self-censorship. The same producers who had so recently promoted bawdiness started vigorously cleaning up *rai* lyrics in order to get their product played on radio and television and to make it palatable to a wider audience. Rachid Baba, the producer of *Rai Rebels*[9] and other acclaimed *rai* releases for the U.S. market, explained without a hint of irony: "In the beginning, I let a *cheb* sing the words as he wanted. Now I pay attention. When he sings a vulgarity, I say 'Stop.' If he doesn't obey, I cut it during the mixing" (quoted by Virolle-Souibès 1989:60). The mainstreaming did succeed in increasing *rai*'s audience, for many who were previously put off by *rai*'s "dirty" reputation now found it pleasantly acceptable.

RAI AND THE DISCOURSE OF WORLD MUSIC

U.S. World Music publicity—the CD or cassette jackets, the record reviews, and the critical articles—never tells such stories about *rai*'s self-censorship or its complex relation to the state. Instead, World Beat discourse on *rai* since its U.S. arrival in 1988 has generally promoted it as a vehicle of resistance and compared its role within Algerian society to that of U.S. or British rock music at oppositional moments—Elvis in the mid-1950s, the Beatles and Stones of the late 1960s, the Sex Pistols of the late 1970s. It is advertised as "the music of . . . Algerian rebel youth,"[10] and commentators claim that Cheb Khaled "is to *rai* what Elvis was to rock" (Bizot and Dimerdji 1988:93) and that *rai* is a kind of "North African punk" (Eyre 1992:19). Although there is some truth to such claims, they are essentially based on a projection of a white, Eurocentric model of the culture wars onto Algeria. Such a move allows us—World Music fans—to identify with the Algerian *rai* audience by assimilating their struggles to our models. We can thus sympathize with *rai* audiences who seem to be fighting battles we have already fought—as teenagers demanding more sexual freedom—or are still fighting—as rock fans opposed to religious fundamentalism or official puritanism.

This is not to deride some positive effects of *rai*'s late-1980s arrival on the U.S. World Music scene, which until then had largely ignored or excluded Arabo-Islamic musics. The reputation that Arab musicians like Palestinian American *'ud* and violin virtuoso Simon Shaheen, Sudanese singer Abdel Aziz El Mubarak, and Moroccan *gnawa* artist Hassan Hakmoun have since gained in the West was greatly enabled by *rai*'s breakthrough. But that opening depended in part on a crucial discursive absence. World Music publicity has treated *rai* as a strictly Algerian phenomenon, as a musical genre that has merely absorbed Western influences. A more subversive reading would see *rai* as part of the wider endeavor to bring about "the gradual dissolution of 'white' culture by all the peoples who, having been forcibly subjected to it, have assimilated the tricks, the techniques necessary to contaminate it" (Goytisolo 1987b:38). It is symptomatic, therefore, that World Music publicity ignores the role of *rai* in France, where it has served as a central mode of cultural expression in minority struggles. Perhaps this silence can be attributed to the fact that it is much easier for benevolent white World Music fans to align with (imagined) young rockers or punks fighting the same battles as "us" than it is to express solidarity with racialized Others combating European racism.

THE VARIETIES OF FRANCO-MAGHREBI IDENTITY

> The diaspora experience is defined, not by essence or purity, but by the recognition of a necessary heterogeneity and diversity: by a conception of "identity" which lives with and through, not despite, difference; by *hybridity*. —Stuart Hall (1989:80)

As pop *rai* won over Algerian youth, it simultaneously gained adherents among Maghrebi immigrants in France and their offspring—the *Beurs,* as the second generation had come to be known. *Rai* emerged as a crucial cultural vehicle for a minority striving to carve out a space for itself in an inhospitable, racist environment. It became a veritable token of Maghrebi ethnic identity, and presence, in France.

In the summer of 1981, a series of dramatic events involving young Franco-Maghrebis was rapidly transformed by the media into staged spectacles that variously stunned, scared, and titillated an uncomprehending French public. Known as *rodeos,* they took place in the impoverished *banlieues* (suburbs) that encircle French cities and are where the bulk of the Franco-Maghrebi population is concentrated. Young *banlieusards* stole big-engined cars and proceeded to race and perform stunts at dusk for enthusiastic spectators. Before the police could catch them, they would stop, douse the vehicles with gasoline, and torch them. During July and August some 250 vehicles were immolated in these dramatic moments of defiance that were aimed at the hated police and that represented an angry affirmation of the minority's ghettoized existence (Jazouli 1992:17–22).

This startling display of the drastic problems and incendiary mood of young *banlieue* Franco-Maghrebis was followed by a flurry of organizing and networking by Arab militants. Grassroots groups proliferated as the massive demonstrations organized in 1983 and 1984 thrust the socioeconomic problems and the racist treatment of *franco-maghrébins* upon the national stage. The French public could no longer pretend that the Arabs living in its midst were simply immigrant workers whose presence would be temporary. Here was a militant, visible generation of Maghrebis who spoke French fluently, who were permanent residents, not "visitors," and who were laying claim to full citizenship rights and equal participation in French cultural life.

But who, precisely, are these Franco-Maghrebis, whom French racist discourse usually lumps together into catchall categories like immigrants, Muslims, Maghrebis, Arabs, or foreigners? In fact they are a very heterogeneous group that encompasses Algerians, Moroccans, and Tunisians; Arabs and Berbers; citizens, "legal" noncitizen residents, and "illegals"; immigrants born in the Maghreb and their offspring born in France; *harkis* who fought for France during the Algerian War and their descendants, and Algerians who backed the FLN. An estimated 1.5 million North African "foreigners" (noncitizens) live in France, and tens of thousands more (no one is sure of the total) reside there without legal permission.[11] About one million French citizens are of Maghrebi origin, including from 400,000 to 600,000 *harkis* and their offspring (Lanier 1991:16–17; Etienne 1989:107). If we include Jews of North African ancestry, many of whom still identify with the Maghreb, this adds another 300,000 persons (Morin 1991:535). We are speaking, then, of between 2.5 and 3.5 million persons, out of a total population of 60 million.

Economic Conditions

The bulk of the Franco-Maghrebi population, both immigrant and citizen, is concentrated in the multiethnic *banlieues*. These isolated modernist architectural nightmares—bleak zones of high-rises, minimal public facilities, substandard schooling, and exceptional rates of unemployment (70 percent of the children of immigrants in Lyons aged sixteen to twenty-five have no jobs [Begag 1990:6])—are the true loci of the "immigrant" problem.

Conditions in the *banlieues* are closely tied to the recent restructuring and "rationalization" of the French economy. The economy is moving in a "post-Fordist" direction: gradual state disengagement from economic affairs and the privatization of former state enterprises; decline of trade-union influence as well as of local administrative effectiveness; swelling of the service sector; diminution or flight of large-scale industries employing unskilled labor; the rise of industries using little unskilled labor.[12] The impact of these changes on the immigrant workforce is revealing: between 1973 and 1985 the proportion of working "immigrants" employed in industry fell from 45 percent to 36 percent, and in construction from 35 percent to 26 percent, while "immigrant" participation in the lower-paying service sector rose from 20 percent to 37.5 percent (Lanier 1991:20).

The spatial marginalization of the Maghrebi population in France also reflects a socioeconomic shift toward the "ethnicization" of the labor force and an increased dependence on undocumented and "reserve" labor in the new era of "flexible specialization" (Naïr 1992:39–46).[13] One facet of this shift is that the total number of working North African males has decreased by about 5 percent since 1975, whereas the number of Maghrebi women workers has shot up dramatically (by over 150 percent) during the same period. The fall in male employment and the coincident rise in the female workforce is integral to the process of economic restructuring, in which employers tap a "reserve army" of women and youth to maintain profits and ensure flexibility of labor allocation. This transformation in the makeup of the labor force is due in part to the government's halting of immigration in 1974 (until then predominantly a Maghrebi male activity) and its shift to a policy of family reunification (mainly involving Maghrebi women and youth). So sharp was the demographic turnabout that by 1982 more than 44 percent of the Maghrebi population in France was under seventeen years of age, compared with 22 percent for the population as a whole (Talha 1991:497–99).

Authenticity and Hybridity

We employ the term Franco-Maghrebi here as a convenient descriptive device. Although one occasionally encounters the designation *franco-maghrébin,* ethnic groups in France typically do not define themselves in terms of hyphenated identities. Whether one's background is Italian, Spanish, Jewish, or Polish, one is expected to be assimilated, to be simply "French." This requirement has proved difficult for residents and citizens of Third World origins to live up to. It is particularly problematic for North Africans, because memories of recent colonial violence in Algeria remain so vivid and because so many French people believe that the Maghrebis' Islamic heritage makes them unassimilable. Citizens or not, French Arabs tend to be regarded as foreigners.

Many first-generation immigrants would agree, at least in part, with this designation. They have never felt "at home" in France, and dream of returning to their villages of birth as they slowly lay aside savings to build homes there for comfortable retirement. Such *immigrés* often retain an image of an Algeria or a Morocco that continues to uphold the revered traditions and Islamic values. Then there are those Franco-Maghrebis, both immigrants and citizens, who have reacted to French exclusivism by practicing their own form of isolationism. These are the ethnonationalists, most prominent among them the militant Islamists.

But advocates of a separatist "authenticity" are probably a small minority. Most Franco-Maghrebis, particularly the younger generation and especially those with citizenship, dream neither of returning to the motherland nor of establishing an isolated Maghrebi or Islamic enclave in France. Although all have felt the sting of racism, few have contemplated departing France for a "home" in an unfamiliar North Africa. Instead, their project is to create livable zones for themselves within French society. Most therefore favor some form of integration that does not entail total assimilation and the abandonment of their "Arabness." They seek to negotiate integration on their own terms, maintaining their right to be different.

In the wake of the upsurge of Arab militancy in the early 1980s, Franco-Maghrebis born in France began to be known as *Beurs,* a *verlan*[14] term made by reversing the sounds of *arabe.* Today many educated French Arabs consider this tag pejorative and lacking in geographic specificity. They prefer the rather cumbersome appellation "youths originating from North African immigration" (*jeunes issues de l'immigration maghrébine*).[15] Others simply refer to themselves as Algerians or as French. But none of these terms seem to capture the complex positionality of those who feel located somewhere "in-between." As one educated young Franco-Maghrebi told us:

> We don't consider ourselves completely Algerian or completely French. Our parents are Arabs. We were born in France (and visited Algeria only a few times). So what are we? French? Arab? In the eyes of the French we are Arabs. But when we visit Algeria, some people call us emigrants and say we've rejected our culture. We've even had stones thrown at us [in Algeria].

Such ambiguity is demonstrated in the various avenues of integration Franco-Maghrebis have chosen to travel, all of which could be considered, in their different ways, paths of hybridity.[16]

At one end of the hybridity spectrum are the quasi-assimilationists, who tend to see France as the height of civilization, who frequently change their names from Karima to Karine or Boubker to Bob, and who practice a kind of hyperconformism to French societal norms. Members of this group tend to be successful, upwardly mobile, and well educated, and frequently are of *harki* or *kabyle* (Algerian Berber) background. They also have organized politically, most notably within the framework of France-Plus, an electoral pressure group that pushes for Franco-Maghrebi electoral representation on all party tickets except those of Le Pen's National Front and the Communists. Even Franco-Maghrebis who disapprove of France-Plus's middle-of-the-road orientation admit it has markedly increased Arab visibility and influence in the political arena. France-Plus managed to get 390 *Beurs* elected, about equally divided between parties of the Right and the Left, in the municipal elections of 1989, a major gain over 1983, when only 12 *Beurs* were voted in (Begag 1990:9). Two "*Beurettes,*" Nora Zaïdi of the Socialist Party and Djida Tazdaït of the Greens, were elected to the European Parliament in 1989. France-Plus, however, lacks a social base in the *banlieues,* and is viewed as representing the interests of the "*beurgeoisie*" (Aïchoune 1992:15).

SOS-Racisme, France-Plus's chief competitor in the political sphere, occupies an intermediate position. Founded in 1985 by activists with close ties to the ruling Socialist Party, SOS-Racisme built on the wave of *Beur* militancy of the early 1980s, at the same time channeling and neutralizing its energies. The emergence of this multiethnic organization, according to many militants, represented a blunting of the Maghrebi-Arab specificity and orientation of earlier anti-racist struggles (Jazouli 1992; Aïchoune 1991). SOS-Racisme managed to deploy its connections with officialdom, superior organizing skills, media savvy, and ability to attract the financial support of government agencies, so as to position itself as *the* hegemonic group within the anti-racist movement. It gradually shifted the concerns of the anti-racist movement away from a platform stressing immigrants' rights to one that emphasizes individual ethics and diffuse "multiculturalism" (Jazouli 1992). SOS-Racisme evolved into the mediagenic organization of the anti-racist "establishment," the favorite of the ruling (until March 1993) Socialist Party. Although a vocal critic of racism, SOS-Racisme has often argued for quasi-assimilationist positions. Like France-Plus, it enjoys little grassroots support in the *banlieues.*

Arabs who have felt defeated or overwhelmed by an impossible social and economic environment have followed yet another route. These are the "delinquents," chiefly from the impoverished *banlieues,* whose response to the lack of decent educational or employment opportunities has been a resort to petty criminality, random acts of violence, rage, and drug use. Many of these Franco-Maghrebis regard the battle to establish a meaningful identity and comfortable space of existence as utterly hopeless. Yet the position of this group is unstable and contradictory, its members capable of actions, like the *rodeos,* at once nihilist and oppositional.

The opposite end of the spectrum from the *beurgeoisie* is populated by a diffuse array of community-based political and cultural groups that operate fairly autonomously, outside the framework of any overarching umbrella organization. It is these groups that carry on much of the organized activity with a specifically Franco-Maghrebi character. Franco-Maghrebis who hold this perspective aggressively assert their right to a place in France, regard racism as French society's problem, and reject out of hand the notion that they, the Arabs, are the "problem," as racist discourse would have it (see Gilroy 1987:11). They consider themselves French citizens, just like anyone else, and they lay claim to the French heritage of democracy and freedom of speech. Their attitude might be summed up by the slogan "We're here, we're Beur, get used to it!"[17] They advocate a kind of affirmative identity politics that, at the same time, promotes syncretizing rather than essentializing practices.

HYBRIDITY IN PRACTICE: RAMADAN NIGHTS IN THE DIASPORA

Rai played a significant part in the story of Franco-Arab mobilization and identity formation. It was aired widely on the local radio stations, such as the celebrated Radio Beur in Paris, that sprang up to serve and instill pride into French North African communities. The music gained greater public visibility as a consequence of the upsurge of Franco-Arab anti-racist struggles of the 1980s, particularly when SOS-Racisme sponsored multicultural concerts featuring *rai.* Prominent Algerian *rai* performers started touring France, and young Franco-Maghrebis began forming their own *rai* bands.

Salah Eddine Bariki's study of Franco-Maghrebi radio stations, carried out in Marseilles—the site of France's largest concentration of Arabs—in 1984, highlights *rai*'s role in the complicated, syncretic processes of Franco-Maghrebi identity formation (Bariki 1986). The most popular radio programming, he discovered, was during Ramadan Nights, the evenings of feasting and celebration following daytime fasting during the holy month, when listeners stayed up late and called radio stations to request songs, tell jokes, engage in political or religious debates, or discuss the meaning of Ramadan for North Africans in France. Almost all callers to Arab stations spoke in "Musulman," as they termed the Arabic spoken in France (meaning they were probably immigrants rather than French-born). Bariki's survey of the everyday practices and beliefs of Marseilles's Arab radio audience showed that most drank alcohol, few condemned mixed marriages (with non-Muslims), about a third had eaten pork, and less than half fasted during Ramadan. But most of them still observed Ramadan, if rather idiosyncratically by orthodox standards. Many made special efforts to buy meat that was *halâl* (slaughtered according to strict Islamic precepts) during the holidays, and a large number claimed they did not drink alcohol for forty days prior to the holy month. Both practices were immigrant innovations.

Participants in the survey described Ramadan Nights radio programming as a nostalgia-laden return to an ambience resembling what they remembered or had heard about Ramadan celebrations in the home country—a time of plentiful food and pleasant relations between parents and children. The evenings of North African entertainment reduced the "burden of exile" by establishing a mood of community closeness. Many radio listeners reaffirmed their ethnic presence by phoning the station to dedicate a song to a relative or friend. Bariki's study shows that the near unanimous favorite of Ramadan radio audiences was Algeria's "King of Rai," Cheb Khaled.

That Arabs of Marseilles selected Cheb Khaled as their favorite vocalist during Ramadan merely underscores the complicated and contradictory nature of North African identity construction in France. For ever since launching his career at the age of fourteen in the mid-1970s, Cheb Khaled has cultivated the image of a swaggering, dissolute, worldly cabaret singer. "When I sing *rai,*" Khaled proclaims, "I talk about things directly; I drink alcohol; I love a woman; I am suffering. I speak to the point . . . I like Julio Iglesias. But he just sings about women, whereas [I sing] about alcohol, bad luck and women" (Eyre 1991:44; Bizot 1988:88).

Although not sentiments one normally associates with Ramadan observance in the Arab-Islamic countries, they are consistent with *rai*'s demimonde, anti-puritanical heritage in Algeria. (Recall Cheikha Rimitti's song about "eating" during Ramadan.) According to Hocine Benkheira, during the mid-1980s Cheb Khaled typically opened his concerts in Algeria with a number about Muhammad, then followed it with songs about drink, women, and so on. Whether Khaled's subject was whiskey or the Prophet, the audience danced—and no one present considered this blasphemous (Benkheira 1986:176). Such attitudes corresponded with cultural life in a tolerant country where, despite official puritanism and a growing Islamist movement, mosque attendance remained comparatively low and alcohol was consumed in open view of the street at the numerous taverns in central Algiers and Oran (Kapil 1990:36).

In the spring of 1992, we made friends with twenty-three-year old Sonia, "modern" in outlook, a student of English at the University of Avignon, and recently married to Jeannot, the son of a *harki*. Her father left Algeria at age fourteen to work in France. Sonia is in charge of the family grocery store, and supplements her income by flipping Big Macs at Avignon's Golden Arches. She sells liquor in her shop—located in a rundown Maghrebi district where the usual clientele includes addicts and prostitutes—reasoning that although the Qur'an forbids handling alcohol, it is permissible to dispense wine sealed in glass or plastic bottles. But she does not peddle pork, which she would have to touch, an act that would be *harâm* (morally prohibited). Sonia fasts during Ramadan, but finds Islam's five daily prayers too cumbersome to integrate into everyday activities. "You've got to adapt to the society where you live," Sonia asserts, "but if I didn't observe Muslim holidays, there would be nothing to set me apart from any other French person."

Another young Franco-Maghrebi woman we met, *rai* singer Chaba Aïcha, feels strongly about being a Muslim although she does not cover her hair or pray five times daily. She fasts at Ramadan and observes dietary laws for forty days before Ramadan. In her opinion, Islam forbids alcohol not because of its substance but because of its effects. Therefore, she reasons, if one can maintain proper behavior, it is permissible to imbibe.

Such syncretizing attitudes and practices reflect a general secularizing trend within Franco-Maghrebi communities, in the course of which Islam—like Arab cuisine, language, and music—has become for many more a question of ethnic identification than of belief (Jazouli 1992:133–34). Despite unceasing alarms raised by the mainstream press, the extent of militant Islamist mobilization in France is quite limited, and by some estimates, only 5 percent of the "potential" Islamic population are actually practicing, orthodox Muslims (Singer 1988:861; Etienne 1989:259–60).[18] Islamic observances like Ramadan, however, are widely commemorated—but in novel "ethnicized" forms (Safran 1986:104). The focus of Ramadan has shifted away from daily fasting and praying to the celebratory nighttime meal. In this regard, the Franco-Maghrebi community resembles French society at large, which observes all former religious holidays chiefly as secular feasts. The head of the Paris mosque, for instance, has suggested that on 'Id al-Kabir (the commemoration of Abraham's sacrifice of a ram instead of his son), Muslim families slaughter chickens in the privacy of their homes rather than violate health laws and offend popular prejudice by slaughtering rams according to orthodox precepts (Brisebarre 1989). Lacoste-Dujardin (1992) reports that it is increasingly common for Franco-Maghrebis to imbibe champagne on festive occasions, including religious feasts like 'Id al-Kabir.

The secular, modern, and socially progressive lyrics and ambiance associated with *rai* therefore appeal to young Franco-Arabs like Sonia, who desire to belong to a collectivity within France that endorses a tolerant sense of Arabo-Islamic identity. The sentiments of singers like Cheb Khaled resonate with the younger generation's dislike of the strictures imposed by their elders and Islamist orthodoxy:

> I am against Islamic fundamentalists. Young people want to progress. Even now, I can't smoke in front of my father, not even a cigarette. Young people who want to speak with a girl or live with her can't talk about it with their parents. In rai music, people can express themselves. We break taboos. That's why fundamentalists don't like what we're doing. (quoted in Eyre 1991:45)

But Khaled is not anti-Islam per se. "I'm a muslim man, I love God, but I don't practice and I don't pray," he explains (Goldman 1993). Meanwhile, other *rai* artists incorporate religious themes into their songs. Cheb Anouar's "Bi'r Zem Zem" (from the video *La ballade d'Anouar*), for instance, refers to the famous well in Mecca that figures prominently in the hajj ritual. Anouar sings to his mother about leading the proper life and one day making the hajj. Vendors of *rai* cassettes and videos at Avignon's weekly Arab *sûq* (open-air market) claimed that "Bi'r Zem Zem" was merely Anouar's attempt to cash in on the heretofore ignored "Islamic" market niche. Many stalls in Avignon's *sûq* carry Islamist cassettes featuring Qur'anic recitations, sermons, and how-to guides for proper Islamic conduct, hard by *rai* recordings of Cheb Mami or Chaba Fadela that extol the virtues of libertine lifestyles.

HYBRIDITY IN PRACTICE: WOMEN AND RAI

The analysis of *rai*'s uses within the North African diaspora reveals a great deal, not only about the changing valence of religion and tradition in Franco-Maghrebi identity construction, but also about gender relations, as the following examples illustrate.

Most of the women were sitting on low cushions along the wall at one end of the rented room in the Avignon *banlieue*. Those who felt uncomfortable squatting close to the floor were supported by chairs on the other side of the room. Older women were decked out in long, empire-waisted, shiny polyester Algerian dresses and gold marriage belts. Some younger ones were similarly clad in "traditional" outfits, while others sported slacks or miniskirts plus accessories like geometric earrings or necklaces hung with miniature pastel-colored pacifiers (a 1992 teenage fashion craze throughout Europe). Some women had flown in from Algeria specially for the wedding, while others had traveled north from Marseilles or south from St. Etienne. Only five of the sixty women present were not of North African origin.

Rai provided the sound track for the wedding festivities, but no one was paying much attention to the singers or the lyrics. "If you want to know the name of the singer or the song," they said, "go look at the cassettes." I picked up a bag full of home-dubbed tapes.[19] Most contained minimal or no information, but several Cheb Khaled tapes were clearly marked. When Khaled's 1992 hit "Didi" came on, many younger women jumped up to dance. The room was hopping when a power outage stopped us short.

Someone threw open the windows looking onto the courtyard where the men were gathered. A *rai* singer named Cheb Kader[20] started his set, accompanied by a single instrumentalist on a keyboard synthesizer equipped with drum machine. The dancing inside took up in earnest: a throng of shimmering sequins and beads, provençal skirts, satin and linen, bare shoulders and legs. Dance styles resembled what I had seen in northeastern Morocco in 1986, but occasionally younger women broke into disco steps and some girls seemed to be imitating cabaret belly dancers.

After midnight, over bowls of *chorba* and *tajine,* I asked some chicly accoutered lycée girls whether they liked the music. Not very much. What did they listen to? Funk—African American. But they supposed that when their turns came, their weddings would be like this one. I tried to imagine James Brown's "Funky Drummer" blaring out amid the crowd of matrons who had flown in from Algeria for this gender-segregated event.

Rai was passé for, but tolerated by, the under-twenty set. But to the twenty-three-year-old bride and her generation, it signified a strong attachment to Algerian roots. The older women regarded *rai* as merely familiar Arabic music—perhaps not their first choice, but good for dancing. *Rai* was the musical form of expression uniting the generations in this community celebration.

Weddings like this remain major sites for *rai* performance and consumption. *Beur* radio stations in the major cities also serve up *rai* on a regular basis, often as part of astonishing sets that also feature African American funk, tunes from Berber Kabylia, Caribbean reggae, rap, and Zairean *soukous*. *Rai* is also disseminated via video technologies. Several videotapes sold in Arab stores and market stands feature live concert footage of *chebs* (male *rai* singers) at festivals in Oran or on European tour. Others show *chaba*s or older *cheikha*s in staged settings, like Cheikha Rimitti's television-studio "wedding" performance.

Another video genre that focuses on gender relations is the narrative music video dealing with romantic love. Cheb Anouar's above-mentioned video, *La ballade d'Anouar*, not only pays homage to Mecca but also features numbers depicting teenage dating and the pain of separation from one's lover. Videos from the famous married couple of *rai*, Chaba Fadela and Cheb Sahraoui, often narrativize romantic relationships between boyfriend and girlfriend, in stereotypically Western settings.

Such videos advocate a rejection of the "traditional" and patriarchal family power relations that continue to define the lives of so many young Franco-Maghrebi women. In fact, differences of opinion on how to integrate into French culture often focus on gender issues. The controversy about the appropriate behavior for women seems exacerbated both by the preference of French employers for female, as opposed to male, Franco-Maghrebi labor and the tendency of French society and media to treat young Franco-Maghrebi women as "model" citizens while subjecting Arab men to overt discrimination and denigration (Jazouli 1992:179). Many ostensibly "integrated" Franco-Maghrebi males, who haunt the nightclubs and have white girlfriends, invoke traditional values when dealing with their own sisters and zealously police their movements in and outside the home. Parents, too, often attempt to uphold ethnic identity, at least within the domestic sphere, by insisting on controlling their daughters' extradomestic activities, by trying to choose their marriage partners, and by requiring that they wait on their brothers and fathers hand and foot when at home.

Even young, unmarried Franco-Maghrebi women who appear completely at ease in French society assert that they would face tremendous problems if their families found out that they had been sitting with a man at a café. And for such young women, marriage to a non-Muslim would automatically cause a radical break with their families.[21]

Hence romantic love, involving dating before marriage and the option of choosing one's marriage partner without the interference of kin, is regarded as liberatory by many Franco-Maghrebi youth (as well as young people in North Africa).[22] But paradoxically, whereas many *rai* songs and videos promote romance as well as more freedom for women, the jackets of *rai* cassettes seem governed by normative codes that confine Maghrebi women to the private realm. The *cheb*'s photograph almost invariably adorns his cassette, but tapes by *chaba*s typically feature picturesque Algerian countryside vistas or photographs of women—sometimes lissome surfer girls with lush blonde hair and deep tans—who are more "conventionally" beautiful—by Western standards—than the *chaba*s who sing the music contained within.

Before we traveled to France, we heard several explanations for this absence in the World Music publicity on *rai.* An Algerian student claimed that the celebrated Chaba Zahouania, with the distinctive, vigorously husky voice and ribald lyrics, was unmarried, and forbidden by her family in Algeria to perform in public or to be photographed for album jackets. What resemblance, we wondered, did Zahouania bear to the exquisitely beautiful and exotic chiffon-draped belly dancer on the cover of her suggestively titled U.S. release, *Nights Without Sleeping?*[23] We then came across another explanation: Zahouania did not sing in public because she was a divorcée with four children who did not want her ex-husband's family to be able to argue in court that she was an unfit mother and thereby win custody of the children (M. Rosen 1990:23).[24] Wandering Paris' Arab district of Goutte d'Or in the summer of 1992, we found dozens of Chaba Zahouania cassettes for sale, none with a photograph of the elusive singer. But we did discover a video featuring Chaba Zahouania performing live before a television studio set. Zahouania looked about forty and wore a modest, Western-style dress. Thick glasses magnified her conventional plainness. Later, acquaintances from the Netherlands told us that in an interview with a Dutch paper, Chaba Zahouania explained that her picture was not displayed on cassettes because she considered herself ugly! Perhaps *rai*'s advocacy of greater freedom for women is held back as much by the internalization of Western standards of beauty as by "patriarchal" constraints.

We met *rai* artist Chaba Aïcha after seeing her perform, complete with disco globe and fog machine, at a modest hall near Avignon in August 1992. She claimed that *rai* is the music of women who have a great deal of experience in life, and that mothers with no husbands have traditionally sung *rai* to support their children. Aïcha's repertoire includes tunes about problematic love affairs, unemployment, parental restrictions, and undocumented immigrants. Her close-cropped hairdo and butch outfits projected an image unlike that of any other *chaba* we have come across, and reminded us of k.d. lang. Even the androgynous, progressive Chaba Aïcha did not want her photo to appear on the cover of her first release—but the Marseilles-based recording company insisted.[25] The photos of another female of *rai,* the chubby—by Western standards—Chaba Fadela, also show up on cassettes. She usually wears unassuming dress (although sometimes a black leather jacket) and is always accompanied by her husband, *rai* singer Cheb Sahraoui.

In marked contrast to the *chabas*' public propriety, Franco-Maghrebi *rappeuse* Saliha strikes a pose that is at once defiant and seductive. On the cover of her 1991 recording, *Unique,* Saliha is fitted out in a sleek black mini, hands encased in black leather half-gloves. Romantic love as liberation does not feature prominently in the hip-hop emanating from the *banlieues,* nor does a wholesome image "sell" in the rap market. Yet French rappers appear unable to escape conventional expectations regarding female looks.

FROM RAI THING TO RAP THANG

By the mid-1980s, *rai* was breaking out of the strictly "ethnic" boundaries that characterized its uses in the Marseilles of Bariki's study. It gained greater public visibility during the upsurge of Franco-Arab struggles and through SOS-Racisme's concerts, which gained it an audience among antiracist whites. In the late 1980s and early 1990s, *rai*'s star rose in French World Music circuits and then, via Paris, it was propelled into the international World Beat market.[26] By 1990, when Islamist campaigns against *rai,* as well as the lure of higher earnings and global exposure, prompted several of its leading figures (Cheb Khaled, Cheb Mami, Chaba Fadela, and Cheb Sahraoui) to relocate from Algeria to France, Paris became a major *rai* center.

More recently, *rai*'s fortunes in France have varied according to the trends within the Franco-Maghrebi community. For their part, the "*beur-*

geoisie" and their benevolent white liberal and Socialist allies continue to sponsor concerts and festivals featuring Arab music, including *rai*. Such events, which celebrate the "authentic" culture or folklore of "the people," represent efforts to disguise the liberals' lack of a social base in the *banlieues*. State monies for such concerts were abundant under Socialist rule.

At the grassroots level, *rai*'s core audience has been somewhat diminished. It is now the music of choice principally for recent immigrants and "les jeunes issues de l'immigration maghrébine" over the age of twenty-five. *Rai* performers continue to tour the French-Arab communities, performing at modest local dance halls and at weddings. But none of the major figures—Cheb Mami, Cheb Kader, Chaba Fadela and Cheb Sahraoui, or Chaba Zahouania—managed to capitalize on their momentary successes on the World Music scene between 1988 and 1990, when a number of *rai* recordings were released on various U.S. or international labels. Crossover success remains limited.

The exception is Cheb Khaled, who after years of performing for adoring Franco-Maghrebi audiences has finally, and spectacularly, "crossed over" into the French and international pop scene. His 1992 LP release, *Khaled*,[27] is a remarkable recording that manages to incorporate an impressive mélange of styles—traditional "folk" and "pop" *rai*, funk and reggae, flamenco and cabaret. But it is the hit single "Didi" that propelled Khaled into the international pop arena. Opening to *derbouka* rhythms, "Didi" switches to a deep-bass hip-hop underpinning, and is constructed around an instantly recognizable instrumental hook and a hummable chorus. In the spring of 1992 it was a dance-hall favorite throughout France.[28] The "Didi" video, aired frequently on French television and a key ingredient in the song's success, is a rapid-fire, MTV-style, cut-and-mix of images of a Moorish *mashrabiya* (wooden latticework screen), evocations of a Sufi music circle, and hip-hop steps performed by a multiethnic team of miniskirted dancers.[29]

In July 1992, some Franco-Maghrebi women we met in Avignon told us that mainstream French nightclubs and discos had finally, in the past two or three months, begun playing Arab music—but only Khaled. The Franco-Maghrebi men sitting with us had to take their word for it, for Arab men are still regularly turned away at the doors of French clubs. The first Arab voice to penetrate French discos failed to open the gates either for his Arab brothers who wish to dance there or for the discs of other *chab*s and *chaba*s. It should be stressed that a key ingredient in the success of "Didi"—besides its intrinsic qualities—was Barclay's heavy promotion. A subsidiary of Virgin Records, Barclay is one of the big six recording companies (along with BMG, EMI, PolyGram, Sony, and Warner) that control 83 percent of the French market (Laing 1992:129). Without such backing, commercial triumph is likely to continue to elude other *rai* artists.

As Khaled (who has now dropped the title Cheb, with its *rai* associations) captivated non-Arab music fans in France and elsewhere in Europe, he was abandoned by some of his original devotees. Some asserted that this occurred after Khaled was interviewed on television, where he expressed the same views about wine and women that he voices in his songs. Although Franco-Maghrebi fans did not object to Khaled singing about such subjects, some were offended when he discussed them on the air. Others claim that Khaled demonstrated disrespect for community values when he canceled a number of concerts scheduled for Arab audiences due to drunkenness and when he released a music video featuring "scantily dressed" dancers. Still others said that Khaled had "sold out" to Western commercialism.

Although such complaints were voiced frequently in the summer of 1992, *Khaled* appeared to be selling briskly in the music stores we visited in Arab quarters in Paris and Marseilles. Meanwhile, "Didi" went high in the charts throughout Europe, sold well in the *sûqs* of northern Morocco, and ruled the airwaves in Israel, Jordan, and Lebanon. In October and November 1992, "Didi" occupied the number 1 spot on Egypt's official Top 40, and by May 1993, *Khaled* was said to have sold 2.5 million tapes there (de Neys 1993). By the spring of 1993, "Didi" was a certified global phenomenon (although one that seems to have bypassed the United States), and with the aid of video broadcasts on European and Asian MTV had sold 4.5 million copies (Dickey and de Koster 1993).

It is not yet clear what this unprecedented international popularity for a Franco-Maghrebi singer will ultimately mean. Will Khaled's move out of "ethnic" space contribute to a corrosion of dominant/white French culture, or will hegemonic Western forces deploy Khaled as a convenient spokesman against "backward" Algerian traditions and Islamic "fundamentalism"?

Ironically, even as Khaled's reputation soared, French Arab youth had already largely abandoned *rai* for rap. This conversation with a group of twenty-something Franco-Maghrebis in Avignon suggests some of the continuities and differences between Khaled's *rai* and the new *rap français:*

> *Mehmed:* Everyone listens to *rai.* It creates a festive atmosphere. Rap is for adolescents, fifteen to twenty years old, who have hard lives and

feel lost. Rap is for their generation. *Rai* only talks about love, but rap speaks about society and how to change it.
Malika: I object. Rappers talk about their society because they are not doing well. Rappers are guys who don't have work, who don't have much, and they project messages about changing society. But in certain songs of Cheb Khaled, when you see that he speaks of love, of alcohol, of everything that is taboo in our culture, well, it's clear that he also wants a change. They're not only love songs. If they were, why would some of them be banned in Algeria? Umm Kalthum sings love songs and they're not banned.[30] *Rai* songs evoke emancipated, libertine women. They, too, contain messages.
Salah: Rap tries to change daily life, but *rai* tries to change a culture. Both rap and *rai* reclaim something which has been kept from us.

In a number titled "Do the Raï Thing," Malek Sultan of the rap group I AM likewise equates the social significance of *rai* and rap when he dubs Cheb Khaled "le Public Enemy arabe."[31] But this resemblance was all but lost on the second- and third-generation Franco-Maghrebi boys, between six and ten, at a birthday party Joan Gross attended in an Avignon *banlieue.* "No Arab music!" the boys yelled, whenever their mothers put "Didi" on the tape recorder. The moms appeased them with hip-hop, but periodically snuck the funky "Didi" back on the player. Eventually the boys were break dancing to the arabesque grooves of "le Public Enemy arabe."

RAPATTITUDE

The late 1980s found the French media again training their lenses on the menacing youth of the *banlieues.* The focus of renewed concern was not *rodeo*s but the apparent danger of suburban ghettos going the way of South Central Los Angeles and the South Bronx. What had become visible to the media, particularly after a wave of riots in *banlieues chaudes* like Vaulx-en-Velin and Sartrouville during 1990 and 1991, and the *banlieusard*-organized lycée strikes, demonstrations, and attendant "anarchic" violence of the fall of 1990, were the gangs (*bandes*) and their associated practices: "tagging," drug use, petty crime, and rap music.[32] The right-wing press sounded the alert, luridly suggesting links between *banlieue* youth and crack, AIDS, gang warfare, and welfare scrounging, all of which, the press suggested, inhered in immigrant culture. There were even intimations in the extreme-Right *Minute-La France* that the big (immigrant) drug dealers of Marseilles were using profits from heroin sales to finance "certain Arab movements in France" (Folch 1992:19). In this latest version of the French nightmare, it was the illegible "tags" (*le graff*) of the *banlieue* posses that threatened to deface all the walls and monuments of *la civilisation française*.

For their part, most members of the French gangs or "posses," who give themselves names like Black Tiger Force or Black Dragons and turn out in continental hip-hop garb—Air Jordans, baseball caps, and baggy pants—regard themselves as part of an oppositional youth movement whose sonic expression is rap music. This new multiracial orientation reflects the ethnically diverse character of the predominantly "immigrant" *banlieues*. The *bandes,* whose argot is a distinctive blend of French *verlan* and U.S. hip-hop vernacular,[33] often include Arabs (*rebeus* or *beurs* in *verlan*), Jews (*feujs,* from *juifs*), Blacks (*renois,* from *noires*), Portuguese (*tos*), and white French. The posses are vigorously anti-racist, and many try to project a positive image that marks them off from the *caillera*s (from *racailles*), "riffraff," gangs involved in criminal activities like drug dealing and theft (Aïchoune 1991:79, 89). Franco-Maghrebis belonging to the *bandes* of the 1990s therefore appear markedly different from the "delinquent" Maghrebi youth of the early 1980s, whom Adil Jazouli (1982) described as being incapable of fashioning coherent identities, as trapped between two distinct cultural poles (French and Arab), neither of which could accommodate them.

French rappers achieved a remarkable proficiency (by U.S. standards) and media visibility by the early 1990s.[34] Coming from *banlieue* backgrounds, *rappeurs* and *rappeuses* attempt to express, as well as to shape and mobilize, the sentiments of ghetto youth.[35] Their most salient messages are anti-racist, including the assertion of the need for interracial solidarity, for the unity of "Black, Blanc, *Beur.*" French rap groups, like the *bandes* of the *banlieues* but unlike rap groups or youth gangs in the United States, tend to be multiracial; the Marseilles rap group I AM, for instance, includes whites, Blacks, and Arabs. Their messages and historical sensibilities, however, tend to be pro-Black African; the backing tracks, as in U.S. rap, are composed primarily of sampled African American riffs and beats. Yet while it articulates pro-Blackness, French rap is largely devoid of the Black nationalism so hegemonic within African American hip-hop. Saint Denis rappers Supreme NTM have even criticized Louis Farrakhan (head of the Nation of Islam, promoted by U.S. rappers Public Enemy and Ice Cube), asserting that he is an agent of hatred just like Le Pen ("Blanc et Noir"). Such a contentious claim would be virtually unthinkable in the U.S. hip-hop nation.[36]

But although they are anti-Le Pen, French rappers refuse to define themselves in terms of a hegemonic political discourse of Right, Center, or Left. They thereby manifest the disdain for traditional "politics" that is typical of the "new social movements" (Mercer 1990:44). Rappers propose multiracial alliance and anti-racism as the alternative to the "old" politics, and often present music and dancing as the chief means to achieve these utopian ideals. According to *Beurette* rapper Saliha, "Seul le beat aujourd'hui nous lie et nous unit" ("Today only the beat links and unites us").[37] Rappers express total disdain for the state—"ce putain d'état," as I AM dubs it[38]—and the police. They dream of more money being allocated to the *banlieues* and of a cutoff in funds to the army while advocating equal rights for immigrants.[39] French homeboys and homegirls refuse all media discourses that brand them as criminals and barbarians. They promote a renewed spirit of militancy, anger, and menace, and self-consciously distinguish themselves from the pacifistic and mediagenic image projected by the state-friendly anti-racists of SOS-Racisme.[40]

The largest single constituent of the multiethnic *banlieue* posses and rap audiences is probably Franco-Maghrebi youth. Arab rappers (like Saliha, Malek Sultan of I AM, members of MCM 90, and Prophètes de Vacarme) occupy a significant position in the movement, although Black rappers appear to be preeminent. Rap numbers, whether by Black, white, or Maghrebi artists, are typically peppered with samples from Arabic music, positive references to Palestine and Islam, and the occasional Arabic expression ("Allahu akbar," "Salaam"). The name of one of the foremost rap groups, Supreme NTM, is short for *Nique ta mère* (Fuck your mother). This designation is symptomatic of the degree to which street slang has adopted Arabic terms (*nique,* sometimes spelled *nik,* is Arabic for "fuck").

But despite Maghrebis' significant involvement in the French rap scene, rap lyrics make few references to the history of French colonialism in the Maghreb. Instead, like U.S. hip-hop, French rap expresses a hegemonic Afrocentric historical sensibility concerned mainly with sub-Saharan—not North or Arab—Africa. North Africa is mentioned only in the context of Afrocentric claims about the Black origins of civilization in ancient Egypt. (Most of I AM's members carry Pharaonic "tags": Kheops, Akhenaton, Imhotep, and Divin Kephren.) Rappers compose rhymes about the history of slavery, humanity's origins in Africa, Europe's destruction of African civilizations, and the struggle against apartheid—but almost none concerning Arabo-Islamic civilization,[41] colonial violence in North Africa, or the

FLN-led independence struggle in Algeria.[42] Perhaps this absence stems in part from rap's roots in a diasporic, Afrocentric form of cultural expression that does not usually deal with specifically "Arab" subjects.[43] This hesitancy of otherwise militant rappers seems to echo the incapacity of society at large to confront the bloody colonial history that still poisons race relations in the metropole. The fact that a significant portion of rap's audience is composed of descendants of *harkis* (who fought alongside the *colons* in the Algerian War) also doubtless contributes to *rappeurs*' reticence concerning colonialism in Algeria.

While the Right fulminated about crack, rap, and immigrant hordes, the Socialist establishment's tactic was to try to co-opt the youth subculture. "Le rap, le graff; I believe in this generation," intoned Jack Lang, hip-hop's loudest elite cheerleader, during his tenure as culture minister. Lang's attempts to appropriate rap included arranging museum space for graffiti artists, subsidizing tours by hard-core rappers NTM, and inviting rap artists to perform at a prime minister's garden party before nonplussed National Assembly members (Riding 1992; James 1991). His justification was typically elitist: "A man of the theater such as myself would tell you that rap bears a relationship to *la commedia dell'arte* as it was practiced in the sixteenth and seventeenth century" (Labi et al. 1990).[44] But if such sponsorship earned hip-hoppers greater publicity, there are few signs that *banlieusard* youth are about to be tamed. "What gratitude should I have for France," raps NTM's Joey Starr, "I, whom they consider a barbarian?"[45]

MOOR BETTER BLUES

Beyond the realms of *rai* and rap, Franco-Maghrebis have actively invaded, created, or influenced an impressive range of expressive forms, from the humble local supermarket—where canned couscous or tabbouleh may be purchased—to the pinnacle of high culture, the Paris Opera—where we find the star dancer Kader Bélarbi (Videau 1991:39). The fiction of Tahar Ben Jelloun (1987 winner of France's most prestigious literary award, the Prix Goncourt), Driss Chraïbi, and Abdelkebir Khatibi crowds the "Francophone" shelves in the bookstores (Hargreaves 1989). Arab comedians are making inroads as well. Tunisian-born Lilia is a prominent figure on the Paris stage, and the television and video sketches of the well-known comedy trio Les Inconnus frequently revolve around the misadventures of its *Beur* member.[46] The 1990–91 television season was enlivened by "La

Famille Ramdan," a Cosby-ish sitcom (the oldest son was a doctor) about a *Beur* family (Hargreaves 1991). The most successful French Arab comedian, Smaïn, is often described as the successor to the late, and now canonical, figure Coluche.[47]

But it is to popular music, and not just in genres like *rai* and rap, that the Franco-Maghrebi contribution has been especially rich, complex, and contradictory. Among the expressive cultural forms, popular music seems particularly amenable to syncretization and cross-fertilization, because it is relatively unconstrained by the generic rules that fetter traditional or elite genres (see Malkmus and Armes 1991:23; Barber 1987). Take the startlingly innovative heavy-metal band Dazibao, whose Moroccan-born vocalist, Jamil, sings screeching Arabic vocals that cascade over grunge-metal. Dazibao performed in June 1992 at a free outdoor music festival organized to keep Marseilles's heavily "Maghrebized" 13th and 14th arrondissements "cooled off."[48] Although the band inspired white head-bangers to thrash about wildly, they seem to have left inner-city North Africans unmoved, despite Jamil's between-song exhortations (in French) to be proud of one's Arabic heritage.

During the same month Radio Beur in Aix-en-Provence held a fundraiser on its first anniversary, attended by a casually attired but well-heeled, college-town Maghrebi crowd able to pay the 100 francs (approximately twenty dollars) admission. The show's emotional peak was Parisian-Algerian blues-jazz-funk crooner Jimmy Oihid's performance (in French) of "Ballade pour les enfants," his famous tribute to the Palestinians.[49] The spots dimmed as hundreds of Bic lighters flickered on. Many sang along with the chorus as the dance floor swayed solemnly to the lament's measured beat. Although hybridized Franco-Maghrebis may care little for Arab nationalism or Maghrebi "traditions," even the *beurgeoisie* identifies strongly with Palestinian militancy.

There are other styles and cultural tendencies as well. Sapho, a French New Wave jazz/rock singer raised in a Jewish household in Marrakesh, actively celebrates her "Oriental heritage" as the source of her musical inspiration and performs with North African string musicians and sub-Saharan percussionists (Billard 1987). Mano Negra, whose members are of Spanish, Corsican, and Moroccan backgrounds, belt out polyglot (Arabic, French, Spanish, and English) tunes to a frenetic bouillabaisse of punk, rockabilly, reggae, flamenco, and *rai* styles—something like The Clash gone pan-Mediterranean. Until recently the Franco-Maghrebi rock group Carte de

Séjour (meaning "residence card") vocalized in both French and Arabic, and churned out guitar riffs tinged with subtle arabesques; their former leader, Rachid Taha, continues to record in this vein as a solo artist. Finally, there is the Franco-Tunisian Amina, France's representative at the mainstream 1991 Eurovision contest, who sings cabaret ballads and disco-funk in French, Spanish, and Arabic, and is backed by a band composed of Euro-French, West African, and North African musicians.[50] Amina proclaims, "I will continue preaching for the mixture of cultures. . . . The more hybridization we have, the less we'll hear about claims to [a pure] culture" (Attaf 1991:52).

EL HARBA WAYN? (TO ESCAPE, BUT WHERE?)

Franco-Maghrebis deploy such syncretizing mechanisms to carve out a space for themselves where they can identify simultaneously with French and Arab cultures while rejecting French ethnocentrism and Algerian conservatism. Yet at times the pressures from both French racists and Algerian traditionalists seem overwhelming, and the Franco-Maghrebi border "zone" shrinks to a "line." Potent memories of racist brutality, colonial and postcolonial, are relived with each new threat and attack. Older Maghrebis still recall the horrific police massacre of three hundred to four hundred Algerian immigrants in Paris in October 1961, after a demonstration organized in favor of the FLN—probably this century's bloodiest racial atrocity against immigrants to occur in the West. The younger generation still remembers Habib Grimzi, an Algerian killed when French soldiers tossed him from a speeding train in November 1983, and carried his picture at the head of the 100,000-strong anti-racist march on Paris in December 1983. Similar incidents are a constant feature of Franco-Maghrebi existence, with over 250 Arabs killed in racist attacks since 1985 (Alcalay 1993:12).[51]

Franco-Maghrebis felt especially vulnerable and beleaguered during the 1991 Gulf War, when French newspaper headlines howled about "the Arab Threat in France" and "Arab Terrorism in France," and Michel Poniatowski, who was interior minister during Giscard d'Estaing's presidency, suggested the mass expulsion of immigrants (Attaf 1991:55). A poll in *Le Figaro,* taken during the war, showed that 70 percent of all French "Muslims" (i.e., Arabs)[52] feared they would become targets of terrorist attacks, and more than half felt that the war could lead France to deport Muslim immigrants (LaFranchi 1991; see also Ben Jelloun 1991). Rumors raged through southeastern France about Arab immigrants arming themselves and attacking whites, and caused a run on guns and ammunition by panicky French natives (Leblond 1991; Cambio 1991). During this period of heightened tensions, France-Plus urged Franco-Maghrebis to remain calm and not to organize demonstrations, and Arab stations like Radio-Gazelle in Marseilles and Radio-Soleil in Paris decided not to air recordings like "Vas-y Saddam!," the song by Algerian Mohammed Mazouni that was so wildly popular across the Mediterranean (Bernard 1991). To its credit, SOS-Racisme came out against the war, but it lost many liberal supporters as well as significant financial backing (Lhomea 1991).

Meanwhile, back in Algeria, hybrid cultural forms were also under assault from conservative forces who branded popular music—especially *rai*—not merely as "noise" but also as "illicit" and "immoral." *Rai* artists and consumers came under intense pressure in the wake of the sweeping municipal electoral victories of the Islamist party, Le Front Islamique du Salut (the Islamic Salvation Front, known as FIS), in 1990. The FIS-dominated city council of Oran canceled funding for the annual *rai* festival scheduled for August 1990, and its mayor banned a Cheb Mami concert on the grounds that his lyrics were offensive. Cheb Mami, Cheb Sahraoui, and other *rai* artists who returned from France to perform that summer were harassed and sometimes physically threatened by Islamists. As the Islamist movement emerged as a significant forum of expression for alienated Algerian youth in the late 1980s and early 1990s, it reportedly cut into *rai*'s audience, reducing it, according to some accounts, by over 50 percent.[53]

During Ramadan 1991 (which fell during March) FIS mounted a vigorous campaign against the public performance of music (*rai* and other genres). Fourteen persons were injured in Algiers on March 21 when young Islamists, attempting to torch a performance hall and halt a concert, clashed with police. On March 24, crowds led by FIS activists threw bottles and stones at another concert audience, injuring several fans.[54] An anti-*rai* plank was central to FIS's successful platform in the December 1991 elections (Ireland 1992). Franco-Maghrebi writer Mohamed Kacimi, attending a Friday prayer service in late 1990 at an Algiers mosque, reports hearing FIS second-in-command Ali Benhadj make the following remark: "As for the secularists, pseudo-democrats, atheists, feminists and francophones, and other evil-doers [*suppôts de Satan*], the day we gain power we'll put boats at their disposal which will take them to their motherland—France."[55] The crowd, according Kacimi, was entranced (Attaf 1991:55). Writing at the time of the Gulf War, Kacimi wondered where—given virulent French anti-Arab sentiment and the rise of religious-based intolerance in Algeria—*franco-maghrébins* should go.

Kacimi's question recalls Cheb Khaled's celebrated song of alienated fury, "El harba wayn?" (To escape, but where?), released when *rai* was at its peak of popularity in Algeria. It was reportedly taken up as an anthem by rioting Algerian youths during the violent October 1988 urban insurgencies that resulted in over five hundred civilian deaths (M. Rosen 1990:23). (Many rioters were since won over by FIS.) It goes:

> Where has youth gone?
> Where are the brave ones?
> The rich gorge themselves,
> The poor work themselves to death,
> The Islamic charlatans show their true face.
> So what's the solution? We'll check it out.
> You can always cry or complain
> Or escape. But where?[56]

Rai and rap are both possible "lines of flight" (Deleuze and Guattari 1983a) for Franco-Maghrebis, cultural borderzones of syncretism and creative interminglings of French and Arab. At once "ethnic" and French, they are fronts in the wider cultural-political struggle to recast French national identity and force a kind of genetic mutation in French culture. Both *rai* and rap are practices of "interculturation" (Mercer 1987) or "transculturation," which George Yúdice describes as "a dynamic whereby different cultural matrices impact reciprocally—though not from equal positions—on each other, not to produce a single syncretic culture but rather a heterogeneous ensemble" (1992:209).[57]

We should distinguish, within this heterogeneous ensemble, the relatively "defensive" and "ethnic" deployment of *rai* music by immigrants and twenty-plus Franco-Maghrebis, and the more assertive and multiethnic uses of rap by the younger generation of French Arabs. *Rai* represents a more cautious and separatist sensibility insofar as it reproduces cultural linkages with a remembered Algeria. With its cultural roots in Algeria, *rai* offers a kind of protective shield for immigrants who are experiencing the disruptions, dislocations, and insecurities of migration, who feel vulnerable to racist discrimination and economic marginality, and who wish to maintain an originary, imaginary communal identification. *Rai* is one tool that immigrants use in their attempts to "widen the margins," to expand their sphere of existence and identity beyond the claustrophobic confines imposed by the status of manual laborers (Balibar 1992). *Rai* performance and consumption re-create a relatively free and protected cultural zone, not unlike that of contemporary Oran or Algiers, in which Algerians in France can relax and feel "at home." *Rai* performances are also ritual occasions for the expression of pride and protest, where, as in music performances among African Americans and Black British, a "moral, even a political community" is defined (Gilroy 1990:275, 277).

It is *rai*'s association with a progressive vision of Algeria—the contemporary, relaxed, sophisticated, tolerant, and urban image of the homeland that *rai* audiences selectively privilege—that attracts over-twenty, non-immigrant, French-born Maghrebis. Equally important are *rai*'s modern, syncretic-pop sound and its danceability. The synthesizers, drum machines, and advanced production techniques combine to produce a musical texture that audiences regard as proof that Euro-Arab music is not quaintly "folkloric," but is as modern and advanced as any popular European music. As Khaled remarked about his "American sound" on the album *Khaled:*

> I said to myself, if rock musicians in Europe can take our instruments and rhythms for their music, then why can't I do the same? I wanted to show people in France, where there's a lot of racism—they don't like us there, and that's a fact—that we can do anything they can, and better. (Goldman 1993)[58]

On the other hand, because *rai* is (virtually) always sung in Arabic and every recording is recognizably "Arab" in instrumentation and melody, it always carries an unmistakable air of "otherness" to the Western ear. Today's *rai* is an expression of cosmopolitan "modernity" that self-consciously distances and distinguishes itself from Euro-pop (see Urla 1993). Franco-Maghrebis' attachments to *rai* also stem from its function as a marker of ethnic difference and its ability to evoke solidarity. *Rai* therefore manages to be at once "ethnic" and "intercultural."

Rap music, by contrast, is deployed in more volatile and intrusive ways, and expresses and mobilizes new forms of identity. It serves as the badge of a multiethnic minority youth subcultural movement that participates in the struggle against the new racism's attempts to impose rigid boundaries around French national culture. Rap is a key weapon in minority youths' attempts to invade from the margins and "dehomogenize" the French cultural core. (Khaled has invaded, too, but in a less threatening or incendiary manner.) Unlike the sometimes nostalgic and community-based appeal of *rai,* rap is aggressively deterritorializing and anti-nostalgic, even as it reterritorializes a multiethnic space. Rappers combine elements of the African-Caribbean musical diaspora with the specific concerns of the multiethnic French minorities, linking the diasporic Mediterranean to the diasporic Black Atlantic (see Gilroy 1992b, 1993). It remains to be seen, however, whether rap will fully open up to assertions of Maghrebi identity, or will remain an ensemble that is heavily weighted toward the diasporic African cultural matrix.

The cultural milieus associated with both rap and *rai* provide alternative heterogeneous discourses, clearing larger spaces in which formerly colonized subjects can live the multiplicity inherent in diasporic existences. In some of those intercultural zones, they contribute to the corrosion and mutation of dominant French identity. Maybe one day the "decent" people in France will listen avidly to the sounds of Chaba Zahouania or I AM, and consider the speeches of Le Pen and Chirac to be obnoxious "noise." Maybe one day French natives will decipher the graffiti, and learn that *l'humanité* and الإنسانيّة are synonyms, not mutually exclusive.

POSTSCRIPT

In January 1992, the Algerian regime canceled the second round of national elections after first-round results indicated that FIS would be the resounding winner. A military government with a civilian veneer was established, and quickly became embroiled in a "dirty war" against the Islamist militants.[59] Faced with daily attacks by Islamist guerrillas, who by the fall of 1992 were killing about one policeman per day,[60] the shaky regime attempted to enlist *rai* in an effort to win popular support. After disbanding FIS and dismissing Islamist mayors and city councils, the government permitted the annual *rai* festival to be held, once again, in Oran in the summer of 1992. On Thursday nights state-run television broadcast *rai* music videos on the program *Bled musique* (Country Music). Devout Muslims frequently called in to complain that the program promoted corrupt Western values and was not "educational." They were particularly scandalized by the seductive dancing and miniskirts of Khaled's "Didi" video.

In 1994, after three years of struggle and a death toll of between ten thousand and fifteen thousand (Reuters, November 1, 1994), militant Islamists declared a sentence of death for "vulgar" singers. In September, Berber singer Lounes Matoub was kidnapped (but eventually released unharmed), and the popular *rai* singer Cheb Hasni was assassinated in front of his home in Oran. Although the twenty-six-year-old artist had remained in Algeria, he was a favorite among Franco-Maghrebis and had toured France, Scandinavia, Canada, and the United States (*Sud Ouest* [*Gers*], September 30, 1994). Several thousand fans and musicians reportedly joined in Cheb Hasni's funeral procession, carrying his portrait and chanting "Algeria free and democratic"—a cry that indicted all factions in the dirty war.

Meanwhile Khaled, riding on the sensational success of "Didi," toured the Arab world in the spring of 1993. But he was still unwelcome in Algeria, where he reportedly remains wanted for avoiding military service. A *Newsweek* report on the tour, "Rai Rocks the Mosques: Arab Pop Music Has Fundamentalists All Shook Up," resembled World Music discourse for its focus on Islamist antipathy to Khaled and its avoidance of Khaled's base in the Arab community in France (Dickey and Koster 1993). The article suggests how the Western media may attempt to promote Khaled as a counterweight to Islamic "fundamentalism."

But we can be sure that the media will not boost Khaled as an opponent of French racism, recently invigorated by the Right's landslide electoral victory in March 1993. If Le Pen's popularity is on the wane, it is because the "respectable" Right has essentially embraced the National Front's program. The first few days of the Edouard Balladur premiership saw three young men killed by police in a space of four days (April 4–8), including a Maghrebi and a Zairean, and violent protest demonstrations. Since then, French police have been carrying out sweeps to round up undocumented immigrants and "delinquents." French Interior Minister Charles Pasqua introduced legislation to tighten immigration laws considerably, and his popularity rose accordingly, as many French citizens blamed rising crime rates and high unemployment (10.9 percent) on immigrants (read Arabs). Most recently, Jacques Chirac, the intrepid enemy of immigrant noise and smell, was elected French president.

NOTES

Thanks to Ruth Frankenberg, Smadar Lavie, Lata Mani, Fred Pfeil, and Miriam Rosen for their acute comments on various permutations of this piece. We are also grateful to Sonia Saouchi and her family, and to Aref al-Farra for loaning us a copy of the "Didi" video. Research for this article was funded in part by Oregon State University's College of Liberal Arts. The first version was presented in November 1991 at the American Anthropological Association meetings in Chicago and the Middle East Studies Association meetings in Washington, D.C.; shorter versions appeared in *Middle East Report* 22, no. 5 (1992) and in *Diaspora* 3, no. 1 (1994).

1 *Le Monde* (April 4, 1987), quoted in Stora 1992:217 (our translation).

2 The figure of one million Arabs killed is commonly cited; our figure for French casualties comes from Dupuy and Dupuy (1986).

3 Etienne Balibar contends that the two European ideological schemata of colonialism and anti-Semitism converge in the racism against minority populations of Arab-Islamic origin, "so that imagery of racial superiority and imagery of cultural and religious rivalry reinforce each other" (1991a:12).

4 Koulberg (1991:34) shows that, amid the media onslaught, it was ignored that 48 percent of French Muslims actually opposed wearing the *hijab.* A new furor over headscarves erupted in September–October 1994, after Education Minister François Bayrou issued a new ban on Islamic scarves and other "ostentatious religious symbols." In early October, Franco-Maghrebi students and their supporters clashed with teachers, parents, and police in Maintes-la-Jolie and in Lille (west and north of the capital). More than a dozen students were expelled for not complying with the new dress code.

5 One of the polls also found that 24 percent believe there are too many Jews in France. A March 1992 report by the National Consultative Commission on the Rights of Man found that nearly half of those polled expressed open antipathy toward North Africans, and 40 percent claimed to dislike North Africans born in France (*Minute-La France* [April 8–14, 1992]:15).

6 For more background on French racism, see Balibar (1992), Ben Jelloun (1984), Lloyd and Waters (1991), Taguieff (1991), and Wieviorka (1992).

7 On Cheikha Rimitti, see Virolle-Souibès (1993).

8 Muslims are required to abstain from sex as well as food from sunup to sundown during the month of Ramadan.

9 Virgin, 1988. Rachid Baba also produced *Pop Rai Rachid Style: Rai Rebels (Vol. 2)* (Virgin, 1990), Chaba Fadela's *You Are Mine* (Mango, 1988), and Chaba Fadela and Cheb Sahraoui's *Hana Hana* (Island, 1989). The liner notes and song translations that accompany *Pop Rai Rachid Style* make a point of emphasizing that alcohol consumption and risqué female behavior are associated with *rai.*

10 This is how the 1990 World of Music and Dance Festival program advertised Chaba Fadela and Cheb Sahraoui (WOMAD 1990). Thanks to Rosemary Coombe for providing this source.

11 Estimates of "illegals" (Arab and others) in France range from 300,000 to 1 million (*al-Hayât* [April 30, 1993]:9). When the new Socialist government proclaimed amnesty for undocumented residents in 1981, 131,000 came forward to claim citizenship (Lanier 1991:14).

12 This sketch is based on Balibar (1992), Naïr (1992), and Wieviorka (1992).

13 For an introduction to "flexible specialization" or post-Fordism, see Harvey (1991) and Hall (1991b).

14 A type of slang that originated in criminal circles and is now used extensively by *banlieusard* youth, especially around Paris (see Sherzer 1976).

15 Some so-called *Beurs* are French citizens, some are foreign residents, and others are binationals. When we were in France in 1992, Algerians born in France after Janu-

ary 1, 1963, automatically received French citizenship, whereas those born before this date remained Algerian citizens. Children of Tunisian and Moroccan immigrants had to decide whether to opt for French citizenship at age twenty-one (Begag 1990:4). Since the Right came to power in the 1993 elections, these regulations have become more restrictive.

16 Sociologist Adil Jazouli's typology (1982) of Franco-Maghrebi cultural orientations was very helpful in constructing this spectrum of hybridity.

17 Adapted from Queer Nation's slogan: "We're here, we're queer, get used to it!" Our discussions with members of La Rose des Sables, a Franco-Maghrebi theater group from Valence, helped us understand this orientation.

18 We are told, however, that adherence to Islamist groups has been on the rise since we left France.

19 The "I" in this section is Gross; McMurray and Swedenburg didn't attend this event.

20 A local musician, not the Cheb Kader heard on U.S. *rai* releases (*From Oran to Paris,* Shanachie, 1990).

21 We realize that this does not tally with the Marseilles radio listeners' opinions on mixed marriages, discussed earlier. This leads us to believe that Bariki (1986) mainly questioned young men about their views on their own marriages, and not parents about their children's marriages.

22 Moroccan feminist Fatima Mernissi, for instance, regards the independent, companionate heterosexual marriage unit based on romantic love, in which partners are equal and share love for each other, as a real threat to the "Muslim system" (1987:8).

23 Island, 1990.

24 McMurray and Swedenburg reproduced these stories uncritically in their 1991 article (1991:40).

25 *Maman cherie* (Contact Music, 1991).

26 See Bizot (1987) for an early account of the Parisian World Music scene.

27 Barclay, 1992.

28 See Dominique Guillerm's review of "Didi" in *Max* (May 1992:21). The album was recorded in Los Angeles with producers Don Was and Michael Brooks of 4AD Records. Don Was, a member of Was (Not Was), is well-known in the U.S. music industry for his production work with Bonnie Raitt, the B-52's, and Mick Jagger.

29 Since this writing, Khaled has released a new album (Mango, 1994) called *N'ssi N'ssi.* For an appreciative assessment, see Christgau (1994).

30 The late Umm Kalthum, most popular of all Egyptian singers, was probably the most canonical of those with a classical orientation. Among her lyrics: "Come and we will finish our love in one night." Muhammad 'Abd al-Wahhab, one of the few Egyptian singers who ranks with Umm Kalthum in terms of popularity and classicist orientation, sang "Life is a cigarette and a cup [of wine and liquor]." Neither singer, however, has a reputation for being "vulgar" (Armbrust 1992:534).

31 From . . . *De la Planète Mars* (Labelle Noir/Virgin, 1991).

32 So-called delinquent youth seem to provide the media with ready suspects whenever violence erupts in the *banlieues.* See, for instance, Tourancheau (1991) on the

March 1991 Sartrouville riots and Moreira (1990) on the November 1990 Vaulx-en-Velin riots, as well as the sensationalist media treatment of the "*Bandes de Zoulous*" (Vivier 1991c).

33 See Aïchoune (1991) for a flavor of the everyday speech of *banlieusard* posses.

34 Useful discussions of French rap are Lapassade (1991), Leibowitz (1992), Mézouane (1990), and Vivier (1991a, 1991b, 1991c, 1991d).

35 Our analysis is based primarily on the releases of Supreme NTM (*Authentik,* Epic, 1991) and I AM (. . . *De la Planète Mars,* Labelle Noir, 1991)—two of France's best-known rap groups—as well as two important anthologies (*Rapattitude,* Labelle Noir, 1990 and *Rapattitude 2,* Labelle Noir, 1992) and a recording by Franco-Maghrebi *rappeuse* Saliha (*Unique,* Virgin, 1991). We do not discuss the more celebrated and musically innovative rapper MC Solaar, whose lyrics are less confrontational.

36 As evidenced, for instance, by the angry reactions when presidential candidate Bill Clinton equated black nationalist rapper Sister Souljah with neo-Nazi David Duke.

37 From her song "Danse le beat."

38 On "Non Soumis à l'Etat."

39 On I AM's "Le Nouveau Président" and "Red, Black and Green."

40 For instance, NTM's "Freestyle."

41 One interesting exception is Siria Khan's "La Main de Fatma," on *Rapattitude 2.*

42 With the exception of Prophètes du Vacarme's politically ambivalent "Kameleon" on *Rapattitude 2.*

43 Although many prominent U.S. rappers are avowed Muslims (Brand Nubian, Ice Cube, Poor Righteous Teachers, Rakim of Eric B and Rakim, Professor Griff, Big Daddy Kane, Wu Tang Clan, Nas), their rhymes almost never deal with specifically Arab subjects, except for an occasional mention of Palestine.

44 Other liberal "intellos" also feel compelled to establish rap's pedigree by comparing it with other canonical examples of verbal artistic performances. Mézouane (1990:5) compares rappers with the West African griots, the *meddahs* (itinerant Berber poets), the *berrahs* (traditional *rai* announcers), and the reciters of *la chanson de geste* of the European Middle Ages. Georges Lapassade, the ethnographer of hip-hop who teaches at Paris VIII, likens rap performance to a Moroccan call-and-response ritual (*aît* and *daqa*) and the rapper to an Arab *majdoub* (a tranced-out religious ecstatic) (Loupias 1990). Another commentator claims that "the importance of rap today for the Black community perhaps approaches that of the story tellers of the nineteenth century in our [*sic*] society" (Bouillier 1990:2).

45 On "Quelle Gratitude?"

46 One of their jokes: "What is the difference between 'migration' and 'immigration'?" Answer: "La migration c'est les oiseaux qui volent; l'immigration c'est les arabes qui volent" (Migration is birds that fly; immigration is Arabs who steal).

47 One of Smaïn's stand-up routines opens: "Okay, all French people in the audience, put your hands in the air. Now, all North Africans in the audience, take your hands out of their pockets."

48 Sayad et al. (1991) gives a breakdown on immigration to Marseilles by arrondissement.

49 On *Salam Alikoum* (Musidisc, 1992).

50 Amina played the prostitute in Bertolucci's *The Sheltering Sky,* a film she subsequently condemned as orientalist. She was the only Arab artist to participate in the remake of "Give Peace a Chance," an all-star recording organized by Julian Lennon to mobilize opinion against the 1991 Gulf War that went virtually unremarked in the United States. Her single U.S. release is *Yalil* (Mango, 1989).

51 On the 1961 massacre, see Aïchoune (1991), Ben Jelloun (1984), Cockburn (1991), Einaudi (1991), and Hargreaves (1989); on racist violence in the 1980s, see Aïchoune (1991), Giudice (1992), and Jazouli (1992).

52 Although the Muslim population in France includes a growing number of Turks, as well as some Pakistanis and Black Africans, in this context "Muslim" means Arab.

53 Our thanks to the late Philip Shehadeh for this information.

54 *Foreign Broadcast Information Service,* Near East and South Asia Daily Reports, March 27, 1991, p. 5; *Libération,* March 28, 1991, p. 33. We heard quite different interpretations of this event from Algerians living in Seattle. An engineer who loves *rai* and despises FIS returned from a visit to Algiers in March 1991 and claimed that several people were killed in one FIS attack on a music audience, and that one performance hall was burned down. We have been unable to confirm this story. A graduate student who is a sharp critic of the FLN claimed that the state was the aggressor in this battle, that it actively encouraged music performances during Ramadan in order to harass and provoke the Islamists. For instance, he claimed, the state would issue permits for concerts to be held during Ramadan prayer times, and it specifically promoted events at venues located next to mosques.

55 FIS's program would allow only widowed or divorced women, particularly those with children to support, to hold paid employment. In late December 1991, FIS leader Muhammad Said told a huge crowd that it was time for Algerian women in big cities to start wearing scarves to cover their hair and to stop looking like "cheap merchandise that is bought and sold" (Ibrahim 1991).

56 Adapted from Steve Arra's translation on the liner notes to Cheb Khaled's release *Fuir mais où?*

57 Yúdice draws this definition from the work of Cuban theorist Fernando Ortiz and Uruguayan theorist Angel Rama.

58 Goldman's article (1993) is unique in the music industry's coverage of Cheb Khaled for its mention of anti-Arab racism in France.

59 Useful accounts of the civil conflict in Algeria are Howe (1992), Bekkar (1992), Roberts (1994), and Human Rights Watch (1994).

60 According to a BBC news report, October 11, 1992. This should be understood in light of governmental repression of the Islamists. By March 1992, some twelve thousand Algerians had been banished to internment camps in the southern desert, and between one thousand and three thousand were still being held there in October 1993. Approximately twenty thousand Algerians had been jailed by late 1993, thirteen Islamists had been executed, and torture was rampant.

TOURISM IN THE BALINESE BORDERZONE

EDWARD M. BRUNER

In this essay, I use the concept of borderzones to better understand and conceptualize Western tourism to the less developed regions of the Third World. Although many tourist destinations are in First World countries, I focus on travel to the Third World.

International tourism is an exchange system of vast proportions, one characterized by a transfer of images, signs, symbols, power, money, goods, people, and services (Lanfant 1989; V. L. Smith 1989). The tourism industry is aggressive in ever seeking new attractions for its clients, so there are tours not only to Bali, which has been a tourist destination for over seventy years,[1] but also to places that formerly were difficult to access, such as Kalimantan, New Guinea, the Amazon, and even the South Pole. Tourism has no respect for national boundaries, except in those few countries that for one reason or another restrict tourism (e.g., Myanmar, Albania, Bhutan). Wherever ethnographers go or have gone, tourists have already been there or are sure to follow. And where tourism establishes itself, our traditional anthropological subject matter, the peoples and cultures of the world, becomes commercialized, marketed, and sold to an eager audience of international tourists.

International mass tourism has precipitated one of the largest population movements in the world, in which literally millions of temporary travelers from the industrialized nations seek in the margins of the Third World a figment of their imagination—the exotic, the erotic, the primitive, the happy savage. Bali, for example, is depicted in the tourist literature as a tropical paradise of haunting beauty, an unspoiled beach, an isle of mystery and enchantment, an exotic South Seas island of dreams, where the people live untouched by civilization, close to nature, with a culture that is artistic, static, harmonious, and well integrated.[2] We recognize the trope of the vanishing primitive, the pastoral allegory, the quest for origins (Clifford 1986; Bruner 1993). This romantic characterization not only suppresses the true conditions of Balinese life; it also depicts a culture that never existed (Boon 1977, 1990; Picard 1992; Vickers 1989). The excesses of the descriptions of Bali and many other Third World tourist sites echo Orientalist discourse and anthropological monographs based on a hypothetical ethnographic present. Indeed, the "happy primitive" image was a means of colonial control, one that was in part constructed by ethnography itself. It is ironic, however, that tourists are now chasing the ethnographer's discarded discourse, pursuing an ahistorical vision that anthropologists have long abandoned.

Tourism occurs in a zone physically located in an ever-shifting strip or border on the edges of Third World destination countries. This border is not natural; it is not just there, waiting for the tourists to discover it, for all touristic borderzones are constructed. The parties involved are the tourists who travel from the industrialized nations with already formed images in their heads of the primitive peoples they will see; the "natives," or indigenous population, in their exotic setting; and the multinational travel companies, airlines, hotels, tour agencies, and government bureaucracies that construct and profit from building the touristic infrastructure.

The concept of borderzones used in this paper differs from the usage by Gloria Anzaldúa (1987), Guillermo Gómez-Peña, Emily Hicks (1991), and Coco Fusco (1989), who theorize based upon the U.S.-Mexican border, which is a site of migration between two national states. In touristic borderzones there are no immigrant tourists, almost by definition, but rather a recurring wave of temporary travelers, an ever-changing moving population. The tourists are always present and are always "there," but are always in motion, and they change constantly. The category and presence of tourists are permanent, but the actual individuals come and go, they flow across the border like each new freshman class in college, an ever-renewing source. The native or the resident population is more or less permanent, but as I visualize the touristic border, the natives have to break out of their normal routines to meet the tourists: to dance for them, to sell them souvenirs, or to display themselves and their cultures for the tourists' gaze and for sale. The touristic borderzone is like empty space, an empty stage waiting for performance time, for the audience of tourists and for the native performers. The natives, too, then, move in and out of the touristic borderzone. But the perceptions of the two groups are not the same, because what for the tourists is a zone of leisure and exoticization, is for the natives a site of work and cash income.

What is advertised as unspoiled and undiscovered in the touristic borderzone has been carefully manufactured and sold. The Balinese and other Third World peoples recognize the touristic thirst for the exotic and the unpolluted, so they present themselves and their cultures to conform to the tourist image. Tourists come from the outside to see the primitives; from the inside, paradoxically—from the native perspective—tourism is a route to economic development and a means of livelihood (Lanfant et al. 1995). The predicament is that the more modern the locals, the less interesting they are to the Occidental tourist, and the less their income is derived from tourism. Intellectuals and artists like Anzaldúa and Gómez-Peña theorize about the U.S.-Mexican border, but the situation is so different for those who are the object of the tourist gaze in the underdeveloped Third World, for peoples like the Balinese—if they step out of their assigned roles in exotica, they may lose their major source of income. What most native peoples do in this situation is to collaborate in a touristic co-production.

Professional anthropologists until recently had a very ambivalent attitude toward tourism (see Crick 1995). As intellectuals, anthropologists denigrated tourism as commercial, inauthentic, and tacky. Touristic culture, they felt, was simply a truncated version of a fuller, more authentic native culture located elsewhere. For ethnography, tourism was an embarrassment, an impostor. The stuff of ethnography, what we studied and wrote about in our monographs, was the real culture. Even with the questioning of ethnographic authority (Clifford 1983), anthropology as a profession still has not been entirely clear on what stance to take toward tourism and touristic culture.

Renato Rosaldo (1989:208) provides a theoretical key: "borderlands should be regarded not as analytically empty transitional zones but as sites of creative cultural production"—and, I would add, as sites of struggle. The touristic borderzone is a creative space, a site for the invention of culture on a massive scale, a festive liberated zone, one that anthropology should investigate, not denigrate. To ask how the culture presented for tourists compares with culture we ethnographers have traditionally studied is just the wrong question, one that leads to a theoretical dead end in the never-never land of essentialized nostalgia. The tourists are the ones who desire the uncontaminated precolonial past,[3] the so-called pure culture, so versions of that hypothetical past are invented and presented for tourist consumption. As scholars, anthropologists should study the recent construction of "authentic" culture for a tourist audience, not intellectualize it or judge it or criticize it as yet another Derridian instance of lost origins. Tourists do not travel to experience the new postcolonial[4] subject, the emerging nation in process of economic development; they yearn for their image of a precolonial past.

From the perspective of the geographies of identity, the Western elite travel to the margins of the Third World, to the ends of empire, to the borderzone between their civilized selves and the exotic Other, to explore a fantasyland of the Western imaginary. Curiously, the Other, the postcolonial subject, has already traveled in the opposite direction, for the Jamaican, the Pakistani, the Malay, the Algerian is already established in the centers of Western power (Buck-Morss 1987). Paradoxically, then, the Western elite spend thousands of dollars and travel thousands of miles to find what they already have.

Many Western peoples, of all social classes, make a desperate effort not to "see" the Third World presence in their midst, for they segregate themselves in safe and exclusive neighborhoods, or move to the suburbs if they can afford to do so, or insulate themselves by alternative means. When they do see the Third World peoples who surround them, it is with a very selective vision emphasizing poverty, drugs, crime, and gangs to the neglect of those Other who have become middle class; or the Other may be performers, entertainers, athletes, or servants. Western peoples enjoy ethnic restaurants and performances as long as they are in their proper "space/place."

Although the elite try to avoid the Other in First World cities, making a conscious attempt not to see, to overlook—an absence of sight—when they go to the touristic borderzones they do so with the specific objective of looking, for in tourism there is a voyeurism, an overabundance of seeing, a cornucopia of visualization—almost a pathology, a scopophilia. The Other in *our* geography is a sight of disgust; the Other in *their* geography is a source of pleasure. In *our* place, the Other is a pollution; in *their* place, the Other is romantic, beautiful, exotic. In *our* geography, the elite pay not to see the Other, keeping them distant or hidden, whereas in *their* geography, the Western elite pay for the privilege of viewing and photographing. There is a racialization at home and a primitivization over there, in exotica.

I have consciously exaggerated the differences for emphasis, but I do understand that First and Third World peoples intermingle and circulate in each other's spaces and I do understand that there is upward mobility. For a large segment of the Western elite, however, the essential paradox remains—in First World cities the Other is a social problem; in Third World places the Other is an object of desire. At home the industrialized peoples of the First World avoid the very peoples that they pay enormous sums to see and photograph in Africa or Indonesia. This is actually an old phenomenon, at least a century old in the United States, where Native Americans on their reservations become exoticized and romanticized, whereas the very same peoples as urban neighbors are considered drunks and undesirables.

The industrialized First World splits the Other into two spaces. Their space is made safe by the military, the government, and eventually by the tourist industry; the Other becomes domesticated, reworked for the tourists, frozen in time, or out of time, in past time or no time, performing a Western version of their culture, essentially as entertainers. In First World space the Other is dangerous, associated with pathology and violence, with bad neighborhoods and crime. Western peoples fail to see the joy and beauty of the Other in First World space, just as they fail to see the poverty and suffering of the Other in Third World space.

For the Western tourist, the Orientalist stereotype is dominant in Third World space, and tourists go there to collect souvenirs and photographs to show to their friends at home. They go for adventure, for experience, for status, for education, to explore and collect the image of the exotic Other. But the Other is already here at home, in the flesh, outside on the street, in a neighborhood across town, waiting for us. Tourists bring back a disembodied, decontextualized, sanitized, hypothetical Other, one they can possess and control through the stories they tell about how the souvenirs were acquired and the photographs taken. Tourists place the postcolonial subject in a new narrative frame, in stories in which the tourists become the traveling heroes and the Other, the objects of their search. Narrative mastery is the means to fix meaning, encapsulate, and control the Other, stop motion and time, and exert power.

METHODOLOGY

My project, in this essay, is to explore cultural production in the touristic borderzone, to learn how the Balinese and other Indonesian peoples respond to tourism, and to study how American tourists experience Indonesia. James Clifford (1989b:183) asks the right questions, for we need to know "How do different populations, classes, and genders travel? What kinds of knowledges, stories, and theories do they produce? A crucial research agenda opens up."

In order to investigate these matters, I decided to become a tour guide to

Indonesia, primarily for methodological reasons (E. Cohen 1985a).[5] Tour groups assemble in their area of origin—in, say, San Francisco or London—travel together, see the sights together, eat their meals together, become a tightly knit unit, and disband at the end of the trip. It is difficult to penetrate the tour group from the outside at midpoint in their voyage. Since the tour group is a traveling social unit, I felt that the best way to study tourism was to travel with the group and to share the adventures of a common journey. As a guide, I would be an insider, and would be there to observe and record the tourists' reactions, behaviors, and interpretations. I wanted to learn if tourists buy into the hyperbole of tourist advertising, or if they are really on a quest for authenticity, as MacCannell (1976) claims, or if they have given up the quest and have become post-tourists (Urry 1990), or if tourists play at reality (E. Cohen 1985b). The approach is ethnographic. Standard ethnographic practice tells us to study cultural content in the social context of its reception, which in this case is the tour group, although as a guide/ethnographer my subject position was not that of a classical ethnographer.

Because there are many different forms of tourism, it would be appropriate to describe my particular tours to Indonesia. Briefly, the tours were an upscale version of what has been called cultural or educational tourism (see Graburn and Jafari 1991; Nash and Smith 1991). The agency advertised that their tours were led by "noted scholars," a reading list had been distributed in advance, and the front page of the tourist brochure for Indonesia presented a biographical sketch of my academic qualifications, stressing that I was an anthropology professor, had conducted three years of fieldwork in Indonesia, and spoke the language. One way to put it was that the tour agency was not only selling Indonesia, they were selling me, at least in my capacity as a scholar. Another way to put it was that tourism had co-opted ethnography. I was relatively straightforward with the tourists, telling them that I was an anthropology professor interested in Indonesia and also in tourism; I must admit, however, that I did not tell the tourists I was studying them. This was a tour with a tour guide professor and tourist students, ostensibly there to learn. University alumni associations and museums often organize such tours with faculty lecturers; indeed, the frequency of alumni tours is growing. Many anthropologists have led such tours, but few mention it and even fewer write about it or incorporate the experience into their academic discourse, a situation that poses the question, Why the silence? I suggest that tourism as a subject matter is perceived as somehow tainted:

too popular, too commercial, and not worthy of serious scholarship. To become involved in the touristic enterprise is considered by the discipline to be in some sense unprofessional.

A sociological profile of those on the Indonesia tours shows that they were clearly older and more affluent than most tourists. The average age was about fifty. Almost half were retired, about one-third were divorced or widowed women traveling alone, all except one had a college education, everyone had taken previous tours, and most were business or professional persons. There were physicians, executives, a lawyer, an engineer, and two professors. If, as MacCannell (1976) says, tourists are alienated beings who lead such shallow lives that they have to seek authenticity elsewhere, one would never know it from these tourists. These were successful and affluent persons, quite secure about their identity, and they were traveling at a stage in their lives when they had the leisure and the income to do so. Tourism for them was consumption, and a tour to Indonesia was an expensive status marker (Bourdieu 1984).

I turn now to the analysis of several encounters between the members of the tour group and various Indonesians, as well as to the story of the confrontation of the tourists with Hildred Geertz in Bali in 1986. My point is to demonstrate innovation and creativity in the touristic borderzone.

AN INCIDENT IN BALI

In addition to the standard *barong* and *kecak* dances that are on all the tourist itineraries, I had arranged to take the tour group to an *odalan* or temple festival, a ceremony that the Balinese enact for themselves. These events are not ordinarily on the tour schedule, for one is never entirely sure when they will begin, and the local tour agencies are reluctant to include them. I, however, had lived near the temple in the village of Batuan a few years previously and knew the area. We arrived at the temple about 4 P.M. The tourists, dressed in the appropriate ceremonial sash, sat together in a group along the temple wall and observed the scene, as I had instructed them to do. The Balinese do not appear to object to the presence of tourists at their temple ceremonies as long as they are respectfully attired and well behaved. We seemed to be the only tourists there except for one couple dressed very casually who stood off by themselves.

As the crystal sounds of the gamelan music pervaded the early evening glow, I looked across the temple compound and saw Hildred Geertz, the

1. The gamelan orchestra at the temple festival in Batuan, with Hildred Geertz seated across the compound, right rear.

personification of Balinese ethnography, resplendent in full Balinese ceremonial dress (figures 1 and 2).[6] I knew that Geertz was doing research in Batuan, for I had written to her in advance, informing her that after my work with the tour group was completed, I intended to return to Bali, and I looked forward to visiting with her at that time. Although I realized that Geertz was working in the area, I was nevertheless somewhat surprised to see her at this festival.

I crossed the compound to say hello to Geertz, who I have known for over thirty years, and her response was an astonished "I didn't expect you until next month." I replied that indeed I was returning next month, and I offered to introduce her to the tour group. She responded, "Don't introduce me to those tourists, but after your tour is over, be sure to come to my house."[7] As Geertz later recalled the incident, she was "rather busy and didn't want to get involved in polite conversation with people [she] didn't know" (letter, August 5, 1991). As I interpreted the event, Geertz welcomed Ed Bruner, ethnographer, but chose to keep her distance from Ed Bruner, tour guide. After an awkward moment I went back across the compound to sit with the tour group. To ethnography, tourism is indeed like a poor country cousin, or an illegitimate child that one chooses not to recognize.

Unexpectedly, after a brief interval, Geertz came over to our group and asked if we would like to visit the studio of a nearby Balinese artist. I introduced everyone, and the tourists readily agreed. On the way to the artist's house, I asked Geertz why she had changed her mind. She replied that she was working on the life history of Ida Bagus Madé Togog, a Balinese painter, then an old man (and since deceased), who had been an artistic consultant for Gregory Bateson in the 1930s (figure 3). Possibly Togog could sell one of his paintings to the tourists, she explained, and her reason for escorting us was to help the painter, not the tourists. The tourists didn't buy any of his paintings, but I did: a picture of the *barong* dance, which I have on the wall in my bedroom. It was Togog who suggested to Geertz that she should bring her "friends" to buy his pictures. She wrote, "I had already brought a California artist friend, a New York psychiatrist, several anthropologists, an Australian historian, an American composer, and a whole bunch of Harvard students, just to mention a few" (letter, August 5, 1991).

As we walked to Togog's house, I could not help reflecting that here was I, ethnographer qua tour guide, with a group of tourists, and all of us being guided by Hildred Geertz, tour guides guiding tour guides, to the home of a Balinese artist who in his youth had himself been involved with tourism, with Gregory Bateson and the production of tourist art, and who

2. Hildred Geertz at the Batuan festival.

3. Ida Bagus Madé Togog in his home studio with a painting of the *barong* purchased by Edward M. Bruner.

now in his later years was even more involved with tourism. Togog was Bateson's research consultant, but in a sense Bateson was Togog's tourist. While walking to the painter's studio, Geertz pointed to the house that Gregory Bateson and Margaret Mead had occupied during their research in Batuan in the 1930s, and all of us, the tourists and I, stopped to take pictures.

This scene, I said to myself, is paradigmatic: Ed Bruner's version of a Balinese cockfight, a scene to be commemorated, a postmodern pastiche, a meeting of the First and the Third Worlds in the postcolonial borderzone, a site of in-betweenness, of seepage along the borders. In this event, how does one distinguish between ethnography and tourism, between the center and the periphery, between the authentic and the inauthentic? These faded binaries seem so dated, no longer relevant to the work that ethnographers are actually doing in the field.

What arises in ethnography enters into tourism, but the reverse is also true; what arises in tourism enters into and is legitimated by ethnography (Picard 1992; Vickers 1989). Balinese do paint and dance for tourists, but at a later date many of these creative expressions enter into Balinese social and cultural life. In Batuan in the 1970s, for example, a cultural performance called a frog dance was devised for tourists. At the time of its creation, there was no "authentic" counterpart of the dance located elsewhere in Balinese culture; the dance was a commercial invention specifically designed for a tourist audience. It was not a simulation of an original, for there was no original (Baudrillard 1983). It was an example of cultural production in the borderzone. Over a decade later, in the 1980s, while I was living in Batuan, the organizers of a Balinese wedding asked a dance troupe to perform the frog dance at their wedding. What began in tourism entered Balinese ritual, and might eventually be included in an ethnographic description of the culture. Further, dance dramas and other art forms constructed by Westerners have been adopted by the Balinese as their own and have been incorporated into their artistic repertoire. When President Ronald Reagan visited Bali in 1986, a *kecak* dance, one created by the German artist Walter Spies and some Balinese dancers in the 1930s, was selected as emblematic of Bali and was performed in Reagan's honor.

Balinese culture is performed worldwide, not just on the island of Bali. Balinese dance dramas are exported to the concert halls of Sydney, Paris, and New York, and have become part of the international art world. As early as 1931, a *barong* dance was performed at the Colonial Exhibition in Paris and was probably seen by Antonin Artaud (Picard 1990:58). If the Balinese perform at a temple, it is traditional culture and is described in ethnography; at a hotel, it is tourism; and on a concert stage, it is art, according to our Western categories. From the Balinese perspective, however, these are not closed systems. The Balinese, of course, know if they are performing for tourists, for themselves, or for the gods. They are very aware of the differences between audiences, and indeed they have public debates about the impact of tourism on their culture. The Balinese try to keep some sacred performances exclusively for themselves, but their language does not distinguish between sacred and profane, and in practice, over time, there is slippage.[8] Ethnography, tourism, and art as discourse and practice are porous at the borders, and cultural content flows from one arena to the other, sometimes in profound yet subtle ways. Cultural innovation that arises in the borderzone as a creative production for tourists, what anthropologists formerly called "inauthentic" culture, eventually becomes part of Balinese ritual and may subsequently be studied by ethnographers as "authentic" culture.

For example, the *barong* and *rangda* performances (figures 4 and 5) involving trance fascinated early Western visitors and residents more than any other Balinese dance form (Bandem and de Boer 1981:148). Baum, in her novel *A Tale from Bali,* explicitly documents this Western infatuation

4. The *barong*, from a tourist performance of the Denjalan group at Batubulan.

with the *barong* (1937:282). The gifted group of intellectuals and artists who lived in Bali in the 1930s, including Spies, Covarrubias, Belo, McPhee, Bateson, and Mead, were captivated with the *barong* and, in collaboration with the Balinese, commissioned new forms of the *barong* dance. The famous Bateson-Mead 1937 film, *Trance and Dance in Bali,* which is usually regarded as an early photographic record of a Balinese ritual, was actually a film of a tourist performance for foreigners commissioned and paid for by Bateson and Mead. As Jacknis (1988:167–68) and Belo (1960:97–98, 124–27) document, the *barong* ritual filmed by Bateson and Mead was not ancient but had been recently created during the period of their fieldwork, and the story performed had been changed from the *Calon Arang* to the *Kunti Sraya,* a less dangerous form. The *Kunti Sraya barong* dance, after various transformations since the 1930s, is being performed for tourists to this day. Further, for the film, Bateson and Mead changed the dance by having women rather than men hold the krisses, and they commissioned the dance during the day, when the light was good for photography, rather than having the performance in the evening.

The interest of these influential foreigners enhanced the prominence of the *barong* performances in Balinese life to such an extent that the *barong* has become the preeminent tourist performance, and is now paradigmatic of Bali in Western discourse (Vickers 1989). The dance is so popular that it is performed for tourists by three different troupes simultaneously every day in the village of Batubulan and occasionally by other dance troupes as well (e.g., at Singapadu). The *barong* performance shaped by foreign fascination in the 1930s entered ethnographic discourse most prominently in the 1960s, in Clifford Geertz's influential "Religion as a Cultural System" (1966), which takes the *barong* and *rangda* as illustrative of his generalizations about religion. Balinese culture, after all, has been shaped for seventy years by performances for foreigners, so it is not unexpected that the *barong* dance that an earlier generation of ethnographers helped to construct is described by a more recent ethnographer as the incarnation of "the Balinese version of the comic spirit" (Geertz 1973:118) and as emblematic of Balinese religion. Even the Balinese themselves are not entirely sure what is "authentic" and what is touristic, and such scholars as Picard (1992) doubt if such a distinction makes any sense to the Balinese. To overstate the case for emphasis, the Balinese became what ethnographers studied, in that Western interest in the *barong* led the Balinese to modify their culture so that the *barong* became more prominent in their performances.[9]

5. *Rangda,* the witch, from the Denjalan Batubulan performance.

THE TOURIST RESPONSE

To return to the meeting between the tour group and Hildred Geertz, we ask, How did the tourists react to this incident in Bali? One woman said it was "thrilling," and another, that it was the high point of the Indonesia trip. I eventually saw color slide shows presented at home in America by two tourist families, and both included photographs of the Bateson-Mead house, which in itself is not very striking. Slide shows become an occasion for a narrative summary of the tour, a means to personalize a group experience, and an opportunity to tell stories of travel and adventure. From the perspective of these tourists, the presence of Gregory Bateson and Margaret Mead, and of Ed Bruner and Hildred Geertz—to them the pinnacle of scientific authority—gave them the validation that they, although mere tourists, were in the presence of professors who knew the "real" Bali.

In a sense, the decision of the tour agency to include an academic lecturer is a marketing ploy to have a built-in authenticator; thus I, and also Geertz, had become, like the Balinese, tourist objects (Morris 1995). Complexity is multiplied in a many-layered reflexive voyeurism, in a thick touristic description; the tourists were looking at the Balinese, the ethnographers were looking at the Balinese as well as the tourists; the tourists were looking at the ethnographers; and of course the Balinese were looking at everyone. One ethnographer, Bruner, was studying the other ethnographer, Geertz, who, after she had read a draft of this paper, stated, "This is the first time I've ever been an ethnographic object." The tourists were also looking at the other tourists, because the tour group for them was their basic social unit, the group they traveled with and discussed the sights with on a daily basis. What I want to emphasize here is not just the voyeurism, the tourist gaze, but also that all parties—the painter Togog, the ethnographer Geertz, the tour guide Bruner, and the tourists—were not just passive beings, looking or being looked at, but also were active selves interpreting their worlds.

I later learned that Geertz had selected Batuan as the site of her research precisely because the Balinese craft of painting for tourists began there in the 1930s (Geertz 1995). She was as much involved in the study of tourism and the borderzone as I was, and had a similar postmodern perspective. Geertz wrote to me in her letter of August 5, 1991:

> I was by no means "embarrassed" by the entry of your tourists into my Balinese world, for they were, and had been for some years, a common part of it. There was hardly a day in Batuan when foreigners had

> not been around. I had long ago clarified to myself the presence of "other tourists" as a part of my own research or, at least, had learned to live with it. The Balinese never let me forget that I was just one more tourist among the others.

Geertz graciously gave me permission to write about our meeting in Bali, although she felt uncomfortable that she did not have more of an active voice in the presentation of her own views.

BETWEEN TOURISM AND ETHNOGRAPHY

I found aspects of the tour guide role uncomfortable and ambiguous (Bruner 1995). As ethnographer my aim was to study how the tourists experienced the sites, but as guide my assignment was to structure that experience through my commentary. My talk mediated their experience, so that in a sense I found myself studying myself. Like the Kaluli shamans who create the meaning they discover, I created the meaning of Indonesian sites for the tourists, and then I studied that meaning as if I had discovered it. This is not, however, especially unique in ethnographic research (Bruner 1986).

"Tourist" and "ethnographer" are roles that one plays and manipulates. At times, when our tour group approached a new site, the Indonesians would behave toward me as if I were another tourist, and I could rupture that attribution by speaking the Indonesian language, which in effect said, Don't confuse me with these tourists, or I could choose to remain silent and to accept the designation. At other times, by emphasizing my role as a working tour guide, I could identify with the Indonesian performers and locals, saying in effect, as guide and native, We are in the same situation, catering to tourists, who are our source of income. I stressed to the Indonesians that we were on the same side, as it were, in opposition to the tourists, but I was never sure if the Indonesians accepted this alignment.

More disturbing was that during the journey, I would slip back and forth between the touristic and the ethnographic, for I could not always keep them straight. I truly enjoyed these hardy tourists who were, like me, older, college educated, and of either professional or business class. At times I felt myself becoming a tourist, gaping in awe at Borobudur, rushing from the bus to take photographs, enthralled by breathtaking scenery in Sulawesi, luxuriating in the hot showers but complaining about the meals at the hotel in the evening. At other times I felt myself as straight ethnographer, making detailed observations of tourist behavior, dissecting their conversations, and writing my field notes late into the night. Balinese *barong* performers wear masks, but so do ethnographers.

As a tour guide, I felt that what tourism needed was not another sojourn among the exotic savages of the mysterious East, not more clichés and stereotypes, so I tried to demystify traditional tourism, to deconstruct the romantic images of the Indonesians, to reveal the mechanisms of production of tourist performances. But the more I did so, paradoxically, the more I contributed to traditional touristic romanticism. For the tourists, I became the heroic ethnographer, a regular Indiana Jones, the "true" interpreter of the sites and enactments on the tourist itinerary. The tourists were proud that they had their own "authentic" ethnographer as tour guide, compared with those other, more touristy tours, the superficial ones that didn't have their own professor as lecturer. I found myself in the position of "authenticating" the experience for the tourists at the same time I was deconstructing the Balinese cultural performances. The tourists saw me as providing the ultimate backstage, despite my protestations to the contrary.

AUTHENTICITY AND VERISIMILITUDE

In Yogyakarta, the heart of central Javanese culture, the tour agent scheduled a supper and performance at the home of "Princess" Hadinegoro, a relative of the sultan. We arrived in the early evening, the only tourists there, and were served drinks in the living room of the home. We then moved to the dining room, were seated at tables, and enjoyed a buffet supper as a gamelan orchestra played in the courtyard. After supper, we moved to the courtyard and watched a Ramayana ballet, a performance of the old Hindu epic (figure 6). The performers were in colorful costumes, their bodily movements slow and controlled, and the presence of children peering over the courtyard wall added to the ambiance of the evening.

Afterward, when asked how they enjoyed the event, the tourists replied that it was absolutely lovely. I then explained that the invitation to the "home" of a Javanese princess was a gimmick, because it created the impression that they were "guests," which disguised the commercial nature of the attraction; actually they were paying customers, who had in effect gone to a restaurant. The princess ran a business to produce income, and had tour groups to her home an average of twenty days a month. Further, I explained, although the Ramayana ballet was presented as if it were an ancient classical dance, this was not the case. The ballet is not a Javanese

6. Tourists seated at the Ramayana performance at the home of Princess Hadinegoro in Yogyakarta, Java.

genre, and the Ramayana ballet was created in 1961 as a performance for tourists (Laporan 1970), with support from the Indonesian central government of President Sukarno.[10]

The Javanese Ramayana, like the Balinese frog dance, was an example of new cultural production in the borderzone. At the time of its construction, it was somewhat of a theatrical event in Java because it brought together the best of the performing artists from Solo and Yogya and two distinct court traditions, and the ballet was performed at the Prambanan temple.[11] Since that time the artistic standards have declined, and the ballet has been shortened and adopted in a number of tourist settings. The Ramayana, as a dance for tourists, could not use the Javanese language because the foreigners could not understand it; the pace was made faster and the length was kept shorter to hold interest, and the gestures were exaggerated to communicate a story line across wide cultural chasms. Relative to other Javanese dances, the Ramayana was reduced and simplified so that it could be incorporated more readily into a Western system of meaning. In a sense, I told the tourists, the Ramayana is a caricature of a Javanese dance, a postmodern construction in the borderzone, an ancient Hindu epic reworked for foreign consumption.[12]

Well, I asked the tourists, what do you think of the evening now, knowing that the setting and the dance were not as authentic as you had assumed? Their response, all of them, was that nothing I said had detracted from their enjoyment of the evening, that it was still absolutely lovely! "What did you like?" I asked. They replied that it was a good show, that they were the only persons present, that it was stimulating being in an Indonesian home and seeing all the old Dutch and Javanese pictures and memorabilia, that the food was fine, and that the performers were superb.

After this discussion the performers, dressed in their street clothes, came out to meet the tourists, as I had requested. We found that the male lead, a history major at Gajah Mada University, had joined the troupe as a part-time job. His wife of six months was a student at the Dance Academy of the university, and she hoped to become a professional dancer. The tourists asked questions about the dance and contemporary life, I translated, and the session ended with the taking of group photographs. My idea was to remove the performers from roles in the timeless Hindu past, and to show them as modern Indonesians who could interact with the tourists on a more direct and personal basis.

After leaving Java we flew to Bali, to stay at the Bali Hyatt Hotel, a large resort complex on the beach in Sanur that caters primarily to tour groups. The next evening the hotel advertised a rijstaffel dinner with a performance of the Ramayana ballet, at a cost of twenty dollars per person plus service fees. I suggested that our group attend, as it was an opportunity to see the same performance in two settings on two different islands. Following the creation of the Ramayana ballet, the Balinese copied the dance drama in 1962 and adapted it to their own culture. After the dance, I asked the tourists how they enjoyed the evening. One replied that it was too much like Honolulu, then another corrected her and said it was more like Miami Beach. Everyone shared this negative view, and I inquired why. The answer was that they were in a room with three hundred or four hundred other tourists; one Hyatt hotel is like any other; it was too crowded; the buffet lines were too long; there was no feeling of intimacy; and they were too far from the performers to take good photographs. "But," I protested, "this is a Balinese version of the same Ramayana that you enjoyed so much in Yogya. The performers are a diverse group put together by a local producer, but they are good dancers, and the gamelan orchestra is hired as a troupe from one of the villages, so it is the same group that you might hear performing in a temple festival." Despite my arguments, they did not like the performance of the Ramayana ballet at the Bali Hyatt.

The next day in Bali was Nyepi, the one day in the calendrical cycle when all activity stops on the island, and the tourists could not leave the hotel. I felt it was an appropriate time for some extended discussion with the tourists, so I booked a seminar room for our meeting. Our topic was authenticity, and I rather liked the idea of holding a seminar on authenticity at the Bali Hyatt Hotel, a world-class hotbed of international tourism.

When I probed further into the differences between the Javanese and the Balinese versions of the Ramayana, it was apparent that the context was the crucial variable: the atmosphere of a home for just our group as opposed to a tourist hotel with many groups. In Java the audience, the gamelan orchestra, and the performers were on the same level, whereas in Bali there was an elaborate raised stage for the performers and another separate area for the orchestra. There was even a raised platform labeled "photo point," where the tourists could go to take pictures. Both the performances were commercial, but in the first the mercantile dimension was disguised, whereas in the second it was transparent.

These upscale tourists did not object to a performance constructed for tourists, but they demanded that it be a good performance, and they had their aesthetic standards. They were not romantics and were concerned with the artfulness of staged theatricality, not disguised issues of authenticity. What they wanted was a good show. Authenticity, they said, might be an issue in the literature on tourism, but it was not an important issue for them. They pointed out that the Ramayana ballet might be recent, but it was still Indonesian. They recognized that they might be responding to the "authenticity" of the setting, for the differences in context between the performances in a Javanese home and in a Balinese beach hotel were striking. They acknowledged that the Java version was more exclusive, more high-class, held in the home of Javanese royalty; and these tourists were, after all, trying to secure an exclusive tourist experience, of which I was a part. But the Java version was also a better show. The tourists appreciated my historical perspective on the dance and my data on the processes of its production, but my information did not detract from their enjoyment of the evening. I understood their position, and believe they accurately characterized the views of many other tourists.

We had seen a Balinese *barong* performance by the Denjalan group at Batubulan the previous day, and one woman volunteered that she immediately recognized it as the "sacred tourist dance," which she has come to expect on all her tours. Her comment elicited smiles of acknowledgment from the others. After all, if a dance performance begins at precisely 9 A.M.

each day; if there are only tourists and no Balinese in the audience; if they charge admission and sell souvenirs; if it lasts for precisely one hour, after which everyone returns to the tour buses, it doesn't take much to figure out that this is a dance staged for tourists and not for Balinese. I said to the tourists, however, that the Denjalan group had two *barongs,* one of which was a consecrated *barong* with *sakti* (power); that the man in white sprinkling holy water on the stage, playing the part of a Balinese priest, was a Balinese priest, not an actor, and the water he sprinkled was holy; that they sacrificed a chicken on stage as an offering; that the performers recited mantras before the performance; and that the dancers reported that sometimes they did go into trance. For the Balinese the gods are always present. I agreed with the tour group, however, that this was a dance staged for tourists. The tourists, in turn, accepted what was presented to them and had no inclination to look beyond the "staged authenticity" of the Denjalan performance for the "real" *barong.*

The seminar convinced me that the basic metaphor of tourism is theater, and the tourists enter into a willing suspension of disbelief. The key issue for students of tourism then becomes the mechanisms by which a tourist production is made convincing and believable to the tourists, which in effect collapses the problem of authenticity into the problem of verisimilitude (E. Cohen 1988; Bruner 1994). What makes a theatrical or tourist production credible? This is the old anthropological question of how people come to believe in their culture (Crapanzano 1986). It is not just that the Ramayana in Java had fewer tourists and the Ramayana in Bali had more tourists, and was more touristy, which is the dimension that the tourism literature has emphasized. When there are fewer tourists, it is easier to suspend disbelief, to get into the event or site, or to imagine oneself as an adventurer or explorer in a distant land. The performance becomes more believable. Nor is it a question of the authenticity of a performance, which implies the presence of another performance that is more genuine or truer to life. The Ramayana ballet is not a simulacrum; it has no counterpart elsewhere in the culture, and there is no original. Even if there were an original, it would not be of primary concern to the tourists. The problem of focusing so narrowly on the quest for authenticity is that one is always looking elsewhere, over the shoulder or around the bend, which prevents one from taking the Ramayana and the *barong* as serious performances in themselves, ones that deserve to be studied in their own right.[13]

Clearly, what MacCannell wrote in 1976 in his classic book about touristic authenticity did not seem relevant for the tour groups I took to Indonesia, but his comments in 1990 on the ex-primitives and the postmodern tourists staging the touristic enterprise as a co-production, as a kind of contract, seems very provocative, as do Erik Cohen's view of tourist playful self-deception (1985b) and Urry's (1990) notion of the posttourist, although I have never known any other kind of tourist than the one Urry describes. The question emerges of whether what MacCannell, Cohen, and Urry now write seems relevant because the world has changed or because we are for the first time beginning to understand touristic phenomena. The results of my studies of Indonesian tourism suggest that the issue of authenticity in the tourism literature has been overdone, that tourists are not primarily concerned with authenticity, and that it would be more productive to pursue the metaphors of theater and of borders to study touristic verisimilitude.

CONCLUSION

This essay has tried to throw some light on what Taussig has called the epistemic murk of the anthropological predicament, what Hildred Geertz calls the great semiological swamp that we all live within. Postmodern complexities occur not only in the centers of Western power but also in postcolonial borderzones on the periphery, in what used to be the pure, authentic preserve of ethnographic science. Indeed, the border between ethnography and tourism is clouded, porous, and political. Tourism not only shapes Balinese culture but also is now part of Balinese culture—or it could even be said that tourism is Balinese culture (Errington and Gewertz 1989; Picard 1992). Balinese born since the 1930s have lived their entire lives as tourist objects, and in some areas, such as Batuan, any adequate ethnographic account of Balinese economy or ritual would have to take account of tourism.

Balinese performances are exported to the centers of Western power, and they are also enacted every day in a shifting touristic borderzone on the edge of the Third World, a zone of interaction between natives, tourists, and ethnographers. Tour agents are always looking for new products to present to their clients, for new temples or new islands to discover and to "touristify." The Balinese, the Javanese, and other Indonesian peoples in the tourist zone are themselves always experimenting, creating, and playing with new expressive rituals, constantly devising new performances for the tourists. But the new Indonesian culture does not necessarily remain forever fixed in the zone in which it was created. Old ceremonial forms are reworked for tourists, culture produced for tourists enters Balinese ritual, what arises in tourism or ritual may be exported to the concert stages of the West for an international audience, and what was at one historical period "touristic" at a later period becomes "ethnographic."

Anthropology has always recognized that peoples and cultures move, for concepts such as diffusion and migration have had deep roots in the discipline from the beginning, but we may not yet have taken account of the particular nature and the full extent of the movement of peoples and cultures in this postmodern world. The old anthropological metaphor of place, where one culture belongs to one people who are situated in one locality, is being challenged by the new metaphors of diaspora, travel, tourism, and borderzones (Appadurai 1988; Clifford 1989b). I see the challenge as a continuation of the emphasis on practice, performance, movement, and process that has become so prominent in anthropology since the 1960s (Ortner 1984), and I welcome it. It makes ethnography more dynamic, more exciting.

NOTES

An earlier draft of this essay was read at the Department of Performance Studies, New York University, and at the Departments of Anthropology at SUNY Buffalo and at Rice University. I wish to thank Barbara Kirshenblatt-Gimblett, Richard Schechner, Dennis and Barbara Tedlock, Bruce Jackson, George Marcus, and Hildred Geertz for their suggestions. Parts of an earlier draft were presented at the conference Tourism and the Change of Life Styles, Instytut Turystyki, Warsaw, Poland, in 1988. Helpful comments also were made following discussion of the paper at the Cultural Studies reading group at the University of Illinois.

All photographs in this chapter were taken by the author.

1 Specialists might argue about the precise date when tourism began in Bali, but by the time the KPM steamship line initiated weekly service in 1924, and opened the Bali Hotel in 1928, there was international tourism.

2 See Picard 1992; and Vickers 1989. The same exuberant phrases are found in the Balinese travel brochures from the 1930s to the 1990s.

3 Other groups may seek an essentialized precolonial purity—for example, national liberation movements.

4 I use the term "postcolonial" in the sense of "after the colonial era," but I realize that the term is problematic (e.g., see Frankenberg and Mani in this volume).

5 See Bruner 1995 for the economic aspects of the tour guide role.

6 For the Balinese, ceremonial attire at a temple festival is less an expression of individual identity and more a matter of respect toward others, especially the gods and

demons who inhabit the ritual world. The Balinese would expect an ethnographer to dress respectfully.

7 I did return to Bali the next month, and Geertz helped me gather data on Balinese tourism.

8 This is best documented in Picard 1992.

9 This thesis was presented at the annual meetings of the American Folklore Society in Cincinnati, 1985, by Kirshenblatt-Gimblett and Bruner in a paper titled "Tourist Productions and the Semiotics of Authenticity." See also the seminal work of Boon (1977); the scholarly work of Picard (1990); and the popular book by Vickers (1989).

10 I wish to thank Edi Sedyawati for her help in understanding the Ramayana. I am also indebted to I Made Bandem for his help with Balinese performances.

11 The local Javanese guide in Yogya complained in 1987 that there were now so many tourists at the Prambanan temple for the Ramayana performance that the Javanese could no longer attend. He had missed the point completely: that the Ramayana was constructed precisely for a tourist audience, and thus blurred the distinction between performances for tourists and for Javanese.

12 The enactment of the Ramayana, from the performers' point of view, was more a rite of modernity, generating cash income in a market economy.

13 In 1986, after the tourists had left, I saw a Ramayana ballet performed as part of a large, multiple-day temple ceremony, an example again of how a dance created for tourists becomes part of Balinese ceremonial. The Ramayana, however, was held the day following the major temple ritual. Such occurrences are commonplace in Bali.

SONGS LODGED IN SOME HEARTS: DISPLACEMENTS OF WOMEN'S KNOWLEDGE IN KANGRA

KIRIN NARAYAN

Women's suffering—poignant and painful—pervades songs of the genre *pakhaṛu* sung among older upper-caste women in the villages of Kangra, northwestern India. These songs are said to be set in a past era (*pichleyā jamānā*) both remembered and imagined: a time when girls who had not reached puberty were displaced by marriage from their homes of birth; when in-laws in the joint family were excessively strict; when distances could be traversed only on foot or horseback; and when migrant husbands could be missing for years at a time. The songs are sung in a regional dialect called Kangri, which is locally known as Pahari "of the mountains." Each song has a woman at its center and narrates her travails.

In the early 1990s, the women who sang *pakhaṛu* songs were mostly illiterate or semiliterate, roughly thirty-five and older. Younger women and girls who were educated, on the other hand, rejected such sorrowful songs as old-fashioned; they preferred contemporary romantic songs associated with Hindi films. Men and women, adults and children alike contrasted the local "old women's songs" (*jhabrī de gīt*) with film or film-inspired songs (*filmī gīt*) that piped in urban, middle-class prestige through radio, tape recorder, cinema, video, and television. As a college student stated, handing back a notebook in which his mother had helped him transcribe tapes of local songs, "It's only old-fashioned, backward [*pichhleyā*] people who sing songs like this. Progressive [*agleyā*] people sing film songs." Adopting Raymond Williams's framework, such Kangri women's songs of suffering, rooted in displaced social formations, might be viewed as "residual culture" in the context of dominant culture (Williams 1977:121–27; 1991:415–17) that is today disseminated from urban centers in the modern Indian nation-state, and tied in turn to wider transnational power formations.

Compelling currents in contemporary anthropological theory (and cultural studies generally) direct research toward emergent cultural forms associated with metropolitan regions and transnational cultural flows (Appadurai 1990, 1991b; Hannerz 1989). In this context, attention to older women's songs in a mountain dialect might well be mistaken as a misguided quest for bounded cultural authenticity (Handler 1986), a regressive return to the "salvage paradigm" that casts anthropology's subject matter as disappearing (Clifford 1989a), or a form of imperialist nostalgia whereby anthropologists mourn the passing of that which their very presence destroys (R. Rosaldo 1989:68–87). Further, in accepting older women's statements that their songs are being displaced, the documentation of such songs might be seen as an endorsement of "the devolutionary premise in folklore," in which oral traditions are seen as deteriorating through time (Dundes 1969).

This essay is a defense of ethnography about indigenous knowledges locally perceived as being displaced by change. Displacements of knowledge (cf. Abu-Lughod 1991) are tied to rearrangements in power relations. To ignore such knowledge while focusing on the cutting edge of cultural innovation is frequently to ignore the socially marginalized: women, peasants, the old, the poor. While anthropologists are well advised to discard an emphasis on pristine authenticity, taking heed of hybridity, innovation, and global connections, it does not necessarily follow that documenting older traditions that appear to be waning hinges on a quest for authenticity. Rather, such traditions must be analytically reframed amid a widening field of available imaginative possibilities (Bausinger 1990:47). Also, these traditions can in their own right be seen as processual and mixed. Instead of seeing these "residual" traditions as irrelevant to contemporary times, we might also explore whether they have "an alternative or even oppositional relation to the dominant culture" (R. Williams 1977:122).

Songs of women's lives—and especially their suffering—have been documented among women from a variety of castes and regions in India (Bryce 1964; Claus 1991; Dhruvarajan 1989; Junghare 1983:273–75; Narayan 1986, 1993; Raheja and Gold 1994; Rao 1991; Tharu and Lalita 1991:126–42; Trawick 1991). Usually these songs critique a kin-based patriarchal society through an active voicing of women's perspectives. However, within India since the nineteenth century such women's folk knowledges have been increasingly marginalized by a nationalist construction of a sanitized tradition associated with the urban, educated, middle-class women (Banerjee 1989; Chatterjee 1989a). In this essay, I document how locally based, sung representations of village women's lives today compete with images, borne through the media, of the ideal middle-class Indian women. I also discuss how Indian women's activist groups' rediscovery of singing as a political practice underlines the continuing relevance of women's songs of suffering.

KANGRA AND WOMEN'S SONGS

Kangra Valley is perhaps best known for the exquisite miniature paintings that adorn many international museums. Kangra is also now on the international tourist circuit as home to the Dalai Lama, the Tibetan leader and Nobel Peace Prize winner. Today, one can fly into Kangra in an unpressured propeller plane from Delhi, the north Indian plains rising beneath one into the Sivalik Range. After crossing the wooded Sivaliks, the Dhauladhar ("White-Bearing") Mountains loom on the northern horizon, the first range of the Himalaya stretching north. Between the Sivaliks and the Dhauladhar lies Kangra, a mosaic of lush green fields, hamlets, rivers, and a few large pilgrimage and market towns.

Most people who are not tourists cannot afford to fly into Kangra. They usually take the narrow-gauge train from the railway junction in Punjab, or they cram into one of the buses that lurch along the mountain roads. As the air thins and cools, the roads grow less packed. The flat-roofed, cement box architecture of the plains gives way to houses of mud and slate, glimpsed across fields or through clusters of bamboo. Yet since the mid-1980s, these adobe houses increasingly bear television antennas. Also, many older houses are being torn down and new cement houses are built in their stead.

The presence of the outside world is not new. Like most places that at first seem remote, Kangra actually has a long history of interaction with the outside world through trade, pilgrimages, migrations, and invasions. Katoch kings once governed Kangra as a hill state; these rulers were brought under Mughal rule in the mid-sixteenth century, submitted to Sikh domination in 1809, and became part of the British colonial state in 1846. Kangra remained an administrative district of Punjab under British rule and for almost two decades following Indian independence. When post-independence Indian states were rearranged on the basis of language, Kangra's local dialect, *Kangṛī bolī*—evaluated in colonial linguistic surveys as a subdialect of Dogri, "intermediate between standard Panjabi and the Pahari of the lower Himalaya" (Grierson 1916:608)—was politically construed in favor of a hill rather than a plains identity. In 1966, Kangra merged with the adjacent northern hill state of Himachal Pradesh (Parry 1979:11–14).

Kangra's population was over a million in 1991. This population is mostly Hindu, and internally differentiated along the lines of caste. My focus in this paper is on upper-caste women—Brahmans, Rajputs, and traders—from families that have historically been privileged as landowners (even though it is men who have owned the land [Sharma 1980]). Kangra is also home to Sikhs, to nomadic shepherd Gaddi tribes, to Tibetan refugees relocated here in the 1960s, and to Western hippies and tourists interested in Tibetan Buddhism. While Muslims of the Gujar tribes had once formed a sizable segment of Kangra's population, with India's partition from Pakistan and the accompanying riots, many Gujars were slaughtered. In the village that was my base, an old Gujar woman with stubs at her wrists—plundering assassins sliced through bone for gold bracelets—remains a troubling reminder of the largely vanished Muslim presence.

Subsistence farming in Kangra is increasingly backed by a cash economy, with the crucial part of each family's income hinging on remittances sent by men working in the plains and beyond. If women are displaced from their homes of birth through marriage, men tend to be displaced from their homes by the need to earn. In women's songs, husbands are regularly addressed as "employed man" (*naukar, chākar*) or "soldier" (*sipāhi*), for the British army's policy of recruiting from the hill states has made for an enduring association of employment with army life. During my stay, army men came in on leave not just from the adjoining troubled states of Kashmir and Punjab, but also from distant parts of India. Some recalled previous stints in Sikkim or Sri Lanka. Old soldiers who had served in the British army rolled up pants to display battle scars acquired in places like Cairo and Italy. Men in other professions were occasionally reported as off in places as far-flung as Dubai, Mexico, or New Jersey. Women, however, once married, have tended to stay put, looking after the farm and aging parents. Even that small but growing percentage of women who accompany their husbands to their jobs elsewhere tend to remain housebound. As the feminist cultural geographer Doreen Massey has observed, differential access to mobility both reflects and reinforces power (1991:26). This holds, of course, not just between men and women but also for those of us whose economic advantage enables travel to Kangra, while an air ticket abroad would be an unthinkable expense for someone Kangra-based.

"In a village you know everything," observed Sharmaji, a village schoolteacher in his forties, in English. "You read papers, you listen to the radio. But you just don't have the same facilities." We had just been talking about the problems of procuring cooking gas cylinders, a phone call away in the city but a matter of bribes, fake registration, and extensive waits for those villagers who could afford to move beyond firewood. If Sharmaji, an upper-caste schoolteacher with a regular salary, had this sense of disempowerment in terms of Indian and global power structures, this was even more the case with older, illiterate or semiliterate women largely dependent on their men as links to bureaucratic structures and the cash economy. "I perform worship daily, but God doesn't seem to listen anymore," said Gita Devi Pandit, whose family's main wealth was in the form of fields. "These are the times of money [*paise dā jamānā*]. What will happen to my son if he doesn't improve in school and learn how to earn money?" Head bowed with despair as she told me about losing a court case when her adversaries bribed the judge, Brinda Devi Sud observed that we were in a terrible dark era (*ghor kali yuga*) characterized by a lack of sympathy between the powerful and the powerless. A widow eking out her living as postmistress once cross-examined me about the nature of cows and the availability of milk in America. She then remarked in a Pahari aside to another woman present, "It makes me angry when I think of people's lives there and all the hardships we have here!" Switching back to the Hindi in which she addressed me, the postmistress dismissed American economic advantage by recourse to Hindu nationalist chauvinism, which was very much in the air in the fall of 1990 (as Hindu fundamentalists prepared to storm the purported birthplace of the deity Ram in Ayodhya). "But America is the underworld (*pātāl*). That's where the sun goes at night, right? So it must be the underworld. Our Bharat [India] is where all the gods took birth, like Ram. The underworld is where all the demons are, like Ravana, Kumbhakarna, Meghnath. Don't you feel worried about living in the underworld?"

Kangra, then, has always been linked to the outside world, though men's links have tended to be stronger than women's. The multiple cultural currents running through Kangra's history and location surface both in everyday speech and in the framed domains of folklore. Women's songs are not just in Pahari, "of the mountains" (the local gloss for the Kangri dialect), but also mix in Urdu, Punjabi, Hindi, and occasionally English. In terms of prestige, Pahari would be near the bottom as an unwritten dialect, with Hindi and English, the languages of state bureaucracy near the top. The extent of language mixing in songs varies with genre. The genres can be conceived along a continuum from those which are most linguistically conservative to those most open to the languages brought in by outsiders. (It should be kept in mind that a dialect like Pahari is not just internally differentiated; it is also continually integrating expressions from other languages.) *Pakhaṛu* songs stand near the end of the spectrum that employs Pahari, freely mixed with Punjabi and Urdu terms. Dance songs (*nāch gīt*)—a category that can assimilate women's renditions of film songs (*filmī gīt*)—tend to be at the other end of the spectrum, and are often sung in Hindi sprinkled with English terms. Correspondingly, it is older, illiterate and semiliterate women who are most likely to know *pakhaṛu* and young women who specialize in the dance songs. Yet even among these two broadly defined groups of women there was variation explained by "interest" (*sukinnī*). Thus, not all old women knew old songs, and not all young ones knew newer dance songs.

As an auspicious (*mangal*) activity, singing is prescribed for rites of passage such as a boy's birth or annual birthday, thread ceremonies, and weddings of human and divine couples. Communal singing, like ritual, is viewed by older women as a form of vital work (*kām*) through which they perpetuate the social world. If I asked *why* women sang at rites of passage, I was always assured by men and women alike that this was "out of happiness" (*khushi se*). While this glib shorthand turned women singers into choruses at the margins of triumphantly marked male lives, it also served to cloak the subversive potential in songs that were not happy at all. While these songs appeared to have been incorporated by the dominant patriarchal culture, the apparent incorporation shielded the presence of alternative, even oppositional, models of social reality that emphasized women's perspectives (see Messick 1987; Raheja and Gold 1994; Radner and Lanser 1987; R. Williams 1991).

As a social practice, singing is deeply tied to women's sociality and household interdependence. It hinges on women's presence in the village (rather than following their migrant husbands to cities), women's availability for such activity (rather than being responsible to the hours of wage labor), and women's conviction of the need for cooperation in ritual matters. Vidhya Sharma, who was helping me transcribe songs, said about these gatherings for song, "Even if you don't feel like going, you have to go, otherwise when your family's turn comes, no one will come sing for you."

Having come and gone to Kangra for many years since 1975 (my American mother lives there), I, too, had felt the social pressure to sit through women's singing sessions. Bored at first, I turned my attention to making sense of what was being sung during an extended break between college and graduate school in 1980. In 1982, as a graduate student, I spent a summer focusing on wedding songs (Narayan 1987). I thought I would explore wedding songs further during a year of research leave between 1990 and 1991. When I arrived in Kangra, though, my project was rapidly taken charge of by village women. To them I seemed mostly a pitiable, skinny, and displaced girl-spinster, lost between identities, continents, languages, statuses, floundering in need of their help. While I provided the equipment and preliminary questions, older women themselves usually decided at which occasions for communal singing I should be present. They also sang along, choosing songs they wished to preserve on my tapes, and hauled me around to meet and coax other performers for choice songs. I was soon redirected from wedding songs, which emphasize a girl's sorrow at leaving her natal relatives, to *pakhaṛu,* which map out a complex topography of the many sorts of suffering that come with marriage.

As ethnomusicologists have observed, gender and other planes of social differentiation are mapped onto musical spheres (Koskoff 1989). *Pakhaṛu* songs of suffering are thus associated with women rather than with men, particularly high-caste women. The songs given this label are not tied to any particular ritual action, but can be freely launched into during women's gatherings when there are no men present: while communally grinding spices, cutting vegetables, and patting out yeasted *baturas* for a villagewide feast, or when sitting together after ritual worship. *Pakhaṛu* is a name known only to women of Brahman, Rajput, and trading Sud castes, all communities that have traditionally restricted women's movements through purdah while supporting a culture of indoor communal leisure. With land reforms, and a breakdown of the *jajmānī* ritual and economic interdependence between castes, many of these women from landowning families had been forced into the fields or at least into cutting fodder for livestock. Nonetheless, the value of singing together meant that they worked their routines around singing occasions.

Women of agricultural and "untouchable" castes did not recognize the name *pakhaṛu;* their equivalent genre that highlighted women's suffering was the *barsāti* songs sung by groups ankle deep in cold water, transplanting young rice in the monsoon. Low-ranking Rajputs who work in the fields appear to serve as a bridge for the crossing over of texts between *pakhaṛu* and *barsāti* genres. These in fact are often very similar texts, though sung in a different style that employs an emphatically prolonged final note. Another closely related genre of songs were ballads called *ḍholru,* sung by low-caste Dumna basket makers in the month of Chaitra (March/April). For different reasons than *pakhaṛu,* these other sorts of songs also appear to be waning. Since the mid-1980s women sing *barsāti* less and less in the fields, complaining that with the breakdown of caste interdependence and the rise of wage labor, they often work in smaller groups. Dumna basket makers, in turn, do not readily seek out the stigma of a caste that absorbs inauspiciousness (for example, through singing in the month of Chaitra). Basket makers are turning from their caste-based occupations of bamboo work and singing to wage labor.

Like most folklore forms, women's songs in Kangra are learned, shared, and transmitted within small groups. In performance, one or two women usually lead the singing while the others blend in. Before plunging into a particular song, singers often confer in mutters and fragments of melody to plot out the words, the verse order, and the tune. The first line, called the root (*ḍhak*), is the main way of identifying a song when a singer is negotiating for partners to join her. Since the melody is repetitive and each line of text is repeated twice, any listener can join in. For women's songs, then, everyone is simultaneously a potential performer and a member of the audience. Voices joining in a common song, women appear to be dramatizing a shared social destiny and their own solidarity as fellow performers, fellow celebrators, fellow sufferers. At the same time, though, it is also acknowledged that not all women may feel an emotional connection to the same songs. As Brinda Devi Sud observed, "There are always women singing. Anytime you go to a 'function,' women are singing. Some songs you know and some you sing along with. Some songs attract you, they go sit inside your heart. That's how you learn songs."

Women's songs are increasingly located amid competing musical traditions and other gender representations coming from the outside world. While Kangra has never been isolated, and it is clear that "Kangri songs" as they stand are already linguistically and culturally hybrid, sharing themes with bodies of folk songs from other regions of India, there is clearly a new order of magnitude in the exogenously based cultural flows flooding through Kangra today. This is due to diverse factors such as heightened communications with the outer world, greater access to technology, the integration into a market economy that sends men off to work in increasingly distant places, and the spread of government-sponsored education for boys and girls. Clustered in a courtyard around ritual action, women singers regularly vied with both a wedding band and a scratchy loudspeaker blaring renditions of Hindi film songs. Song sessions were sometimes held up because neighboring women drifted in only after viewing *Chitrahaar* and *Chhāya Geet,* television programs of dizzying clips from assorted song-and-dance sequences in films. Increasingly, younger girls chorusing together at weddings sing songs in Hindi, or from Hindi films. "Filmi!" older women sitting beside me would whisper into my ear. "Shut off your tape recorder." (Occasionally, they themselves briskly snapped my microphone or the machine off.)

I now turn to a closer ethnography of several women and their relation—or lack thereof—to older Kangri songs of suffering. Though singing is most often a communal practice, women may sing to themselves in a variety of informal settings. My interest in songs frequently elicited solo performances, by women alone or in an appreciative group. In making sense of songs I had taped, I usually turned to singers for help. Their interpretive style was usually a narrative retelling and clarification of events in the song (see Narayan 1995).

SINGING AS SOLACE AND STRENGTH

"When I can't sleep at night, I lie there thinking about songs from old times," Tayi once confessed. "It gives me solace [*tasalli*]." In 1991, Tayi was in her seventies, a hunched woman with a bulbous nose, freckled face, and luminous brown eyes. She was universally Tayi, "Aunty"; I learned her name, Sita Devi Rana, only when I asked her for it, several weeks before I left. Married at twelve and widowed at fourteen, she had spent her life at the borders of the joint family in which her husband's younger brother is head of the household. Without children of her own, she was nonetheless central to household work and was respected for her knowledge of ritual and folk songs. "Child, there's sorrow in life and there's joy too," she said when I'd already heard a synopsis of her life story and asked if someday I could tape it. "According to your karma, you might be strong or you might be weak. People can take all kinds of things from you. If you're a widow like me, they take everything. But there is one thing that they can't take, and that is your heart [*dil*]. That's your own, that's yours. That's what you keep and what you can make nice." The heart, it seemed, was for Tayi the only inviolable home.

One of the ways of making a heart nice, according to Tayi, was through singing and storytelling. In these activities, she said, there was "wisdom and reflection." Repeatedly, when I reminded Tayi that I'd like to record her life story, she would lift my microphone and sing *pakhaṛu*. Here is a *pakhaṛu* Tayi recorded for me, her voice soft and quavering.[1]

chhoṭi dei ḍālnī bo
    nāpi baja jhūldī e

dhūpe jāndi kamalāi e

chiṭṭiye deie chādar o
mācchi kaḍe sītī e
kinnī chādar ditī o
kinnī chādar sītī e

bāpue chādar ditī o
ammā chādar sītī e
bhāi mere chādara bo
lāi ghare āiā e

ik man boldā o māe
roiā̃ ḍūbi marā e
duā man boldā o māe
bālak bares e

ik man boldā o māe
jahar khāi marā e
duā man boldā o māe
bālak bares e

ika bakh khāi chhodeyā o māe
jala diyā̃ jalakiye
duā bakh rahi giyā o māe
sapaḍe de heṭh e

ammā merī rondī o māe
bāpue mere jhūrade
bhāi mere topde o māe
nadiyā̃ de phere e

bhābho meri kholdi o māe
sire diyā̃ minḍiyā̃
bahanā meri roādi o māe
bāvā̃ diyā̃ joḍiyā̃

A small branch swings,
bent over with weight.
In strong sunshine, it wilts away.

A white veil
is embroidered with the fish stitch.

Who gave the veil?
        Who sewed the veil?

Father gave the veil.
        Mother sewed the veil.
My brother brought the veil
        to the house when he came.

One mind says, Oh mother,
        that drowning by the river bank,
                                I die.
Another mind says, Oh mother,
        I am but a child.

One mind says, Oh mother,
        that eating poison,
                                I die.
Another mind says, Oh mother,
        I am but a child.

One half was eaten, my mother,
        by fish in the water.
Another half is left, my mother,
        crushed beneath a boulder.

My mother weeps, oh mother,
        My father is in despair.
My brother searches, oh mother,
        circling the river.

My brother's wife opens out, oh mother,
        the tight braids in her hair.
My sister weeps, oh mother,
        cradling her arms.

We sat facing each other, legs drawn up on a wooden bench at one corner of the veranda. Other women of the household were transplanting rice, and Tayi's brother-in-law, Pratap Singh, was talking with a hired laborer of the untouchable cobbler caste. In keeping with my conviction that interpretive authority should be shared by eliciting oral literary criticism (Dundes 1966) from a performer, I asked Tayi what was happening in the song.

"In this?" asked Tayi, drawing out a *beedi* and lighting up. As an old and desexualized widow, she was the only woman I knew in Kangra who smoked publicly, even before her male relatives. "In this, she has been married off someplace. She probably says, 'I don't want to stay here.' But her mother and father say, 'You have to stay in this very place.'" Tayi went on to describe how the girl was so sad that she jumped into the water. Her description of the girl's two minds, and of the two halves of her dead body, reminded me of how often women described their identities as split between allegiances to their natal home and the home of their in-laws. "Her brother went looking for her," Tayi continued, "then her mother wept, her father wept, her sister-in-law and sister, they all wept. This was when they heard that half of her was eaten by the fish and the other half was left under the boulder. That's it. This is a song of sorrow."

"She would have been cremated," said Pratap Singh, a stocky man with thick glasses and a gravelly voice. He had unexpectedly turned his attention to us, somewhat to my embarrassment, for usually women sang far from the surveillance of men. "Cremated and then thrown into the water."

"Yes," Tayi said noncommittally. "What else?" Yet as I ran through the words of the song with her, it was clear that this was not a cremation, but a suicide: an ambiguous act that can be interpreted as a woman being pushed to desperation by social forces, or as asserting resistance by slicing short a life she does not want. "So the people from her in-laws' house didn't mourn her at all?" I asked.

"Why should they mourn? They'll get another," said Pratap Singh, taking charge of exegesis. Despite the Widow Remarriage Act passed by the colonial government in 1856, for Kangra Rajputs, as for most upper-caste north Indian villagers, a widower is expected to remarry, whereas a widow must live the rest of her life celibate and marginalized. As Tayi herself once remarked, if it had been she who died at fourteen, her husband might have married as many as six other women by this time. "She destroyed her parent's honor [*izzat*]," Pratap Singh continued. "When honor is destroyed, then parents' love goes, too."

Tayi said nothing. Instead, she started into another song in which a young widow paces back and forth, mourning her absent husband. The implicit link between the two songs led me to ask Tayi several weeks later whether the white veil being sewn for the depressed child bride meant that she had become a widow. The fish stitch on the veil, I thought, also foreshadowed the girl's eventual fate in the water. We were alone in the upstairs kitchen, and Tayi was washing yellow pumpkin blossoms for a vegetable dish. "That's it," agreed Tayi. "When a man dies, his widow receives white clothes from her parents' home. Her brother brings them. She will put these on following the tenth day clothes-washing ceremony after the death." Remembering how Pratap Singh had seen a different meaning in the song, I wondered afresh about the extent to which the prevalent belief that women sang from happiness was a form of what Radner and Lanser (1987) have called "feminist coding," allowing women to camouflage bitter critiques of the kinship structure.

Around a loose framework of songs like this, Tayi gradually told me more details about her past experiences. Her husband, a nineteen-year-old boy, had gone to look after the land in Montgomery (currently Pakistan) that the British government had given the family as a reward for his father's service in World War I. He had been there for some time, and was preparing to return with his possessions assembled, and his mattress tied up with a rope. But unknown attackers hung him from that rope and made off with his possessions. The news came by telegram. As Tayi said, she was only a child of fourteen. Not yet deeply attached to her husband, she did not at first understand what it meant for him to die. Yet his death radically altered her life. Pollution rules prescribed that she bathe in icy water each morning with other widows, and for the first year eat only once a day, even if hunger was afire in her stomach. "You get used to it," she said. "What else can you do?" Perhaps it was because a woman is seen as responsible for her husband's life, protecting it through fasts and rituals, that Tayi's mother-in-law was constantly angry at her son's widow. When work was completed at home, she would send young Tayi off to other people's houses to do their work. Since Tayi had no brother, there was no possibility of returning to her natal home. After a few years, though, her younger brother-in-law, Pratap Singh, married; thus there was another teenage girl in the house. "When she came, my sorrows lifted," said Tayi. "When there is someone to sympathize with, anything can be endured. We have lived together since then. Working together, raising children together." Looking into my sympathetically puckered face, Tayi laughed, adding, "Yes, and singing together. The men were often gone, and we looked after everything together."

Tayi's sister-in-law bore six children. In 1991, the eldest son, Dilip, was retired from the army and lived at home, from which he ran a trucking business. Another two sons were in the army, the daughters had been married away, and the youngest son was unmarried and in government service (he also lived at home). Dilip's wife, Meena Rana, an energetic woman of about forty, had a bawdy sense of humor and wide smile. She was notorious for her outrageous skits during the *giddā,* when the men of a settlement set off with a groom's party, leaving the women alone for a night of raucous merriment in costume. Meena, at birth, was an "extra or useless (*fāltu*) child"—that is, she was one daughter too many. Her mother had given her away to her sister, who, like Tayi, had been widowed young, before bearing children. However, unlike Tayi, this aunt, to whom Meena refers as Masi (mother's sister), had been terribly mistreated by the husband's family. They gave her nothing except a small room for herself, and she was miserably lonely. Adopting a bright little girl brought new energy to her life; she raised sheep and goats, sent Meena to school, showered affection upon her that perhaps lives on in Meena's extreme self-confidence. Yet like all girls, "born to be given away," Meena had to be married off. Now, with responsibilities in the house and on the land, Meena hardly ever sees her aunt-mother.

In December 1990, I accompanied Meena to a wedding at her parents' village—the place where she had been born but had not grown up. After the groom and other men had taken off by bus for the bride's faraway village, a carnival spirit erupted among the women. They dashed from house to house, veils thrown off, catching up on gossip, shouting with laughter, telling dirty jokes. One of the women had everyone in stitches as she described how a shopkeeper near her place had hung up three eggplants together, one long one flanked by two little bulbous ones, and how every woman who passed by had trouble keeping a straight face. At night there were songs and skits in which Meena was a prominent performer. Many of the skits involved phallic replacements—a spoon previously used by the Brahman to feed the sacred fire, a wooden stick used to thump out clothes, a cricket bat—threateningly poked toward the crotches of the groom's female relatives. Late into the night, I was requested to perform "a song from America—disco!" After much urging, I was pulled to my feet. In a fit of inspiration, I slipped a Bonnie Raitt cassette I had been carrying into my recorder. Several women gyrated around with me to the strains of "Love in the Nick of Time." Awkward, embarrassed, clearly disappointing my companions by not singing myself, I could not help smiling at the irony of playing a single American woman's song that derived from the pain of another set of life choices.

The next morning, a groggy group of us sat clustered in the morning sun, waiting for the groom's party to return. The married women all had their gold finery on—hoop earrings with three red stones, large nose rings, necklaces with a broad, flat, heart shape at the end. Perhaps it was the presence of the necklaces, usually locked up in trunks, that inspired one of the songs led by Meena, a chorus of other voices joining in.

darāni jeṭhāni doyo
pānie jo chaliyā̃
age milā bhāi parohnā e

pahale tā onde the bhāiyā
hanḍiyā par hanḍiyā
haṇ kajo bahanā basāri e

nere jāndiyā dhīyā̃ par dhīyā̃
dhīyā̃ par dhiyā̃
tāyi tā bahanā basāri e

gale dā kanḍiyā khoḍī
bhāiyā̃ jo ditā
idi kane dhiyā̃ byāhiyā e

jāndiyā nuā jo
sauhrā je puchhadā
gale dā kanḍiyā kuthu gavāyā e

gangā de nohne sauhriyā jī
jamnā de nohne
gale dā kanḍiyā othu gavāyā

desā pardesā te sauhre
dobe mangvāe
gale dā kanḍiyā najara ni āyā e

sach galayā ni nue
jhūṭ mat galāndī
gale dā kanḍiyā kuthu gavāyā e

sach galāngī jī sauhriyā
jhūṭ ni bolagī
gale dā kanḍiyā bhāie jo ditā

desā pardesā te sauhre
chunhāde mangvāe

nūh gori ḍagiyā chanāi e

uḍi jāiyā kāgā
tu de diyā saneh
bahanā tā ḍangiya chanāi e

rijhiyā rasoi
ḍholi je ditiyā
āi rahiā bahanā de dese e

ḍangeyā de puṭṭi
bahanā chikhā rachāi
bahanā jo dāh duhāyā e

Older and younger sisters-in-law both
set off to fetch water.
Up ahead they met the brother-guest.

"In the past, brother, you used to visit
often on foot.
Now why have you forgotten your sister?"

"Being born to me is daughter after daughter,
daughter after daughter
That's why I've forgotten my sister."

Unfastening her necklace,
she gives it to her brother.
"Marry off your daughters with this."

Returning home, the daughter-in-law is
asked by her father-in-law,
"Where did you lose your necklace?"

"I bathed in the Ganga, father-in-law,
I bathed in the Yamuna River, too:
that's where I lost my necklace."

From countries near and far, father-in-law
sent for divers.
The necklace wasn't to be seen.

"Speak the truth, daughter-in-law,
don't tell lies.

Where did you lose your necklace?"

"I'll tell the truth, father-in-law,
I won't tell lies.
I gave my brother the necklace."

From countries near and far, father-in-law
sent for masons.
The daughter-in-law, the beautiful one, was
bricked into the wall.

"Fly high, crow,
deliver the message.
Your sister is bricked into a wall."

The cooking food
he spilled over.
"I'm coming to my sister's country."

Smashing open the wall,
he prepared his sister's pyre,
He kindled the flame for her cremation.

It wasn't until July that I moved through a backlog of transcriptions to write out this song. By this time, I recognized it as a variant of the basket makers' ballad with the title "Kandi" ("necklace," which in the *dholru* is also the heroine's name [Vyathit 1980:34–37]). I walked through the glare of the afternoon to visit the Pratap Singh household. Meena was tending the cattle. Later, she came in, adjusting her veil in the presence of her father-in-law. I read aloud lines of text to check them with her, as Meena nodded her head. The heroine of this song, it seemed, had gone out with a group of daughters-in-law to fetch water, and intercepted her brother as he entered the village. This song, like the last, plays upon a woman's dual allegiances to both natal and marriage families. Although her brother has forgotten her, she has remained loyal to him. Tayi said, "He was caught up in the entrapping illusion [*māyā*] of his own children." Meena elaborated, "His thoughts were with his responsibilities to his children. So many daughters and a man becomes poor. He has to pay for their weddings. So his sister takes off her necklace and gives it to him."

So many daughters and a man becomes poor. Hearing this, I thought of the slogan used for advertising sex-determination clinics in Kangra towns and the rest of India: "Rs. 500 now or 50,000 later." That is, 500 rupees for learning the identity of a girl child and aborting her, or 50,000 rupees for her marriage in less than twenty years. Although female infanticide was practiced among high-ranking Rajputs in the past (the great-granddaughter of a midwife recalled the pit dug during labor to immediately dispose of a girl child), this was because of hypergamy and the loss of honor entailed in acknowledging one's inferiority in relation to the family one's daughter married into (Parry 1979:213–21). This song seemed to touch on the negative evaluation of female identity both in the natal home, where a daughter is a burden, and in the in-laws' house, where she is dispensable. I asked why the father-in-law was so cavalier in bricking up his daughter-in-law alive. "For a girl from another's house, why should a father-in-law care?" inquired Meena. With this rhetorical question, she wiped the sweat off her face and set about trying to persuade her teenage daughter to accompany her to the fields. What the father-in-law did care about, it seemed, was nonrenewable property like the heroine's necklace, over which he assumed control. Her brother, on the other hand, cared enough to come at once and give his sister a proper cremation. While pollution beliefs require that boiled food be spilled over and the hearth extinguished at news of a relative's death, in the context of this song, I couldn't help likening the spilled food to the uselessly wasted life of a woman devalued by her in-laws.

The violence turned toward a woman by herself or by those around her surfaced in many songs' texts: if it wasn't suicide, a woman was bricked up by her father-in-law, poisoned by her mother-in-law, beaten by her husband. Yet in all these songs that described women as dispensable, the subjective perspective from which the tales were sung simultaneously denied that women were merely objects. The dominant Hindu ideology of women's *pativrata* unquestioning, one-pointed devotion toward and service of the husband and his kin—was put into an ironic frame in such texts: first, the woman's allegiances to her natal family remained highlighted, and second, husbands and their relatives were held culpable for mistreatment. In many songs, the woman did not merely suffer; she sought active ways to change the situation or to wreak revenge on her husband.

I now turn to my last example from Tayi, an unusual song in which an abandoned wife dresses as a man to abduct a mate. Tayi sang this song several days after I'd taped the first, one afternoon as we sat upstairs.

phūl khile phulvāṛī
gori khile ghar apane

jis dhiyāḍe tusā̃ chalde naukarī
mahalā̃ di chaḍhi jānde jandare

mahalā̃ di chaḍhi jānde jandare
bāgānde suki jānde gaṭo pyāre

bārāh tā barasā̃ giyā je hoiyā̃
kucch nahī̃ karde vo vichār pyāre

maradāne siyāndi māi kapaṛe
līle di hoi savārā pyāre

age tā jāndi tīn jane haṭṭiyā
baiṭeyo
karde vo vichār mera pyāre

haṭteyā baiṭheyo banye
tusā̃ kīyā̃ mainjar lāe merā pyāre

ika kahandā hai marad
dūyā̃ kahandā o nār pyāre

ghoṛe te utari gorie
bāe ta pakarī ghoṛi charhāndī

ghore charhānde mūṛhade
mūṛhi ghare jo ānde o pyāre

mahale de khuli jānde jandare
bagānde khiri jānde gaṭo pyāre

gaṭ khili gaṭavāḍiyā
gori khile ghar apane

Flowers blossom in the garden.
The Beautiful One blossoms
in her own home.

The day you go off for work,
The palace house is abandoned
with locks.

The palace house is abandoned with locks.
In the garden, marigolds
wither, my love.

Twelve years pass by,
you never think
of me, my love.

I sew men's clothes
and climb astride
a gray horse, my love.

Proceeding ahead to a shop where
three men sit,
They are pondering
over me, my love.

"Oh, shopkeeper, sitting in the shop,
What are you
discussing?" My love.

"One says, "You're a man,"
the second says, "You're
a woman." My love.

The Beautiful One gets off her horse,
grabs his arm,
seating him on the horse.

Seating him on the horse, she turns.
Turns around, bringing
him home, my love.

The palace house is unlocked.
In the garden, marigolds
blossom, my love.

Marigolds blossom in the marigold garden.
The Beautiful One blossoms
in her own home.

"Like this," finished Tayi.

"And this is a *pakhaṛu?*" I coaxed, "In this, a man goes away . . . ?"

"The man went away," Tayi summarized. "He didn't come back for twelve years. The house was locked up, and flowers withered in the garden. Similarly, Gori, the Beautiful One, withered in her parents' home."

I nodded, thinking of, but not voicing aloud, A. K. Ramanujan's (1991) argument that in South Asian symbolic systems, women and women's genitals are equated with flowers. The abandoned woman withers as she loses her identity as wife, becoming an ambiguous spinster-widow in her parents' home. Similarly, her sexuality withers. An anomalous female, she takes on a transvestite disguise—clothes, horse, "staff"—to accomplish what she desires in the public male sphere.

Tayi continued, "For twelve years, she thought, 'he has no thoughts of me.' Then she sewed man's clothes and took a gray horse. She set off to look for him, with a staff in hand. When she traveled ahead, she saw him sitting in a shop in a distant region. There were three men sitting there. One said, 'This is a man.' Another said, 'This is a woman.' She asked, 'You three people sitting in the shop, what are you thinking about me?' He said, 'One says you're a woman, and the other says you're a man.' "

The man who acknowledges the woman's dual nature is the man whom she recognizes as the one she wants to bring home. It is never made clear whether this is the woman's absent husband, who for twelve years did not think of her; however, this man is now clearly puzzling over her, and it is he whom the heroine abducts, acting as a man to reclaim her identity as sexual woman. "She grabbed him by the arm and sat him down on the horse," said Tayi. "She brought him home. When she brought him home, the locks were opened up. The flowers that had withered in the garden became green again. She, too, was happy that she had returned home. This is what happened." Tayi laughed, freckled face stretching out in a triumphant grin.

FROM SONGS TO BOOKS, MAGAZINES, RADIO, TELEVISION

While my research centered on women who knew beautiful songs such as these, throughout my stay in Kangra, I constantly met women and girls who did not know, and were not interested in, such songs. My closest friend, Vidhya, for example, was an educated young woman who could, if pressed, mumble along with some of the most frequently sung ritual songs. Mostly, though, she prided herself on not knowing any of these "old" songs.

Vidhya and I had met during my first summer visit to Kangra, when I was fifteen, about to take my school-leaving examinations, and she was eighteen, working on a correspondence course for a Hindi degree equivalent to a B.A. We used to walk together in the evenings, whispering and wondering in Hindi about her forthcoming arranged marriage. Now she was a housewife, living with her schoolteacher husband and two sons in a new cement house complete with a chiming doorbell, kitchen counter for gas, and a television. There was a hearth at one corner of the narrow kitchen, and water still had to be fetched from the stream down the hill or the tap by the road. Her mother-in-law had died about a week before I arrived in 1990, and her husband's brothers were all working in administrative jobs elsewhere, so the old joint family courtyard with mud buildings stood deserted with locks on the doors.

A tall, angular woman of thirty-three with close-set, alert black eyes, and a perpetually amused expression, Vidhya was my window into another mode of being a woman in Kangra. Though she attended song sessions for neighbors and relatives, and though she welcomed the chance to earn something by being my assistant, helping with transcriptions, she frankly acknowledged that these local songs did not mean much to her. Reading and television framed her imaginative life. Magazines and books are increasingly expensive in India, so all that Vidhya had to read was the daily Hindi paper, the Hindi *Griha shobha* (Household Beauty) magazine that came once a month, and Hindi novels that her husband occasionally brought home from the high school library.

As with many of the other women I worked with, I became a recipient of confidences only when I, too, had spoken frankly. For example, one sweltering afternoon in June, I walked to Vidhya's in a listless fog. Her husband happened to be home and greeted me with his usual kindness. Later, she escorted me as far as the communal tap, and squatted on a grassy strip for a chat. I told her how trapped I felt by my work, how hard it was to keep forcing myself out to see people and to keep up the discipline of transcribing tapes. I confessed that I had just taken refuge in a light novel. Vidhya laughed, commenting that to everyone a daily routine must sometimes become unbearable. She went on to say, "At night, if I don't read even a little, I can't get to sleep. When the *Griha shobha* comes, I read it all in one day. I tell myself to save it for the whole month, but I can't stop reading. When anyone comes to visit, I have to put down the magazine. 'Why did they have to come just now?' I think. Then, when the children come home and disturb me, I whack them! It's the same with novels. Once I start, I don't want to do anything else. I don't want to cook or wash clothes or anything. I have to read the last page first, just to assure myself that the hero and heroine are still alive, that everything is all right. After that I read every page. . . . I also read the entire newspaper."

What gender representations resided in these media? Flipping through her newspaper during my visits, I found that degenerate Western women were often used to index India's distinctive national identity as framed around chaste and modest *pativrata* women. There were front-page news items about such varied topics as an American brother and sister who married one another and were now being sued by their child; Raquel Welch's cleavage being shamelessly displayed at her child's wedding; the love life of Steffi Graf. Also, the *Griha shobha* magazine, subscribed to in several of the aspiring middle-class households I visited, carried articles on such topics as "Why women don't like to be touched" and "How to respond if your husband teases you" (accept it silently, even if he is joking about how you have been verbally molested in a public place). As we rested together on a double bed under the whirring electric fan one afternoon, Vidhya repeated with shining eyes a short story she had just read in the magazine. The story was titled "*Putradān*" (gift of a son), playing upon the central part of a Hindu wedding ceremony, *Kanyādān,* the gift of a virgin. I summarize Vidhya's retelling from my notes:

> A man and a woman meet in an office where they both work. The woman sets the condition that they will be married only if the wedding entails the gift of a son rather than of a virgin. After marriage, the man comes to live with the woman's parents and serves them as a new daughter-in-law would. He rushes home from work to make tea and serve it to everyone; he does the cooking. After a while the wife begins to despise him for serving tea rather than acting as a man should. So then she gives up her job and they both go to live in their own house, where she thereafter looks after him as a good wife should, and they live happily.

"But the message here is that a man shouldn't do any housework," I said, uncomfortable with the story's ending. "I think this is a dangerous story." Vidhya shook her head, as though I quite missed the point. "No, how can there be a gift of a son?" she inquired. "It's always been a girl who's gifted. How can this change now?" Cherishing our friendship too much for a showdown, I silently thought of the time that I outlined the principle of a couple sharing housework, and Vidhya disagreed. "A man is a man, after all," she had vehemently stated. "He *must* be served." I wrote in my field notes that evening, "I decided not to argue. Even as dear friends we don't see eye to eye on certain points, like men's role as superior, women's place in the house, the necessity of a cement house and a television. . . ."

The television had a place of honor in the front room. Because of the hills around, reception was frequently blurred. Vidhya liked to take a break in the middle of the afternoon so that she could watch a program for housewives. I would sometimes stay, feeling disoriented, as Vidhya avidly took in demonstrations on how to make dainty party sandwiches (which had no place in regional cuisine, in which rolled *rotis* or yeasted *baturus* were eaten) or how to cut decorations from kinds of colored paper one could never buy in the village. In the evenings, Vidhya watched serials, which she greatly enjoyed. These television programs were state monitored, and as Mankekar has observed in her brilliant analysis of television serial watchers in Delhi, the programs promoted a nationalist vision of the Indian woman as a modest, self-sacrificing, middle-class citizen (Mankekar 1993).

Vidhya also loved the radio and Hindi film songs broadcast on it. A genre that brings together Indian classical music, Indian folk music from many regions, and generously mixes in Western pop, rock, disco, rap, and musical instruments and technologies, Hindi film music is deeply hybrid (Manuel 1993:37–59; Marre and Charlton 1985). Sometimes I would arrive to find Vidhya singing to herself in a piercing, high voice reminiscent of film music styles. Though these film songs drew on folk music for inspiration, they did not carry the bitter edge of songs like *pakharu*. Instead, they were largely sentimental and romantic creations of male songwriters—S. D. Burman, Kalyanji, Anandji, Lakshmikant, Pyarelal, and so on—in urban centers. "I have new-new bangles on my hands," was the titillating hit sung everywhere in Kangra in 1990, referring to a bride's attire. "Wait a little, lover, I'm helpless."

The older women with whom I talked were articulate about these changing tastes. "I don't like today's songs," said Tayi. "The girls are in too much of a hurry with their drums. To really sing, you must be tranquil." Another time she stated that the film songs or film-derived songs sung by girls had no wisdom in them (unlike old songs, which did). "My songs aren't film songs," stated eighty-year-old Janaki Devi proudly after I'd been taping jewels of her repertoire. She sniffed, "Humph, *filmi!*" Brinda Devi, another prolific singer, linked the decline of older songs to the shrinking of rituals as more people were drawn into participation in the capitalist workforce. "In the past, weddings would go on for seven to eight days," she said. "We could sit together and sing at our leisure for a full seven or eight days. Now a wedding is over in a day and a half. Where is the singing in that? That's why songs are being forgotten." Her sister, a schoolteacher who did not sing much but was sympathetic to her sister's songs, discerned a border separating the tastes of generations: "The new generation doesn't go on the same road as women in the past. This is why they don't see the truth in these songs. They don't sing them."

There was a Pahari song program on the local radio, with recordings of local songs done by semiprofessional singers in studios. Similarly, Pahari songs (especially dance songs) were taught for performance on the stage in state-sponsored, Hindi local schools. Although Vidhya was frankly not interested in such programs, other young women I met proudly sang set pieces they had picked up from these contexts. However, when songs had been acquired as a set piece of "Kangra culture," singers simply did not have the same kind of engagement as when these were (in the words of a middle-aged schoolteacher) "our life story." Local songs thus were turned into experience-distant quaintness rather than meaningful women's experience; they were bracketed as irrelevant to the "modern" world.

What is to be made of this shift? In a stimulating recent volume, *Recasting Women: Essays in Colonial History,* essays by various Indian historians trace the emergence of a revised form of patriarchy in nineteenth-century India as British colonizers and the indigenous elite sought to redefine an essential "tradition" of which women became emblematic (Sangari and Vaid 1989). Expanding on an earlier article (1989a), in this collection Partha Chatterji (1989b) describes the emergence of the "new" woman as Bengali nationalist discourse responded to colonial charges that Indian tradition was oppressive and barbaric to women. The new, middle-class woman was associated with spiritual refinement and interior spaces (as opposed to Western materialism and the public realm within which their men transacted); she stood for a sanitized tradition that marked India's distinctive essence. Part of her cultivation involved education in a corpus of male-monitored texts in her mother tongue. This education marked Indian women as different from and superior to Western women, older uneducated women, and women of the lower classes (Chatterji 1989b:246). Sumanta Banerjee (1989) expands on how this cultivated women became separated from the lively oral traditions associated with women of lower classes, and how, in turn, through lack of patronage and active suppression, these women's oral traditions were marginalized. He acknowledges that education allowed middle-class women access to a male intellectual sphere even as it served to cultivate a particular construction of womanhood.

> But in the process she lost something else—the potent and vigorous language of women's popular and folk cultural forms, the nimble-witted drollery and gusto that her mothers and grandmothers shared

> with the *panchali* singers and the *jhumur* dances [folklore forms associated with lower class women] of the past. (Banerjee, 1989:168)

While it is sometimes said in jest that "what Bengal thinks today the rest of India will think tomorrow," the process described by Banerjee for nineteenth-century Bengal appears to be extending to Kangra in the late twentieth century. Unlike their Bengali city counterparts a hundred years earlier, Kangra village women have tended to perform together in caste-specific groups rather than relying on a woman's culture purveyed by female entertainers. However, with integration into the state through education, the media, and the market economy, the emerging upper-caste, middle-class women like Vidhya appeared to be subscribing to an evolving nationalist-based construction of cultivated womanhood that does not have a place for a subversive women's folk culture.[2]

CONTINUITIES IN WOMEN'S SUBORDINATION AND THE REDISCOVERY OF SONGS

Can it be that songs of suffering are growing less popular among women because suffering is no longer relevant to women's lives? This was an issue I often wondered about, especially because, when I questioned women about the meanings of particular songs, they often said that things had been this bad in the past, but were not so at present. Can it be that younger woman are not singing such songs because their positions have improved so much that they have nothing to complain about? Do the songs depict a vanished world of patriarchal relations that no longer apply?

Certainly, most of the women I spoke to felt that the condition of women generally had improved with better transport facilities, running water brought in taps closer to the houses, and access to medical care. Amniocentesis or ultrasound technology followed by abortion of female fetuses notwithstanding, many women felt that being able to control fertility was an important advance (though I should add that reproductive decisions were made by the husband and his family). Also, though many expressed frustration that there were few paid jobs for women available, women were increasingly working in banks, schools, and post offices. Increased population pressures, however, meant that even these small employment possibilities were tightening. Explaining why none of her daughters or daughters-in-law worked, Bimlesh Kanta, a primary schoolteacher in her sixties queried, "If even boys aren't getting jobs, who's going to give them to girls?"

Although the condition of women was generally said to be better, the condition of daughters-in-law in particular was often stated to have dramatically improved. "The mothers-in-law of the past" were often said by older women to have been extremely strict. Though I do not reproduce any songs with a cruel mother-in-law here, she was a stock character in many *pakhaṛu*. Time and again, commentaries on songs elicited the statement that mothers-in-law of the past used to stick their daughters-in-law's hands in the fire if displeased. Many women said that now that girls were married off later, after having had some schooling, and there were improved forms of communication and transport with their homes of birth, no mother-in-law would dare do such wicked things. In singing such songs, then, older women were sometimes claiming a moral authority for having survived more arduous times. As Brinda Devi said, "Suppose I bring a daughter-in-law here tomorrow. She'll say, 'Hah! My mother-in-law is terrible! She does this, she does that.' But if I convey these songs to her, then it'll come into her brain, 'Oh, no! Oh, brother! These people had even worse times than me. My situation is good after all! I shouldn't carry on this way.' It's for this reason that stories of the past, the songs of the past, should be listened to, should be sung, transmitted from one person to another, so the singers can say, 'Look at the hardships! These are such wonderful songs. Such touching songs!'"

Some of the practices described in the songs—women tightly braiding their hair, men riding off to work on horses, brothers walking miles to visit a sister, daughters-in-law setting off in a cluster to the village well—have waned. Yet the dual, kin-based identity, the precarious and subordinate position in patriarchal structures described in *pakhaṛu,* have not drastically changed. Marriage and the birth of male children still remain the central, idealized events in a woman's life, even if this woman happens to be educated. Marriages continue to be arranged, and even in the rare cases where women work outside the home, at home they continue to do the domestic work.

Discussing songs with Kangra women, whenever I probed the quick displacement of women's pain to the past alone, most women—even Vidhya, helping me transcribe—would end up agreeing that things weren't all that great today. In the songs discussed here, Tayi and Meena gave their interpretations in the present tense. Yet in other cases, interpretations pointed to the past. For example, after singing about a husband who comes home after twelve years and responds to his wife's joyful meal preparation with irrational anger, Sudha Sud, a schoolteacher in her forties, stated that such things had often happened in the past. "Not now as well?" I asked. "Even now women really are attentive," Brinda Devi, Sudha's serene elder sister put in. "But men, there is some real arrogance in them. They don't give a damn [*nahī̃ mārdā prabhāv*]. Then that irritation burns inside a woman as rage. But what else can she do? She can't do anything about it."

Another time, Sudha and Brinda Devi had together sung a song with the line "You've given birth to girls, mother, now don't give birth to any more," spoken by a son after he has visited a miserable sister in her married home. Commenting on this song, Sudha first said that in the past, boys were preferred because a woman's life was so hard. I immediately thought of families I knew who drew on Western technologies of sex determination now available in Kangra to abort female fetuses; of a local doctor's poignant testimony about the selective neglect of female children (see B. Miller 1981). I asked whether boys weren't still favored. Questioned, Sudha shifted tones. "In the last census you've seen it!" she declared. "Women's rates are down." Indeed, the 1991 census of India found that there were currently 92.9 females for every 100 males, a drop from 93.4 in 1981, which was a staggering number of missing women in a population of 850 million. In short, many songs of suffering contain within them the seeds of critique for present circumstances.

Competing discourses on gender in India today include urban-based feminist movements with the explicit goals not just of critique but of change. Reading Madhu Kishwar's introduction to a collection of articles reprinted from the progressive women's journal *Manushi*, I thought of the irony of striving to create a forum for women to get together and pool experiences when in the villages such practices based around singing are gradually being rejected. She writes:

> . . . getting women together into informal associations, especially those from peasant households, even to start by exchanging stories or engaging in similar activities, is a major step forward. This may slowly build a tradition of women coming together to discuss issues of common concern, relating to each other as women who have common problems and objectives, and developing associations independent of the family. In these and other ways they will finally recognize themselves as independent human beings with inherent human rights. (*Kishwar* 1984:44)

Singing among women certainly involves gathering, pooling common issues, and relating to each other along a plane of shared gender inequalities. Describing a Greek women's lament genre, for example, Anna Caraveli points out that this singing expresses protest in a "poetic voice that recognizes a 'sisterhood of pain' among women, a sense of communal victimization inflicted by either social or natural forces" (1986:181–82). In some respects, such a communal pooling of grievances is akin to the Western feminist practice of "consciousness-raising," which Chris Weedon has described as allowing women "the possibility of interpreting difficulties, problems and inadequacies not as an effect of individual, personal failings, but as a result of socially produced structures" (1987:85). Also, following Norma Alarcón's critique of consciousness-raising, women's singing serves to constitute a feminine subject in opposition to a male one, so that one is likely to "lose sight of the complex and multiple ways in which the subject and object of possible experience are constituted" (1989:361). Collective singing in a village setting, however, differs from consciousness-raising in that instead of actively instigating change through gender solidarity, the singing appears to help women adapt to the constraints placed on their lives while serving as a powerful emotional catharsis. While I only occasionally observed women moved to tears by song, in other parts of India collective singing and weeping about the plight of women in patriarchy go hand in hand. Vanaja Dhruvarajan, an anthropologist, describes singing among Vokkaliga women in a Karnataka village in South India.

> On rare occasions they get together and sing folk songs, the themes of which range from the sorrow felt by parents when the daughters leave the *thavaru* after marriage, brother-sister love, and the agonies suffered by the young bride in the new home to the general predicament of being women. These women get so involved in this singing that most of them cry continuously as the singing is going on. When asked why they did this, the answer was that they felt that they themselves were going through these experiences all over again. (Dhruvarajan 1989:55–56)

The emotional force of such singing among women has inspired some Indian activist groups to use songs as part of an explicit agenda of mobilization for change. The introduction to a Hindi songbook put out by the women's group Jagori acknowledges that women's folk songs have been a medium to express hardships and unfulfilled desires, and goes on to state the importance of singing for the woman's movement. "In these songs we have planted new aspirations and increased our unity, our sense of strength" (Jagori 1990:iii–iv). Though deriving from a folk-song model, the Hindi songs in this collection are different from most folk songs in that they have named authors like Kamla Bhasin and Vibhuti Patel; further, in a strategic use of the ubiquity of film-song culture, most songs' tunes are identified with film hits, such as "My Shoes Are from Japan" (*mere jūte hai jāpāni*). As Madhu Kishwar writes, "Our cultural traditions have tremendous potential within them to combat reactionary and anti-women ideas, if we can identify their points of strength and use them creatively" (1984:47).

CONCLUSION

At a moment when the myth of the exotic has exploded, releasing anthropologists to study continuities between "us" and "them," much important new work examines topics such as diasporic communities, fractured identities, capitalist incursions, metropolitan centers, transregional and transnational flows. In this exciting context of attention to the movement of populations, finance, technologies, ideologies, and the media, articulated most forcefully by Arjun Appadurai in a brilliant series of articles (1990, 1991a, 1991b), it may well seem regressive to pay attention to old women living in remote villages and singing folk songs set in a past era. As Appadurai writes in the afterword of a collection of essays on South Asian folklore, "it may be the idea of a folk world in need of conservation that must be rejected so that there can be a vigorous engagement with the hybrid forms of the world we live in now" (1991a:474). From this vantage, it might seem more relevant to the contemporary world if my scholarly attention were trained on members of the younger generation like gap-toothed, seven-year-old Goma, who, coaxed to sing by adoring sisters, belted out, "I yam a deesco dancer." For me, a partial member of the Indian urban elite and also the metropolitan West, collecting old songs could well be cast as a misguided reinvention of (neo) "imperialist nostalgia" (R. Rosaldo 1989:68–87) and salvage ethnography (Clifford 1989a) that involves mourning and preserving precisely what has been destroyed by the incursion of aliens indexed by an ethnographer's presence.

Yet it is also becoming clear that the recent reorientations of theory to account for transcultural flows need not extend to a complete overhaul in the loci of anthropological research. As Sherry Ortner has cautioned, "by focussing heavily on the points at which 'we' and 'they' intersect . . . we run the danger of implicitly denying the validity or at least the interest, of the worlds of other peoples prior to, or apart from the operations of capitalism, colonialism, or other forms of Western 'penetration'" (1991:186). At this historical moment in which the flows of public culture are rightly included in our analytic frameworks, we must reframe our understandings of the ensuing transformations of cultural knowledge within marginalized communities. Villagers, the aged, women, and folk traditions can also be viewed through lenses of movement and flux, and songs like *pakhaṛu* can be revisioned as irrevocably hybrid and fluid forms rather than as tokens of a frozen, authentic culture associated with a monolithic "folk." We must heed the agency of performers who purvey these traditions as one discourse among a range of coexisting discourses, some locally based, some originating in faraway cultural centers. As Hermann Bausinger has shown in his *Folk Culture in a World of Technology* (1990), technological transformations do not erase folklore but, rather, reframe it in the context of widening horizons of experience that often can lead to an increased self-consciousness about the relationship between folklore and local identity. As Lila Abu-Lughod (1991) has elegantly argued, changes in the modes of resistance dramatized through expressive culture point to changing configurations of power that frame people's lives.

I fear that too single-minded an engagement with emergent cultural forms may lead us increasingly to attend to public male metropolitan genres while overlooking marginalized, ebbing residual knowledges that are the domain of the elderly, peasants, and women. As Appadurai writes in regard to changing agricultural practices and the loss of traditional knowledge among farmers in rural India, "the only valid justification for the wholesale violation and transformation of a traditional way of knowing is if it is accompanied by a widely shared and perceived increase in well-being for the communities whose mental life is being transformed" (1988b:184). Appadurai sees no such increased well-being in the lives of small-scale male farmers or the women in their families, who are losing older forms of self-reliance and cooperation with the incursion of Western technologies. And, as Appadurai states, "knowledge lost . . . is choice foregone" (1988b:177). What is argued for agricultural knowledge holds also for women's knowledge in a patriarchal society. While women's songs of suffering may appear to be "residual" in Raymond Williams' (1977:121–27; 1991:415–17) sense of being rooted to a past social formation, the constraints and injustices around women's lives have not been changed. In voicing an alternative, women-based perspective on society, and sometimes swelling into an actively oppositional critique of dominant patriarchal values, it appears to me that such songs remain relevant to women's experience even as cultural flows from within and outside the state are displacing their imaginative hold. I like to hope that documenting such songs might have relevance to activist movements within India that seek to improve women's social condition, and not merely to Western theories of scholarship (see Mani 1990).

To reiterate the contrast evoked through the ethnography in this essay, I give the last word to two women in Kangra: one who viewed songs of suffering as tied to lived experience, another who saw such songs as old-fashioned cultural artifacts.

Crouched on the wooden bench the same afternoon in 1991 that she had sung about the child widow's suicide, Tayi observed, "You sing about this pain in your heart [*dil*]. Then you get some solace in your heart, that there have been hard times like this for others in the past. It's good to sing songs about pain. They make you remember." After reflecting that the old songs were "full of the past," Tayi went on to say, "Any matters of the past that you've heard and that are good, you should keep passing those along. Take you and me: I should make you understand these things. How are you to know what things have occurred in the past? I should make these take a seat in your heart. Then you'll have solace that these sorts of matters have taken place. . . . A lot of matters are forgotten along with people. But we singers don't forget the matters of the past. We don't forget the old songs. No one forgets matters close to their hearts. I'm an old woman now, but my memory, it's fresh."[3]

Having taped a Pahari song that Sunita, an M.A.-educated young woman had learned from the radio and sang in the high-pitched voice of the films, I prepared to record her ninety-seven-year-old, bedridden grandmother. A woman singer in her fifties had brought me to this village of her birth, urging that I tape the old woman's long, complex songs. Sunita did not know her grandmother's songs. As I fiddled with my cassettes, Sunita mused aloud in Hindi, using the English word "culture." "This is our 'culture,'" she earnestly observed. She turned to a neighbor who had come by, adding, "I suppose it's true that if you lose your 'culture,' it's hard to get it back again."

NOTES

Though personal ties have taken me to Kangra since 1975, the formal fieldwork on which this essay is based took place between September 1990 and September 1991. I am grateful for support from the University of Wisconsin Graduate School funds, an American Institute of Indian Studies Senior Fellowship, and a National Endowment for the Humanities Fellowship. I am also very grateful for the time to write granted by the School of American Research, the Social Science Research Council, the John Simon Guggenheim Foundation, and the University of Wisconsin Graduate School. Thanks to Eytan Bercovitch, Eyal Ben-Ari, Didi Contractor, Richard Flores, Brian Greenberg, Sharon Hutchinson, Smadar Lavie, Maria Lepowsky, Margaret Mills, Ted Swedenburg, and Anna Tsing for their critical readings of this or earlier versions. The extended version published here was finished in 1992, and now, revising in 1995, I regret that I cannot incorporate all the relevant references that have amassed in the last few years.

1 Though Tayi sang this alone and I did not subsequently tape the song from any other women, it appears, in several variants, in earlier song collections made in Kangra by M. S. Randhawa in 1959–61 and by Dr. Gautam Sharma Vyathit in the early 1970s (Randhawa 1963:246–47, 298–99, 300–301; Vyathit 1973:142–43).

2 While this paper focuses on upper-caste women, preliminary explorations with lower-caste women, particularly untouchables, suggests that lower castes may be adopting upper-caste songs made available to them through education, radio programs, and tapes. But this is the subject of another paper.

3 It is with sadness that I revise this paper, knowing that Tayi died in 1993, of cancer of the mouth.

"CULTURAL DEFENSE" AND CRIMINOLOGICAL DISPLACEMENTS: GENDER, RACE, AND (TRANS)NATION IN THE LEGAL SURVEILLANCE OF U.S. DIASPORA ASIANS

KRISTIN KOPTIUCH

> The pleasure of criminology is to displace the Other's unfixed pleasure into the pain of a certain victim and to master her, to keep an eye on her, to induce her to confess herself the proper subject of the law. (Pfohl and Gordon 1987:229)

In 1988 in Brooklyn, New York, Dong Lu Chen, a Chinese immigrant employed as a dishwasher and garment worker, pled guilty to a charge of manslaughter of his allegedly adulterous wife, Jian Wan Chen, also a garment industry worker. In a nonjury trial, Brooklyn Supreme Court Judge Edward Pincus reduced a murder charge to manslaughter and gave Mr. Chen the lightest possible sentence, five years' probation. The judge adjudicated the case in accordance with the defense attorney's argument that the man's uncontrollable violence was driven by "traditional" Chinese notions about the shame infidelity casts upon a husband and his ancestors. Clinching the case was the "expert witness" testimony provided by a white male anthropologist, Burton Pasternak of Hunter College, whose "forceful appearance" persuaded the judge that the immigrant could not escape his originary cultural formation, and hence his actions were culturally excusable (that it is unlawful for a man to murder his wife in contemporary China was apparently beyond the "facts of the case"). Had Chen been residing in his native country, the expert on China surmised, community and kin most likely would have checked the violent reaction provoked by the infringement of his honor. Since such a check was evidently unavailable to Mr. Chen in the United States (begging the question of an enormous Chinese diaspora here), the judicial decision allowed that he could hardly be held entirely responsible for the untoward effects of his culturally prescribed behavior—unfortunately for Mrs. Chen.[1]

The Brooklyn district attorney at the time, Elizabeth Holtzman, whose office was prosecuting the case, issued an angry statement in opposition to Mr. Chen's sentence:

> There should be one standard of justice—not one that depends on the cultural background of a defendant. There may be ***barbaric customs*** in ***various parts of the world***—that cannot excuse criminal conduct here. Anyone who comes to this country must be prepared to live by and obey our laws. And people like Mrs. Chen are entitled to the protection of our laws. This sentence suggests that women's lives, and particularly minority women's lives, are not valued. (emphasis added)

Holtzman's statement certainly redresses the more obviously egregious implications of a double-standard system of justice with respect to gender inequity. Yet the broader logic of her argument implicitly rests on assumptions about cultural difference that can scarcely be differentiated from those at work in the judgment she castigates. Though here scourged (in the voice of white liberal feminism) rather than (paternalistically) patronized, "barbaric customs" are nonetheless attributed to "various [but always elsewhere] parts of the world." This oppositional stance reverses from positive to negative the assessment of "cultural difference" proposed by Mr. Chen's attorney, but it leaves intact many categories of an anachronistic colonial discourse that underpin much of the current debate on race, ethnicity, and gender in a discourse on nation. Holtzman's position also leaves open a lingering legacy that once justified colonial interventions in other worlds: like their colonial predecessors, the great White Men of U.S. criminal justice—who need be neither white nor, as in this case, men, because "White Men" figures a subject-positioning with a specific code of behavior and particular "way of seeing" rather than a genital or racial accident of birth (Doyle 1992:68; Said 1978:227)—have a self-appointed mission to save minority women from minority men.

I wish to develop in this essay a framework for situating a critical cultural study of the broader ramifications of the novel legal strategy known as a "cultural defense," as exemplified in *People* v *Chen*. In the cultural defense, gender violence ordinarily criminalized by U.S. legal science is redefined as "ritual" by authority of anthropological science, and is said to require exceptional standards of judgment. Starting in the mid-1980s, a cultural defense led to substantially reduced culpability and penalties levied against immigrant defendants in several (mostly nonjury) trials. I stress that although judges have not yet formally recognized a cultural defense in any of these cases, the mitigation of criminal charges and leniency in sentencing in all instances indicate that judges' decisions were strongly influenced by defense attorneys' arguments that their clients' unrestrained violence was driven by primordial, culturally prescribed "customary law" radically incommensurate with U.S. juridical norms. Such decisions alert us to the insidious reemergence of an antiquated cultural relativism readied to validate gender and racial/ethnic inequalities in the name of sensitivity to "cultural diversity." It is a bit uncanny to find a colonial discourse operating full swing in a so-called postcolonial age. Yet I take such a discourse to underwrite an emerging cultural debate over the applicability of U.S. criminal law to select groups of recent immigrants in America's diasporas. My project is to intervene in this debate by tracking the historical genealogy of the unacknowledged colonial shadow that darkly haunts uncritical exuberance about the liberatory potential of "multiculturalism" within the law.

In its premise, a cultural defense takes exception to the tried-and-true legal principle "Ignorance is no excuse," on the grounds that the law's universal juridical subject, the ordinary (white, bourgeois) "reasonable man," fails to accommodate the multicultural heterogeneity of the nation today. Yet it is intriguing to note that thus far the application of the cultural defense has been highly selective. Overwhelmingly, immigrant defendants have been, like Mr. Chen, Pacific Rim Asian men (from China, Japan, Laos, Vietnam). Their crimes of violence (beatings, rape, murder) were committed against immigrant Asian women. To immigrant women threatened by domestic violence, particularly those held hostage to abusive husbands by immigration laws that might otherwise place their citizenship in jeopardy, the apparent persuasiveness of a cultural defense delivers the chilling message that D.A. Holzman suggested: their lives and bodies are of little value under U.S. law. It is hardly surprising that Asian women's centers in New York City were besieged by Asian women seeking counsel or refuge from violent husbands immediately after the Chen case; or that anthropologist Pasternak received several requests to testify in similar murder cases, including one involving a Korean man whose attorney was apparently unperturbed that Pasternak's expertise is Chinese culture (Jetter 1989); or that Mr. Chen's attorney, Stuart Orden, has been consulted for advice about similar cases around the country.[2] Cumulatively, cultural defense cases oblige us to ask why sexual/domestic violence is the rubric under which the racialized, gendered figure of "Asia" has presently emerged as an object of U.S. legal discourse.

I situate my study of cultural defense in a legal discursive field opened up by the present transnational reterritorialization of political economy, culture, and identity, and I undertake a historical and ethnographic investigation of exemplary cases of juridical power. My objective is to explore how a distant colonial discourse on culture has been transposed to the U.S. Asian diaspora, where, embraced by the law, colonial constructions of race and gender comprise disciplinary technologies that shape and restrain subaltern subjectivity. At stake, clearly, is not just difference but power; such discursive technologies form the substance of imperial protocols now deployed to counter, if not popular, then demographic, insurgency in what I call the "Third World at home" (Koptiuch 1991).

Since the early 1970s, the modern imperial field has been fractured and deterritorialized by the upheavals of a new transnationalized division of labor and global restructuring of regimes of capital accumulation (Lipietz 1987; Miyoshi 1993; Sassen 1991). Among the effects of these shifts has been a material and metaphoric reterritorialization[3] of people, economy, and culture, which has had the unexpected result of structurally reconstituting the Third World within the First. Through this process of "third-worlding," the United States now interiorizes a new sort of little-explored, imperial frontier located on the borders of neoterritories and destabilized local identities, aftereffects of the tectonic implosion of imperial potency and its fallout of racially cast, multilingual immigration. And abutting the diasporas of exotic Others-come-home are the internal communities constructed anew as Other (by class, race, or gender), whose constituents' struggles for inclusive parity in the hallowed pronominal phrase "*we* the people" have taken on renewed vigor in the postmodern context. Along with occasional bursts outward (e.g., the Gulf War, Haiti), it is here on the interior frontier that imperial power nostalgically seeks its reincarnation, reinventing itself through primitive forms of capital accumulation, social reproduction, counterinsurgency, effectively consolidating the preconditions for the new global division of labor and capital. The "imagined community" (Anderson 1983) of post-World War II national unity has been ruptured by this transnational undertow, and internal fissures have been readied as formerly unimagined battlefields of colonization and resistance. These struggles are most visibly under way in major urban centers, reterritorialized as "global cities" (King 1990; Sassen 1991), where the intensities of social life are most effusive, the effects of social/spatial restructuring most devastating. Yet these struggles, too, have cut to the core of American identity itself, contesting over what subjectivities are most (in)appropriate for inhabitants in the U.S. Third World. The colonial discourse inscribed into the legal strategy of cultural defense, I argue, engages in this contest.

Recognition of the recurrence of a repressed familiarity with the Third-Worlding process, and the emergence of this Other Third World frontier here in the United States, have imploded into American consciousness to provoke the queasy anxiety of what Freud called the uncanny. In Freud's sense, the uncanny is an unsettling awareness of repetition-compulsion (Freud 1962). It is this awareness that constitutes the uncanny for Freud, not the specific nature of the original occurrence. The awareness of the reappearance of the repressed familiarity of that which recurs, provokes an uncanny emotional impulse of anxiety (Hertz 1979). And anxiety abounds today about this most unnatural miscegenation of core and periphery, First and Third Worlds, development and underdevelopment, miscegenation whose hybrid progeny now occupy the same space and time, the two having been compressed, as geographer David Harvey puts it (1989), under conditions of postmodernity. The same Third World that used to keep itself politely elsewhere (assisted by immigration control, imperial subterfuge, and the evening news)—out of sight, out of mind—has somehow, stealthily, crept in around us all like an unexpected, engulfing tide.

Perhaps you're thinking that "Third World" slips off the tongue all too easily these days, a catchall for describing a (distantly familiar) newness perceived and experienced but scarcely comprehended. Even many immigrants had no idea they "belonged" to the Third World until after they got to America (see Rieff 1991:243, 239). And isn't America's Third-Worlding alternately regarded with lyrical hopefulness (will it restore U.S. competitiveness in the global economy?) or with grave trepidation as "the horror, the horror," evoking a *Blade Runner* image that might well have slid off a narrative by Conrad or Coppola's apocalyptic celluloid remake? Either prospect is still indeterminate. Yet other researchers in cultural studies have begun to call attention to America's Third-Worlding in their work. Anthropologist Renato Rosaldo (1988:85) has called it "the implosion of the Third World into the first," sociologist Saskia Sassen (1982) speaks of "peripheralization at the core," and novelist Salman Rushdie (1982) glosses its manifestation in Britain as "the empire within." Literary critic Jean Franco (1985) has identified metropolitan New York as a "Third World city," and journalist David Rieff bluntly titled his book *Los Angeles: Capital of the Third World* (1991). In the press, too, it has become commonplace to find innumerable comparisons, usually cast as unfavorable aspersions, between the United States and various Third World cities and countries (concerning issues of education, health, housing, city planning, policing, etc.).

Bearing in mind Freud's notion of the uncanny, for my own work I have purposefully chosen "Third World" as concept-metaphor to gloss this new practice of Othering here in the United States, neither in order to collapse what are distinctly different historical formations nor to bolster the faltering hegemony of the West by holding closer its constitutive mirror of alterity. However, dislocated to a formerly First World domain, the repetition of the signifier "Third World" grates oxymoronically against its new location, obliging us through this disturbance to forgo the imperious luxury of blindness, sanctioned in the old colonial era, to the nearly inadmissible "truth" that "Third World" is a name, a representation, not a place (see Spivak 1985:149). Here I want to track within the cultural-legal system the historical and spatial slippage of "Third World" as concept-metaphor that specifically names the effects of a process of exploitative incorporation and hegemonic domination—and its contestation by subjugated peoples—that white and especially middle-class Americans, at least, used to be able to believe took place at a safe, reassuring distance.

This expansive, global geographical scale has collapsed into the national, the urban, even the subject itself, and anthropologists and other social theorists have begun to speak, as in this volume, of "geographies of identity" or to take seriously the spatial geography metaphorized as "subject-position" (Bondi 1993). But if the Third World can no longer be mapped off as a space separate from a seigneurial First World, if what social geographer Neil Smith (1984:165) labeled a "swath of satanic geographies" now contains capitalism's uneven development by interiorizing metaphors of space and nature and materializing the exploitative contours of the Third World and its natural natives right here in the West's core, how must we change our concepts, theories, and struggles of a newly spatialized politics of culture to accommodate this shift? How can we excavate the colonial past stratified in Western knowledge, whose repetition-compulsion of the nineteenth-century colonial episteme uncannily seems to have a perfectly current function producing/restraining the U.S. Third World? What strange migratory "field" is this that, in literary critic Homi Bhabha's words, "redraws its frontiers in the menacing, agonistic boundary of cultural difference that never quite adds up, always less than one nation and [always] double" (1990a:318)? What forces propel this strange implosion of the Third World into the First, that finds even those Americans who *never left home* poised on the borderland of worlds, a borderland described by anthropologists Akhil Gupta and James Ferguson as an "interstitial zone of displacement and deterritorialization that shapes the identity of the hybridized subject" (1992:18)?

From Michel Foucault's work we learn that the production of disciplinary subjects is contingent upon forms of knowledge that multiply the effects of power. Colonial discourse theory offers an analytical strategy for pursuing this insight by "excavating the colonial past stratified in Western forms of knowledge" (Sharpe 1989) and deconstructing the colonial discursive forms, representations, and practices that constitute the legitimating discourses of law, culture, and economy. Whereas most colonial discourse studies have focused on its politics and effects for understanding distant Third World colonial contexts,[4] my own project picks up on the rebound of the transnational era and tracks the genealogy and effects of its displacement into the First World, to show how a colonial discourse on culture sustains the contemporary disciplinary practices of the postmodern state.[5] The so-called postcolonial era begins to resemble the nineteenth-century colonial one a good deal more than contemporary observers might otherwise like to acknowledge (see Frankenberg and Mani in this volume; Shohat 1992; Miyoshi 1993).

Foucault's *Discipline and Punish* (1979) provides a starting point for analyzing cultural defense as a technology for the production of gendered, "disciplinary individuals" (see also de Lauretis 1987). Although cultural defense strictly operates within a juridical framework, it does so explicitly as an exception to the "universal norms" that define juridical subjects. By way of cultural difference selectively applied, cultural defense introduces classification, hierarchizes, disqualifies, invalidates; it brings the (patriarchal, colonial) power that once operated on the "underside of the law" into the domain of the law itself, and thereby "undermines the limits that are traced around the law"; it extends the "general forms defined by law to the infinitesimal level of individual lives"; it becomes a "method of training" for immigrants; it invites custom to work alongside the law as a "counter-law" that becomes the "effective and institutionalized content of juridical forms" (Foucault 1979:222–24).

In a criminal case involving Hmong refugees, we find the cultural defense operating in this manner, replete with a resurrection of the early modernist trope of exotic primitivism, through which it no doubt garners some of its more lurid power. Press coverage of cases involving Hmong refugees indulge in primitivist discourse with great relish, constructing a deliriously oxymoronic image of archaic, preliterate Hmong tribals (unable to eke out a living from their tiny garden plots) existing on welfare in the agrobusiness wonderland of California's San Joaquin Valley. Some seventy thousand Hmong now reside in California, having arrived in the United States since the late 1970s, when they were granted refugee status. Reporters wax ethnographic, dwelling on images of primitive Hmong finally "emerging from the mists of time": their naïveté about modern life, their lack of a concept for the passage of time, their belief ("still") in spirits and shamans, traditional curing, ritual sacrifices. Such timeless, primordial representations are undeterred by the fact that many Hmong were actively engaged in the eminently modern cold war: their refugee status was granted to make amends for the reprisals of death or imprisonment they suffered in their homeland for having fought Communists for the CIA in its "secret war" in Laos.

In a nonjury trial in 1985, the Fresno Superior Court heard the case *People v Kong Moua,* in which a Hmong "tribesman" was charged with kidnapping and rape of a Hmong woman.[6] Defense attorneys argued that Mr. Moua had no intent to rape, but simply was carrying out a Hmong cultural ritual, known to anthropologists as "marriage by capture" (invariably, the transliteration *zij poj niam* is always offered as linguistic authentication). In accordance with this ritual, a young man abducts the woman of his choice, with whom he previously had exchanged tokens of affection, and takes her to his family's home, where he "consummates" the marriage. Tradition requires the virtuous bride-to-be to resist her suitor (no man would want a woman who submits willingly), and requires the virile man to ignore her protests. Moua allegedly was surprised to find himself slapped with criminal charges by the college coed with whom he chose to play out this drama. In debating whether this marriage ritual is a valid tradition in the U.S. diaspora, attorneys presented expert testimony on Hmong culture, reviewed a doctoral dissertation in anthropology on Hmong marriage rituals, and conferred with male Hmong clan elders. Criminal charges were dropped, and the judge allowed the defendant to plead guilty to false imprisonment, a misdemeanor, on the grounds that Moua reasonably, if mistakenly, believed that the woman had consented to sexual intercourse—given that no-means-yes is already built into the structure of the ritual. The judge used his discretion to permit Moua to plea-bargain to the lesser charge and sentenced him to ninety days in jail and fined him one thousand dollars, nine hundred dollars of which was to be paid as "dowry" to the family of the victim. The judge had implicitly recognized the cultural defense, and Moua was spared a much harsher prison sentence.

In an era when "date rape" has begun to be taken seriously as a criminal infringement on American women's rights and bodies, and is no longer irreproachably regarded as simply a manly right/rite, does it not seem curious that the Hmong crime victim's recompense, the "dowry," effectively reinserted her into the (punitive) circuit of sexual exchange of women, defined by anthropologists as characterizing (primitive, patriarchal) kin-based systems of social organization (see Rubin 1975)? And if the (dubious) privilege of cultural distinctiveness afforded the Hmong by the cultural defense seems to compensate for their war-torn displacement to the United States, doesn't it nevertheless place Hmong culture in a decidedly deprivileged relation to the still-secure "reasonable man" of U.S. jurisprudence?

It does not seem far-fetched to me to argue that the Hmong are stand-ins for all of Asia (because in the eyes of white racism, all Asians look alike). One of the effects this achieves—and perhaps this is one reason why Asians figure so prominently in cultural defense cases—is to primitivize the inhabitants of Pacific Rim nations, chief competitors of the United States in the global economy. As if by sleight of hand, the law is engaged in a displaced equivalent of Asian-bashing that assists in consolidating the preconditions for a new transnational division of the subject. (Much as consolidating the preconditions for a transnational division of labor is assisted in the United States by a hegemonic discourse on labor that holds up as exemplary other practices of "Asian culture," such as the Japanese "family" firm, so-called Oriental diligence, and reputed selfless lack of individuality.)

Those in favor of the cultural defense argue that it simply recognizes the cultural pluralism of the nation; they regard it as comparable to what are commonly misconstrued as separate legal defenses or standards of reasonableness applied to other population groups with distinctive experiences, such as the so-called battered women's defense and post-traumatic stress disorder of Vietnam veterans. But in most instances thus far, the courts have accommodated the intent and culpability involved in such cases under the standard legal defenses of provocation, diminished capacity, insanity, or justification (e.g., self-defense), without requiring substantive-law redefinitions providing separate standards for battered women that reify the defendants' special experiences as such.[7] Yet on a pious altar of cultural diversity, a cultural defense would seem to offer for sacrifice the standard "reasonable man," in order to open up the juridical subject to a specifically "cultural" heterogeneity. Although the potential to accommodate difference is indeed ultimately desirable, cultural defense, by differentiating the nation's heterogeneous subjects, once again reasserts the privilege of the "normal subject" for which special, mitigating circumstances are simply contingent, not indelibly essentialized as part of its very being. What, then, is at stake in reifying "cultural difference" as an exceptional criterion for distinctive legal recognition? Perhaps this is best illuminated in the last case I will discuss, one of two cases I've learned about whose defendants were women.

In 1985, Fumiko Kimura, a Japanese immigrant woman living in California, attempted to commit what the law calls murder-suicide but what Japanese culture considers the ritual of "parent-child suicide" (*oyaku shinju*), by walking into the ocean at Santa Monica with her two children after learning that for three years her husband had been supporting a mistress, a waitress at the restaurant where he worked. The children drowned, but Mrs. Kimura was saved by passers-by, of whom she later said, "They must have been Caucasians. Otherwise they would have let me die" (cited in Woo 1989). Kimura was charged with two counts of first-degree murder and felony child endangering, and prosecuting attorneys believed they could prove a deliberate, premeditated intent to kill (malice aforethought).[8]

Although Fumiko Kimura's attorney did not attempt to build a case around her cultural background, as in *People* v *Chen,* in preliminary hearings he did establish that although she had lived in the United States for sixteen years, she maintained a "traditional Japanese home": she spoke little English, didn't drive, had few interests or friends outside her family, knew little of her husband's work in the restaurant business, and was a devoted, traditional mother and wife, "waiting up each night to bathe her husband's feet upon his return home from work" (Woo 1989:404). The chief defense was based on psychiatric testimony by several clinical psychiatrists, two familiar with Japanese culture, all of whom found her to be suffering from severe emotional distress, cause enough to consider her "temporarily insane" at the time of the drownings. Psychiatrists minimized any causative role of culture, but theorized that her native Japanese beliefs may have led her to be more vulnerable to stress from her domestic situation.

Among the cultural experts who influenced this case must be included members of the Los Angeles Japanese American community. In the court hearing, Japanese Americans in the audience interceded on Kimura's behalf through her attorney by contesting the accuracy of the court interpreters' translations. Also, when the case was publicized, Mrs. Kimura received an outpouring of support from Japanese Americans, who submitted a petition to the Los Angeles district attorney with over twenty-five thousand signatures, requesting leniency and special consideration of her emotional distress and social isolation, and her "roots in Japanese culture," which "then directed her troubled behavior."[9] Widespread press coverage explained that the ritual of parent-child suicide, committed by a Japanese mother to escape some personal disgrace or shame, occurs frequently in Japan and is popularly considered an honorable way to die, for it would be a disgrace for a mother to take her own life and leave her children motherless. Although parent-child suicide is prohibited under modern Japanese law, the petition stated that it is treated as the equivalent of involuntary manslaughter or a lesser offense, punishable by a light, suspended sentence with probation and supervised rehabilitation.

Though ultimately the court considered cultural background irrelevant in determining Mrs. Kimura's guilt or innocence, and instead based its judgment on psychological testimony, cultural factors were admitted as mitigating factors during sentencing. After plea-bargaining, Kimura was allowed to plead no contest to reduced charges of two counts of voluntary manslaughter. She was sentenced to five years' probation, one year in prison (already served), and psychiatric counseling. The end result was the same as if the case had been decided by a Japanese court: leniency. Thus the California Penal Code required recourse to a "legal fiction" (insanity) available to everyone (Sheybani 1987), disclosing the constitutive relation between pathology and reason that already underpins the way the distinctive U.S. legal culture negotiates, legitimates, and constructs categories of identity and social order (see Coombe 1991). It was entirely unnecessary to appeal to the "cultural fiction" proposed by a cultural defense, concocting what the prosecuting attorney in the Chen murder case perhaps aptly called "anthropological hocus-pocus" (Polman 1989). In effect, behavior that may be considered aggrieved but "normal" in Japanese culture was reclassified for U.S. legal culture as "insane" or, more tellingly, in the translation that plagued the court interpreter in this linguistically troubled case, "mentally unusual" (*People* v *Kimura, Preliminary Hearings* transcript, p. 35).

It is instructive that a *Harvard Law Review* essay arguing in support of cultural defense takes the Kimura case as its first example and paradigmatic case (Cultural Defense 1986). The author's use of feminine personal pronouns as stand-ins for the generic case has the rhetorical effect of giving a feminine cast to all defendants in cultural defense criminal cases, when in fact all but one defendant until that time had been men. By starting the article with the best-known case whose defendant was a woman, the author subtly prejudices the argument in a way that would seem potentially to turn acceptance of cultural defense, as an independent exception to the "ignorance is no excuse" criterion, into an instrument for feminist advocacy of women's rights, again comparing it to the battered women's defense. Feminist and Asian women's advocacy groups argue its effect is precisely the reverse (Eng 1989; Jetter 1989).

Most crucially here, whereas in defending battered women, attorneys represent "American" women as active agents whose subjectivity is constituted through (oppressive) social relations of kinship and legal and other structures, cultural defense cases set up immigrant Third World women as passive victims claimed by an essentialist cultural logic of always-already-Otherness, what Chandra Mohanty (1984) calls the always-already-Third-World-women-as-victim. Indeed, even as perpetrators of domestic violence, Third World men, too, are deprived of historical agency. Their actions are all the more forgivable, given their representation by defense attorneys as hapless blank screens across which prescribed, primordial cultural ritual seemingly enacts itself. The already precarious subjectivity of Third World women and men as active agents is effectively obliterated (Spivak 1988a). Agency is denied in advance by the passivity ascribed to Asians, and triply so to subaltern Asian women, whose divergence from Eurocentric inscriptions is eclipsed as such, in the historical/cultural narrative, by patriarchy, class, and colonialism. Following this ethno-logic, legal discourse on cultural defense resonates with Lata Mani's research into the representation of women in the discourse on *sati* (widow sacrifice) in nineteenth-century colonial India: "official discourse forecloses any possibility of women's agency, thus providing justification for 'civilizing' colonial interventions" (1987:130).

In the Kimura case, the so-called timeless tradition of *oyaku shinju* (glossed as parent-child suicide, though characteristically it has engaged mothers and their children) can be shown to have emerged in early-twentieth-century rural Japan under specific historical conditions. These conditions include shifts in (global and local) political economy and social relations of class and gender, the rise of what historian Kathleen Uno identifies as a new kind of intensified motherhood, and the waning of another cultural "tradition," the adoption by wealthier households of the children of impoverished families (Uno n.d., 1991). By pseudo-archaizing what is clearly not a timeless practice, legal practitioners sidestep more pertinent questions that remain bracketed outside the "facts of the case." What conditions, for instance, make possible the transposition of such so-called traditional practices to the U.S. Asian diaspora, and what does this cultural slippage along immigration routes tell us about the power relations of race, gender, and class *here* that made suicide the desperate last resort for a Japanese immigrant woman? If "suicide is the ultimate act of hostility," in the words of Lillian Kimura (no relation), president of the Japanese American Citizens League in 1993,[10] its attempt by Fumiko Kimura was a self-inflicted and specifically gendered act of "domestic violence." Finally, in her law review essay elucidating the Kimura decision, Woo (1989) persuasively argues the need to historicize U.S. legal culture, yet timelessly validates her assertions about Japanese cultural "traditions" on the ethnographic authority of culture-and-personality anthropologists like Ruth Benedict (1974) and Eiichiro Ishida (1968). The historical timing of each of these anthropologists' books is clearly caught up in important moments of global politics, and the colonialist relations of power/knowledge palpably at play in their work warrants far more critical excavation of the imprint of both U.S. and Japanese Orientalism.

Recent debate over the sensitivity of U.S. jurisprudence to difference and power has drawn critical legal attention to discrimination by sex, gender, race, and disability.[11] But this scholarship, and the growing body of literature specifically arguing the pros and cons of the cultural defense,[12] contain little about how this legal practice transposes a distant colonial discourse to the U.S. Asian diaspora. Under conditions of colonial contestation, sex, gender, race, and tradition have all been crucial sites for controlling and engendering subaltern subjects (Mani 1987; Parker et al. 1992; Sharpe 1993; Stoller 1991). Cultural defense cases are situated at these same sites within the context of the new civilizing mission under way in the U.S. Third World. Here, too, the figure of the Asian woman remains an abiding Orientalist currency, "centerfold to the imperial voyeur" (Stoller 1991:54). How does the law organize the Western pornographic fantasy of Oriental culture to reconstruct the space within which (sexual) violence is permitted, and cover over what Luce Irigaray calls the law's "seduction function" of interpellating U.S. Third World women by subcontracting out to the law-of-the-father as part of its technologies of gender and race (Irigaray 1985:38; Kondo 1990)?

If the cultural defense allegedly marks a discursive *shift* in U.S. jurisprudence toward a more ethnically sensitive, representative inclusiveness, it is imperative to note that its advocates legitimate this claim through *continuities* with colonialist discourses of cultural relativism, Orientalism, and paternalism. Defense attorneys rely upon colonial-era conceptions of "culture," for which they readily find precedent in acculturationist, pluralist sociology and especially in salvage-model, relativist anthropology, both very much regnant today (just examine any introductory textbook). Culture is devised as nonhistorical (timeless) and pre-social (essential, natural), complete with the familiar relativist refrain, "each culture should be judged in its own terms." Lawyers cite scholarly texts, ethnographic studies, and doctoral dissertations as objective sources of knowledge about the cultural "facts of the case," and have called cultural anthropologists as "expert witnesses" for live, authoritative testimony about the powerful effect of beliefs and ritual practices prescribed by their client's originary cultural formation (as in "you can take the man out of China, but not China out of the man"). Invariably, it seems, explanation hinges upon virtually unreconstructed (because ever popular as "common knowledge"?), pre-Edward Said (1978) Orientalist categories of honor and shame, and prefeminist, primitivist tropes such as wildly passionate (but blind) masculinity and passive (but seductive) femininity.

What is going on here? In the name of multicultural sensitivity, advocates of a cultural defense urge the court to expand the law's legitimacy through greater flexibility—yet the only cultural alterity they seem willing to countenance is a highly specific, reified Otherness. What counts as "culture" in this context? The law's own claims of representative *inclusiveness* are premised upon essential, asymmetrical, racially constructed, unified, stable "traditions" of gender difference and cultural identity, all representations that were initially devised by colonial discourses to *exclude* from equal status those Others whose disqualifying difference from Western culture was carefully classified, coded, and hierarchized by the panoptic, disciplinary technologies that sustained colonial rule (see Butler 1990b; Said 1978). The juridical modeling of the cultural defense uncannily repeats this colonial episteme, attributing to all Asians a unitary difference that elides distinctions of gender, race, class, or nation, and investing this imaginary Asia with a repetition-compulsion of colonial desire. So if the law now (mis)recognizes only what Chinese American novelist Amy Tan calls the "American face" of Asian culture (see Tan 1989), it does so on the authority of the social and human sciences that once supplied the legitimating ethic for the West's imperial ventures and collectively produced a domitable "Asia" for American imagination, exploitation, and occupation (see M. L. Pratt 1985 on "Africa"; Asad 1973; Said 1986b; Young 1990).

These colonial discourses have been dusted off for redeployment in the United States as perfectly current resources of power/knowledge in the struggle for hegemony now under way in the "empire within." From a spectacular collapse of space, time, and subjectivity, the law takes license to retrieve a nonhistorical, primitivized, feminized image of Asia that facilitates what Johannes Fabian (1983) calls the "denial of coevalness" between Asia and the United States. No matter that today this official image is decisively belied by Pacific Rim Asia's status as the chief global competitor of the United States, or that the passivity ascribed to timeless Orientals is flatly contradicted by the Asian (and other) immigrants' arrival in the United States from imperial outposts as political refugees or on their own economic initiative. Does their current patent engagement in transnational events make it imperative to tuck these aliens back into colonialist narratives? The limits of these narratives are obliquely glimpsed at the point of crisis, where any notion of *post*colonial discourse becomes its own "white mythology" (Young 1990). Thus situated, the law's mobilization of new deployments of gender, race, and ethnicity goes well beyond the court's rhetoric of multicultural sensitivity. Rather, the exigencies of political rule at a time of slipping U.S. white males' political and economic hegemony, and the unstable indeterminacy of national identity in a transnational era, have required more careful attention by the state's ideological apparatuses to the construction of identities willing to be subjected to the laws of an efficient imperial policy in this decidedly not *post*colonial "Third World at home."

I propose that if it can be shown—as I think it can—the subject now (re)produced by, and (mis)recognized as, culturally Other by the law, was historically constituted *as subaltern* by the very relations of power and discursive practices through which the law now claims to "represent" immigrants *more equally,* then a cultural defense clearly introduces into the law a complex and formidable disciplinary technology that deserves critical scrutiny by those concerned with counterhegemonic politics. Coded more innocuously as "culture," the law sustains "flexible accumulations" of racist, sexist, and colonialist forms of knowledge that underwrite the cultural defense as a disciplinary technology for the production of gendered, racialized, juridical subjects appropriate for a Third-Worlded United States (much as the current transnational flexibility in production, labor markets, and consumption attempts to redress the accumulation crisis in late capitalism). It is my position that unless cultural defense is disentangled from its self-legitimation in colonial knowledge, its promise of a truly multicultural politics can only prove less than salutary, regardless of its potential strategic value in undermining immigrant subordination.[13]

My reading of the cultural defense thus far has been primarily discursive. I am concerned with identifying the categories, definitions, and representations of "traditional" Asian cultures generated by legal officials and cultural spokespersons (in the courts these most often have been male elders), which they take to be *cause* enough for criminological displacements, and which I take as the *effects* of imperial exigencies of rule under conditions of contestation. By tracking the colonialist narrative that threads its way through the history of Western encounters with "the Orient," my project aims to uncover its sedimentation in what counts as "knowledge" about Asian culture that the law is currently willing to sanction, whereby a cultural defense commutes "crime" to "ritual" (see Spivak 1988a). My concern is not so much with the accuracy of accounts of cultural practices as "authentic" traditions, as with a pursuit of their (re)definition *as* "traditional" in the U.S. context. Does cultural "tradition," in this instance, name the effects of subaltern insurgency and global upheavals that in the first place uprooted many of these people now displaced in American diasporas (see Sharpe 1991; Spivak 1985, 1988a)? In the displacement operation described here, ritual obviates criminological charge as it slides across hyper-culturalized transnational borderlands. It deploys positivist, humanist, realist social science to place the Asian Other more firmly into the sights/sites of surveillance of the law's normalizing strategies (see Pfohl and Gordon 1987). Backed up by the force of law *here* in the United States, colonialist models of Asian culture, which were devised *elsewhere* as part of the protocols of imperialist appropriation, surely take on a renewed but unmistakably different relation to the materialist forms of imperialism now operating in a post-Fordist, transnationalized political economy of "flexible accumulation" (Harvey 1989) and culturalized commodity circuits.

It is important to trace such discursive movements between cultures in order to examine the place and function of colonialist representations of culture, and to show how the repositioning of gender and race is performatively staged, through a legal discourse on nation and multiculturalism, at this historical juncture of the transnational era. This procedure enables us to see that in a first register, the cultural defense racializes colonial relations that constitute the Third World at home, through a juridical structuring of essential, stable Asian identity engendered by a culturalist logic of always-already Otherness. In a second register, it implicates those relations in the now familiar narratives of sexual violence already chartered by First World feminist outrage (e.g., Gordon 1988). This second register eclipses the first, for it, too, constructs immigrant Asian women as always-already passive victims, whose oppression is taken as symptomatic of always-elsewhere, barbaric, misogynous custom, imported via displaced authority of colonial discourses that themselves too often remain unexamined (see Mohanty 1984; Mani 1989; Sharpe 1991). Liberal feminist condemnation of the cultural defense, such as Holzman's statement quoted earlier, as a double standard of justice that fails to protect immigrant women, provides a sexual-equality alibi that reinstates here in the United States a lingering legacy that once justified colonial interventions in other worlds: the self-appointed "civilizing mission" of nineteenth-century colonial administrators as "white men saving brown women from brown men" (Gayatri Spivak's gloss for the British colonialists' understanding of their intervention into the practice of *sati* in nineteenth-century India, 1988a:297; see also Mani 1987; Sharpe 1989).

Fortunately, in my opinion, what Chela Sandoval (1991) identifies as an "oppositional consciousness" of U.S. Third World feminism has begun to interrupt these two officializing normative registers, raising questions that cannot be asked by either (e.g., Anzaldúa 1987, 1990; hooks 1992; Mohanty 1984; Mohanty et al. 1991; Volpp 1994). This interruption occurs in defiance of the injunction by which Third World women are engendered agentless by the laws of father and state, and in subversion of the pseudo-archaic regimes of interdictions that render them intelligible only as speechless subalterns (Spivak 1988a; also Alarcón 1990a; B. Parry 1987). Such an oppositional consciousness obliges an interrogation into how the dominant image of the "immigrant Third World woman" enables and sustains a sovereign self-representation for (white, middle-class) women whose identity politics would still have them positioned (metaphorically, materially) elsewhere, as if "the West" could still be (self)contained and geographically locatable in this era of transnational reterritorialization, a reassuring raft of stability in a menacing sea of difference.

As I begin to research ways that U.S. Asian diasporic communities have organized and aligned themselves around the pros and cons of the cultural defense, I am not in the least surprised to find that many of these other narratives are comprised of representations of various "Asias" that often, at first glance, are equally essentialist, ahistorical, and confabulated as those entertained by the law. These strategies of cultural self-representation are engaged in a politics of location that charts the multiple positionalities of subjectivities that, like the new writing by radical women of color, confound and "go beyond an oppositional theory of the subject" (Alarcón 1990a:366), and transform the "satanic geographies" of a Third-Worlded United States into homelands for hybrid Americans. The legal terrain of the cultural defense thereby becomes a contradictory battleground, one of the terrains on which the struggle is currently waged for multiple subjectivities that, once again, have fractured the ever-inadequate identity named by "we, the people." Attending to these performances of narrative and counternarrative of the nation's self-generation can undermine colonialist and criminological displacements.

NOTES

Earlier versions of this paper benefited from discussion after its presentation at conferences at the City University of New York and Rutgers University, the American Ethnological Society, and the Social and Behavioral Sciences Program at Arizona State University West, Phoenix. I would especially like to thank Rosemary Coombe, Elissa Krauss, Smadar Lavie, Holly Maguigan, Lata Mani, and Jenny Sharpe.

1 *People* v *Chen,* Supreme Court of the State of New York, Kings County, Indictment no. 7774/87, 1989. Reduced charges and sentences were handed down in two other murder cases in which a cultural defense informally influenced the outcome for male defendants. One involved Laotians (*People* v *Aphaylath,* 510 N.Y.S. 2nd 83, Court of Appeals, 1986); the other, Hmong (*People* v *Tou Moua,* Case no. 328106-0, Fresno Superior Court, 1985).

2 Telephone interview, August 5, 1993.

3 In this analysis I have adapted the notions of deterritorialization and reterritorialization devised by Deleuze and Guattari in their "schizoanalysis" of both libidinal and political economies (1983b). These notions are theorized differently as global Fordism by the French regulationists (Lipietz 1987), or more optimistically as flexible specialization (Piore and Sabel 1984). See the lucid and cautionary critique of these formulations by Julie Graham (1991).

4 For example, work by Bhabha, Guha, Mani, Mohanty, O'Hanlon, Said, Spivak, Stoller, Williams and Chrisman, and Young.

5 Young has called for such a project (1990:175; see also Mani 1989; B. Parry 1987; Sharpe 1993).

6 *People* v *Kong Moua,* Case no. 315972-0, Fresno Superior Court. Several other such cases apparently were resolved in pretrial hearings, according to press reports.

7 In some states, courts have recognized a distinct "reasonable battered woman" standard. Feminist legal scholar Holly Maguigan, in her extended discussion of the legal debates around this issue (1991), argues that such attempts are ill-conceived theoretically, fail to eliminate judicial bias, and flatly do not work as guarantors of fair trials for battered women.

8 *People* v *Kimura,* Los Angeles Superior Court, Case no. A-091133, 1985, *Preliminary Hearings* transcript. Deborah Woo has discussed this case at length (1989), although there is a great deal more to be said about the fascinating complications she raises. Leti Volpp (1994) has most fully addressed the case of *People* v *Helen Wu,* in which a Chinese woman was tried in a parent-child suicide attempt (286 Cal. Rptr. 868, California Court of Appeals 1991).

9 The petition is fully cited in Woo (1989:404). Woo reports that support for Kimura was less than unified: Issei (first-generation) Japanese immigrants were most sympathetic to her situation; other Japanese Americans felt Kimura should be subject to American legal standards, which "would facilitate a long overdue acceptance of Japanese Americans as Americans rather than as culturally unassimilable foreigners"; and still others found disturbing the public attention drawn to this single case in light of other social problems deserving of attention (p. 426).

10 Telephone interview, September 3, 1993.

11 For example, Bartlett and Kennedy 1991; Delgado 1985; Gordon 1988; MacKinnon 1987; Minow 1990; and Rhode 1989.

12 For starters, Choi 1990; Gallin 1994; Magnarella 1991; Cultural Defense 1986; Renteln 1993; Rimonte 1991; Rosen 1991; Sams 1986; Sherman 1986; Sheybani 1987; Thompson 1985; Volpp 1994; Woo 1989; and many newspaper reports.

13 Volpp (1994) has provided a politically sophisticated analysis of the cultural defense, in which she advocates a considered, but not formalized, admission of cultural testimony in cases where cultural information would further the "value of antisubordination" of marginalized groups such as immigrant women.

THE FIGURE OF THE X: AN ELABORATION OF THE DU BOISIAN AUTOBIOGRAPHICAL EXAMPLE

NAHUM D. CHANDLER

In his introduction to the 1990 edition of *The Souls of Black Folk* (hereinafter referred to as *Souls,* followed by page number[s]; see Du Bois 1990), to which I shall return, the writer John Edgar Wideman adduces the order of the problematic that we must bring into focus:

> Like Freud's excavations of the unconscious, Einstein's revelations of the physical universe, Marx's explorations of the economic foundations of social organization, Du Bois's insights have profoundly altered the way we look at ourselves. The problem of the twentieth century is the problem of the color-line. With this utterance the unconscious, relativity, class warfare are all implicated. Du Bois posits a shift of cataclysmic proportions, demanding a reorientation of consciousness as radical as that required by physics at the atomic level. (Wideman 1986:xii)

I would suggest that Du Bois's discourse should and must alter our self-understanding. It carries this force, not only because it specifies a (mundane or ontic) historical generality—for example, the historical modalities of "the color-line"—of the concept of race and the practice of racial distinction, that would find its pertinence in the entire field of a specific historiographical investigation—for example, that which Du Bois called "the twentieth century." (I do not think Wideman's formulation leaves the question to rest at such an order of relative radicality.) His discourse also broaches an investigation of the constitution of identity as such. I would tend to colloquialize this question as subatomic.

For what emerges at the very inception of Du Bois's discourse and remains throughout his entire itinerary is his conception of the necessity that in order to think the possibility of something like an African American subject, one must be able to think not only the actual social practices that give our historical modernity its specific character (for example, the operation of practices under the sign of race) but also the most radical possibility of identity (what I shall strategically call, in this essay, the question of difference or the question of the other). This possibility would not be simply those practices which organize our specific historicity—for example, the practice of racial distinction in all its modalities (conceptual, political, economic, etc.). For although we cannot avoid a passage through the constitutive deployment of racial distinction in the historical field proper to the African American subject, and although in one sense our modernity cannot rigorously be thought as something other than a racialized historicity, the force of the practice of racial distinction itself (simply) (or, for example, the concept of the commodity or the concept of the unconscious) would not remain radical. We must also give an account of that structure of possibility in which the practice of racial distinction opens, and to which the concept of race, and hence racist practice, is a certain kind of response—a violent, destructive, response. This possibility would be the possibility of difference, of the other. In another discourse we might say: the question of being or the movement of *différance*.

Yet the particular richness of Du Bois's discourse must be continually, and hence gradually, (re)emphasized.[1] The innovation of Du Bois's approach was opened by his manner of proceeding. We might summarize the pathway of Du Bois's innovation in the following terms. His thinking of historicity in general was developed according to a methodological protocol that required him to attempt to think the particulars, the minute historical specifics, that which we often call the micrological, of a specific historicity, the history and status of that which we call African American (or Negro). His concern was to specify, at all levels of generality, the systemic site or structures that organized the emergence of the African American or Negro as subject.

This concern to think the micrological, while remaining preoccupied with the most general possible formulation of the question of the Negro, led Du Bois to question the status (in every sense) or foundation of the Negro or African American. A concern with the question of the *status* rather than only or primarily the question of the *quiddity* (or empirical modes of existence) of the African American subject (both collectively and individually) remains the decisive meditation of "The Conservation of Races" (Du Bois 1982g) and emerges as the distilled and governing problematic of "Strivings of the Negro People" (Du Bois 1897), both written in 1897, a year that was pivotal for Du Bois (the latter work was revised and republished in 1903 as the opening, and governing, chapter of *Souls*).

His concern with the question of status was Du Bois's central conceptual innovation in discourses on the African American or Negro (see Spillars 1991b:63–64).

In trying to formulate the problem of the status of the African American subject, Du Bois was led to the question of how to think the status of the problem of that which we call race and, beyond (yet partly on the basis of) this particular historical problem, the problem of the status of difference in general. Beyond simply empirical or so-called "real" history, at the core of the question of race and our historicity, was another question, one for which Du Bois never proposed a proper name. In this essay, for reasons of strategy and economy, I call it the question of the other, of the general possibility of difference. The problem was how to situate the question of difference, how to situate to each other the relation of sameness and difference.

This led Du Bois to raise the question of how our entire historicity and "our" world are constituted, in both a historical sense and a transcendental sense (in the nonfoundational sense of the ultratranscendental elaborated by Derrida 1976:61). This question was similar in its conceptual aspects to the questions posed by Marx and Freud; indeed, it is from this standpoint that we must approach Du Bois's "discovery" of the discourses of these two thinkers in the later part of his itinerary. For we must recall the generality of the problem of racial distinction for Du Bois:[2] in its innermost interstices, the structural economy (a certain oppositional logic or principle) at stake here is such that, even if it is not called by the name "race," its pertinence extends at least to all that we can call "modern" or "modernity."[3]

This conjunction of the historical and the ultratranscendental, organized and motivated, with a certain rigor, a decisive contribution of Du Bois's discourse: his description of the movement and force of the practice of racial difference as simultaneously revelatory and productive of the difference that is (the chance, or the possibility, or) the movement of the constitution of subjectivity in general. Du Bois is thus led to think the "originary" moment in the constitution of racial distinction or racialized social difference, thought as a subjective practice that is not reducible to the intentionality of the subject, and in the constitution of the African American subject, thought in terms of its concept or possibility (hence in terms of subjectivity in general) as a unique structure of repetition. An analytical formulation of this structure recognizes each "originary" or inaugural moment as a re-inaugration. The precision and rigor with which Du Bois sifts this originary structure out of the play of the ensemble of relations that is our racialized "modern" subjectivities remains unsurpassed in twentieth-century thought.

I submit that Du Bois decided that these questions could be thought in no better way than by thinking, in as exact and thorough a manner possible, the questions posed by the actuality of the African American subject, the history of the experience of African Americans, the structures of historicity that are the histories of African Americans. These questions, as formulated in Du Bois's discourse in all their specificity, can be succinctly and powerfully gathered into the question of the general possibility of a being, specifically a subject, like an African American. Thus, Du Bois was led to return to that with which he began, but in a new way.[4] According to his own exigencies, then, his own protocols, Du Bois, perhaps in a manner that was not ordered simply by intention, was trying to give an account, an empirical account that would also be an account of that which we sometimes call meaning or the symbolic,[5] of the mode of being of African Americans in the United States, formulated a strategic method for thinking along with the question of the subject, the historical question of racial distinction, and the ultratranscendental question of difference. Under the force of palpable necessity, the abusive practice of racism, and for strategic reasons whose economy will be elaborated in due course in this essay (in a word, having to do with the status of heterogeneity or what I call the problem of purity in the Negro-Black-Afro-or-African American case), Du Bois took the status of the African American subject as an exemplary theme by which to trace the theme (or develop the topic) of the problem of racial distinction and, hence, the problem of difference in general. For similar practical and strategic reasons, in this regard Du Bois could do no better than to question himself.

Late in his life, in his 1940 autobiography *Dusk of Dawn* (1975a), Du Bois called this strategy the "autobiography of a concept," specifically the "autobiography of a race concept"; indeed, the text was subtitled *An Essay Toward an Autobiography of a Race Concept.* Du Bois wrote:

> I seem to see a way of elucidating the inner meaning and significance of that race problem by explaining it in terms of the one human life that I know best. I have written then what is meant to be not so much my autobiography as the autobiography of a concept of race, elucidated, magnified and doubtless distorted in the thoughts and deeds which were mine. (*Dusk:* 2)[6]

I emphasize, however, that one of my central suggestions in this essay is that the development of the methodological strategy for thinking the status of our *socius* that Du Bois called an "autobiography of a concept" was first broached in the opening paragraphs of *Souls* (Du Bois 1986b).

> Between me and the other world there is ever an unasked question: unasked by some through feelings of delicacy; by others through the difficulty of rightly framing it. All nevertheless, flutter round it. They approach me in a half-hesitant sort of way, eye me curiously or compassionately, and then, instead of saying directly, How does it feel to be a problem? they say, I know an excellent colored man in my town; or I fought at Mechanicsville; or, Do not these Southern outrages make your blood boil? At these I smile, or am interested, or reduce the boiling to a simmer, as the occasion may require. To the real question, How does it feel to be a problem? I answer seldom a word.
>
> And yet, being a problem is a strange experience,—peculiar even for one who has never been anything else, save perhaps in babyhood and in Europe. It is in the early days of rollicking boyhood that the revelation first bursts upon one, all in a day as it were. I remember well when the shadow swept across me. I was a little thing, away up in the hills of New England, where the dark Housatonic winds between Hoosac and Tagkanic to the sea. In a wee wooden schoolhouse, something put it into the boys' and girls' heads to buy gorgeous visiting-cards—ten cents a package—and exchange. The exchange was merry, till one girl, a tall newcomer, refused my card,—refused it peremptorily, with a glance. Then it dawned upon me with a certain suddenness that I was different from the others; or like mayhap, in heart and life and longing, but shut out from their world by a vast veil. I had thereafter no desire to tear down that veil, to creep through; I held all beyond it in common contempt, and lived above it in a region of blue sky and great wandering shadows. That sky was bluest when I could beat my mates at examination-time, or beat them at a foot-race, or even beat their stringy heads. Alas, with the years all this fine contempt began to fade; for the worlds I longed for were theirs not mine. But they should not keep these prizes I said; some, all, I would wrest from them. Just how I would do it I could never decide: by reading law, by healing the sick, by telling the wonderful tales that swam in my head,—some way. With other black boys the strife was not so fiercely sunny: their youth shrunk into tasteless sycophancy, or into silent hatred of the pale world around them and mocking distrust of everything white; or wasted itself in a bitter cry, Why did God make me an outcast and a

> stranger in mine own house? The shades of the prison-house closed round about us all: walls strait and stubborn to the whitest, but relentlessly narrow, tall and unscalable to sons of night who must plod darkly on in resignation, or beat unavailing palms against the stone, or steadily, half hopelessly, watch the streak of blue above. (*Souls*:7–8)[7]

In a 1904 commentary on *Souls,* Du Bois called attention to its ground in a certain autobiographical organization.[8] Of the many changes from its 1897 original publication as an essay (Du Bois 1897) to its 1903 publication as the opening chapter of *Souls,* only one change (the addition of a letter: the phrase "the world I longed for" in the second paragraph was changed to "the world*s* I longed for") in these opening paragraphs was introduced. Although richly significant in one sense (introducing a semantic inflection that, as a description, both retains and displaces an oppositional structure), by its minuteness this change does not contest but, rather, tends to affirm what I am proposing here: that Du Bois never questioned the general method of inquiry, a certain sort of autobiographical inquiry, adumbrated in these opening paragraphs. In the multiple and heterogeneous movements of Du Bois's itinerary over some six and a half decades, he never questioned the approach he put forth in these opening paragraphs.

Indeed, this formulation, this reflection upon the autobiographical, was a decisive aspect of Du Bois's entire itinerary and of all the subsequent diverse problematics he approached. Not only is it affirmed through his practice in other essays in *Souls,* but his subsequent writings return to this approach again and again (see Du Bois 1968, 1975a, 1975c, 1982a, 1982b, 1982c, 1986a; Andrews 1985). At his death in 1963, Du Bois was still pursuing the writing of the autobiographical (see Aptheker in Du Bois 1968:5–6). The historian Thomas Holt touched a radical chord, one with which any reading of Du Bois must reckon or resonate, when he wrote that Du Bois's "own life became the text, the point of departure, for each of his major explorations of race, culture, and politics" (Holt 1990:307). It is the implication of a confirmation of the fecundity of Du Bois's strategy, relating to how we understand our entire modernity, that motivates the reading I am outlining here.

SITUATING THE EXAMPLE: CONCEPT

I. In order to properly situate the strategy of this methodology of Du Bois's (for he had many others), it must be recognized that the autobiographical *example* in Du Bois's methodology is approached at a level of distinctive generality. I have chosen to elucidate this question of the example with one example from Du Bois's discourse: from the *Dusk of Dawn* text of 1940 (1975a), a passage of some fourteen pages in the pivotal chapter, "The Concept of Race" (*Dusk:* 97–133). The passage in question is principally concerned with Du Bois's desedimentation of his family genealogy (*Dusk:* 103–17). And this desedimentation is at once a desedimentation of the history and possibility of an African American subject (such as Du Bois), of the concept and practice of racial distinction, and of the general possibility of difference.

The first theme I wish to underline is that the elaboration of the autobiographical in *Dusk,* as well as elsewhere in Du Bois's work, is nothing less than a radical formulation of the status of the example that bears implications for any methodology of interpretive practice. It formulates, with regard to the subject in general, what I call here (by analogy) the subatomic. To formulate this theme I will, initially, proceed through a reading of the five-page opening chapter of *Dusk,* which Du Bois enigmatically calls "The Plot" (*Dusk:* 3–7).

In a general sense Du Bois's "autobiography of a concept" does not offer a reduction of historicity to the (individual or collective) subject, nor a simple elimination of the subject from the production of historicity; rather, it resituates the structure of subjectivity, it resituates the intentionality (or consciousness) of the subject. He innovates in a domain that Althusser (1971b) and Foucault (1984) have since claimed as their own: (1) the subject is possible only in the space or spacing of a system of distinctions or practices; however, (2) the system itself does not simply precede, in its root possibility or opening (and above all analytically), the constitution of the subject. Everything in Du Bois's demonstration is played out between, as this between, of the movement or structure of the constitution of the subject.

If Du Bois has to justify the choice of his example with reference to a certain empirical order as an indispensable guardrail against saying anything whatsoever (see Derrida 1967a:158), and if we must note that this empirical order is always privileged by Du Bois throughout his many different projects (see *Souls:* 83–99; Du Bois 1901a, 1901b, 1901c, 1904, 1973, 1976, 1980a, 1980b, 1980c, 1982d, 1982e, 1982g; see also Du Bois 1982a), we must not understand this privilege as claiming (explicitly or implicitly) an ultimate, pure, or first-order status for such an order of phenomena or a first-order truth for our knowledge of such an order of phenomena. In the passage from *Dusk* quoted earlier, we must not understand Du Bois's reference to "the one human life I know best" as claiming a first-order truth for his self-knowledge.

If Du Bois explicitly followed a method of reflection upon himself, of reflection upon his constitution as an individual subject, his stated intention in this passage is anything but *simply* the elaboration of a self-possessive and self-possessed narrative subject, although there is certainly a subject at work or play here. Thus Du Bois writes: "I have written what is meant to be *not* so much *my* autobiography as the autobiography of a concept of race. . ." (*Dusk:* 2). I call it the autobiography of a (conceptual) problematic (conceptual here is anything but *simply* ideal or mental; see Althusser 1970:55–70). We should note here what Du Bois wrote to Paul G. Partington in a letter dated March 31, 1961: "*Dusk of Dawn* was not an autobiography. It had a great many autobiographical notes, but it was distinctly the story of a theory of race and how it had developed in my own life" (Partington 1977:201).

Moreover, Du Bois explicitly distinguishes the order of intentionality or subjectivity organized by the self-conscious motivations and practices of the subject (here marked as individual) from another order of "intentionality" or subjectivity (if it still makes sense to call it by this name), that is not reducible simply to the order of subjective intention, but is also organized as a certain kind of structural domain that I am calling "between" (structural is anything but static; a rethinking of the concept of structure is posed here; the reference is to the movement of *différance* elucidated in Derrida's discourse. See Chandler 1993; Derrida 1976:27–73; 1982b:17–27, esp. 24; 1982c). Thus, Du Bois explicitly indicates that his intention as (an individual) subject does not *constitute,* pure and simple, the phenomenon being described (the experience of an individual subject). Rather, this subjectivity, this experience, the organization of intentionality, as well as sense in general—insofar as it is the specific object of Du Bois's inquiry—is itself situated in terms of a systemic possibility. However, if this is so, Du Bois practices a recognition, if he does not name it, of the necessity that in order for racial distinction to operate as an iterable distinction, as a system of repetitive marks, it can do so only *in* the making of subjects—in the making and not before. Du Bois analytically positions the relationship between these two orders of intentionality, the experiential and the systemic, in such a way that the latter is "elucidated, magnified and doubtless distorted" in the former: the order of "thoughts and deeds" is interpreted in terms of how it is situated in relation to another order, the order of a "concept" of racial distinction. Yet, the concept acquires its possibility only as a text, as a system of practices, in the actual making of subjects. At the level of the subject, this "between" perhaps can be most specifically and generally elucidated at once in the demonstrative style of the autobiographical.[9]

The order of "concept" put forth in *Dusk* by Du Bois must be carefully situated, for just as it responds to the so-called empirical, it is not simply empirical. Neither is it simply ideal. It responds, it seems to me, to a problematic similar to that which led Edmund Husserl to elucidate what he came to call the phenomenological.

I suggest, if only by analogy (because a detailed exploration of the relation of Du Bois's and Husserl's problematics remains to be undertaken), that the problematic that Derrida (in his early work) has so carefully situated as organizing Husserl's early work is also at stake, and is decisive in organizing Du Bois's formulation of the domain of which he wishes to inquire, although it is proposed in distinctly different ways in the respective discourses of these two thinkers. Derrida writes of Husserl:

> Husserl . . . [sought] to *maintain* simultaneously the normative autonomy of logical or mathematical identity as concerns all factual consciousness, and its original dependence in relation to a subjectivity *in general;* in general but *concretely.* Thus he had to navigate between the Scylla and Charybdis of logicizing structuralism and psychologistic geneticism (even in the subtle and pernicious form of the "transcendental psychologism" attributed to Kant). He had to open up a new direction of philosophical attention and permit the discovery of a concrete, but nonempirical, intentionality, a "transcendental experience" which would be "constitutive", that is, like all intentionality, simultaneously productive and revelatory, active and passive. The original unity, the common root of activity and passivity is from quite early on the very possibility of meaning for Husserl. And this common root will ceaselessly be experienced as the common root of structure *and* genesis, which is dogmatically presupposed by all the *ulterior* problematics and dissociations concerning them. . . . [The problem of how to situate this unity is nothing other than] the problem which is already Husserl's [in the 1890s], that is the problem of the *foundation of objectivity.* (Derrida 1978d:158–59; emphasis in original)

Derrida goes on to trace how this problem of Husserl's overran its epistemological frame to become the question of the foundation and emergence of phenomenality in general, of the phenomenality of the phenomenon (Derrida 1978d:162–64).

Du Bois's problem, of course, was to specify a distinct orientation of description of the social. This concern might be construed as primarily epistemological. Yet, this problem was produced not as an abstract question or as a philosophical exposition, but as a pivotal moment of a practical effort to think—which is not simply to describe—simultaneously the order of the constitution of the African American subject and the order of the phenomenon of the systemic practice of racial distinction. Thus, Du Bois was concerned with *concrete* social practice—but concrete *in its most general implications.* In the closing paragraphs of the first chapter of *Dusk,* a chapter in which Du Bois maps out the questions that organize, for him, the discourse that follows, he specifically remarks this motif of the general: "Negroes must eat and strive, and still hold unfaltering commerce with the stars" (*Dusk:* 7).

His trajectory was moving in a direction precisely otherwise than that of Husserl. Yet, to the extent that the question of the foundation of objectivity, especially as Husserl raised it, as possible only by an irreducible passage through history and the subject (unlike the formulations of Kant, for example; see Derrida's elucidation of this question in Husserl's work, Derrida 1978c: 39–42), broaches the question of the structure of the subject, and Du Bois's question, a question of the possibility of the radical difference of the subject, raises not only, in Du Bois's phrase, the social question of "the scope of chance and unreason in human action" (*Dusk:* 7) but also the question of the chance of truth in general (Du Bois raises this question throughout his career; see 1975b, 1977, 1982, 1982g, 1990), a discreet crossing and intermixing of the respective problematics and itineraries of Husserl and Du Bois can be recognized.

In a certain specific sense, Du Bois's question concerned the roots of phenomenal being from its inception. Two specific questions arise, already in 1897, and remain at work throughout his entire itinerary. For example, in 1940: Who, or what, is an African American or Negro? What is race, and the practice of racial distinction? (Du Bois 1897, 1968, 1975a, 1986c). The form of these questions—not only their frame as the epistemological question of science, "what is . . . ," but also the autobiographical mode of their elaboration—raises the ultratranscendental question of the basis truth, or the status of difference. What Du Bois's discourse points to again and again, in part as a result of this double preoccupation of his thinking with specific historical questions along with the general problematics embedded within them, is an order of constitution in which the subject is neither the beginning nor the end of historicity. Yet without the subject, historicity, which is the very matrix of the example, would in turn have no example itself, and hence no meaning.

Since Du Bois does not state this proposition literally as a theme, I propose it as an interpretation, support for which I note in his practice: the style of his consistent preoccupation with the example, specifically the autobiographical example. The staging of the autobiographical example, the responsibility it demands as a demonstration, seems to resolutely insist that any recognition of a meaning of history in general can only be articulated by the risky and unavoidable passage by way of the micrological or the subatomic (see *Dusk:* 18, 49, 51–53, 64–65, 67, 95–96). The subject is *situated* in history and historicity, yet the very possibility of historicity is situated in the structure that opens the possibility of subjective practice. (Later I will recognize this structure, at the level of the subject, under the heading of what Du Bois early on called "second-sight.") In the opening chapter of *Dusk,* Du Bois poignantly situated his autobiographical subject thus:

> In the folds of this European civilization I was born and shall die, imprisoned, conditioned, depressed, exalted and inspired. Integrally a part of it and yet, much more significant, one of its rejected parts; one who expressed in life and action and made vocal to many, a single whirlpool of social entanglement and inner psychological paradox, which always seem to me more *significant for the meaning of the world today* than other similar and related problems. Little indeed did I do, or could I conceivably have done, to make this problem or loose it. Crucified on the vast wheel of time, I flew round and round with the Zeitgeist, waving my pen and lifting faint voices to explain, expound and exhort; to see, foresee and prophesy, to the few who could or would listen. Thus very evidently to me and to others I did little to create my day or greatly change it; but *I did exemplify it and thus for all time my life is significant for all lives of men.* (*Dusk:* 3–4; emphasis added)

In a general sense, then, we can say that Du Bois's concept of the example, of the autobiographical, of the "autobiography of a concept"—specifically, the "autobiography of a race concept"—is precisely other than a reduction of history or historicity to the subject (individual or collective), or of the subject (in whatever empirical modality) to the (a)historical. It retains each inflection of these oppositions in a certain (nonoppositional) way.

II. In order to further clarify the status of the example in Du Bois's discourse, we must give the general sense of the "autobiography of a concept" just outlined specification along two interwoven pathways. One we may call ultratranscendental. The other we may call historical.

First, Du Bois's discourse seems to recognize that in order to give an account of the specific historicity (the "particular social problem"; *Dusk:* 4; "the problem of the color-line" *Souls:* 16; "the world-wide domination of white Europe"; *Dusk:* 3) that organizes this autobiography (and to give such an account is the only way to avoid simply assuming this historicity and, hence, analytically presupposing that which is descriptively found), this historicity (this particularity) must itself be situated in terms of its general possibility. In order to think the question of this historicity, to give an account of it in its root, the question of its general possibility must be formulated. This question leads, certainly in Du Bois's discourse, to the formulation of a question that, in its radicality, broaches a questioning of the status of the relation of identity and difference as such. We can call this the question of difference. We can also call this the question of identity. It has a transcendental resonance. I suggest that we can elucidate a discourse that we can call "ultratranscendental" in its interstices (see Derrida 1976:61 regarding situating the ultratranscendental invoked here). Du Bois formulates the (ultra) transcendental question as follows.

> What now was this particular social problem which through the chances of birth and existence, became so peculiarly mine? *At bottom and in essence it was as old as human life.* Yet in its revelation, through the nineteenth century, it was significantly and fatally new [we will take account of this "newness" below]: *the differences between men;* differences in their appearance, in their physique, in their thoughts and customs; differences so great and impelling that always from the beginning of time they thrust themselves forward upon the consciousness of all living things. Culture among human beings came to be and had to be built upon knowledge and recognition of these differences.
> (*Dusk:* 4; emphasis added)

The question in its root concerned the implication for human experience, for what we may call subjectivity in general, of the general possibility of difference, specifically as marked in human difference. It concerned how humans understood, or made sense of, the general possibility of difference. What is the ultimate status of such differences? Whence difference (itself or in general)? It is in the space of this problematic that the particular historicity that is our own, and that aspect of it which occupies Du Bois's investigations, opens.

Second, Du Bois's discourse sketches a brief history of the unfolding of the question of difference in our historicity and as our historicity. Thus, as Du Bois puts it, although operating throughout human history (indeed, perhaps as history or historicity itself), the question of social difference "in its revelation, through the nineteenth century," as a "particular social problem" of our modernity, our imperial and colonial nexus, "was significantly and fatally new" (*Dusk:* 4).[10] Continuing his twofold elaboration (in terms of the concept of race and of the African American subject) of the status of his "autobiography of a concept of race" in the passage quoted in extenso above, Du Bois develops a historical schema for situating the ultratranscendental problematic adduced therein.

> But after the scientific method had been conceived in the seventeenth century it [the scientific method] came toward the end of the eighteenth century to be applied to man and to man as he appeared then, with no wide or intensive inquiry into what he had been or how he had lived in the past. In the nineteenth century however came the revolution of conceiving the world not as permanent structure but as changing growth and then the study of man as changing and developing physical and social entity had to begin. But the mind clung desperately to the idea that basic racial differences between human beings had suffered no change; and it clung to this idea not simply from inertia and unconscious action but from the fact that because of the modern African slave trade a tremendous economic structure and eventually the industrial revolution had been based upon racial differences between men. (*Dusk:* 4–5)

If we recall my suggestion above that the question was how difference was to be understood, we can recapitulate three statements, thus far, from Du Bois's historical schema and take note of a certain sort of conceptual ambiguity. First, Du Bois suggests that eighteenth-century European discourse produced a static (perhaps hierarchical and typological) conception of "differences between men," based upon a certain reading of the way humans "appeared" at that time in a sort of global scenography. Second, Du Bois seems to suggest further that this conception could, and should, have been challenged by a thinking of the world as historical that was affirmed in the nineteenth century. Third, in the passage, as quoted so far, Du Bois suggests that this conception of differences as static persisted, despite this challenge, because of its ability to function in the production of modern systems of privilege and subordination. We should also note here a certain ambiguity in Du Bois's usage of the terms "culture" and "racial" to describe the problem of (human) difference in the three paragraphs quoted above.

Elsewhere,[11] in a reading of Anthony Appiah's reading of Du Bois on the concept of race (Appiah 1986, 1992), I develop the suggestion that Du Bois's analytic and political usage of the concept of race was strongly and decisively inflected with a social valence that situated the concept as a distinction of meaning, the ambiguous descriptive value of which, in Du Bois's discourse as well as in any other, derived from its status as simultaneously real "as" a meaningful distinction (one with brute, often murderous, effects) and as other than "real" as a meaningful distinction (the functionality and force of which is such that it is not necessarily limited by what we may take to be empirical facts). It is this social valence that is most consistently and rigorously elucidated by Du Bois over the course of his entire productivity.

At this point, however, it seems to me that Du Bois's discourse suggests that the problem of human difference formulates the specific historical site of the problematic that he wishes to elucidate. While recognizing the (apparent) ambiguity in Du Bois's usage of the terms "culture" and "race" (see Holt 1990:321, fns. 3, 5, 6), I suggest that what was decisive for Du Bois was the way in which difference was situated. Differences, he seems to suggest, were taken as signs of primordial or ultimate homogeneous identities. Although Du Bois's schema implies that (what we now often call) cultural difference became "racialized," in a strict sense his formulation suggests that the question of whether difference was conceived under the concept of "culture" or "race" (or "civilization") would not be radical. The decisive question, Du Bois's discourse seems to suggest, should be whether difference was conceived in an oppositional or a categorical manner. Du Bois thus describes our racialized historicity as one premised on "the idea that [there are] *basic* racial differences between human beings" (emphasis added).

This structural distinction, Du Bois goes on to suggest, was elaborated into an apparently simple but exceedingly complex social hieroglyphic. It is at the nexus of the play and the production of this hieroglyphic that Du Bois locates the systemic site of his emergence as an individual subject.

> . . . and this racial difference had now been rationalized into a difference mainly of skin color. Thus in the latter part of the nineteenth century when I was born and grew to manhood, color had become an

> abiding and unchangeable fact chiefly because a mass of self-conscious instincts and unconscious prejudices had arranged themselves rank on rank in its defense. Government, work, religion and education became based upon and determined by the color line. The future of mankind was implicit in the race and color of men.
>
> Already in my boyhood this matter of color loomed significantly. My skin was darker than that of my school mates. My family confined itself not entirely but largely to people of this same darker hue. Even when in fact the color was lighter, this was an unimportant variation from the norm. (*Dusk:* 5)

According to Du Bois's text, this social hieroglyphic sediments, as a sign, as a meaningful distinction, reference to an entire social order and subject positions therein. His text specifies the constitutive force of the distinction. It is not the sign itself or its status as a sign that is decisive but, rather, how it is situated. First, Du Bois outlines the general pertinence of the sign of skin color to the entirety of the specific historical field in which he was born: an "abiding and unchangeable fact" inscribed in and inscribing "government, work, religion and education." Second—and this point is crucial to our reading Du Bois responsibly—he indicates that the distinction in question, skin color distinction as a sign of racial difference that is understood in turn as a sign of fundamental human difference, was not of the ultimate importance: "even when in fact the color was lighter, this was an unimportant variation from the norm."

Although a distinction among humans according to skin color has its own specific functional effects and modes of meaningful signification, for Du Bois it was not the color that was crucial but the way in which color was understood. What grouped differences of lighter and darker skin color as one kind or type was the constitutive force of a distinction premised on the idea of the oppositional or singular coherence of another kind or type. Du Bois suggests that the "norm," the distinction or difference in question, was organized as an oppositional distinction. It gave a constitutive sense to this social field. What we must highlight here is that in the process of his description, Du Bois outlines how, according to a certain kind of distinction (an oppositional distinction), social or subject positions were produced (he gives the examples of "school" and the "family" arenas). What Du Bois's text literally describes in this opening chapter of *Dusk* is the concrete or empirical social embeddedness, the sedimented meaningfulness, the specific historical pathway in his "life" or "experience," of this sort of distinction.[12]

Having thus specified the levels of generality on which Du Bois situates the strategy that he called "autobiography of a concept," we can now turn to the example of this strategy in Du Bois's work that I have chosen to privilege in this essay.

SITUATING THE EXAMPLE: AUTOBIOGRAPHY

Over the course of the three chapters preceding the fifth chapter of *Dusk,* Du Bois gives a narrative account of his coming of age in the United States at the end of the nineteenth century. The chapter headings are as follows: Chapter Two, "A New England Boy and Reconstruction"; Chapter Three, "Education in the Last Decades of the Nineteenth Century"; Chapter Four, "Science and Empire." What is distinctive is that this account of a coming of age is not concerned with the canonical motifs of such narratives such as the becoming of a sexual, religious, or class subject. It is an account of a racial coming of age (and, of course, each of the canonical motifs is inflected in the latter). In these chapters Du Bois describes the familial and communal matrix by which he was situated as a racial subject from his "youth" (Chapter Two); the all-pervasive conception of evolutionism that coordinated not just his formal "education" but also a social conception of human difference quite generally operative in the United States in the late nineteenth century (Chapter Three); and his response—both institutional and conceptual—to the limits of general scientific conceptualizations of human difference and social practice as such conceptualizations were organized in an age of empire (Chapter Four).

In each case, Du Bois outlines, in the first person, a structure of experience that he does not name as such, but that, in its operative coordinates, is the same as what he (very early in his itinerary) called "the gift of second sight" (*Souls:* 8). A certain sense (which Du Bois called "double consciousness" in *Souls*) of this structure, called into formation by a certain experience of (or position in) the practice of racial distinction, is the pivotal recognition in this coming of age narrative.

> Had it not been for the race problem early thrust upon me and enveloping me, I should have probably been an unquestioning worshiper at the shrine of the social order and economic development into which I was born. But just that part of that order which seemed to most of my fellows nearest perfection, seemed to me most inequitable and wrong; starting from that critique, I gradually as the years went by found other

> things to question in my environment. At first, however, my criticism was confined to the relation of my people to the world movement. I was not questioning the world movement itself. What the white world was doing, its goals and ideals, I had not doubted were quite right. What was wrong was that I and people like me and thousands of others who might have my ability and aspiration, were refused permission to be part of this world. (*Dusk:* 26–27; see also 13–15, 51–52, 54)[13]

It was this structure of experience, self-consciously and strategically apprehended as a path of inquiry and understanding by Du Bois, that opened for him a critical (or desedimentative) space within the system of racial distinctions.[14] As such, this structure of experience, operated epistemologically, according to a methodology that Du Bois, as we have been noting, called the "autobiography of a concept," makes possible the demonstration, the desedimentation, of the presuppositions of the concept of race and the practices that produce or operate it, that Du Bois carries out in the telling of his family genealogy. Situated in the interim between Nietzsche and Foucault, Du Bois's discourse is certainly "genealogy" *avant la lettre* (see Foucault 1977: esp. 80–83; Nietszche 1989). We shall attempt to recognize the innovations of Du Bois's approach as we attempt to retell his telling.

Du Bois opens the chapter titled "The Concept of Race" with the following statement:

> I want now to turn aside from the personal annals of this biography to consider the conception which is after all my main subject. The concept of race lacks something in personal interest, but personal interest in my case has always depended upon this race concept and I wish to examine this now. (*Dusk:* 97)

His concern is "the history of the development of the race concept in the world and particularly in America" (*Dusk:* 97).

Du Bois begins by mapping out the conceptual context or the racial problematic (in every sense: political, economic, epistemological, etc.) into which he was born. There was one central and decisive aspect of this problematic. Racial distinctions were considered to be absolutely original, determinate, fixed, permanent, eternal, in the order of things, natural. Ultimately, the difference that was called racial was conceptualized as radically decidable as one thing or the other.

In setting the stage for his desedimentation of his racialized biography, Du Bois describes his inscription into a racial logic of opposition thus:

> So far I have spoken of "race" and race problems quite as a matter of course without explanation or definition. That was our method in the nineteenth century. Just as I was born a member of a colored family, so too I was born a member of the colored race. That was obvious and no definition was needed. Later I adopted the designation "Negro" for the race to which I belong. It seemed more definite and logical. At the same time I was of course aware that all members of the Negro race were not black and that the pictures of my race which were current were not authentic nor fair portraits. But all that was incidental. *The world was divided into great primary groups of folk who belonged naturally together through heredity of physical traits and cultural affinity.* (*Dusk:* 100; emphasis added)

As the denouement of his genealogical demonstration and at the inception of his formulation of the question of his relationship to Africa, Du Bois re-emphasizes the oppositional character of the system of racial distinction in the Americas (and Europe and its colonies in general, perhaps) at the turn of the century.

> I was born in the century when the walls of race were clear and straight; when the world consisted of mutually exclusive races; and even though the edges might be blurred, there was no question of exact definition and understanding of the meaning of the word. (*Dusk:* 116)

In terms of logic and metaphysics (that is, philosophy and science)—and I wish to emphasize this subcontext (which has no strictly delimitable margins)—the distinction was considered to be oppositional. The schema that organized its deepest conceptual resources, a certain understanding of being (see Heidegger 1969), was formulated in Aristotle's *Metaphysics* (1005b11–34) as the so-called law of contradiction (or noncontradiction) and restated, for example, in one entire aspect of Hegel's project (see Hegel 1976; 1977; Derrida 1976, 1978a, 1978b, 1981a, 1981c).

Du Bois indicates that initially he accepted the logic of this system of distinctions, although he never accepted the specific historical teleology derived from it, which placed a European race at the pinnacle of civilization (and eternally so) (*Dusk:* 51, 98–99; see also 1982f). Indeed, the "uplift" of the "Negro" race, according to the terms of this logic, provided the ground for his conception of his lifework.[15] Yet, Du Bois records that early on, he began to question this system of distinctions. His privileged example, that which led him to question this racialized logic, recognized through a mode of reflection that we have provisionally named "second-sight," was the problem (first of all autobiographical) of what I will provisionally and strategically call (in part following Du Bois; see *Dusk:* 103) "intermixture."

Along with the first theme of Du Bois's concept of the example, which we explored above, the character and implication of the concept of intermixture is the second theme that I wish to emphasize in this essay.

Du Bois describes two provocations that lead him to question the logic of racial opposition. First, citing a shuttling instability of the grounds claimed for the distinctions proposed by social Darwinism, phrenology, and degenerationist speculation, Du Bois notes that he began to question the scientificity or truth claimed for the object of description. "The first thing that brought me to my senses in all this racial discussion was the continuous change in the proofs and arguments advanced" (*Dusk:* 99). This persistent change in the *epistemological* grounds claimed for the object, at the very least, made the object itself—"race"—problematic (ambiguous, not readily susceptible to evidence). Second, and far more important, according to the emphasis of Du Bois's elaboration in this text, this epistemological ambiguity, when combined with a certain *experience,* brought the concept of race into radical question for Du Bois. "All this theory, however, was disturbed by certain facts in America, and by my European experience. Despite everything, race lines were not fixed and fast" (*Dusk:* 101). Du Bois specifies this nonoppositional heterogeneity in two ways. First, there is the motif of internal differentiation, the subatomic, if you will: "Within the Negro group especially there were people of all colors" (*Dusk:* 101).[16] Second, there is also the motif of the crossing of boundaries (in every sense of the word), a form of interlacing: "In Europe my friendships and close contact with white folk made my own ideas waver. The eternal walls between races did not seem so stern and exclusive. I began to emphasize the cultural aspects of race" (*Dusk:* 102).[17]

Du Bois inaugurates the telling of his family history with this sentence: "There is, of course, nothing more fascinating than the question of the various types of mankind and their intermixture" (*Dusk:* 103). Yet he suggests in this text, first published in 1940, that in the Americas, "where we have had the most astonishing modern mixture of human types, scientific study of the results and circumstances of this intermixture has not only lagged but been almost non-existent. We have not only not studied race and race mixture in America, but we have tried almost by legal process to stop such study" (*Dusk:* 103). We do not have to assume that only a utilitarian motivation is at work in the process of racial distinction to recognize (1) the distinct historical generality that Du Bois attributes to its functioning, pertinent to our entire modernity, and (2) the way in which he understands it to inscribe scholarship in its folds as well as to be susceptible to description by scholarship. Du Bois writes:

> [E]ver since the African slave trade and before the rise of modern biology and sociology, we have been afraid in America that scientific study in this direction might lead to conclusions with which we were loath to agree; and this fear was in reality because the economic foundation of the modern world was based on the recognition and preservation of so-called racial distinctions. In accordance with this, not only Negro slavery could be justified but the Asiatic coolie profitably used and the labor classes in white countries kept in their places by low wage. (*Dusk:* 103)

Although he never explicitly makes a declaration in the terms we are proposing here, the strategic importance for Du Bois of the problem of intermixture in the desedimentation of the problem of racial distinction is registered in every inflection of the passage just quoted. In the context of a global system (colonialism [and now its aftermath]) of proclaimed oppositional (racial) distinctions, intermixture as the very organization of all that we may call "modernity" (see also, for example, R. T. Smith 1988: 3–4), calls into question the logic of that system.

Although phenomenally ubiquitous, recognition of intermixture in the Americas has been suppressed by, for example, whites and Blacks. "[O]n the one hand, the white folk have bitterly resented even a hint of the facts of this intermingling; while black folk have recoiled in natural hesitation and affected disdain in admitting what they know" (*Dusk:* 104). Du Bois marks this response and a counterresponse in his autobiography:

> I early began to take a direct interest in my own family as a group and became curious as to that physical descent which so long I had taken for granted quite unquestioningly. But I did not at first think of any but my Negro ancestors. I knew little and cared less of the white forebears of my father. But this chauvinism gradually changed. (*Dusk:* 103)

Given (1) the operability of (oppositional) racial distinctions in the modern world, (2) what Du Bois considered to be the paucity of studies of "racial intermixture" relative to its phenomenal ubiquity, and especially

(3) the capacity of "intermixture" to overthrow the entire oppositional logic by which racial distinctions were conceptually organized (certainly in America) at the turn of the century, Du Bois considered the study of intermixture of signal importance. But to arrive at such an insight or recognition, he had first to desediment his own inscription within the logic of racial distinction. He had to formulate a conceptual change with regard to himself. As noted above, the pivotal pathway by which he was able to produce such a formulation was a form of "experience" that I have described as "second-sight," produced by a certain position within the practice of racial distinction. It led him to recognize the nonabsoluteness of racial distinction in practice. The innovation of Du Bois's insight or double sight was that he not only took it as a basis for resituating his personal understanding and behavior, but also recognized its general relevance for the way in which the entire system of racial distinctions was organized in the "modern" or "colonial" world. To recognize and situate the heterogeneous structure of the Americas, the modern world, and identity as such, Du Bois first had to recognize and situate his own heterogeneous origins, the nonreducible heterogeneity of his own constitution.

It is at this multiply layered juncture that Du Bois situates the telling of his autobiographical problematic, as a telling example. He proposes a genealogy of his family. "It is for this reason that it has occurred to me just here to *illustrate* the way in which Africa and Europe have been united in my family" (*Dusk:* 103; emphasis added). Then comes the crucial claim of the value of this example, its phenomenal generality, with regard to the historical field in which it operates: "There is nothing unusual about this interracial history. It has been duplicated thousands of times" (*Dusk:* 103; see R. T. Smith 1988:82–109; Gutman 1976).

> I am, therefore, relating the history of my family and centering it around my maternal great-great-grandfather, Tom Burghardt, and my paternal grandfather, Alexander Du Bois. (*Dusk:* 104)

This narrative provides a genealogical account of Du Bois's family for five generations on his maternal side and eight on his paternal side. What is distinctive about this narrative in terms of the strategic method and problematic that we have been mapping in this essay is that Du Bois has recalled his paternal genealogy, which he had formerly set aside because of its heritage of intermixture. In this recollection he places it alongside his maternal genealogy, the genealogy that records the matrix of kinship in

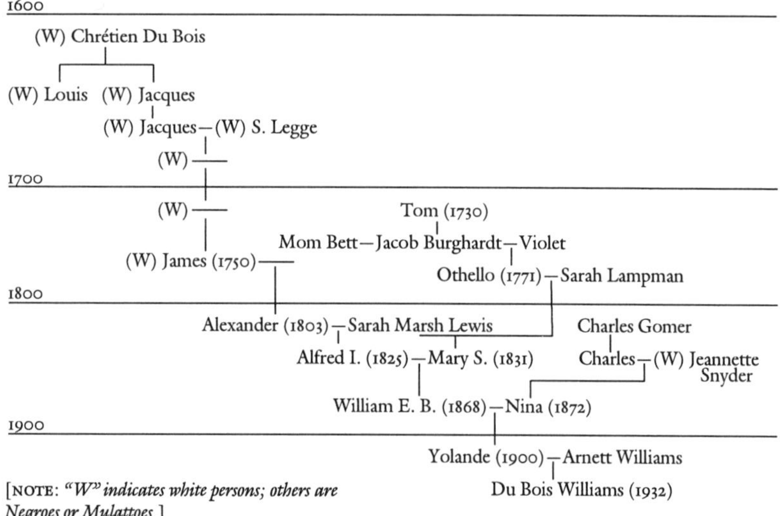

Genealogical chart of the family of W.E.B. Du Bois (from W.E.B. Du Bois, *Dusk of Dawn: An Essay Toward an Autobiography of a Race Concept*).

which Du Bois was actually raised. As early as the fourteenth chapter of *Souls* (182–83; and Du Bois repeats this African reference in *Dusk:* 114–15), Du Bois had privileged his maternal line, emphasizing both the maternal and the supposed African origin of that line. Yet, it should be noted that Du Bois approaches both the maternal and the paternal lines under the heading of patriarchy. On the one hand, we recognize here the replication of an old and tenacious sexist kinship discourse that must be brought into question. On the other hand, part of the value of Du Bois's narrative is its ironic effect, its paradoxical desedimentation of ("white") paternity. By desedimenting his "mixed" paternity, he raises questions about any "pure" (paternal) genealogy, and ultimately any notion of "pure" origin in general.[18] Hence, because the desedimentation of Du Bois's paternal genealogy allows us to negotiate all the effects to which we have been alluding, for reasons of strategy and economy I focus in the reading that follows that aspect of his narrative. Although my reading is partial, its effects, I suggest, are general. It is not a disavowal of the maternal that leads us to focus on the paternal, for it is precisely the force of the maternal in the paternal line, marked by a certain absence, a certain X, that will lead to the effects that we are attempting to bring into relief.

Du Bois focuses the inaugurating moment of his narrative around his paternal great-grandfather, Dr. James Du Bois, a physician, landholder, and slaveholder based on Long Cay in the Bahamas. He was a fifth-generation descendant of a French Huguenot farmer, whom Du Bois has come to know as Chrétien Du Bois. Let us read the narrative.

> My paternal great-grandfather, Dr. James Du Bois was white[19] and descended from Chrétien Du Bois who was a French Huguenot farmer and perhaps artisan and resided at Wicres near Lille in French Flanders. It is doubtful if he had any ancestors among the nobility, although his white American descendants love to think so. He had two, possibly three, sons of whom Louis and Jacques came to America to escape religious persecution. Jacques went from France first to Leiden in the Netherlands, where he was married and had several children, including a second Jacques or James. In 1674 that family came to America and settled at Kingston, New York. James Du Bois appears in the Du Bois family genealogy as a descendant of Jacques in the fifth generation, although the exact line of descent is not clear; but my grandfather's written testimony establishes that James was a physician and a landholder along the Hudson and in the West Indies. He was born in 1750, or later. He may have been a loyalist refugee. One such refugee, Isaac Du Bois, was given a grant of five hundred acres in Eleuthera after the Revolutionary War. The career of Dr. James Du Bois was chiefly as a plantation proprietor and slave owner in the Bahama Islands with his headquarters at Long Cay. Cousins of his named Gilbert also had plantations near. (*Dusk:* 105)

The first pivotal event of the narrative occurs here. Dr. James Du Bois "never married, but had one of his slaves as his common-law wife, a small brown-skinned woman born on the island" (*Dusk:* 105). Du Bois does not know a proper name for this woman, who was his paternal great-grandmother. He records, marks, but does not explicitly re-mark this absence. She appears under the sign of absence, an invisible X. Yet, according to the narrative, this unnameable, invisible difference produces a radical displacement of identity. Two sons were born, Alexander and John.

> Alexander, my grandfather, was born in 1803, and about 1810, possibly because of the death of the mother, the father brought both these boys to America and planned to give them the education of gentlemen.[20] They were white enough in appearance to give no inkling of their

> African descent. They were entered in the private Episcopal school at Chesire, Connecticut, which still exists there and has trained many famous men. (*Dusk:* 105–6).

At this moment the second pivotal event of the narrative occurs. "Dr. James Du Bois used often to visit his sons there, but about 1812, on his return from a visit, he had a stroke of apoplexy and died. He left no will and his estate descended to a cousin" (*Dusk:* 106). The boys were removed from school, bound out as apprentices, and cut off from the "white Du Bois family." This connection was never renewed.

These two narrative moments set the stage for a richly paradoxical narrative meditation by (W.E.B.) Du Bois focused upon the process of racial inscription of his paternal grandfather, Alexander.

> Alexander Du Bois thus started with a good common school and perhaps some high school training and with the instincts of a gentleman of his day. Naturally he passed through inner turmoil. He became a rebel, bitter at his lot in life, resentful at being classed as a Negro and yet implacable in his attitude toward whites. . . . If Alexander Du Bois, following the footsteps of Alexander Hamilton, had come from the West Indies to the United States, stayed with the white group and married and begotten children among them, anyone in after years who had suggested his Negro descent would have been unable to prove it[21] and quite possibly would have been laughed to scorn, or sued for libel. . . .[22] Alexander Du Bois did differently from Hamilton. He married into the colored group and his oldest son allied himself with a Negro clan but four generations removed from Africa. (*Dusk:* 106–7)

I will not follow this paternal narrative any further except to note two facts that I consider pertinent. First, in the part of his narrative that immediately follows the passage just quoted, Du Bois describes his grandfather's negotiation of the system of racial distinctions in the United States. Initially, it seems Alexander attempted to maintain a position of openness in the negotiation of his "racial" identity. For example, he joined a nonsegregated church, but eventually he left this congregation to join a segregated church movement—perhaps, Du Bois surmises, due to some extreme racial insult. Second, of the account of the maternal side of Du Bois's genealogy (*Dusk:* 109–15), beginning with his maternal great-great-grandfather Tom Burghardt (whom Du Bois describes as "an African Negro" [*Dusk:* 110]), the central fact that bears upon our analysis is that, as Du Bois writes: "I was brought up in the Burghardt clan and this fact determined largely my life and 'race'. The white relationships and connections were quite lost and indeed unknown until long years later" (*Dusk:* 112–14).

Du Bois's narrative of the inscription of his grandfather as a racial subject is exceedingly rich with regard to the inflections of racial distinction that it sediments in its telling. We shall not be able to be responsible to all of them or to any of them fully. Rather, I focus all too briefly on two aspects that I consider decisive: the relationship between choice and system or classification, and displacement of classification. Du Bois's discourse marks both aspects.

First, choice is coherent only as system or structure. Du Bois suggests that Alexander, by emigrating to the United States, could have had a certain limited flexibility in his negotiation of the race lines due to his physical appearance. Yet we know that even this apparent choice was governed by the system of racial distinctions operative at the time. And at this juncture we can recognize the operation of the structure, the logic of a system of racial distinctions that Du Bois describes. For we can recognize the systemic governance of Alexander's apparent choice in this fact: the decisive question is not whether Alexander truly had a choice. Rather, what matters is that the choice is either one or the other; that one cannot coherently and according to the operative systemic practices be both; that one cannot be neither.

Second, however, we must recognize that the categories do not simply preexist the subject. Alexander, as subject, had to be produced as a certain subject. For example, he had to be either "schooled" (as a "white gentleman" or as a "mulatto apprentice [shoemaker]") or deschooled (as a prepubescent mulatto boy or as a "former" white-gentleman-in-the-making). He had to be made, and in this making the historicity of the "system" is marked. It is both reproduced and rendered open to a movement of transformation, or even contestation. This contestation is possible (and a certain transformation is indeed irreducible) because it shutters itself from its own most original properties, its very possibility, its structure of intermixture (no identity can acquire its coherence without this constitutive detour through the other), in order to consolidate and reproduce itself; yet this structure of intermixture remains operative and functioning, sedimenting its irreducible difference, its X, in the very space of purity.

It is the ironic play of this X that Du Bois desediments in his autobiographical genealogy. Hence the desedimentative force of Du Bois's narrative is such that it has the logical force to overthrow the very concept of race that coordinates its problematic. The possibility of his genealogy and the structure that organizes it, the structure of intermixture, indicates that there is no stability of distinction at the root. There are no absolute criteria that would delimit Du Bois's grandfather as either black or white, and likewise for Du Bois. The irony is that socially defined as a Negro, Du Bois was somehow led—by second sight, he tells us—to recognize the ultimate nonpertinence not only of that designation but of all such designations.

Thus, by its fidelity to its theme and the form of its telling, the autobiographical, Du Bois's discourse, it seems to me, comes upon a rather profound and profoundly original structure. Stated at the level of the subject, Du Bois desediments the "fact" that "the other" is, quite literally, himself. Yet this is "true" in a double sense: (1) he is other than himself, his subject position fashioned through the other, by the structure or play of a certain X; and (2) that which he thought was other is he himself. This original structure would be as true for a "white" as for a "Black" Du Bois.

Although Du Bois is concerned to specify the relevance of his autobiographical exploration to the Americas, it would, by analogy at least, question any notion of hereditary or genealogical purity regardless of the historical domain in which it was proposed. From this standpoint, intermixture would not be historically delimitable only to the Americas or the colonial context. Further, I have been suggesting in this essay that Du Bois's discourse also formulates a structure, one that I have provisionally called "intermixture," following Du Bois,[23] that would be general to the operation of identity or difference as such, and hence not simply delimitable to any particular historical field. Rather, it would allow that historical field to open, as such, and with the configuration original to it.[24]

THE SIGNIFICATION OF THE EXAMPLE

There is a valence in Du Bois's discourse that encourages, to the extent that it does not state, the generalization I am proposing of the formulation of the problematic I have outlined therein. Indeed, if we return to the opening chapter of *Dusk,* with regard to the historical generalization I have proposed (the suggestion that the problematics of the constitution of the African American subject might be relevant to the constitution of both the "subaltern" in general and a "white" or "European or Euro-American subject"), Du Bois explicitly highlights this distinctive valence, in a way that in itself could authorize our preoccupation with the generalizing aspects of his discourse. I must note here that this generalization is produced in an autobiographical situating of the status of the autobiographical. Du Bois outlines an itinerary of desedimentation and affirmation that remains the fecund site of our responsibility. This site has been called the domain of the subaltern (Spivak 1988b). I propose no name as such. Our responsibility remains the rigorous thinking of the generality described therein.

> As I grew older, and saw the peoples of the land and of the world, the problem changed from a simple thing of color, to a broader, deeper matter of social condition: to millions of folk born of dark slaves, with the slave heritage in mind and home; millions of people spawned in compulsory ignorance; to a whole problem of the uplift of the darker races. (*Dusk:* 5)

The palpable effects of the force of this social distinction ("the problem") as Du Bois describes it are enough to blight the eye, to render the spirit jaundiced, to set conviction on a path of forceful revenge. Yet we must tease out an implication that would authorize an overrunning of all the embedded oppositions of our racialized *socius* while nonetheless positioning our sense of possibility at the fecund conjuncture of responsibility and generosity. What we may find is that the same structures which position certain historical subjects under the backbreaking and discouraging violence of enforced racialized subordination (for example, that of an African American or Negro subject), the ultratranscendental structure that marks its possibility, and the historical structures that organize its specific motivation (the distinction of these two structures would not be a true one whose functioning could be logically regulated; see Derrida 1990:959) also produce another experience of violence, another distinctive historical subject positioning (for example, that of a Euro-American or white subject), whose most distinctive sign may be that it unfolds under the cloak of normalcy—that is, as an unmarked sign.[25]

Let me summarize an argument developed at length elsewhere,[26] and perhaps too elliptically. If I mark the force inscribing the first historical experience of (racialized) violence by the name "the force of the double," then that force which inscribes the second historical experience of (racialized) violence is what I call "the double force of the force of the double." If there is such a movement as the force of the double, then it is itself at least double. What is registered here is the strange and powerful play of a certain asymmetry and symmetry (see Derrida 1978b). The point I wish to make is that while it retains the historical specificity of its topical concern with the experience of African Americans, a demonstration like Du Bois's will also demonstrate the processes through which a Euro-American or white subject is constituted (see Spillars 1991a).[27] The crucial distinction is that they are historically positioned differently with respect to those structures, particularly the specific character of the violence of this process. Yet they nonetheless are marked and constituted by the very same process, in the movement of racial distinction.

By this theme we can recognize two generalized implications of Du Bois's demonstration. The structural aspects of the process that is brought into relief by his discourse, those aspects constitutive of his subject position as an African American, (1) would be relevant to discussions of any historical identity and (2) would provide a rigorous pathway for the elucidation of a heterogeneous structure as operative at every level of generality of such an identity. Hence they would desediment the root presuppositions of canonical philosophical conceptions of identity (see Aristotle *Metaphysics* 1005b11–34)[28] (still widely afoot even when categorically, and hence naively, disavowed), and could overthrow the hegemony of an essentialist understanding of difference or sameness when elaborated with respect to the openness of its style, as I have tried to do here.

I have tried to give an account of that peculiar double or "between" at work in Du Bois's text, the specificity of this conjuncture, at once individual and general, historical and (ultra) transcendental, Afro and Euro (Black and white), to which he calls attention when he writes of "my problem of human difference, of the color line, of social degradation" and of the unavoidable force of the practice of racial difference "for me and many millions, who with me have had their lives shaped by this course of events" (*Dusk:* 6, 7). Both this problem and this force are simultaneously (ultra) transcendental and historical, inscribing, if they mark any part thereof, an entire historical field without partiality. Thus, as I have suggested, these millions surely could not be limited simply to a given identity. Although the differences of subject positions must be given an account, Du Bois's methodological practice and his strategic choice of an "autobiographical" account of a concept, of the practices organized around a concept of race, prove remarkably resourceful in elucidating and elaborating such a general account.

What is striking is that this familial demonstration produces effects at all levels of conceptual generality; it displaces a logic of racial distinction pertinent to our entire historical modernity, but it also displaces the proclaimed governing pertinence of a traditional philosophical schema, a logic of opposition, by which identity and difference in general have been understood. And in this order of generality, which here I have called the ultratranscendental, it would by analogy be conceptually pertinent to the way we talk of any identity or difference (e.g., gender, cultural).

Thus, although we are, so to speak, looking at Du Bois, looking at his own constitution as a subject, this is anything but an itinerary in simple self-reflection. It refers to what Spivak has called for as an act of "deidentification": a sort of self-reflexive account that is precisely a referring of the subject to those structures that mark and organize its emergence. In her own autobiographical gesture, Spivak writes:

> I'm interested in a sort of deconstructive homeopathy, a deconstructing of identity by identities . . . I believe that the way to counter the authority of either objective disinterested positioning or the attitude of there being no author (and these two opposed positions legitimize each other) is by thinking of oneself as an example of certain kinds of historical, psychosexual narratives that one must in fact use, however micrologically, in order to do deontological work in the humanities. When one represents oneself in such a way, it becomes, curiously enough, a deidentification of oneself, a claiming of an identity from a text that comes from somewhere else. (Spivak and Rooney 1989:130)

Performing her own masterful "reformation of mastery," to borrow and reform Houston Baker's phrase (Baker 1987; see also Clark 1991:42), in an interpellation of Derrida's discourse (Derrida 1978a), Spivak continues her appeal, recalling, in a contemporary discourse, the order of generality that I have tried to elucidate in Du Bois's discourse.

> A mother tongue is something that has a history before we are born. We are inserted into it; it has the possibility of being activated by what can be colloquially called motives. Therefore, although unmotivated it's not capricious. We are inserted into it, and, without intent, we "make it our own". We intend within it; we critique intentions within it; we play with it through signification as well as reference; and then we leave it as much without intent for the use of others after our deaths. To an extent, the way in which one conceives of oneself as representative or as an example of something is this awareness that what is one's own, supposedly what is proper to one, has a history.

> That history is unmotivated but not capricious and is larger in outline than we are, and I think that this [such self-representation] is quite different from the idea of talking about oneself. (Spivak 1989:130–31; see entire discussion, 127–31)

Indeed, the force of this essay is intended to suggest just how different from simple self-reflexivity, from solipsism in general, is such an elucidation of the autobiographical example.

However, if only by the form of his reflection, the autobiographical, Du Bois's discourse resolutely resists the absolute reduction of the subject. He seems to recognize by this style, far better than Althusser, for example (even because of the Althusserian protocol; see Althusser 1971b: 170–76), that there is a historical field only if there is such a thing as a (yet displaced and decentered) subject. Du Bois recognizes by his practice, if not by a declaration, that sense, especially epistemological sense—that which is often called truth—remains only because it is at risk and open in something like a subject.

By example, Du Bois asks us to look at ourselves in a radically other way.[29]

NOTES

This essay is dedicated to the memory of my dear friend Dwayne Hoskins.

Sections of this essay were initially prepared for the sessions at the Annual Meetings of the American Anthropological Association, on "Displacement, Diaspora, and the Geographies of Identity," in Chicago, November 20–24, 1991, organized by Smadar Lavie and Ted R. Swedenburg, and on "The Transnational Subjectivities of Africans in the Diaspora" in San Francisco, December 2–6, 1992, organized by Helan E. Page and Donna D. Daniels. Portions of this essay were presented at the Workshop on the Politics of Race and the Reproduction of Racial Ideologies, University of Chicago, May 2, 1992, and at conferences organized by the Department of German Studies at Emory University, March 25–27, 1993, and the Centre for Research in Ethnic Relations at the University of Warwick, May 21–23, 1993. Smadar Lavie and Robert Gooding-Williams read this essay in its entirety and gave me distinct and principled responses, for which I am most appreciative and will benefit beyond this text. I thank David Goldberg for our continuing dialogue; Abebe Zegeye and Julia Maxted for the wonderful invitation to Warwick; Angelika Bammer for her unfailing generosity, of which her sense of critical responsibility and the invitation to Emory have been such a small part; Thomas Holt for the freedom and openness of his response to Du Bois, which teaches by example; and Sue Hemberger, intellectual confidante and friend.

Where applicable, all references to texts by W.E.B. Du Bois are to *The Complete*

Published Works of W.E.B. Du Bois, compiled and edited by Herbert Aptheker, published by Kraus-Thomson, White Plains, N.Y., in 35 vols. (1973–1986). Where a reference is to a volume published as part of the *Complete Published Works,* the title is followed by *CPW.*

1 I should perhaps offer, as a form of generosity and a certain caution, an overture to the reader. I have written in a manner self-consciously concerned to encourage—at times, and according to a certain protocol—a nonlinear reading of this essay, attempting at times to recognize that certain problematics cannot be rigorously formulated or thought declaratively, but acquire their most sustainable formulation by indirection, delayed resonance, open-ended-return-traversal of passages, and so on. Patricia Williams has written of her own approach in writing:

> I am trying to create a genre of legal writing to fill in the gaps of traditional legal scholarship. I would like to write in a way that reveals the intersubjectivity of legal constructions, that forces the reader both to participate in the construction of meaning and to be conscious of that process. Thus, in attempting to fill the gaps in the discourse of commercial exchange, I hope that the gaps in my own writing will be self-consciously filled by the reader, as an act of forced mirroring of meaning-invention. To this end, I exploit all sorts of literary devices, including parody, parable, and poetry (Williams 1991:7–8).

Although I do not claim to fill any gaps by my style, and the range of rhetorical forms at work in the essay at hand is not as richly multiple as Williams' text, the principle by which I have written recognizes the same structures as operative in the reading/writing of this essay. It doubtless should be noted that the problem of style I have just outlined is the space in which Du Bois has made some of his most lasting contributions. The form of the autobiographical, in all its heterogeneity, is one such form or style.

2 As Du Bois explicitly suggested on more than one occasion and across several decades, the theme or question of race, the movement of the strange and powerful economy that organizes the movement of the practice of racial distinction, takes us close to the root of what we consider constitutive of our world, of our modernity, of our common colonial nexus. Thus, the implication of an elaboration of this question will remain excessive to all the particular historical domains in which we might seek to simply situate it. For example, the most general and decisive implications of perhaps the most commonly cited of Du Bois's formulations of this question, to which I have already referred, are seldom made the focus of a thematic questioning. At the beginning of the second chapter of *Souls,* which is a meditation on the aftermath of the Civil War and the project that was summed up in the Freedman's Bureau (the thesis of which—that the question of Negro slavery and the question of Negro freedom were the principal issues of the Civil War and Reconstruction, respectively, has come to majesterial fruition in the great text of Eric Foner's *Reconstruction: America's Unfinished Revolution 1863–1877* [1988]), a chapter that thus inaugurates and situates the historiographical and ethnological itinerary through the post-Emancipation South developed over the course of the following twelve essays as first and foremost

a reflection on a historical *problem,* Du Bois writes that "the problem of the twentieth century is the problem of the color-line,—the relation of the darker to the lighter races of men in Asia and Africa, in America and the islands of the sea." This sentence is often quoted. However, and decisively, the next sentence (not often quoted and seldom thought) opens with a formulation that recontextualizes the entire problematic: "It was a *phase* of this problem that caused the Civil War" (*Souls:* 16; emphasis added).

Perhaps the problem of race is the problem of our century, but its structures far exceed such limits: in this formulation, a rethinking of the contextual status of the problem of race (in every sense) and a resituating of the American Civil War in the context of the historical unfolding of global (European) colonialism (then at the moment of its consolidation in Africa) and the history of imperialism was simultaneously proposed. Forty years later Du Bois repeats the formulation. Despite its functionalist conceptualization and its restriction to a particular form of social practice, given a certain concern with the implications of the discourse of Marx (and the dominant readings thereof at the time), its continuity and faithfulness to a question should be remarked: "[T]he economic foundation of the modern world was based on the recognition and preservation of so-called racial distinctions. In accordance with this, not only Negro slavery could be justified, but the Asiatic coolie profitably used and the labor classes in white countries kept in their places by low wage" (*Dusk of Dawn* [hereinafter *Dusk,* followed by page number(s)] 103; see Du Bois 1975a).

No single structural domain or practice can situate the heterogeneity of the problematic adumbrated in these lines. Yet its pertinence remains for the entirety of our historicity. This heterogeneous problematic can only be made the topic of a thematic questioning, the only justification of which is a strategic calculation. Du Bois, at the very inception of his itinerary, undertook such a calculation and formulated a strategic line of questioning by which he could desediment those structures buried, in the American context, around an axis of denial (in every possible sense of this word) with regard to the ensemble of practices and concept-metaphors organized around the sign of race. The strategy, developed by Du Bois, that I have thought to privilege in this essay is that which focuses specifically on those processes which fashion the subject of sense. Du Bois called it the "autobiography of a concept." This genealogy of Du Bois's formulation of the color-line as a problem of modernity was first broached as it is outlined here at the annual meeting of the American Anthropological Association in November 1991.

3 Several superb essays by Cornel West mark the inauguration of a contemporary rethinking of this question (see West 1982, 1987, 1988). Although begun independently, my initial efforts in this domain were subsequently encouraged by West's contributions (see Chandler 1988). More recently, a discussion in October 1991 focused around a presentation by David Theo Goldberg (Goldberg 1993) as part of the workshop on "The Politics of Race and the Reproduction of Racial Ideologies" at the University of Chicago, convened by Professors Thomas Holt and Kenneth Warren, contributed to my thoughts along these lines. I wish to thank Professor Goldberg for generously sharing with me his extensive work along these lines prior to its pub-

lication and beyond the workshop. His work, which one might locate at the nexus of moral philosophy and cultural history, remains a distinctive contribution.

4 This new way, I hope to suggest later, opened onto the historical question that we now sometimes call the problem of the subaltern in a global sense.

5 "With the best will the factual outline of a life misses the essence of its spirit. Thus in my life the chief fact has been race—not so much scientific race, as that deep conviction of myriads of men that congenital differences among the masses of human beings absolutely condition the individual destiny of every member of a group" (*Dusk:* 139).

6 Let us note that Du Bois does not seem to consider here that this "concept" or "conceptual problematic" might not "be," as such, except as the "thoughts and deeds" or, more generally, the practices of a particular subject or subjects, even as it is not reducible to (the intentionality of) those thoughts and deeds or practices, and hence that the structures that make possible the emergence and functioning of this concept (or any concept, any practice—indeed, historicity in general) might not have any phenomenal status other than in such "magnifications and distortions" as those registered in his "autobiography." Hence, three notes that would help to situate an ambivalence in Du Bois's text can be placed here, to be taken up later.

First, the opening of Du Bois's autobiography that we quote here is called "Apology" (*Dusk:* 1–2). Second, this must be juxtaposed with Gayatri Spivak's suggestion that a decisive post-Enlightenment epistemological problem, a problem given by the sedimentations of an Enlightenment concept of objectivity, is how to account for the production of a general concept or objectivity (in an epistemological—that is, an already reduced—frame we might say "truth") that nonetheless is or must be constituted in a subjective genesis (see Spivak 1990). Third, both of the two points above have been exhaustively formulated in Derrida's tracing of the problem of genesis in Edmund Husserl's itinerary (Derrida 1954, 1978c, 1978d). Indeed, Derrida made this question his own and the site for the emergence of all his subsequent discourse. It is a rethinking of the transcendental (where the distinction transcendental–worldly cannot be absolute) that Derrida undertakes there. The essence of the accomplishment of these texts, for me, is Derrida's elaboration of the absolutely interlaced necessity of history for the logos and of the logos for history. The critical edge for philosophy of course is Derrida's insistence on the necessity and risks of the "historical" status of the logos—indeed, in the movement of the production of ideality, such as mathematical truths. This poses a new thinking that is surely a rethinking of that which has been called materiality or empiricism in general.

I have ventured this essay under the general aim of one guiding question: Is it possible for the most particular or subjective "history" to tell the most general of truths, perhaps precisely because such histories do distort and magnify in particular sorts of ways?

7 I should cite the entirety of the opening four paragraphs of this opening chapter of *Souls.* Moreover, a formal protocol of pronouns could be traced throughout the entirety of the text. Stepto (1979) provides some suggestions in this regard.

8 "The Souls of Black Folk is a series of fourteen essays written under various circumstances and for different purposes during a period of seven years. It has therefore, considerable, perhaps too great, diversity. There are bits of history and biography, some description of scenes and persons, something of controversy and criticism, some statistics and a bit of storytelling. All this leads to rather abrupt transitions of style, tone and viewpoint and, too, without doubt, to a distinct sense of incompleteness and sketchiness. On the other hand, there is a unity in the book, not simply the general unity of the larger topic, but a unity of purpose in the distinctly subjective note that runs through each essay" (Du Bois 1977:9).

9 Although his emphasis occurs according to a different trajectory, Derrida's formulation of his own affinity for the problematic of the autobiographical is apposite here. I say this ironically, of course, with a double edge, since with regard to the history of African American autobiographical practices, Derrida's contributions arrive quite late on the scene in which these practices have emerged (see Andrews 1986, 1989; Gates 1991), yet he remains a thinker whose work offers one of the strongest possible justifications for recognizing the remarkable resources of the autobiographical (see Derrida 1986). In the course of trying to situate his work as giving up neither philosophy nor literature, "perhaps seeking obscurely a place from which the history of this frontier could be thought or even displaced," Derrida states in a 1988 interview: "'Autobiography' is perhaps the least inadequate name, because it remains for me the most enigmatic, the most open, even today" (Derrida 1989:34; one should cite the entire discussion in which it is embedded, at least).

10 "A man lives today not only in his physical environment and in the social environment of ideas and customs, laws and ideals; but that total environment is subjected to a new sociophysical environment of other groups, whose social environment he shares but in part" (*Dusk:* 134–35).

11 Although I may yet elaborate this reading of Appiah in a separate review essay, along with a reading of Adolph Reed's essay on Du Bois (Reed 1992), I propose a reading of his texts cited here along with other readings of Du Bois's early work in the opening chapters of an unpublished manuscript "The Problem of Purity: The Question of Social Difference and African American Identity in the Early Work of W.E.B. Du Bois, 1897–1915."

12 Here we must recognize Du Bois's pioneering role, articulated in *Souls,* in describing the split or double structure of colonial and postcolonial geographic spaces, such as the two-part character of the colonial town remarked later by Frantz Fanon (1968), Edward Said (1983), Abdul R. JanMohamed (1983), and Bernard Cohn (1987a:422–62; 1987b); or remarked, for example, in the description given of the American South by Zora Neale Hurston (1935) and of the urban North by Joe Gibbs St. Clair Drake (1965; see also Drake and Cayton 1993). Here is where a certain conceptualization of transnationality must disrupt the metaphor of geographical homogeneity that can be implied by the semantic gathering of the word "transnational"; likewise, such a (re)conceptualization would question the presupposition of nation implied therein.

13 Oblique and limited in this initial formulation, the unfolding and specification of

this space of critique is the central teleological motif in *Dusk*. Here I will specify only two key aspects, for this book and this motif in it deserve an entire essay specifically on this question. First, Du Bois explicitly goes on in the narrative of *Dusk* to develop a deep and far-reaching motif of the "White world," culminating in the masterful Chapter Six, "The White World" (134–72). Second, as I suggest below, in this essay, Du Bois elaborates this space of critique as a question of the ground of the very terms of human distinction, especially in the pivotal Chapter Five of *Dusk:* "The Concept of Race."

14 Contrary to many thinkers (e.g., Appiah 1986, 1992), Du Bois never seemed to assume the possibility of simply stepping outside or beyond systems of racial distinction. An entire paradoxical economy, elaborated nowhere as richly as in the work of Du Bois with regard to racial distinction, and in the work of Derrida with regard to philosophical distinction, would demonstrate that such an assumption is at best simply naive and at worst politically suspect. Below, I touch on the ensemble of paradoxes at stake here. See note 16.

15 "[W]hen I came to Harvard [in 1889, at the age of twenty-one] the theory of race separation was quite in my blood. I did not seek contact with my white fellow students. On the whole I rather avoided them. I took it for granted that we were training ourselves for different careers in worlds largely different. There was not the slightest idea of the permanent subordination and inequality of my world" (*Dusk:* 101).

16 Du Bois elaborates, in the sentences following the one just quoted, an acute recognition and negotiation of the paradoxes that lay in wait for anyone who would attempt a coherent response to the logic of racial distinction. A simple declaration of neutrality with regard to a "racial" distinction (and all social distinction would be at least symbolic, and hence semiotic) without a systematic strategy for challenging the existing hierarchy of value would (1) leave that hierarchy in place and (2) intensify its force by reinstating its governing schema, the logic of homogeneity, without recognizing it as such, because all racial distinction (no matter how pragmatically fluid) is founded, in its deepest root, upon the logic of opposition, and hence is always hierarchical.

In order to bring such a system into question, according to whatever purpose or in terms of whatever order of generality, a difference, and especially the irreducible radicality of its possibility, must be adduced:

> Then too, there were plenty of my colored friends who resented my ultra "race" loyalty and ridiculed it. They pointed out that I was not a "Negro" but a mulatto; that I was not a Southerner but a Northerner, and my object was to be an American and not a Negro; that race distinctions must go. I agreed with this in part and as an ideal, but I saw it leading to inner racial distinction in the colored group. I resented the defensive mechanism of avoiding too dark companions in order to escape notice and discrimination in public. As a sheer matter of taste I wanted the color of my group to be visible. I hotly championed the inclusion of two black schoolmates whose names were not usually on the invitation list to our social affairs." (*Dusk:* 101–2)

The set of paradoxes inscribed in this passage mark the coordinates of an ethical challenge that frames all of Du Bois's formulations of the problematic of racial distinction. This ensemble of "racial" paradoxes also inscribes a quite general problematic (see Derrida 1978a, 1981b, 1981c:207, fns. 24, 25).

17 That Du Bois specifies Europe as distinct from America is both an act of generosity and a critique. To recognize an openness in Europe is to recognize a heterogeneity among "white folk" and, moreover, to respond in kind. To specifically leave aside America in this acknowledgment can be nothing less than the harshest of judgments. Du Bois had already stated this theme in the second paragraph of the opening chapter of *Souls* (7).

18 I shall not dwell here on the general fact that Du Bois's account follows conceptions of kinship (such as tracing kinship by bifurcated parental lines, use of common "English" kin terms, conceptualizing the notion of family around a nuclear unit, etc.) that have been found to be quite common and general in the United States and the English-speaking Caribbean (see R. T. Smith 1988; Schneider 1980, 1984). However, I must also note the quite particular fact that Du Bois's discussion records (1) the tendency, where so-called intermixture occurs, to trace the general family line according to a racial bifurcation, through either one or the other racial category, leading to (a) the forgetting of the other line and (b) the polarization of the difference between these two lines; and (2) a deliberate questioning of the logic of this tendency as its central theme.

19 We must recall here a crucial insight of the late James Baldwin: that there is no such thing as a "white" person; that "white" Americans became white only upon the construction of such a category in the United States, and in relation to the construction of "Black" people and "red" people (see Baldwin 1984; but many of Baldwin's insights along these lines could be adduced; see also Baldwin and Mead 1971 and Baldwin 1990 generally; and see Morrison 1992; Roediger 1991). Moreover, Baldwin noted this crucial irony: these immigrants usually came to America because they were not "white" in their own country (see Orsi 1992 for another twist in this paradoxical structure). Above all, we must note here, for elaboration elsewhere, that Du Bois was one of the first twentieth-century writers to recognize this problematic and to make it a theme (see Du Bois 1982b).

20 We could perhaps amend this to read "[white] gentlemen."

21 Raymond Smith's work in Jamaica and Guyana, and to some extent the West Indies in general, which should be understood as both continuous and discontinuous with the United States with regard to the general domain that anthropologists have typically understood as "kinship," records several similar histories (Smith 1988:82–109; see also Craton and Walvin 1970; Craton 1978, 1979; Gutman 1976).

22 The question of legality is central to the structure of racial distinction. Law will always err on or insure the side of distinctions. Du Bois has already qualified his narrative at its inception with this statement: "Absolute legal proof of facts like these here set down is naturally unobtainable" (*Dusk:* 104). At the point in his text at which we have broken off for this note, Du Bois gave a contemporary specification

to what we might call the law of racial distinction: "Indeed the legal advisors of the publishers of my last book could write: 'We may assume as a general proposition that it is libelous to state erroneously that a white man or woman has colored blood'" (*Dusk:* 106–7).

23 But I have also strategically proposed several other names, none simply commensurate with the others, such as "between," "the other," and the (force of the) "double" (which, because it is "first" of all "internal," is never only double).

24 Again, this refers first of all to a new thinking of structure, one that I have called "ultratranscendental," following Derrida (1976:61); one that he has also called "grammatological." The crucial innovation of Derrida's elaboration of this new thinking of structure in *Of Grammatology* is his formulation of structure in such a way that system does not simply preexist iterable mark as an already constituted transcendental field (see esp. Derrida 1976:62–65).

25 We must position at this juncture both Du Bois's long answer to the question "What is Africa to me?" (*Dusk:* 116–33, esp. 116–17) and his enigmatic yet profoundly transgressive response (*Dusk:* 134–72) to his ("White") interlocutor(s) on the question of what the "us" is that comprises "America." Romantic, perhaps, in the hope he has for the "uplift of the darker races," Du Bois could only be accused of maintaining a fundamental commitment to a concept of race as biological fact by a naive or willful reading. Although not motivated as a response to any particular discourse—indeed, my reading issues from a first concern to assume a certain responsibility for the questions that motivated Du Bois's discourse, and not necessarily his answers—the reading I have outlined in this essay suggests that Appiah's reading (Appiah 1986, 1992) of Du Bois's response to the first question quoted above (What is Africa to me?) is a severe misapprehension of the questions that organized Du Bois's discourse and an unjustified and unacknowledged reduction of Du Bois's answer.

For example, the genealogical desedimentation that I have traced in this essay precedes and prepares the stage for Du Bois's response to this question, yet Appiah's reading of it does not refer at all to the deessentializing narrative of the paternal line or the discourse of the previous chapters that prepares us to follow its movement. Nor could his reading open itself up to the movement of the dialogue that Du Bois goes on to elaborate between "himself" and a "white" interlocutor in the very next chapter, "The White World." For example, Du Bois writes: "[Interlocutor]: '—oh Hell! Honest to God, what do you think Asia and Africa would do to us, if they got a chance?'; [Narrator]: 'Skin us alive,' I answer cheerfully, loving the 'us'" (*Dusk:* 167).

26 I develop this argument thematically in *The Problem of Purity* (see note 11).

27 Hortense Spillars (1991a) offers a brilliant reading of William Faulkner's *Absalom, Absalom!* along these lines, but seems to claim a special value for the non-United States Americas in the analytic recognition of heterogeneity in the constitution of racialized subject position. And, although she elsewhere recognizes the pivotal contribution of Du Bois (e.g., 1991b), she does not do so in the essay cited here. Indeed, she privileges mestizo America in a way that replicates an old motif that is produced by the very racialist discourse she sets out to critique. This gesture was already

produced by Retamar (1989) in the opening paragraphs of his essay, and even by Martí (1977), whose text figures centrally in Retamar's; both Martí's and Retamar's discourses are central to Spillars' essay. That Du Bois had raised the question of intermixture persistently throughout his itinerary (e.g., Du Bois 1982b), and that the writing of Faulkner's text (see Faulkner 1972 [1936]) and Du Bois's (first published in 1940) were so temporally proximate suggests the relevance of Du Bois's discourse to her analysis.

28 Even Hegel, in the *Science of Logic,* writes of the "presence" of A in the third, in his discussion of the "law of the excluded middle" (1976:438–39).

29 See also Derrida 1992.

CROSSCURRENTS, CROSSTALK: RACE, "POSTCOLONIALITY," AND THE POLITICS OF LOCATION

RUTH FRANKENBERG AND LATA MANI

This essay had its immediate point of origin in the invitation to contribute to a lecture series on "Postcoloniality and California" in the spring of 1991. Commonplace as the term "postcoloniality" has rapidly become in literature, anthropology, and cultural studies in recent times, the title begged a number of questions about the notion of "postcoloniality" and its efficacy, in relation either to California in particular, or to the United States in general. If the concept of "postcoloniality" is spreading like brushfire through the terrain of cultural theory, what we propose by way of remedy is a carefully strategized "controlled burn" approach that begins by posing the following questions.

What does "postcoloniality" mean, for whom does it resonate, and why? What are the risks and effects of too hastily globalizing the concept?[1] In what senses, for example, are India, Britain, and the United States "postcolonial" locations? What are the multiple implications of "post-ness" in relation to "colonialism," in the context, for example, of the persistence and current escalation of racism? We will argue that rigorous attention to that which neo-Gramscians and Althusserians call "conjuncture," and some feminists describe as a "politics of location," is critical to specifying both the limits and the value of the term "postcolonial." In this essay we sketch the beginnings of what we call a "feminist conjuncturalist" approach to the issue of which spaces and subjects might be conceived as "postcolonial," and in what senses such a description might hold.[2]

NOTES ON THE TERM "POSTCOLONIAL," OR WHAT WE THINK IT MEANS, ANYWAY

India

"Postcolonial" implies independence from Britain; birth of the nation-state; end of territorial colonialism; inauguration of a path of economic development characterized by the growth of indigenous capitalism; neocolonial relationship to the capitalist world; aid from socialist countries and horizontal assistance from other Third World countries not aligned to either the First or the Second World.

Britain

"Postcolonial" signals loss of colonies; decline of empire; and the appearance on British landscapes of a significant number of people from the former colonies: "We are here because you were there." The transition from a society of predominantly white ethnic groups to one that is multiracial. The "Other" no longer geographically distanced—out there—but within, and over time shaping inner city landscape and culture in significant ways. Samosas at the National Theatre Café. Race riots.

United States

Here, the term "postcolonial" sticks in our throats. White settler colony, multiracial society. Colonization of Native Americans, Africans imported as slaves, Mexicans incorporated by a border moving south, Asians imported and migrating to labor, white Europeans migrating to labor. U.S. imperialist foreign policy brings new immigrants who are "here because the United States was/is there," among them Central Americans, Koreans, Pilipinos, Vietnamese, and Cambodians. The particular relation of past territorial domination and current racial composition that is discernible in Britain, and that lends a particular meaning to the term "postcolonial," does not, we feel, obtain here. Other characterizations, other periodizations seem necessary in naming, for this place, the shifts expressed by the term "postcolonial" in the British and Indian cases: the serious calling into question of white/Western dominance by the groundswell of movements of resistance, and the emergence of struggles for collective self-determination most frequently articulated in nationalist terms.

"Post-civil rights" is a possible candidate for signaling this double articulation in the U.S. context. Let us emphasize at the outset that we use the term "post-civil rights" broadly, to refer to the impact of struggles by African American, American Indian, La Raza, and Asian American communities that stretched from the mid-1950s to the 1970s, movements that Michael Omi and Howard Winant have credited with collectively producing a "'great transformation' of racial awareness, racial meaning, racial subjectivity" (1986:90).[3] However, "post-Civil Rights" would grasp only one strand of our description of the United States. The term would have to be conjugated with another, one that would name the experience of recent immigrants/refugees borne here on the trails of U.S. imperialist adventures, groups whose stories are unfolding in a tense, complicated relation—at times compatible, at times contradictory—with the post-civil rights United States.

POST- WHAT?!

We are quite aware that the terms "postcolonial" and "post-civil rights" are, in important senses, incommensurable. First, "colonial" refers to a system of domination, whereas "civil rights" designates collective struggle against a system or systems of domination. Strictly speaking, the analogous term to "post-civil rights" would be "post-decolonization struggle." Conversely, the term analogous to "postcolonial" at its most literal would be "post-racist." This in turn underscores the dangers of a literalist reading of the word "postcolonial." It seems to us that placing the terms "postcolonial" and "post-civil rights" alongside one another immediately serves to clarify some of the temporal and conceptual ambiguities of the "post" in both cases. From the vantage point of the United States today, it draws attention to the unfinished nature of the processes designated by both terms. It undermines, specifically, the sense of completion often implied by the "post" in "postcolonial," and which, if political conservatives could have their way, they would settle upon the "post" in "post-civil rights." In doing so, it helps to clarify that the "posts" in both cases do not signal an "after" but, rather, mark spaces of ongoing contestation enabled by decolonization struggles both globally and locally. Finally, "post-civil rights" has not, to our knowledge, been used to name or claim identity. Questions of subject formation have, on the other hand, been integral to a consideration of the "postcolonial" (see, e.g., Said 1986a; Bhabha 1989; Harasym 1990). Accordingly, in this essay we move between considering "postcolonial" as periodization and as axis of subjectivity. By contrast, "post-civil rights" is developed here as a form of periodization that we believe to be particularly helpful in coming to terms with the ideological and political landscape of the United States today.[4]

POSTCOLONIAL(ITY?): A STATE OF BEING?

Taking the word apart with the help of the dictionary, we find that "post," in the sense that it interests us here, means variously "after in time," "later," "following," or "after in space." Without benefit of the dictionary, we take it that "colonization" and "colonialism" indicate a system of domination, in particular one involving geographical and/or racial distanciation between the rulers and the ruled, and one that, like all systems of domination, has interlinked political, economic, and discursive dimensions. The suffix "i-t-y," in English "ity," in French "ité," and in Latin "itas," is said to mean "character," "condition," or "state," with "state" defined as "a set of circumstances or attributes characterizing a person or thing at a given time," a "way or form of being." This confirms the suffix "ity" in "postcoloniality" as connoting a condition that is evenly developed rather than internally disparate, disarrayed, or contradictory.

Dictionary explorations of course mean little, in the sense that there is no collective unconscious, nor even a common Spellcheck and thesaurus in the hard drive, by means of which cultural critics continually confirm their intended meanings through reference to Webster's. But it seems to us that this staged form of attention to both prefix and suffix dramatizes the crux of what is problematic in the concept of "postcoloniality." The first problem lies with the "post." It means "after in time." But what happened during that time—presumably, in this instance, a time between "colonialism" or "coloniality" and now? In what senses are we now situated "after" "coloniality" in the sense of "coloniality" being "over and done with"? What about "the colonial" is over, and for whom? This is not a rhetorical but a genuine question, for it seems to us that in relation to colonialism, some things are over, others are transformed, and still others apparently are unreconstructed. What, by the way, happened to "neocolonialism" in all of this talk of the colonial and the post? In short, what do we too hastily elide when we invoke the "postcolonial," especially as an "ity," as a condition, state, way, or form of being spread evenly over an area without specified borders or unevenness or contradiction?

AUTOBIOGRAPHICAL RIFF: LATA

As things go, I qualify rather well for the appellation "postcolonial." I was born and raised in post-independence Bombay, singing the Indian national anthem in school assemblies, standing to it in movie theaters, submitting endless unsuccessful entries to essay competitions on the theme "India's unity lies in her diversity." In my youth the colonial period was just that—a demarcatable historical phenomenon. Its greatest significance, we learned, lay in its incitement and provocation of a national liberation movement whose heroes we encountered, sometimes daily, as street names, as marble busts in school yards, or as statues presiding over busy intersections, home to pigeons and the poor. Yes, I think, there *is* a way in which my sense of self—my subject position, if you will—takes shape within a "postcolonial" context, one also constituted by, among other things, my gender, class, and thoroughly urban upbringing.

And yet there is something about the privileging of the concept of "postcoloniality," the particular way in which it is globalized, as a description either of the world or of identity, that makes me exceedingly anxious. I think about Native American friends who rightly cringe at the suggestion that the Americas are "postcolonial." I ponder the fact that Black and Chicano critics have in the main not rushed to embrace the term as adequate to their present condition. I wonder if it is significant that the theorists most associated with the term—Edward Said, Gayatri Spivak, and Homi Bhabha—are themselves first-generation diasporic intellectuals, displaced to the United States and United Kingdom from an elsewhere that shaped them in fundamental ways. At this point in my musings, I recognize two strategies that I could adopt in pursuing the question further. I could explore the historico-intellectual and political biographies of Said, Spivak, and Bhabha and their relation to their theoretical production, tracing the disjunctions between their own formulation of the issues and the politics of their reception within the Western academy. Alternatively, I could explore my disquiet about "postcoloniality" in relation to stories that narrate my own experiences and those of others with whom I debate such things.

> Identity is neither continuous nor continuously interrupted but constantly framed between the simultaneous vectors of similarity, continuity and difference. (Hall, in Chabram and Fregoso 1990:206)

Stuart Hall's formulation, which charts a path between an essentialist and a rigorously poststructuralist conception of identity, captures the complex and dynamic interplay of modes of Othering and racialization within and against which, for instance, my own sense of self and construction by others can be understood.

Incident 1: It is dark and pouring rain. I curse, unprepared as I am for the downpour and for the fact that buildings on campus are locked at 5 P.M. for reasons of safety. I am keeping a colleague waiting, and there is no phone nearby. I decide to knock on the window of the office closest to the entrance. The gentleman, white and in his mid-forties, is on the phone and gestures impatiently for me to wait. Although he is less than a minute, it feels much longer, and I hop from foot to foot in the vain hope of dodging the raindrops. Placing the receiver on the cradle, he comes to the door. Opening it a crack, he asks me irritatedly what I want. Surprised that he needs an explanation, I ask to be let in, stating that I am to meet someone in the building and had forgotten that the doors were locked at 5 P.M. Refusing to open the door any further, he states flatly that he cannot let anyone in off the street, God knows what I might do. I stand there gaping at him, shocked and taken aback.

Incident 2: Later that same week I am hurrying to my car, loaded down with books. I hope that luck is on my side and some kindly soul will let me into the building that borders the parking lot, thereby saving me the trouble of walking all the way around it. I dare not assume too much, given my experience earlier in the week. As I approach the door, I notice a Pilipina woman cleaning the corridor. She looks up at me, smiles, and without a word opens the door for me.

Occurring as they did back to back, these incidents illustrated for me what we otherwise experience in more undramatic ways: that identity is both relational and situated. Not having interviewed either the professor or the cleaning lady, I cannot claim to have their account of the incidents. My comments therefore are to be understood as my account of their constructions of me. In the first case my colleague refused to let me in, presumably concluding that I did not look like someone who had legitimate business in a university building at that time of the evening. I did not, I suppose, look like an authority figure. My clothes or books, which could have signified either class or profession, were clearly not sufficient clues as to who or what I might be. Race appears to have overriden class. In the latter incident, however, it took the Pilipina worker less than thirty seconds to size me up. With similar visual clues and no request from me, she appears to have deemed it safe or appropriate to allow me to enter the building. Class appears to have determined her decision.

These incidents clarified for me a general confusion I had been experiencing in my institutional life: the contrast between the warm response to me of people who explicitly knew what my business was at the university, and the wariness of those who did not, and whose suspicions required an explanation or an ID card in order to be allayed. I should stress here that I am not singling out any particular institution as an especially reprehensible site of racism, but am drawing on some of my experiences to think through my inscription into racist as well as colonial and postcolonial discourses.

My initial naïveté and surprise in response to such incidents as I have just described speaks to my own "postcolonial" and class identity. Not having grown up as the Other of my society, I do not expect to be positioned as such. Indeed, this fundamental difference in life experience has led to my own sense of the importance of specifying the differences between those of us from the geographical Third World and those of us who came to adulthood as people of color in the West. Attention to such differences is crucial if we are not to falsely equalize groups with very different relations to the U.S. power structure. We need to be wary of the possibility that university affirmative action or diversity agendas may be met by filling positions with people trained elsewhere, a strategy common in the business world, and one further enabled by the 1991 Immigration Act. In sum, as many have pointed out, the "Other" is not a homogeneous entity.

Having said that, however, what has been instructive to me is the extent to which modes of racialization specific to the history of certain Others are available for extension to other Others. The best instance of this comes from a story of an Arab woman who was told by a prospective employer in the midst of job negotiations, "I will not haggle over your head." As she put it, she felt dumbstruck as the discourse of slavery, of the trade in human beings as property, reemerged in context of the bargaining that is an integral part of all hiring and is usually assumed to be a process that is at least nominally one among equals, not between master and slave.

The eruption in unexpected places of elements of the discourse of slavery or of the Other as trespasser or potential thief does not in any way undo the specificities of our positionings, but does point to the necessity that any consideration of "postcolonial" identity must necessarily engage the vectors of similarity, continuity, and difference. For the "postcolonial," we will argue, is no unifying moment. Not only are we positioned differently in relation to what is called up by that term, but disjunction must be central to our understanding of it. (For an analysis of contemporary culture that proposes the centrality of disjuncture, see Appadurai 1990.)

AUTOBIOGRAPHICAL RIFF: RUTH

Like Bombay, India, my home—Manchester, England—has a Victoria Station. Two ends of the same imperial line. My first twenty years were shaped both by British imperialism and by the diasporas that sprang from its demise. Thus, in my childhood in the late 1950s and 1960s, some of my toys, clothes, and combs were marked "Empire Made." Colonial encounters marked the English language: I used, and still use, words transformed from Hindi and other Indian languages: shampoo, dungarees, pajamas, cushy. As a small girl my favorite bedtime stories were about Epaminondas, the "naughty picanniny" who lived on a plantation and who, according to his mother—illustrated in the books as large, cheerful, and wearing bright dresses, a white apron, and a headscarf—"didn't have the sense he was borned with." Among my dolls was a black, cuddly golliwog, Sambo crossed with a teddy bear. In one of my proudest moments, my sister and I marched down the aisle of our Unitarian chapel dressed in feathered headdresses and fringed tunics made of old curtains and, beating out a rhythmn on drums that my father had brought back from Kenya, sang to the assembled congregation something that claimed to be "The Huron Indian Christmas Carol." It began, "Twas in the moon of wintertime/when all the birds had fled . . . ."[5]

Postcolonial times brought imperialist nostalgia, crudely slapstick television shows like "Up the Jungle," "It Ain't 'Alf Hot, Mum," and "The Black and White Minstrel Show," in which white men went into blackface as East Indians and African Americans, and the more recent, more upscale "Jewel in the Crown" serial drama in the early 1980s.

For many white Britons, the "Other" was more palatable confined within the white imaginary than in person. During my teens Enoch Powell made his infamous "rivers of blood" speech, marshaling the white population's fear and hatred of immigrants of color, as South Asians, transported to East Africa by the British at the height of empire, were caught in the crossfire of Ugandan and Kenyan nationalism and came to the "mother country." There they found themselves joining African Caribbeans in, among other things, selling bus tickets and emptying hospital bedpans. I remember newspaper articles about Indian and Pakistani "multi-occupied houses," where new immigrant families would work, and sleep, in shifts. The moral of these stories was not, however, that the United Kingdom was less than hospitable to its new arrivals, but that South Asians were dirty and uncivilized. There were court cases about whether turbans were or were not an appropriate adjunct to a bus conductor's uniform or an adequate substitute for a motorcyclist's helmet.

Raised left-wing, my first involvements as a student activist were with

Rock Against Racism and the Anti-Nazi League, massive youth movements in response to an upswing of racist violence and electoral success by neo-Nazi parties around the country. Our chants of "Black and White, Unite and Fight!" and "Never Again!" scrambled together a "Just Say No!" approach to racism with another "moment of glory" in British popular memory—World War II and the fight against Hitler.

This is, of course, a partial and idiosyncratic history. But my point here is that in my own, and most likely in my white compatriots', subject formation a tangle of images and practices, colonial and "postcolonial," from the relatively benign to the brutal, are jostling for position. This has several implications for the present reexamination of "postcoloniality." First, it suggests that periodizing colonialism and its "posts" is not a simple task. There is no evidence here of a smooth march in formation such that, as the economics and politics of domination are transformed, the discursive aspects of colonization follow along and change from colonial to "postcolonial" forms. The white subject, in short, remains enamored of colonial imagery long after the heyday of direct rule, in ways that are both different and the same, changed and not changed much at all.

Second, it is in this context that colonial discourses can plausibly be hauled out apparently unchanged, and redeployed. Telling examples of this, so to speak, renewable energy source were British and U.S. descriptions of Saddam Hussein, his army, and Arab people in general during the recent period of military engagement with Iraq. Here, the rhetoric of colonialism and racism was so evident as to require few if any skills in cultural criticism. The British press, for example, referred to the Iraqi army as, among other things, "hordes," and to the troops as "bastards of Baghdad," "mad dogs," "blindly obedient," "ruthless," and "fanatical." Meanwhile, the British forces were "lionhearts," "heroes," "dare-devils," and "young knights of the skies" (*Guardian Weekly* 1991). In Bellevue, Washington, a Republican state senator insisted on local radio that "there's no such thing as a moderate Arab." And on National Public Radio, during the period of U.S. bombing of Iraq, a white woman American "expert" on the Arab world confidently described "the" Arab psyche as fundamentally narcissistic, yet low in self-esteem. This tragic contradiction, she felt, explained both why Saddam Hussein had gone to war and why future wars and future Saddam Husseins were an inevitability for which the United States and its allies must be prepared. In short, although the period of the buildup to armed conflict between the U.S.-European force and the Iraqi army was relatively brief, it provided ample time for a dramatic resurgence of elements of colonial discourse, premised for their form on notions of essential, ontological difference between the Other and the Western "self" (extremist and irrational versus calm and rational, infantile narcissism versus maturity), and for their content on orientalist categories (ruthlessness, fanaticism, Oriental despotism, etc.) (Said 1978).

Moreover, colonial discourses in the white imaginary are dispersed across space as well as time, evoking images from British colonization of India and Africa, as well as from the history of the United States as a settler, slave-owning colony. As in the incidents and events Lata Mani has described here, my own psyche and material experiences have been, and continue to be, assailed both by my own country's engagements with colonialism and by those of others.

All of this suggests that white, Western "postcolonial" subjects are still interpellated by classical colonialism itself. Which raises questions: When does "colonial" become "post"? And what, in this context, does "post" mean? This kind of bricolage cannot, we feel, be fully explained by reference to "postmodernity" and thence, by extension, to the "postcolonial." For even in the heyday of direct-rule colonization, colonial fiction, museum exhibits, travel accounts, and even "discoveries" at times shared this same disrespect for location and veracity (see, e.g., Hulme 1986; M. L. Pratt 1985; Mullen 1987; Grewal 1990).

Stuart Hall makes an observation about time and social transformation that is helpful here. He argues that history consists of

> processes with different timescales, all convened in the same conjuncture. Political time, the time of régimes and elections, is short: "A week is a long time in politics." Economic time, sociological time, so to speak, has a longer durée. Cultural time is even slower, more glacial. All human action has both its subjective and its objective side. (Hall 1991: 61)

This observation certainly confirms one part of what I am claiming here about white subject formation and cultural context in Britain: both form and content continue to echo colonialism well after the decline, if not the demise, of the British Empire. However, we would add some further observations to those of Hall, beginning by noting in passing that we take it that "culture" here refers to structures of thinking, not to "style"—for style, as we know, changes rapidly. We would suggest that perhaps cultural time is paced differently, according to one's location in relation to systems of domination. Thus, the "afterlife" of colonial discourse is very different for the colonizer and for the colonized. Finally, perhaps for each of us there are multiple time pathways, variously paced, so that cultural change is simultaneously slow and fast, not just across communities but within socially and historically positioned selves. (For a fuller discussion of this point with respect to white American female subjectivity, see Frankenberg 1993.)

SOMETHING "POSTCOLONIAL" IS HAPPENING —BUT WHAT, WHERE, AND TO WHOM?

It is this notion of a political, economic, and discursive shift, one that is decisive without being definitive, that we would like to argue regarding the term "postcolonial." For it enables us to concede the shift effected by decolonization without claiming either a complete rupture in social, economic, and political relations and forms of knowledge (an end to racial inequality, economic self-sufficiency for new nations, "the end of History") or its opposite, admittedly argued by few, that the present is nothing more than a mere repetition of the past.

The distinction between "decisive" and "definitive" seems to us important, given the enabling status accorded to decolonization in discussions of the new ethnography, contemporary cultural theory, the crisis in the humanities, and, more recently, in Robert Young's important discussion of the emergence of poststructuralism (Young 1990). Although we are generally in sympathy both with the direction of such discussion and with the ethical impulses that motivate it, we are wary of certain tendencies within the debate (see also Mani 1991). We would like to note two concerns in particular.

Robert Young's *White Mythologies: Writing History and the West* is a fine example of a project that embodies both the promises and some of the problems of the rethinking currently under way. Young makes a compelling argument for considering the impact of the Algerian War of Independence on French political and philosophical thought. However, his powerful critique of ethnocentrism is undermined by his general tendency to read anticolonial movements as primarily engaging the logic of Western philosophy. Thus it seems, at times, that a key object and achievement of the Algerian War of Independence was the overthrow of the Hegelian dialectic! An argument that a critique of colonial discourses is implicitly a critique of the West becomes in effect an argument that a critique of colonial discourses is primarily and fundamentally a critique of the West. In failing to specify and delimit its own project, *White Mythologies* ironically ends up universalizing, and thus compromising, its own critique. One is tempted to wonder whether we have merely taken a detour to return to the position of the Other as resource for rethinking the Western Self, only this time it is not the Other as "ourselves undressed" so much as "ourselves disassembled."[6]

We would also urge a greater awareness than is sometimes evident in such debate that, despite the impact in certain quarters of the critique of specific textual practices and philosophical presumptions, elsewhere much remains the same—it's business as usual. The integrity of the Subject may have been exposed as a ruse of bourgeois ideology by philosophers and cultural critics, but law, to take one powerful institution, still operates as though this were not the case. To cite one example, the legitimacy of land rights claims of indigenous or Fourth World peoples turns on ahistorical conceptions of culture and essentialist notions of identity. An American anthropologist, having recently discovered Benedict Anderson (1983), can unwittingly create complications for Maori land claims by arguing that Maori traditions are "invented" (Hanson 1990). The point here is not so much that anti-essentialist conceptions of identity are reactionary as that, so long as other conceptions of identity have effectivity in the world, we necessarily need to engage them (Clifford 1988b; Legaré 1990). A position of abstract theoreticism that adjudicates between positions solely on the basis of "theoretical correctness" seems to us to aggrandize theory while failing to grasp the complex and contradictory workings of power/knowledge.

Returning to our conception of the term "postcolonial," then, we would like to accent the ambiguity of the "post" in "postcolonial" and underscore the twin processes that are evoked by it: colonization/decolonization. We would argue that "postcolonial" marks a decisive, though not definitive, shift that stages contemporary encounters between India and Britain and between white Britons and their non-white Others, though not always in the same way or to the same degree.

Location is in many respects key in determining the importance of "postcolonial" as an axis staging cross-racial encounters. In Britain, at least, it seems to us that the "postcolonial" is an axis with effectivity. The memory and legacies of colonization/decolonization form one axis through which social relations and subjectivities are shaped. The operation of the "postcolonial" axis—of the memories and legacies of colonization/decolonization—may be either explicit or implicit. When we argue that the axis of colonization/decolonization stages cross-racial encounters in Britain, we suggest that whether through negation, denial, affirmation, repression, or evasion, the history condensed in the sentence "We are here because you were there" is necessarily engaged. To say this is not to indicate anything about how this history of colonization/decolonization is engaged. One need only point to the positions taken on *Satanic Verses* (Rushdie 1989) by Salman Rushdie, the Bradford fundamentalists, the irate white conservatives, the confused and then outraged white liberals, and the feminist group Women Against Fundamentalism, to note something of the range of possible ways of negotiating this history (for a sense of the debate, see Appigignanesi and Maitland 1989; Women Against Fundamentalism 1989; Connelly 1991; and for Rushdie's shifting position, Rushdie 1991:393–432). The example of *Satanic Verses* serves to clarify another point. It is not our claim that colonization/decolonization is the only axis with effectivity in the British context. For obviously, positions on the Rushdie controversy were equally shaped by other axes, among them gender, race, religion, sexuality, and political orientation.

The "postcolonial" as an axis of subject formation is not constructed simply in dialogue with dominant white society; it is an effect of engagement between particular subjects, white society, region of origin, and region of religious and/or political affiliation—what Paul Gilroy (1990/91) describes as "the dialectics of diasporic identification." Thus, many African or South Asian Muslims in Britain would include in this matrix the home of their religion, the Middle East. Similarly, the films of Isaac Julien and the Black film collective Sankofa—for instance, *Passion of Remembrance* and *Looking for Langston*—are transatlantic meditations on African Caribbean political and sexual identity. The struggle of African Americans in the United States becomes a political resource for forging imagined diasporic communities. The engagement of colonization/decolonization thus has transnational dimensions, its local expressions multiply inflected by regional and global affinities and considerations, in turn crosscut by class, race, gender, sexuality, and so on.

Not all places in this transnational circuit are, however, similarly "postcolonial." The active, subjective, inescapable, everyday engagements with the legacies of colonization/decolonization that are part of the British matrix for reggae, bhangra rap, Hanif Qureshi's screenplays, or Homi Bhabha's conception of "hybridity" (Bhabha 1985) are not the terms of theoretical, artistic, or political endeavors in India. As noted earlier and argued more fully elsewhere (Mani 1990), in India, it is the nation-state and its failure to represent anything other than narrow sectional interests that provides grist for the mill of politics and theory. We are not claiming here that India is not "postcolonial"—that would be an absurd proposition; rather, that it is not "postcolonial" in the same way. The hand of the past in the shape of the present is multiply refracted such that the term "postcolonial" fails to grasp the ways in which people are driven to apprehend the world and their relation to it.

MEANWHILE, BACK AT THE RANCH IN THE GOOD OLD U.S.A.

We suggested at the very beginning of this essay that "post-civil rights" may be to the United States what "postcolonial" is to Britain: a name for a decisive though hardly definitive shift that implicitly or explicitly structures, whether through affirmation, negation, denial, repression, or evasion, relations between the races. We use the term "civil rights" here to signal a range of struggles including those against segregation, for voting rights and political representation, for institutional and economic equality, as well as the cultural renaissance and cultural nationalisms of the late 1960s and early 1970s. Like "postcolonial," "post-civil rights" retains the ambiguity, perhaps more immediately telling, given that this is our backyard, of the "post" in relation to civil rights: the way it simultaneously signals both the fight against entrenched institutional and cultural racism, and the need for continued struggles for racial equality. Whether one is Left or Right on the political spectrum, for or against affirmative action, for or against an ethnic studies requirement, it seems to us that we all necessarily do battle on a discursive and political terrain that is distinctly "post-civil rights." This was abundantly evident in the debates surrounding the nomination of Clarence Thomas to the Supreme Court and the challenge to it presented by Anita Hill's allegations of sexual harassment. Indeed, the concerted effort by the Reagan and Bush administrations to dismantle the gains of the civil rights movement is testimony to the shifts effected by it and to the power of the term to signify both the history of colonial and racist domination and collective resistance to it.

The history of the 1950s and 1960s civil rights movements is, however, the narrative of the domination and resistance of established communities of color in this country: the original Native Americans, African Americans,

Latino/Chicanos, Asian Americans. To this we must add the tales of recent immigrants/refugees, who, rather more like Asians and African Caribbeans in Britain, represent the return of the repressed on the borders of the imperialist center. They also negotiate a "post-civil rights" U.S. landscape. Their travel to the United States has been occasioned by a history related to, but distinct from, that of people of color already here. Their historical experiences stretch existing categories—"Hispanic," "Asian"—inflecting them with new meanings. Relations between recent immigrants/refugees and those already here, whether whites or people of color, are constituted through discourses that draw heavily on colonial and racist rhetoric in both form and content. Such mutual ignorance and parochialism in the context of economic depression and state-supported nativism can be, and have been, explosive. Nothing but the most complex and historically specific conceptions of identity and subjectivity can sufficiently grasp the present situation and articulate a politics adequate to it.

MULTIPLE AXES, CONJUNCTURES, AND POLITICS OF LOCATION

Thus far in this essay, we have attempted to situate the term "postcolonial" in time and space, pointing to differences in its effectivity in a range of contexts. In this final section, we wish to take our argument a step further, suggesting that it is also necessary to view colonial/postcolonial relations as coconstructed with other axes of domination and resistance—that the "postcolonial" is in effect a construct internally differentiated by its intersections with other unfolding relations. We propose here the value of what we will term a "feminist conjuncturalist" approach, drawing tools and inspiration from both Marxist cultural criticism and U.S. Third World feminism (for one definition of the latter, see Sandoval 1991:18, n. 3). We believe such a framework serves well our goal of benefiting from the analytical space opened up by the term "postcolonial" while avoiding the dangers of failing to delimit it. It enables us to argue that at given moments and locations, the axis of colonization/decolonization might be the most salient one, and at other times, not so.

Since the 1970s there has been under way in feminism a process of decentering the white/Western subject (whether male or female) that has been at times similar to, enabling of, and indebted to, but most often separate from, the projects of poststructuralist and "postcolonial" cultural criticism.

Since the late 1960s, U.S. women of color, frequently speaking simultaneously from "within and against" both women's liberation and antiracist movements, have insisted upon the need to analyze and challenge systems of domination, and concomitant constructions of subjecthood, not singly but multiply.[7] More recently, and following their lead, U.S. white feminists have made parallel arguments.

From the inception of second wave feminism in the late 1960s and early 1970s, black women activists like Frances Beale, Toni Cade, Florynce Kennedy, and later the Combahee River Collective argued that race and gender domination (and in Combahee's case, class and sexuality also) were inseparably involved in their experience of subordination (Beale 1970; Cade 1970; Kennedy 1970; Combahee 1979). And as Norma Alarcón argues in her essay on the 1981 anthology *This Bridge Called My Back: Writings by Radical Women of Color:*

> As speaking subjects of a new discursive formation, many of *Bridge*'s writers were aware of the displacement of their subjectivity across a multiplicity of discourses: feminist/lesbian, nationalist, racial, socioeconomic, historical, etc. The peculiarity of their displacement implies a multiplicity of positions from which they are driven to grasp or understand themselves and their relations with the "real" in the Althusserian sense of the word. (1990a: 356)

Parallel with Alarcón, and exemplifying for our purposes the move by some white feminist critics to follow the analytical direction proposed by U.S. Third World feminisms, Teresa de Lauretis writes:

> What is emerging in feminist writings is . . . the concept of multiple, shifting, and often self-contradictory identity . . . an identity made up of heterogeneous and heteronomous representations of gender, race, and class, and often indeed across languages and cultures; an identity that one decides to reclaim from a history of multiple assimilations, and that one insists on as a strategy. (1986:8)

What is significant to us here is the emphasis, within feminist theorizing, on the complexity of effective links between intersecting axes of domination, and the concomitant complexity of subjectivity and political agency. Moreover, as de Lauretis adds, axes of domination and of representation at times clash or contradict, whereas at other times they may be mutually supporting or mutually irrelevant. Each axis involves the unfolding of both material and discursive relations. To this list we would add that this unfolding, this displacement of subjectivities, is "variously and contradictorily paced." For we have argued that the discursive legacy of "colonization/decolonization" is radically nondiachronic. We have also indicated the interplay of different axes of domination/resistance and history—for instance, when U.S. race and class relations, and Indian "postcolonial" relations, may hail the same subject in mutually contradictory or supportive ways.

Although not the direction or intent of any of the feminists named and quoted above, it should be recognized that notions of "multiplicity" have at times led critics down the very problematic path of what one might call "neorelativism," such that it is sometimes argued that "we" are all decentered, multiple, "minor," or "mestiza" in exactly comparable ways. It becomes critical, then, to maintain a sharp analysis of the relationship between subjectivity and power, subjectivity and specific relations of domination and subordination. In this regard, some feminist theorists have argued for attention to the "politics of location," to "the historical, geographic, cultural, psychic and imaginative boundaries which provide the ground for political definition and self-definition. . . . [L]ocation forces and enables specific modes of reading and knowing the dominant" (Mohanty 1987:31, 42).

However, these problems do in a sense arise out of the current state of feminist theorization of subjectivity and systems of domination. For feminist theory—by no means a unified terrain—has vacillated over how to analyze the relationships between the multiple axes of oppression that it names. Thus, feminism seems to comprise at least four tendencies. First we can distinguish a white feminist "rear guard" that continues to argue for the primacy of gender domination, as well as a second "neo-rearguard" tendency, again especially by white feminists, to reabsorb notions of multiply determined subjectivity under the single "mistress narrative" of gender domination.

Third, other theorists and activists, frequently but not exclusively women of color, responding both to the prioritization of gender in "hegemonic" feminism, and to the pervasive sexism and/or heterosexism and/or racism of other movements, insist on the "simultaneity" of the workings of axes of domination (Combahee 1979; Zavella 1987). This insistence on a nonhierarchical analysis of how oppression works was born of political practice and has been critical to coalition building. It is, in fact, articulated in response to prior elisions and erasures in analyses of subject and social formation, whether in feminism, La Raza, Black Power, the Marxist left, or elsewhere. There is finally a fourth tendency that is an outgrowth of the third. This builds on and further complicates the ideas of "simultaneity" and "multiplicity" to examine how oppression may be experienced in specifiably complex and shifting relationships to different axes of domination (Moraga and Anzaldúa 1981; Sandoval 1991). Lest this four-part map be taken to describe a straightforward diachronic unfolding, it is important to point out that the editors and contributors to *This Bridge Called My Back,* the 1981 anthology to which Alarcón's article refers, were already practitioners of the fourth tendency, that of complex, multiply engaged, yet locally focused analyses.

Building complex analyses, avoiding erasure, specifying location. Feminist analysts of this kind share a great deal, some consciously and others not, with "postmodern conjuncturalism" as described by Lawrence Grossberg (1989) in his avowedly partial intellectual history of the Birmingham Centre for Contemporary Cultural Studies during Stuart Hall's tenure as director. We find postmodern conjuncturalism helpful to our current project because, like the feminist developments just noted, it firmly centers the analysis of subject formation and cultural practice within matrices of domination and subordination. Moreover, it does so in a way that neither conceives domination in single-axis terms ("Even at their most concrete, relations of power are always multiple and contradictory") nor falsely equalizes the effects of these relations on subjects:

> A conjunctural theory of power is not claiming . . . that all such relations of power are equal, equally determining, or equally liveable; these are questions that depend on the analysis of the specific, concrete conjuncture.[8]

Also key for our purposes, postmodern conjuncturalism asserts that there is an effective but not determining relationship between subjects and their histories, a relationship that is complex, shifting, yet not "free." The concept of articulation links subjects and structures dynamically, such that practices, meanings, and identities "are forged by people operating within the limits of their real conditions and the historically articulated 'tendential lines of force.'" (Grossberg 1989:136).

This framework intersects with feminist appropriations of Althusser, such as de Lauretis' insistence on "an identity that one *decides* to reclaim" (emphasis added), and, stating even more succinctly the dialectic of agency and context, Alarcón's conceptualization of subjects "driven to grasp" their subject positions across a shifting, though not randomly shifting, field.

> The concept of articulation within postmodern conjuncturalism foregrounds the production of contexts, the ongoing effort by which particular practices are removed from and inserted into different structures of relationships, the construction of one set of relationships out of another, the continuous struggle to reposition practices within a shifting field of forces. (Grossberg 1989:137)

This brings us full circle to one of our arguments about the term "postcolonial." For we have noted the complex temporal and spatial repositioning and recombining of practices and signifiers from the histories of racism and colonization, in the construction of contexts and identities in the United States and Britain. We have emphasized the ways practices may be given new meanings, and create "new subjects," in different locations.

Finally, postmodern conjuncturalism's call for attention to the "tendential lines of force," its insistence that the meanings and effectivity of particular practices and relations of power are dependent on historical moment and locale, underscores our other central argument about the term "postcolonial." For we have argued that the concept must be carefully specified, used to describe moments, social formations, subject positions, and practices that arise out of an unfolding axis of colonization/decolonization, interwoven with the unfolding of other axes, in uneven, unequal relations with one another.

The affinities between U.S. feminist developments we have described and a conjuncturalist approach to cultural studies are all the more interesting once one notes the context in which the latter came into being. For the theoretical appropriations of Althusser and Gramsci we draw on here, like U.S. Third World feminism, were not developed as part of an abstract "race for theory." Rather, they were generated out of the endeavor of a group of scholar-critic-activists (including Stuart Hall and Paul Gilroy) to analyze racial domination and resistance in 1970s Britain—a Britain in which, to adapt the title of a book published by Birmingham Centre scholars in 1982, "the Empire struck back" (Centre for Contemporary Cultural Studies 1982). In short, British conjuncturalist analysis emerges from and speaks to a postcolonial Britain, just as U.S. Third World feminism develops out of and addresses a post-civil rights United States.

What we have attempted in this essay is to sketch in outline a feminist conjuncturalist reading of the term "postcolonial" in three locations—India, Britain, and the United States. We wish to emphasize once again that we have not undertaken here a general reading of the "postcolonial" that is applicable to all places at all times. Not only are we inadequately placed to undertake such a task, but we would argue against the idea that there is such a thing as *the* "postcolonial" in any simple sense. This does not mean, however, that we are against theorizing the term, nor that it is without utility. Rather, as we have said, we would argue that the notion of the "postcolonial" is best understood in the context of a rigorous politics of location, of a rigorous conjuncturalism. There are, then, moments and spaces in which subjects are "driven to grasp" their positioning and subjecthood as "postcolonial"; yet there are other contexts in which to use the term as the organizing principle of one's analysis is precisely to "fail to grasp the specificity" of the location or the moment.

NOTES

A brief comment on the method, scope, and limits of our essay may be useful at the outset. We do not seek here to "master" the term "postcolonial" or its (changing and disputable) meanings. Rather, we present a set of concerns about how the term is being deployed, and propose—but by no means finalize—possibilities opened by a feminist/conjuncturalist approach to the term. The analytical work of this essay moves in and through several interlinked registers, more readily recognizable at some times than at others, as "theory" in academic terms. The autobiographical (but analytical) fragments, as much as the more conventionally analytical (but equally partial and situated) sections of the essay, thus provide pieces of the same argument, cross-referenced but not wholly transcoded. Neither should be seen as more or less than theory, more or less than story; by the same token, neither mode of enunciation is more "transparent," more "real(ist)" than the other.

We would like to thank Chetan Bhatt, Rosa Linda Fregoso, Lisa Lowe, Ted Swedenburg, and Kamala Visweswaran for their comments on earlier incarnations of this essay. It was first published in *Cultural Studies* (Spring 1993).

1 In his analysis of artistic and literary production in sub-Saharan Africa and the reception of the former in the United States, Kwame Anthony Appiah (1991) makes a persuasive argument about the importance of circumscribing the postcolonial and specifying its relation to postmodernism.

2 We note with pleasure the publication of Ella Shohat, "Notes on the Postcolonial," *Social Text* (Spring 1992): 99–113, which appeared while our article was under review, and some of whose concerns about the term "postcolonial" intersect with our own.

3 Omi and Winant state that the phrase "great transformation" is taken from Karl Pol-

yani, and deployed by them to indicate the epochal nature of the transformation under consideration in their text (1986:172, n. 2).

4 The terms "postcolonial" and "post-civil rights," as we use them, are periodizations that name the initiation of particular struggles. These struggles were, of course, to develop in heterogeneous directions—for example, socialism and bourgeois nationalism in the case of India, cultural nationalism and revolutionary race-class struggle in the example of the United States.

5 "Twas in the moon of wintertime/When all the birds had fled/That mighty Gitchee-manitou/Sent angel choirs instead/Before their light the stars grew dim/And wandering hunters heard the hymn/"Jesus, your king is born/Jesus is born/In excelsis gloria."

6 We refer here to Michelle Rosaldo's 1980 essay, "The Use and Abuse of Anthropology: Reflections on Feminism and Cross Cultural Understanding." In it Rosaldo argues that 1970s feminist anthropologists frequently viewed their studies of the status of women in "non-Western" societies as occasions to examine themselves "undressed"—that is, to analyze world cultures in explicitly or implicitly evolutionary terms.

7 Parallel debates have gone on in Britain. See the journals *Spare Rib* and *Outwrite,* as well as Amos et al. 1984; Bhavnani and Coulson 1986; S. Grewal et al. 1988.

8 Grossberg 1989:138. Further citations from this piece will be included in the text.

BIBLIOGRAPHY

Abu-Lughod, Lila. 1991. "The Romance of Resistance: Tracing Transformations of Power Through Bedouin Women." In Peggy R. Sanday and Ruth G. Goodenough, eds., *Beyond the Second Sex,* 313–37. Philadelphia: University of Pennsylvania Press.

———. 1986. *Veiled Sentiments: Honor and Poetry in a Bedouin Society.* Berkeley: University of California Press.

Aharoni, ʿAda. 1985. *The Second Exodus.* Tel Aviv: ʿEked Books (in Hebrew).

Aïchoune, Farid. 1992. "Une mouvance en question." *Qantara* 3 (April–June): 14–15.

———. 1991. *Nés en banlieue.* Paris: Editions Ramsay.

Alarcón, Norma. 1992. "T(r)opographies of Hunger: Dislocation of Chicana Feminism." Presented at "Multiple Tongues: Centering Discourse by People of Color." University of California at Los Angeles, January 30.

———. 1990a. "The Theoretical Subject(s) of *This Bridge Called My Back* and Anglo-American Feminism." In Gloria Anzaldúa, ed., *Making Face, Making Soul: Haciendo Caras,* 356–69. San Francisco: Aunt Lute Foundation.

———. 1990b. "Chicana Feminisms: In the Tracks of the Native Woman." *Cultural Studies* 4 (October): 248–56.

Alcalay, Ammiel. 1993. *After Jews and Arabs: Remaking Levantine Culture.* Minneapolis: University of Minnesota Press.

Althusser, Louis. 1971a. *Lenin and Philosophy and Other Essays.* Trans. Ben Brewster. New York: Monthly Review Press.

———. 1971b. "Ideology and Ideological State Apparatuses (Notes Towards an Investigation) (January–April 1969)." In Althusser, *Lenin and Philosophy and Other Essays,* 27–86. Trans. Ben Brewster. New York: Monthly Review Press.

———. 1970. *For Marx.* Trans. Ben Brewster. New York: Pantheon.

Amos, Valerie, et al., eds. 1984. *Many Voices, One Chant.* Spec. iss. *Feminist Review* 17 (Summer).

Anderson, Benedict. 1983. *Imagined Communities: Reflections on the Origin and Spread of Nationalism.* London: Verso.

Andrews, William L. 1989. "Toward a Poetics of Afro-American Autobiography." In Houston A. Baker, Jr., and Patricia Redmond, eds., *Afro-American Literary Study in the 1990s.* 78–104. Chicago: University of Chicago Press.

———. 1986. *To Tell a Free Story: The First Century of Afro-American Autobiography, 1760–1865*. Urbana: University of Illinois Press.

———. 1985. "Checklist of Du Bois's Autobiographical Writings." In William L. Andrews, ed., *Critical Essays on W.E.B. Du Bois,* 226–30. Boston: G. K. Hall.

Anzaldúa, Gloria, ed. 1990. *Making Face, Making Soul: Haciendo Caras.* San Francisco: Aunt Lute Foundation.

———. 1987. *Borderlands/La Frontera: The New Mestiza.* San Francisco: Spinsters/Aunt Lute Foundation.

Apiryon. (Ramat Gan). 1989. "Statement of Purpose." No. 15, p. 2 (in Hebrew).

Appadurai, Arjun. 1991a. Afterword. In A. Appadurai, F. J. Korom, and M. A. Mills, eds., *Gender, Genre, and Power in South Asian Expressive Traditions,* 467–75. Philadelphia: University of Pennsylvania Press.

———. 1991b. "Global Ethnoscapes: Notes and Queries for a Transnational Anthropology." In Richard Fox, ed., *Recapturing Anthropology,* 191–210. Santa Fe: School of American Research Press.

———. 1990. "Disjuncture and Difference in the Global Cultural Economy." *Public Culture* 2(2):1–24.

———. 1988a. "Putting Hierarchy in Its Place." *Cultural Anthropology* 3(1):36–49.

———. 1988b. "Transformations in the Culture of Agriculture." In Carla Borden, ed., *Contemporary Indian Tradition,* 173–86. Washington, D.C.: Smithsonian Institution Press.

Appiah, Kwame Anthony. 1992. "Illusions of Race." In Kwame Anthony Appiah, *In My Father's House: Africa in the Philosophy of Culture,* 28–46. New York: Oxford University Press.

———. 1991. "Is the Post- in Postmodernism the Post- in Postcolonial?" *Critical Inquiry* 17 (2):336–57.

———. 1986. "The Uncompleted Argument: Du Bois and the Illusion of Race." In Henry Louis Gates, Jr., ed., "Race," *Writing and Difference,* 21–37. Chicago: University of Chicago Press.

Appigignanesi, Lisa, and Sara Maitland, eds. 1989. *The Rushdie File.* London: ICA.

Apter, Emily. In press. "Ethnographic Travesties: Colonial Fiction, French Feminism, and the Case of Elissa Rhaïs." Davis Center Papers.

ʿAraidi, Naʿim. 1985. *Back to the Village*. Tel Aviv: ʿAm ʿOved (in Hebrew).

Aristotle. 1966. *Metaphysics.* Trans. Hippocrates G. Apostle. Grinnell, Iowa: Peripatetic Press.

Armbrust, Walter. 1992. "The National Vernacular: Folklore and Egyptian Popular Culture." *Michigan Quarterly Review* 31 (4):525–42.

Asad, Talal. In press. "Ethnographic Representation, Statistics and Modern Power." *Social Research.*

———. 1990. "Ethnography, Literature, and Politics: Some Readings and Uses of Salman Rushdie's *The Satanic Verses.*" *Cultural Anthropology* 5 (3):239–69.

———, ed. 1973. *Anthropology and the Colonial Encounter.* London: Ithaca Press.

Atran, Scott. 1989. "The Surrogate Colonization of Palestine, 1917–1939." *American Ethnologist* 16 (4):719–44.

Attaf, Rabha. 1991. "Ecoutez: Comment ferons-nous la paix?" *Actuel* (February):49–57.

Azoulay, Eliane. 1991. "La Déchirure: Rachid Taha." *Télérama* (February 13):17.

Baker, Houston. 1987. *Modernism and the Harlem Rennaissance*. Chicago: University of Chicago Press.

Baldwin, James. 1990. *The Price of the Ticket*. New York: St. Martin's/Marek.

———. 1984. "On Being 'White' and Other Lies." *Essence* (April)

Baldwin, James, and Margaret Mead. 1971. *A Rap on Race*. New York: J. B. Lippincott.

Balibar, Etienne. 1992. *Les Frontières de la démocratie*. Paris: La Découverte.

———. 1991a. "Es gibt keinen Staat in Europa: Racism and Politics in Europe Today." *New Left Review* 186:5–19.

———. 1991b. "Is There a Neo-Racism?" In Etienne Balibar and Immanuel Wallerstein, eds., *Race, Nation, Class: Ambiguous Identities*, 17–28. London: Verso.

Ballas, Shimʿon. 1990. *And He's an Other*. Tel Aviv: Zmora-Bitan (in Hebrew).

———. 1984. *The Last Winter*. Jerusalem: Keter (in Hebrew).

Bandem, I. Made, and F. de Boer. 1981. *Kaja and Kelod: Balinese Dance in Transition*. Kuala Lumpur: Oxford University Press.

Banerjee, Sumanta. 1989. "Marginalization of Women's Popular Culture in Nineteenth Century Bengal." In K. Sangari and S. Vaid, eds., *Recasting Women*, 127–79. New Delhi: Kali for Women.

Barber, Karin. 1987. "Popular Arts in Africa." *African Studies Review* 30 (3):1–78.

Bariki, Salah Eddine. 1986. "Identité religieuse, identité culturelle en situation immigrée." In Jean-Robert Henry et al., eds., *Nouveaux Enjeux culturels au Maghreb*, 427–45. Paris: Editions du CNRS.

Bartlett, Katherine, and Rosanne Kennedy, eds. 1991. *Feminist Legal Theory: Readings in Law and Gender*. Boulder, Colo.: Westview Press.

Baudrillard, Jean. 1983. *Simulations*. New York: Semiotext(e).

Baum, Vicki. 1937. *A Tale from Bali*. Singapore: Oxford University Press.

Bausinger, Hermann. 1990. *Folk Culture in a World of Technology*. Trans. Elke Dettmer. Bloomington: Indiana University Press.

Beale, Frances. 1970. "Double Jeopardy: To Be Black and Female." In Toni Cade, ed., *The Black Woman: An Anthology*, 90–100. New York: Mentor.

Bean, L. J., and D. Theodoratus. 1978. "Western Pomo and Northeastern Pomo." In *Handbook of North American Indians*. Vol. 8. Washington, D.C.: Smithsonian Institution Press.

Begag, Azouz. 1990. "'The Beurs,' Children of North-African Immigrants in France: The Issue of Integration." *Journal of Ethnic Studies* 18 (1):1–14.

Behar, Ruth, and Deborah Gordon. 1995. *Women Writing Culture*. Berkeley: University of California Press.

Beinin, Joel. 1990. *Was the Red Flag Flying There? Marxist Politics and the Arab-Israeli Conflict in Egypt and Israel, 1948–1965*. Berkeley: University of California Press.

Bekkar, Rabia. 1992. "Taking up Space in Tlemcen: The Islamist Occupation of Urban Algeria." *Middle East Report* 22 (6):11–15 (interview by Hannah Davis).

Belo, Jane. 1960. *Trance in Bali*. New York: Columbia University Press.

Belsey, Catherine. 1980. *Critical Practice*. London: Methuen.

Ben-David, Joseph. 1970. "Ethnic Differences or Social Change?" In S. N. Eisenstadt, R. Bar Yosef, and C. Adler, eds., *Integration and Development in Israel,* 368–87. New York: Praeger.

Ben Jelloun, Tahar. 1991. "I Am an Arab, I Am Suspect." *Nation* (April 15):482–84.

———. 1984. *Hospitalité française. Racisme et immigration maghrébine*. Paris: Editions de Seuil.

Ben-Rafael, Eliezer. 1982. *The Emergence of Ethnicity: Cultural Groups and Social Conflict in Israel*. Westport, Conn.: Greenwood Press.

Benedict, Ruth. 1974. *The Chrysanthemum and the Sword: Patterns of Japanese Culture*. New York: New American Library.

Benjamin, Walter. 1985. "Allegory and Trauerspiel." In *The Origin of German Tragic Drama,* 159–235. Trans. J. Osborne. London: Verso.

Benkheira, Mohamed Hocine. 1986. "De la musique avant toute chose: Remarques sur le raï." *Peuples méditerranéens/Mediterranean Peoples* 35–36:173–77.

Bernard, Philippe. 1991. "Les Beurs, entre la fierté et la crainte." *Le Monde* (January 17):5.

Bhabha, Homi. 1990a. "DissemiNation: Time, Narrative, and the Margins of the Modern Nation." In Homi Bhabha, ed., *Nation and Narration,* 291–322. London: Routledge.

———. 1990b. "The Third Space: Interview with Homi Babha." In Jonathan Rutherford, ed., *Identity: Community, Culture, Difference,* 207–21. London: Lawrence and Wishart.

———. 1989. "Location, Intervention, Incommensurability: A Conversation with Homi Bhabha." *Emergences* 1 (Fall):63–88.

———. 1985. "Signs Taken for Wonders: Questions of Ambivalence and Authority Under a Tree Outside Delhi, May 1817." *Critical Inquiry* 12 (1):144–65.

———. 1984. "Of Mimicry and Man: The Ambivalence of Colonial Discourse." *October* 28:125–33.

———. 1983. "The Other Question—The Stereotype and Colonial Discourse." *Screen* 24 (6):18–36.

Bhavnani, Kum Kum, and Margaret Coulson. 1986. "Transforming Socialist-Feminism: The Challenge of Racism." *Feminist Review* 23 (Summer):81–92.

Billard, François. 1987. "Rock, Sapho." *Jazz Magazine* 359 (March):24–25.

Biton, Erez. 1990. *A Bird Between Continents.* Tel Aviv: Hakibbutz Hame'uhad (in Hebrew).

Bizot, Jean-François. 1988. "Sex and Soul in the Maghreb." *The Face* 98:86–93.

———. 1987. "Ces Musiciens grandissent la France." *Actuel* (June):145–55.

Bizot, Jean-François, and Fadia Dimerdji. 1988. "Le Blues de l'espoir." *Actuel* (March):92–99, 132–33.

Bondi, Liz. 1993. "Locating Identity Politics." In Michael Keith and Steve Pile, eds., *Place and the Politics of Identity,* 84–101. London: Routledge.

Boon, James. 1990. *Affinities and Extremes: Crisscrossing the Bittersweet Ethnology of East Indies History, Hindu-Balinese Culture, and Indo-European Allure*. Chicago: University of Chicago Press.

———. 1977. *The Anthropological Romance of Bali, 1597–1972: Dynamic Perspectives in Marriage and Caste, Politics and Religion*. New York: Cambridge University Press.

Bouillier, Grégoire. 1990. "Urban Rap." *Dire* 12 (Fall):2–10.

Bourdieu, Pierre. 1984. *Distinction: A Social Critique of the Judgement of Taste*. Cambridge, Mass.: Harvard University Press.

Brisebarre, Anne-Marie. 1989. "La célébration de l'Ayd El'Kebir en France: Les enjeux du sacrifice." *Archives des sciences sociales des religions* 68 (1) (July–September):9–25.

Bruner, Edward M. 1995. "The Ethnographer/Tourist in Indonesia." In Marie-Françoise Lanfant, Edward M. Bruner, and John Allcock, eds., *International Tourism: Identity and Change*, 224–41. London: Sage.

———. 1994. "Abraham Lincoln as Authentic Reproduction: A Critique of Postmodernism." *American Anthropologist* 96(2):397–415.

———. 1993. "Epilogue: Creative Persona and the Problem of Authenticity." In Smadar Lavie, Kirin Narayan, and Renato Rosaldo, eds., *Creativity/Anthropology*, 321–34. Ithaca, N.Y.: Cornell University Press.

———. 1986a. "Experience and Its Expressions." In Victor Turner and Edward Bruner, eds., *The Anthropology of Experience*, 3–30. Urbana: University of Illinois Press.

———. 1986b. "Ethnography as Narrative." In Victor Turner and Edward Bruner, eds., *The Anthropology of Experience*. Urbana: University of Illinois Press.

Bryce, L. W. 1964. *Women's Folksongs of Rajputana*. New Delhi: National Book Trust.

Buck-Morss, Susan. 1989. *The Dialectics of Seeing: Walter Benjamin and the Arcades Project*. Cambridge, Mass.: MIT Press.

———. 1987. "Semiotic Boundaries and the Politics of Meaning: Modernity on Tour—A Village in Transition." In Marcus G. Raskin and Herbert J. Bernstein, eds., *New Ways of Knowing: The Sciences, Society, and Reconstructive Knowledge*, 200–36. Totowa, N.J.: Rowman and Littlefield.

Butler, Judith. 1992. "Contingent Foundations: Feminism and the Question of 'Postmodernism.'" In Judith Butler and Joan Scott, *Feminists Theorize the Political*, 3–21. New York: Routledge.

———. 1990a. "Gender Trouble, Feminist Theory, and Psychoanalytic Discourse." In Linda J. Nicholson, ed., *Feminism/Postmodernism*, 324–40. New York: Routledge.

———. 1990b. *Gender Trouble: Feminism and the Subversion of Identity*. London: Routledge.

Cade, Toni. 1970. "On the Issue of Roles." In Toni Cade, ed., *The Black Woman: An Anthology*, 101–10. New York: Mentor.

Cambio, Sam. 1991. "Marseille: Verification d'une rumeur." *Actuel* (February):33–38.

Caraveli, Anna. 1986. "The Bitter Wounding: The Lament as Social Protest in Rural Greece." In Jill Dubisch, ed., *Gender and Power in Rural Greece*, 169–94. Princeton: Princeton University Press.

Carrio, David. 1990. Personal communication (Spring).

Carrio, Juanita. 1965–91. Personal communications.

Castoriadis, Cornelius. 1987. *The Imaginary Institution of Society*. Trans. Kathleen Blamey. Cambridge, Mass.: MIT Press.

Centre for Contemporary Cultural Studies. 1982. *The Empire Strikes Back: Race and Racism in 70s Britain*. London: Hutchinson.

Chabram, Angie, and Rosa Linda Fregoso. 1990. "Chicano/a Cultural Representations: Reframing Alternative Critical Discourses." *Cultural Studies* 4 (3):203–12.

Chandler, Nahum. 1993. "Between." *Assemblage: A Critical Journal of Architecture and Design Culture* 20 (April):26–27. 1991. "The Force of the Double: A Reading of W. E. B. DuBois' Role on the Question of the African-American Subject." Presented at the Annual Meetings of the American Anthropological Association, Chicago, November 22.

———. 1988. "Writing Absence: On Some Assumptions of Africanist Discourse in the West" Unpublished manuscript.

———. n.d. "The Question of Social Difference and African-American Social Identity in the Early Work of W. E. B. DuBois, 1897–1915. Unpublished Manuscript.

Chang, Grace. 1994. "Undocumented Latinas: Welfare Burdens or Beasts of Burden?" *Socialist Review* 24 (3):151–85.

Chappell, Violet Parrish. 1989. Personal communication. (Spring).

Charef, Mehdi. 1989. *Tea in the Harem*. Trans. Ed Emery. London: Serpent's Tail.

Chatterjee, Partha. 1989a. "Colonialism, Nationalism, and Colonized Women: The Contest in India." *American Ethnologist* 16:622–33.

———. 1989b. "The Nationalist Resolution of the Women's Question." In K. Sangari and S. Vaid, eds., *Recasting Women*, 233–53. New Delhi: Kali for Women.

———. 1986. *Nationalist Thought and the Colonial World—A Derivative Discourse?* London: Zed Books.

Choi, Carolyn. 1990. "Application of a Cultural Defense in Criminal Proceedings." *UCLA Pacific Basin Law Journal* 8(1/2):80–90.

Chow, Rey. 1990. "The Politics and Pedagogy of Asian Literatures in American Universities." *Differences* 2 (3):29–51.

Christgau, Robert. 1994. "Goat-God Rising." *Village Voice* (April 26):67.

Clark, V.C.vC. 1991. "Developing Diaspora Literacy and Marasa Consciousness." In Hortense Spillars, ed., *Comparative American Identities: Race, Sex, and Nationality in the Modern Text*, 40–61. New York: Routledge.

Claus, Peter. 1991. "Kin Songs." In A. Appadurai, F. J. Korom, and M. A. Mills, eds., *Gender, Genre, and Power in South Asian Expressive Traditions*, 136–77. Philadelphia: University of Pennsylvania Press.

Clifford, James. 1989a. "The Others: Beyond the 'Salvage' Paradigm." *Third Text* 6:73–77.

———. 1989b. "Notes on Travel and Theory." *Inscriptions* 5:177–88.

———. 1988a. *The Predicament of Culture: Twentieth-Century Ethnography, Literature, and Art*. Cambridge, Mass.: Harvard University Press.

———. 1988b. "Identity in Mashpee." In *The Predicament of Culture: Twentieth-Century Ethnography, Literature, and Art*. Cambridge, Mass.: Harvard University Press.

———. 1986. "On Ethnographic Allegory." In James Clifford and George E. Marcus, eds., *Writing Culture: The Poetics and Politics of Ethnography*, 98–121. Berkeley: University of California Press.

———. 1983. "On Ethnographic Authority." *Representations* 1:118–46.

Cockburn, Alexander. 1991. "Beat the Devil." *Nation* (December 23):802–3.

———. 1988. "Beat the Devil." *Nation* (October 10):300–301.

Cohen, Erik. 1988. "Authenticity and Commoditization in Tourism." *Annals of Tourism Research* 15:371–86.

———. 1985a. "Tourist Guides: Pathfinders, Mediators, and Animators." *Annals of Tourism Research* 12 (1).

———. 1985b. "Tourism as Play." *Religion* 15:291–304.

Cohen, Robin. 1987. *The New Helots: Migrants in the International Division of Labour.* Aldershot, U.K.: Grower.

Cohn, Bernard. 1987a. *An Anthropologist Among the Historians and Other Essays.* Delhi: Oxford University Press.

———. 1987b. "Lectures on Colonial Societies." University of Chicago, October–December.

Combahee River Collective. 1979. "A Black Feminist Statement, April 1977." In Zillah R. Eisenstein, ed., *Capitalist Patriarchy and the Case for Socialist Feminism.* New York: Monthly Review Press.

Commission on Wartime Relocation and Internment of Civilians. 1982. *Personal Justice Denied.* Washington, D.C.: U.S. Government Printing Office.

Connelly, Clara. 1991. "Washing Our Linen: One Year of Women Against Fundamentalism." *Feminist Review* 37 (Spring):68–77.

Coombe, Rosemary J. 1991. "Contesting the Self: Negotiating Subjectivities in Nineteenth-Century Ontario Defamation Trials." *Studies in Law, Politics, and Society* 11:3–40.

Coombes, Annie E. 1992. "Inventing the 'Postcolonial': Hybridity and Constituency in Contemporary Curating." *New Formations* 18:39–52.

Coon, Carleton S. 1951. *Caravan: The Story of the Middle East.* New York: Holt.

Cormezano-Goren, Yitshak. 1986. *Blanche.* Tel Aviv: 'Am 'Oved (in Hebrew).

———. 1978. *Alexandrian Summer.* Tel Aviv: 'Am 'Oved (in Hebrew).

Cornell, Drucilla. 1992. *Beyond Accommodation: Ethical Feminism, Deconstruction and the Law.* New York: Routledge.

Crapanzano, Vincent. 1986. "Hermes' Dilemma: The Masking of Subversion in Ethnographic Description." In James Clifford and George E. Marcus, eds., *Writing Culture: The Poetics and Politics of Ethnography,* 51–76. Berkeley: University of California Press.

Craton, Michael. 1979. "Changing Patterns of Slave Families in the British West Indies." *Journal of Interdisciplinary History* 10:1–35.

———. 1978. *Searching for the Invisible Man: Slaves and Plantation Life in Jamaica.* Cambridge, Mass.: Harvard University Press.

Craton, Michael, and James Walvin. 1970. *A Jamaica Plantation: The History of Worthy Park 1670–1979.* London: W. H. Allen.

Crick, Malcolm. 1995. "The Anthropologist as Tourist: An Identity in Question." In Marie-Françoise Lanfant, Edward M. Bruner, and John Allcock, eds., *International Tourism: Identity and Change,* 205–223. London: Sage.

"The Cultural Defense in the Criminal Law." *Harvard Law Review* 99 (April):1293–1311.

Curry, James. 1993. "The Flexibility Fetish: A Review Essay on Flexible Specialisation." *Capital and Class* 50:99–126.

De Lauretis, Teresa. 1987. *Technologies of Gender: Essays on Theory, Film, and Fiction*. Bloomington: Indiana University Press.

———. 1986. "Feminist Studies, Cultural Studies: Issues, Terms and Contexts." In Teresa de Lauretis, ed., *Feminist Studies/Critical Studies*, 1–19. Bloomington: Indiana University Press.

De Neys, Anne. 1993. "Rai Rocks Egyptian Pop." *Al-Ahram Weekly* (May 13–19):9.

Deleuze, Gilles, and Félix Guattari. 1987. *A Thousand Plateaus*. Trans. Brian Massumi. Minneapolis: University of Minnesota Press.

———. 1986. *Kafka: Toward a Minor Literature*. Trans. Dana Polan. Minneapolis: University of Minnesota Press.

———. 1983a. "Rhizome." Trans. John Johnston. In *On the Line*, 1–65. New York: Semiotext(e).

———. 1983b. *Anti-Oedipus: Capitalism and Schizophrenia*. Trans. Robert Hurley et al. Minneapolis: University of Minnesota Press.

Delgado, Richard. 1985. "'Rotten Social Background': Should the Criminal Law Recognize a Defense of Severe Environmental Deprivation?" *Law and Inequality* 3 (9):9–90.

Derrida, Jacques. 1992. *The Other Heading: Reflections on Today's Europe*. Trans. Pascale-Anne Brault and Michael B. Naas. Bloomington: Indiana University Press.

———. 1990. "Force of Law: The 'Mystical Foundation of Authority.'" Trans. Mary Quaintance. *Cardozo Law Review* 11 (5–6):919–1045.

———. 1989. "'This Strange Institution Called Literature': An Interview with Jacques Derrida." Trans. Geoffrey Bennington and Rachel Bowlby. In Jacques Derrida, *Acts of Literature*, 33–75. Ed. Derek Attridge. New York: Routledge.

———. 1986. *Glas*. Trans. John P. Leavey, Jr., and Richard Rand. Lincoln: University of Nebraska Press.

———. 1982a. *Margins of Philosophy*. Trans. Alan Bass. Chicago: University of Chicago Press.

———. 1982b. "Différance." In Jacques Derrida, *Margins of Philosophy*, 1–27. Trans. Alan Bass. Chicago: University of Chicago Press.

———. 1982c. "Ousia and Gramme: A Note to a Footnote from Being and Time." In Jacques Derrida, *Margins of Philosophy*, 29–67. Trans. Alan Bass. Chicago: University of Chicago Press.

———. 1981a. "Outwork, Prefacing." In Jacques Derrida, *Dissemination*, 287–366. Trans. Barbara Johnson. Chicago: University of Chicago Press.

———. 1981b. "Positions." In Jacques Derrida, *Positions*, 37–96. Trans. Alan Bass. Chicago: University of Chicago Press (interview with Jean-Louis Houdebine and Guy Scarpetta).

———. 1981c. "The Double Session." In Jacques Derrida, *Dissemination*, 173–286. Trans. Barbara Johnson. Chicago: University of Chicago Press.

———. 1978a. "From Restricted to General Economy: A Hegelianism Without Reserve."

In Jacques Derrida, *Writing and Difference,* 251–77. Trans. Alan Bass. Chicago: University of Chicago Press.

———. 1978b. "Violence and Metaphysics: An Essay on the Thought of Emmanuel Levinas." In Jacques Derrida, *Writing and Difference,* 79–153. Trans. Alan Bass. Chicago: University of Chicago Press.

———. 1978c. *Edmund Husserl's* Origin of Geometry*: An Introduction.* Trans. John P. Leavey, Jr. Stonybrook, N.Y.: Nicholas Hays.

———. 1978d. "'Genesis and Structure' and Phenomenology." In Jacques Derrida, *Writing and Difference,* 154–68. Trans. Alan Bass. Chicago: University of Chicago Press.

———. 1976. *Of Grammatology.* Trans. Gayatri Chakravorty Spivak. Chicago: University of Chicago Press.

———. 1954. *Le problème de la genèse dans la philosophie de Husserl.* Paris: Presses Universitaires de France.

Deshen, Shlomo. 1970. *Immigrant Voters in Israel: Parties and Congregations in a Local Election Campaign.* Manchester: Manchester University Press.

Deshen, Shlomo, and Moshe Shokeid. 1974. *The Predicament of Homecoming: Cultural and Social Life of North African Immigrants in Israel.* Ithaca, N.Y.: Cornell University Press.

Dhruvarajan, Vanaja. 1989. *Hindu Women and the Power of Ideology.* Granby, Mass.: Bergin and Garvey.

Dickey, Christopher, and Beatrix de Koster. 1993. "Rai Rocks the Mosques: Arab Pop Has Fundamentalists All Shook Up." *Newsweek* (April 26):53.

Dolan, Jill. 1990. "'Lesbian' Subjectivity in Realism: Dragging at the Margins of Structure and Ideology." In Sue-Ellen Case, ed., *Performing Feminisms.* Baltimore: Johns Hopkins University Press.

———. 1988. *The Feminist Spectator as Critic.* Ann Arbor: University of Michigan Press.

Dominguez, Virginia. 1989. *People as Subject, People as Object: Selfhood and Peoplehood in Contemporary Israel.* Madison: University of Wisconsin Press.

Doyle, James M. 1992. "'It's the Third World Down There!': The Colonialist Vocation and American Criminal Justice." *Harvard Civil Rights-Civil Liberties Law Review* 27:71–123.

Drake, Joe Gibbs St. Clair. 1965. *The Social and Economic Status of the Negro in the United States. Daedalus* 94.

Drake, Joe Gibbs St. Clair, and Horace Cayton. 1993. *Black Metropolis: A Study of Negro Life in a Northern City.* Repr. of 1970 ed. Chicago: University of Chicago Press.

Drozdiak, William. 1991. "French at Odds over Immigrants." *Washington Post* (July 12): A24.

Du Bois. W. E. B. 1990 [1903]. *The Souls of Black Folk.* New York: Vintage Books/Library of America. Also repr. in CPW. Ed. Herbert Aptheker. Millwood, N.Y.: Kraus-Thomson, 1973.

———. 1986a [1938]. "A Pageant in Seven Decades, 1878–1938." In W.E.B. Du Bois, *Pamphlets and Leaflets.* CPW. Ed. Herbert Aptheker. Vol. 244–74. White Plains, N.Y.: Kraus-Thomson.

———. 1986b [1903]. "Of Our Spiritual Strivings." In W.E.B. Du Bois, *The Souls of Black Folk,* 7–15. New York: Vintage Books/Library of America. Also repr. CPW. Ed. Herbert Aptheker. Vol. 1–12. Millwood, N.Y.: Kraus-Thomson, 1973.

———. 1986c [1897]. "The Conservation of Races." In *Pamphlets and Leaflets.* CPW. Ed. Herbert Aptheker. Vol. 1–8. White Plains, N.Y.: Kraus-Thomson.

———. 1982a [1944]. "My Evolving Program for Negro Freedom." In *Writings by W.E.B. Du Bois in Non-Periodical Literature Edited by Others.* CPW. Ed. Herbert Aptheker. Vol. 216–41. Millwood, N.Y.: Kraus-Thomson.

———. 1982b [1910]. "The Souls of White Folk." In *Writings by W.E.B. Du Bois in Periodicals Edited by Others,* vol. 2, 1910–1934. CPW. Ed. Herbert Aptheker. Vol. 25–29. Millwood, N.Y.: Kraus-Thomson.

———. 1982c [1904]. "Credo." In *Writings by W.E.B. Du Bois in Periodicals Edited by Others.* Vol. 1, 1891–1909. CPW. Ed. Herbert Aptheker. Vol. 229–30. Millwood, N.Y.: Kraus-Thomson.

———. 1982d [1901]. "The Problem of Housing the Negro." In *Writings by W.E.B. Du Bois in Periodicals Edited by Others,* Vol. 1, 1891–1909. CPW. Ed. Herbert Aptheker. Vol. 92–96, 100–104, 117–25, 131–38. Millwood, N.Y.: Kraus-Thomson.

———. 1982e [1900]. "The Twelfth Census and the Negro Problems." In *Writings by W.E.B. Du Bois in Periodicals Edited by Others,* Vol. 1, 1891–1909. CPW. Ed. Herbert Aptheker. Vol. 69–72. Millwood, N.Y.: Kraus-Thomson.

———. 1982f [1900]. "To the Nations of the World." In *Writings by W.E.B. Du Bois in Non-Periodical Literature Edited by Others.* CPW. Ed. Herbert Aptheker. Vol. 11–12. Millwood, N.Y.: Kraus-Thomson.

———. 1982g [1898]. "The Study of Negro Problems." In *Writings by W.E.B. Du Bois in Periodicals Edited by Others,* Vol. 1, 1891–1909. CPW. Ed. Herbert Aptheker. Vol. 40–52. Millwood, N.Y.: Kraus-Thomson.

———. 1980a [1901]. "Testimony: General and Industrial Education." In *Contributions by W.E.B. Du Bois in Government Publications and Proceedings.* CPW. Ed. Herbert Aptheker. Vol. 65–94. Millwood, N.Y.: Kraus-Thomson.

———. 1980b [1901]. "The Negro Landholder of Georgia." In *Contributions by W.E.B. Du Bois in Government Publications and Proceedings.* CPW. Ed. Herbert Aptheker. Vol. 95–228. Millwood, N.Y.: Kraus-Thomson.

———. 1980c [1898]. "The Negroes of Farmville, Virginia: A Social Study." In *Contributions by W.E.B. Du Bois in Government Publications and Proceedings.* CPW. Ed. Herbert Aptheker. Vol. 5–44. Millwood, N.Y.: Kraus-Thomson.

———. 1977 [1904]. "The Souls of Black Folk." In *Book Reviews by W.E.B. Du Bois.* CPW. Ed. Herbert Aptheker. Vol. 9, Millwood, N.Y.: Kraus-Thomson.

———. 1976 [1935]. *Black Reconstruction in America: An Essay Toward a History of the Part Which Black Folk Played in the Attempt to Reconstruct Democracy in America, 1860–1880.* CPW. Ed. Herbert Aptheker. Millwood, N.Y.: Kraus-Thomson.

———. 1975a [1940]. *Dusk of Dawn: An Essay Toward an Autobiography of a Race Concept.* CPW. Ed. Herbert Aptheker. Millwood, N.Y.: Kraus-Thomson.

———. 1975b [1939]. *Black Folk Then and Now: An Essay in the History and Sociology of the Negro Race.* CPW. Ed. Herbert Aptheker. Millwood, N.Y.: Kraus-Thomson.

———. 1975c [1921]. *Darkwater: Voices from Within the Veil.* CPW. Ed. Herbert Aptheker. Millwood, N.Y.: Kraus-Thomson.

———. 1973 [1899]. "The Philadelphia Negro; A Social Study . . . Together with a Special Report on Domestic Service by Isabel Eaton." CPW. Ed. Herbert Aptheker. Millwood, N.Y.: Kraus-Thomson.

———. 1969. *The Souls of Black Folk.* Reprint of 1903 ed. New York: New American Library.

———. 1968. *The Autobiography of W.E.B. Du Bois: A Soliloquy on Viewing My Life from the Last Decade of Its First Century.* CPW. New York: International Publishers.

———. 1904. "The Atlanta Conferences." *Voice of the Negro* 1 (March):85–90.

———. 1901a. "The Freedman's Bureau." *Atlantic Monthly* 87 (March):354–65.

———. 1901b. "The Negro as He Really Is." *World's Work* 2 (June):848–66.

———. 1901c. "The Relation of the Negroes to the Whites in the South." *Annals of the American Academy of Political and Social Science* 18 (July):121–40.

———. 1897. "Strivings of the Negro People." *Atlantic Monthly* 80 (August):194–98.

DuBois, Cora. 1971 [1939]. "The 1870 Ghost Dance." In R. F. Heizer and M. A. Whipple, eds., *The California Indians,* 496–99. Berkeley: University of California Press.

Dundes, Alan. 1969. "The Devolutionary Premise in Folklore Theory." *Journal of the Folklore Institute* 6:5–19.

———. 1966. "Metafolklore and Oral Literary Criticism." *The Monist* 60:505–16.

Dupuy, R. Ernest, and Trevor N. Dupuy. 1986. *The Encyclopedia of Military History.* New York: Harper & Row.

Einaudi, Jean-Luc. 1991. *La Bataille de Paris, 17 octobre 1961.* Paris: Editions du Seuil.

Eisenstadt, Shmuel N. 1967. *Israeli Society: Background, Development, and Problems.* London: Weidenfeld and Nicholson.

———. 1953. *The Absorption of Immigrants.* London: Routledge and Kegan Paul.

Eng, Pat. 1989. "Asians, Domestic Violence, and Criminal Injustice." *New Asian Times* (September): 2.

Epstein, Steven. 1987. "Gay Politics, Ethnic Identity: The Limits of Social Construction." *Socialist Review* 17 (3/4):9–54.

Errington, Frederick, and Deborah Gewertz. 1989. "Tourism and Anthropology in a Post-Modern World." *Oceania* 60:37–54.

Etienne, Bruno. 1991. *La France et l'Islam.* Paris: Hachette.

Eyre, Banning. 1992. "Rai: North African Punk." *Option* 42:19–20.

———. 1991. "A King in Exile: The Royal Rai of Cheb Khaled." *Option* 39:42–45.

Fabian, Johannes. 1983. *Time and the Other: How Anthropology Makes Its Object.* New York: Columbia University Press.

Fanon, Frantz. 1968. *The Wretched of the Earth.* Trans. Constance Farrington. New York: Grove Press.

Faulkner, William. 1972 [1936]. *Absalom, Absalom!* New York: Vintage Books.

Flores, Juan, and George Yúdice. 1991. "Living Borders/Buscando America: Language of Latino Self-Formation." *Social Text* 24:57–84.

Folch, Arnaud. 1992. "Petit glossaire de la chasse aux vilains racistes." *Minute-La France* 1565 (April 8):17–21.

Foner, Eric. 1988. *Reconstruction: America's Unfinished Revolution, 1863–1877.* New York: Harper & Row.

Foucault, Michel. 1984. "Afterword: The Subject and Power." Trans. Leslie Sawyer. In Hubert L. Dreyfus and Paul Rabinow, *Michel Foucault: Beyond Structuralism and Hermeneutics.* Berkeley: University of California Press.

———. 1980. *Power/Knowledge: Selected Interviews and Other Writings.* New York: Pantheon.

———. 1979. *Discipline and Punish: The Birth of the Prison.* New York: Vintage.

———. 1977. "Nietzsche, Genealogy, History." Trans. Donald F. Bouchard and Sherry Simon. In Paul Rabinow, ed., *The Foucault Reader,* 333–39. New York: Pantheon.

Franco, Jean. 1985. "New York Is a Third World City." *Tabloid* 9:12–19.

Frankenberg, Ruth. 1993. *White Women, Race Matters: The Social Construction of Whiteness.* Minneapolis: University of Minnesota Press.

Fraser, Nancy, and Linda J. Nicholson. 1990. "Social Criticism Without Philosophy: An Encounter Between Feminism and Postmodernism." In Fraser and Nicholson, eds., *Feminism/Postmodernism,* 19–38. New York: Routledge.

Freud, Sigmund. 1962 [1919]. "The Uncanny." In *The Standard Edition of the Complete Psychological Works of Sigmund Freud.* Ed. James Strachey. Vol. 17, 219–52. London: Hogarth Press and the Institute of Psychoanalysis.

Fuentes, Annette, and Barbara Ehrenreich. 1983. *Women in the Global Factory.* Boston: South End Press.

Fusco, Coco. 1989. "The Border Art Workshop/Taller de Arte Fronterizo, Interview with Guillermo Gomez-Peña and Emily Hicks." *Third Text* 7:53–76.

Fuss, Diana. 1989. *Essentially Speaking: Feminism, Nature, and Difference.* New York: Routledge.

Gabriel, Teshome. 1989. "Theses on Memory and Identity: The Search for the Origins of the Nile River." *Emergences* 1:131–38.

Gal, Susan. 1991. "Between Speech and Silence: The Problematics of Research on Language and Gender." In Micaela di Leonardo, ed., *Gender at the Crossroads of Knowledge,* 175–203. Berkeley: University of California Press.

Gallin, Alice. 1994. "Cultural Defense: Undermining the Policies Against Domestic Violence." *Boston College Law Review* 35 (3):723–45.

Gates, Henry Louis Jr., ed., 1991. *Bearing Witness: Selections from African American Autobiography in the Twentieth Century.* New York: Pantheon.

———, ed. 1986. *"Race," Writing, and Difference.* Chicago: University of Chicago Press.

Geertz, Clifford. 1973. *The Interpretation of Cultures.* New York: Basic Books.

———. 1966. "Religion as a Cultural System." In M. Banton, ed., *Anthropological Approaches to the Study of Religion.* London: Tavistock.

Geertz, Hildred. 1995. *Images of Power: Balinese Paintings Made for Gregory Bateson and Margaret Mead.* Honolulu: University of Hawaii Press.

Ghanayim, Muhammad Hamza. 1988. "The Land of Fire." *Politika* 278:24–66 (in Hebrew).

Gilroy, Paul. 1993. *The Black Atlantic: Modernity and Double Consciousness.* London: Verso.

———. 1992a. "Masters, Slaves, and the Antinomies of Modernity." Talk given at the Center for Comparative Studies in History, Culture and Society, University of California at Davis, April 6.

———. 1992b. "Cultural Studies and Ethnic Absolutism." In Lawrence Grossberg et al., eds., *Cultural Studies,* 187–98. New York: Routledge.

———. 1990/91. " 'It Ain't Where You're from, It's Where You're at': The Dialectics of Diasporic Identification." *Third Text* 13 (Winter):3–16.

———. 1990. "One Nation Under a Groove. The Cultural Politics of 'Race' and Racism in Britain." In David Theo Goldberg, ed., *Anatomy of Racism,* 263–82. Minneapolis: University of Minnesota Press.

———. 1987. *"There Ain't No Black in the Union Jack": The Cultural Politics of "Race" and Nation.* London: Hutchinson.

Giudice, Fausto. 1992. *Arabicide: Une chronique française 1970–1991.* Paris: La Découverte.

Goldberg, David Theo. 1993. *Racist Culture: Philosophy and the Politics of Meaning.* Oxford: Basil Blackwell.

Goldberg, Harvey. 1972. *Cave Dwellers and Citrus Growers: A Jewish Community in Libya and Israel.* Cambridge: Cambridge University Press.

Goldman, Antony. 1993. "The Man from Oran." *Focus on Africa* (April):81.

Gong, Ted. 1980. "Approaching Cultural Change Through Literature: From Chinese to Chinese American." *Amerasia Journal* 7 (1):73–88.

Gorce, Paul-Marie de la. 1991. "Chirac joue du tam-tam." *Jeune Afrique* (July 3–9):30–31.

Gordon, Linda. 1988. *Heroes of Their Own Lives: The Politics and History of Family Violence.* New York: Viking Penguin.

Goytisolo, Juan. 1987a. *Landscapes After the Battle.* Trans. Helen Lane. New York: Seaver Books.

———. 1987b. *Space in Motion.* Trans. Helen Lane. New York: Lumen Books.

Graburn, Nelson H. H., and Jafar Jafari. 1991. "Introduction: Tourism Social Science." *Annals of Tourism Research* 18 (1):1–11.

Graham, Julie. 1991. "Fordism/Post-Fordism, Marxism/Post-Marxism: The Second Cultural Divide?" *Rethinking Marxism* 4(1):39–58.

Gramsci, Antonio. 1971. *Selections from the Prison Notebooks.* New York: International Publishers.

Grewal, Inderpal. 1990. "The Guidebook and the Museum: Imperialism, Education, and Nationalism in the British Museum." *Culture and Education in Victorian England.* Spec. iss. *Bucknell Review,* 195–217.

Grewal, Shabnam, et al., eds. 1988. *Charting the Journey: Writings by Black and Third World Women.* London: Sheba Feminist Publishers.

Grierson, Sir G. A. 1916. *Linguistic Survey of India.* Vol. 9, pt. 4. Calcutta: Office of the Superintendent of Government Printing.

Grossberg, Lawrence. 1989. "The Formation of Cultural Studies: An American in Birmingham." *Strategies* 2:114–49.

Grossman, David. 1987. "Yellow Wind." *Politika* 230:12–71 (in Hebrew).

Guardian Weekly. 1991. February 3:4.

Guha, Ranajit. 1983. "The Prose of Counter-Insurgency." In Ranajit Guha, ed., *Subaltern Studies II: Writings on South Asian History and Society,* 1–42. Delhi: Oxford University Press.

Gupta, Akhil, and James Ferguson. 1992. "Beyond 'Culture': Space, Identity, and the Politics of Difference." *Cultural Anthropology* 7 (1):6–23.

Gutman, Herbert G. 1976. *The Black Family in Slavery and Freedom, 1750–1925.* New York: Vintage Books.

Ha'aretz (Tel Aviv). 1990a. "A Protest Conference Against Escalation of Ruining of Houses in the Arab Sector Will Be Held in July." June 17:A4 (in Hebrew).

———. 1990b. "The Cost of Cumulative Lag." July 8:B3 (in Hebrew).

———. 1990c. "Ghetto Facing Ghetto." August 12:B3 (in Hebrew).

———. 1990d. "The Housing Distress: Poured Kerosene on Himself and His Son." July 17:A5 (in Hebrew).

Ha'ir (Tel Aviv). 1990. July 13:Classified section (in Hebrew).

Hagedorn, Jessica. 1990. "Introduction to Tenement Lover." In Misha Berson, ed., *Between Two Worlds.* New York: Theater Communications Group.

Hall, Stuart. 1992. "Cultural Studies and Its Theoretical Legacies." In Lawrence Grossberg, Cary Nelson, and Paula Treichler, eds., *Cultural Studies,* 227–94. New York: Routledge.

———. 1991a. "Brave New World: The Debate About Post-Fordism." *Socialist Review* 21(1):57–64.

———. 1991b. "Europe's Other Self." *Marxism Today* 35 (8):18–19.

———. 1989. "Cultural Identity and Cinematic Representation." *Framework* 36:68–81.

———. 1988a. "Minimal Selves." *ICA Documents* 6:44–46.

———. 1988b. "New Ethnicities." *ICA Documents* 7:27–31.

Hall, Stuart, and Tony Jefferson, eds. 1976. *Resistance Through Rituals: Youth Subcultures in Post War Britain.* London: Hutchinson.

Handler, Richard. 1986. "Authenticity." *Anthropology Today* 2:2–5.

Hannerz, Ulf. 1989. "Notes on the Global Ecumene." *Public Culture* 1:66–75.

Hanson, Allan. 1990. "Probably Not: A Reply to Jean Jackson's 'Is There a Way to Talk About Making Culture Without Making Enemies?'" Presented at American Ethnological Society, 113th Annual Spring Meeting, Charleston, S.C., March 15.

Harasym, Sarah, ed. 1990. *The Post-Colonial Critic: Interviews, Strategies, Dialogues: Gayatri Chakravorty Spivak.* New York: Routledge.

Haraway, Donna. 1985. "A Manifesto for Cyborgs: Science, Technology, and Socialist Feminism in the 1980s." *Socialist Review* 80:65–107.

Hargreaves, Alec G. 1991. "La Famille Ramdan: Un Sit-com 'pur beur'?" *Hommes et migrations* 1147 (October):60–66.

———. 1989. "Resistance and Identity in Beur Narratives." *Modern Fiction Studies* 35 (1):87–102.

Harvey, David. 1991. "Flexibility: Threat or Opportunity?" *Socialist Review* 21 (1):65–77.

———. 1989. *The Condition of Postmodernity.* Oxford: Basil Blackwell.

Hegel, George Wilhelm Friedrich. 1977. *Phenomenology of Spirit.* Trans. A. V. Miller. Oxford: Oxford University Press.

———. 1976. *Science of Logic.* Trans. A. V. Miller. New York: Humanities Press.

Heidegger, Martin. 1969. *Identity and Difference.* Trans. Joan Stambaugh. New York: Harper & Row.

Henry, Edward. 1988. *Chant the Names of God: Music and Culture in Bhojpuri-Speaking India.* San Diego: San Diego State University Press.

Herrera-Sobek, María. 1990. *The Mexican Corrido: A Feminist Analysis.* Bloomington: Indiana University Press.

Hertz, Neil. 1979. "Freud and the Sandman." In Josué V. Harari, ed., *Textual Strategies: Perspectives in Post-Structuralist Criticism,* 296–321. Ithaca, N.Y.: Cornell University Press.

Hever, Hannan. 1990. "*Alpayim,* Double Portion: Hannan Hever Replies to Reuven Snir's Article in *Alpayim.*" *Kol Ha'ir* (Jerusalem), May 18 (in Hebrew).

———. 1989. "To Hit Achilles' Heel." *Alpayim* 1:186–93 (in Hebrew).

———. 1987. "Hebrew in an Israel Arab Hand: Six Miniatures on Anton Shammas's Arabesques." *Cultural Critique* 7:47–76.

Hicks, Emily. 1991. *Border Writing: The Multidimensional Text.* Minneapolis: University of Minnesota Press.

Holt, Thomas C. 1990. "The Political Uses of Alienation: W.E.B. Du Bois on Politics, Race, and Culture, 1905–1940." *American Quarterly* 42 (2):301–23.

hooks, bell. 1992. *Black Looks: Race and Representation.* Boston: South End Press.

———. 1990. "Postmodern Blackness." In *Yearning: Race, Gender, and Cultural Politics,* 23–31. Boston: South End Press.

Howe, John. 1992. "The Crisis of Algerian Nationalism and the Rise of Islamic Integralism." *New Left Review* 196:85–100.

Hull, Gloria T., Patricia B. Scott, and Barbara Smith, eds. 1982. *All the Women Are White, All the Blacks Are Men, But Some of Us Are Brave.* Westbury, N.Y.: Feminist Press.

Hulme, Peter. 1986. *Colonial Encounters.* New York: Methuen.

Human Rights Watch/Middle East. 1994. *Human Rights Abuses in Algeria: No One Is Spared.* New York: Human Rights Watch.

Hurston, Zora Neale. 1935. *Mules and Men.* New York: J. B. Lippincott.

Hussein, Taha. 1975. *The Future of Culture in Egypt.* Trans. Sidney Glazer. New York: Octagon Books.

Hwang, David Henry. 1990. "As the Crow Flies." In Misha Berson, ed., *Between Two Worlds.* New York: Theater Communications Group.

Ibrahim, Youssef M. 1991. "In Algeria, Clear Plans to Lay Down Islamic Law." *New York Times* (December 31):A4.

Ireland, Doug. 1992. "Press Clips." *Village Voice* (January 14):8.

Irigaray, Luce. 1985. *Speculum of the Other Woman.* Trans. Gillian C. Gill. Ithaca, N.Y.: Cornell University Press.

Ishida, Eiichiro. 1974. *Japanese Culture: A Study of Origins and Characteristics.* Honolulu: University Press of Hawaii.

Jacknis, Ira. 1988. "Margaret Mead and Gregory Bateson in Bali: Their Use of Photography and Film." *Cultural Anthropology* 3 (2):160–77.

Jagori. 1990. *Todo bandan; buland irade mil jul gayen; narivadei geeto ka sankalan*. Nai Dilli: Jagori (in Hindi).

James, Barry. 1991. "French Rap and the Art of Vandalism." *International Herald Tribune* (July 4):6.

Jameson, Fredric. 1991. *Postmodernism, or, The Cultural Logic of Late Capitalism*. Durham, N.C.: Duke University Press.

———. 1988. "Cognitive Mapping." In Cary Nelson and Lawrence Grossberg, eds., *Marxism and the Interpretation of Culture*, 347–57. Urbana: University of Illinois Press.

JanMohamed, Abdul R. 1992. "Worldliness-Without-World, Homelessness-as-Home: Toward a Definition of the Specular Border Intellectual." In Michael Sprinker, ed., *Edward Said: A Critical Reader*. London: Basil Blackwell.

———. 1985. "The Economy of the Manichean Allegory: The Function of Racial Difference in Colonialist Literature." *Critical Inquiry* 12 (1):59–87.

———. 1983. *Manichean Aesthetics: The Politics of Literature in Colonial Africa*. Amherst: University of Massachusetts Press.

Jazouli, Adil. 1992. *Les Années banlieues*. Paris: Editions du Seuil.

———. 1982. *La Nouvelle génération de l'immigration maghrébine: Essai d'analyse sociologique*. Paris: Centre d'Information et d'Etudes sur les Migrations.

Jeater, Diana. 1992. "Roast Beef and Reggae Music: The Passing of Whiteness." *New Formations* 18:107–21.

Jetter, Alexis. 1989. "Fear Is Legacy of Wife Killing in Chinatown." *Newsday* (November 26):4.

Joseph, May. 1991a. "Hybridity, Ambivalence, and Post-Colonial Theater: Hanif Khureishi's *Birds of Passage*." Presented at weekly seminar of Minority Discourse Research Group, Humanities Research Institute, University of California, Irvine, October 29.

———. 1991b. "Borders, Memory, and Post-Coloniality in Mustapha Matura's Writing." Presented at weekly seminar of Minority Discourse Research Group, Humanities Research Institute, University of California, Irvine, October 29.

Julien, Isaac, and Kobena Mercer. 1988. "De Margins and de centre." *Screen* 29 (4):2–10.

Junghare, Indira. 1983. "Songs of the Mahars: An Untouchable Caste of Maharashtra, India." *Ethnomusicology* 27:271–95.

Kahanov, Jacqueline. 1978. *Eastern Sun*. Tel Aviv: Yariv Publishers and Hadar Press (in Hebrew).

Kapil, Arun. 1990. "Algeria's Elections Show Islamist Strength." *Middle East Report* 20 (5):31–36.

Kaplan, Caren. 1992. "Resisting Autobiography: Out-Law Genres and Transnational Feminist Subjects." In Julia Watson and Sidonie Smith, eds., *De/Colonizing the Subject: Politics and Gender in Women's Autobiographical Practice*, 115–38. Minneapolis: University of Minnesota Press.

Kearney, Michael. 1991. "Borders and Boundaries of State and Self at the End of Empire." *Journal of Historical Sociology* 4(1):52–74.

Kennedy, Florynce. 1970. "Institutionalized Oppression vs. the Female." In Robin Morgan, ed., *Sisterhood Is Powerful: An Anthology of Writings from the Women's Liberation Movement,* 492–50. New York: Vintage.

Kim, Elaine. 1990. "Defining Asian American Realities Through Literature." In Abdul JanMohamed and David Lloyd, eds., *The Nature and Context of Minority Discourse.* Oxford: Oxford University Press.

King, Anthony. 1990. *Global Cities: Post-Imperialism and the Internationalization of London.* London: Routledge.

Kingston, Maxine Hong. 1977. *The Woman Warrior.* New York: Vintage.

Kirshenblatt-Gimblett, Barbara, and Edward M. Bruner. 1985. "Tourist Productions and the Semiotics of Authenticity." Paper presented at the meetings of the American Folklore Society, Cincinnati, Ohio.

Kishwar, Madhu. 1984. Introduction. In M. Kishwar and R. Vanita, eds., *In Search of Answers: Indian Women's Voices from Manushi,* 1–48. London: Zed Books.

Kondo, Dorinne. 1990. "M. Butterfly: Orientalism, Gender, and a Critique of Essentialist Identity." *Cultural Critique* 16 (Fall):5–27.

Koptiuch, Kristin. 1991. "Third-Worlding at Home." *Social Text* 28:87–99.

Koskoff, Ellen. 1989. "An Introduction to Women, Music, and Culture." In E. Koskoff, ed., *Women and Music in Cross-Cultural Perspective,* 1–24. Urbana: University of Illinois Press.

Koulberg, André. 1991. *L'Affaire du voile islamique: Comment perdre une bataille symbolique.* Marseilles: Fenêtre sur Cour.

Kristeva, Julia. 1980. *Desire in Language: A Semiotic Approach to Literature and Art.* Ed. Leon S. Roudiez. Trans. Thomas Gora, Alice Jardine, and Leon S. Roudiez. New York: Columbia University Press.

Kwong, Dan. 1991. Closing remarks. Treasure in the House Performance Festival of Asian Pacific Art, Highways Performance Space, Santa Monica, Calif., Sept. 14.

Labi, Philippe, Marc Daum, and Crazy J.-M. 1990. "Jack Lang: Je crois à la culture rap." *VSD* (October 31):40–41.

Lacan, Jacques. 1977. *Ecrits.* Trans. Alan Sheridan. New York: W. W. Norton.

Lacoste-Dujardin, Camille. 1992. *Yasmina et les autres de Nanterre et d'ailleurs: Filles de parents maghrébins en France.* Paris: Editions La Découverte.

LaFranchi, Howard. 1991. "Immigrants Cool Toward Saddam—and the Coalition." *Christian Science Monitor* (January 3):4.

Laing, Dave. 1992. "'Sadeness', Scorpions and Single Markets: National and Transnational Trends in European Popular Music." *Popular Music* 11 (2):127–40.

Lanfant, Marie-Françoise. 1989. "International Tourism Resists the Crisis." In A. Olszewska and K. Roberts, eds., *Leisure and Life-Style: A Comparative Analysis of Free Time.* London: Sage.

Lanfant, Marie-Françoise, Edward M. Bruner, and John Allcock, eds. 1995. *International Tourism: Identity and Change.* London: Sage.

Lanier, Pierre. 1991. *Les Nouveaux visages de l'immigration.* Lyons: Chronique Sociale.

Lapassade, Georges. 1991. "Qu'est-ce que le hip-hop?" *Hommes et migrations* 1147 (October):31–34.

Laporan, Seminar Sendra Tari Ramayana Nasional, Tahun 1970. Panitia Penjelenggara.

Lavie, Smadar. 1992. Blow-ups in the Borderzones: Third World Israeli Authors' Gropings for Home." *New Formations* 18:84–105.

———. 1991. "Arrival of the New Cultured Tenants: Soviet Immigration to Israel and the Displacing of the Sephardi Jews." *Times Literary Supplement* 4602 (June 14):11.

———. 1990. *The Poetics of Military Occupation: Mzeina Allegories of Bedouin Identity Under Israeli and Egyptian Rule.* Berkeley: University of California Press.

Lavie, Smedar, and Ted Swedenburg. 1992. "Displacement, Diaspora, and Geographies of Identity." Presented at weekly seminar of Minority Discourse Research Group, Humanities Research Institute, University of California, Irvine.

Leblond, Renaud. 1991. "Les Folles rumeurs de grasse." *L'Express* (January 24):61.

Lee, Lisa Ling. 1991. Interview. October 4.

Legaré, Evelyn. 1990. "Native American Identity: The Need to Be Other." Presented at American Ethnological Society, 113th Annual Spring Meeting, Charleston, S.C., March 14.

Leibowitz, Nicole. 1992. "Attali: 'Le Rap remplace le bal.'" *Le Nouvel Observateur* (June 18):20.

Lévi-Strauss, Claude. 1966. *The Savage Mind.* Chicago: University of Chicago Press.

Lhomea, Jean-Yves. 1991. "Un Entretien avec le président de SOS-Racisme." *Le Monde* (June 8):3.

Limón, José E. 1992. *Mexican Ballads, Chicano Poems: History and Influence in Mexican-American Social Poetry.* Berkeley: University of California Press.

Lipietz, Alain. 1987. *Mirages and Miracles: The Crises of Global Fordism.* Trans. David Macey. London: Verso.

Lloyd, Cathie, and Hazel Waters. 1991. "France: One Culture, One People?" *Race and Class* 32 (3):49–65.

Lloyd, David. 1992. "Ethnic Cultures, Minority Discourse, and the State." Presented at weekly seminar of Minority Discourse Research Group, Humanities Research Institute, University of California, Irvine, February 21.

Lorde, Audre. 1984. "The Master's Tools Will Never Dismantle the Master's House." In *Sister Outsider: Essays and Speeches by Audre Lorde,* 110–13. Freedom, Calif.: Crossing Press.

Los Angeles Times. 1990. "'Doughball' an Uneven Outing at East West," December 21.

Loupias, Bernard. 1990. "Le Rap français trouve ses mots." *Liberation* (October 20–21):44.

Lowe, Lisa. 1991. "Heterogeneity, Hybridity, Multiplicity: Marking Asian American Differences." *Diaspora* 1 (1):24–43.

Lubiano, Wahneema. 1991. "Shuckin' off the African-American Native Other: What's 'Po-Mo' Got to Do with It?" *Cultural Critique* 11 (Spring):149–87.

Lyotard, Jean-François. 1988. *The Differend: Phrases in Dispute.* Minneapolis: University of Minnesota Press.

Ma'ariv (Tel Aviv). 1987. "Racist Contemptuous Graffiti Written on Eretz Biton's Door." (October 11) (in Hebrew).

MacCannell, Dean. 1990. "Cannibal Tours." *Visual Anthropology Review* 6 (2):14–24.

———. 1976. *The Tourist: A New Theory of the Leisure Class.* New York: Schocken.

MacKinnon, Catharine. 1987. *Feminism Unmodified: Discourses on Life and Law.* Cambridge, Mass.: Harvard University Press.

Magnarella, Paul. 1991. "Justice in a Culturally Pluralistic Society: The Cultural Defense on Trial." *Journal of Ethnic Studies* 19 (3):65–84.

Maguigan, Holly. 1991. "Battered Women and Self-Defense: Myths and Misconceptions in Current Reform Proposals." *University of Pennsylvania Law Review* 140 (2):379–486.

Malkki, Liisa. 1992. "National Geographic: The Rooting of People and the Territorialization of National Identity Among Scholars and Refugees." *Cultural Anthropology* 7 (1):24–44.

Malkmus, Lizbeth, and Roy Armes. 1991. *Arab and African Film Making.* London: Zed Press.

Mani, Lata. 1991. "Cultural Theory, Colonial Texts: Reading Eyewitness Accounts of Widow Burning." In Lawrence Grossberg et al., eds., *Cultural Studies,* 392–408. London: Routledge.

———. 1990. "Multiple Mediations: Feminist Scholarship in the Age of Multinational Reception." *Feminist Review* 35 (Summer):24–41.

———. 1989. "Multiple Mediations: Feminist Scholarship in the Age of Multinational Reception." *Inscriptions* 5:1–23.

———. 1987. "Contentious Traditions: The Debate on *SATI* in Colonial India." *Cultural Critique* 7:119–56.

Mankekar, Purnima. 1993. "National Texts and Gendered Lives: An Ethnography of Television Viewers in a North Indian City." *American Ethnologist* 20:543–63.

Mansour, ʿAttallah. 1966. *In a New Light.* Tel Aviv: Karni (in Hebrew).

Manuel, Peter. 1993. *Cassette Culture: Popular Music and Technology in North India.* Chicago: University of Chicago Press.

Manzor-Coates, Lilian. In press. "Witnessing Historia." In *Liberation Theology: A Hermeneutics of Materiality.* Minneapolis: University of Minnesota Press.

Marre, Jeremy, and Hanna Charlton. 1985. "There'll Always Be Stars in the Sky: The Indian Film Music Phenomenon." In *Beats of the Heart: Popular Music of the World,* 136–54. New York: Pantheon.

Martí, José. 1977. "Our America." In José Martí, *"Our America": Writings on Latin America and the Struggle for Cuban Independence,* 84–94. Ed. Philip S. Foner. Trans. Elinor Randall, Juande Onis, and Roslyn Held Foner. New York: Monthly Review Press.

Martin, Biddy, and Chandra Mohanty. 1986. "Feminist Politics: What's Home Got to Do with It?" In Teresa deLauretis, ed., *Feminist Studies, Critical Studies.* Bloomington: Indiana University Press.

Marx, Emmanuel. 1976. *The Context of Violent Behavior: A Social Anthropological Study in an Israel Immigrant Town.* London: Routledge and Kegan Paul.

Massey, Doreen. 1991. "A Global Sense of Place." *Marxism Today* 35 (3) (June):24–29.

McClintock, Anne. 1992. "The Angel of Progress: Pitfalls of the Term 'Post-Colonialism.'" *Social Text* 31/32:84–98.

McKay, Mabel. 1987. Personal communication. Spring.

McMurray, David, and Ted Swedenburg. 1991. "Rai Tide Rising." *Middle East Report* 21(2):39–42.

McRobbie, Angela. 1985. "Strategies of Vigilence: An Interview with Gayatri Chakravorty Spivak." *Block* 10:5–9.

Mercer, Kobena. 1990. "Welcome to the Jungle." In Jonathan Rutherford, ed., *Identity, Community, Culture, Difference,* 43–71. London: Lawrence and Wishart.

———. 1988. "Diaspora Culture and the Dialogic Imagination." In Mbye B. Cham and Claire Andrade-Watkins, eds., *Blackframes: Critical Perspectives on Black Independent Cinema,* 40–61. Cambridge, Mass.: MIT Press.

———. 1987. "Black Hair/Style Politics." *New Formations* 3:33–54.

Mernissi, Fatima. 1987. *Beyond the Veil: Male–Female Dynamics in Modern Muslim Society.* Rev. ed. Bloomington: Indiana University Press.

Messick, Brinkley. 1987. "Subordinate Discourse: Women, Weaving and Gender Relations in North Africa." *American Ethnologist* 14:210–25.

Mézouane, Rabah. 1990. "Le Rap, complainte des maudits." *Le Monde diplomatique* 429 (December):4–5.

Michael, Sami. 1987. *A Trumpet in the Wadi.* Tel Aviv: ʿAm ʿOved (in Hebrew).

———. 1977. *Refuge.* Tel Aviv: ʿAm ʿOved (in Hebrew).

Miller, Barbara D. 1981. *The Endangered Sex: Neglect of Female Children in Rural North India.* Ithaca, N.Y.: Cornell University Press.

Miller, Judith. 1991. "Strangers at the Gate." *New York Times Magazine* (Sept. 15):33–37, 49, 80–81.

Minow, Martha. 1990. *Making All the Difference: Inclusion, Exclusion, and American Law.* Ithaca, N.Y.: Cornell University Press.

Mitter, Swasti. 1986. *Common Fate, Common Bond: Women in the Global Economy.* London: Pluto.

Miyake, Perry. 1991a. "Doughball." Unpublished manuscript.

———. 1991b. Interview. May.

Miyoshi, Masao. 1993. "A Borderless World? From Colonialism to Transnationalism and the Decline of the Nation-State." *Critical Inquiry* 19 (4):726–51.

Mohanty, Chandra Talpede. 1991. "Cartographies of Struggle: Third World Women and the Politics of Feminism." In Chandra Talpade Mohanty et al., eds., *Third World Woman and the Politics of Feminism,* 1–47. Bloomington: Indiana University Press.

———. 1987. "Feminist Encounters: Locating the Politics of Experience." *Copyright* 1:30–44.

———. 1984. "Under Western Eyes: Feminist Scholarship and Colonial Discourses." *boundary 2* 12(3)/13(1):333–58.

Mohanty, Chandra T., A. Russo, and L. Torres, eds. 1991. *Third World Women and the Politics of Feminism.* Bloomington: Indiana University Press.

Montejano, David. 1987. *Anglos and Mexicans in the Making of Texas, 1836–1986.* Austin: University of Texas Press.

Mooney, James. 1965. *The Ghost Dance Religion and the Sioux Outbreak of 1890.* Chicago: University of Chicago Press.

Moraga, Cherríe, and Gloria Anzaldúa. 1981. *This Bridge Called My Back: Writings by Radical Women of Color.* Waterton, Mass.: Persephone Press.

Moreira, Paul. 1990. "La Mal-vie des jeunes." *Le Monde diplomatique* 429 (December):4–5.

Morin, Georges. 1991. "Le Mosaïque des français du Maghreb et des maghrébins de France." In Camille Lacoste and Yves Lacoste, eds., *L'Etat du Maghreb,* 533–37. Paris: Editions La Découverte.

Morley, David, and Kevin Robins. 1990. "No Place like *Heimat:* Images of Home(land) in European Culture." *New Formations* 12:1–21.

Morris, Meaghan. 1995. "Life as Tourist Object." In Marie-Françoise Lanfant, Edward M. Bruner, and John Allcock, eds., *International Tourism: Identity and Change,* 177–191. London: Sage.

Morrison, Toni. 1992. *Playing in the Dark: Whiteness and the Literary Imagination.* Cambridge, Mass.: Harvard University Press.

Mullen, Harryette. 1987. *The Psychoanalysis of Little Black Sambo.* Santa Cruz, Calif.: Occasional Papers, Group for the Critical Study of Colonial Discourse, University of California, Santa Cruz.

Nader, Laura. 1969. "Up the Anthropologist—Perspectives Gained from Studying Up." In Dell Hymes, ed., *Reinventing Anthropology,* 284–311. New York: Pantheon.

Naficy, Hamid. 1991. "The Poetics and Practice of Iranian Nostalgia in Exile." *Diaspora* 1 (3):285–302.

Naïr, Sami. 1992. *Le Regard des vainqueurs: Les Enjeux français de l'immigration.* Paris: Bernard Grasset.

Narayan, Kirin. 1995. "The Practice of Oral Literary Criticism: Women's Songs in Kangra, India." *Journal of American Folklore* 108 (429):1–22.

———. 1994. "Women's Songs, Women's Lives: A View from Kangra." *Manushi: A Journal about Women and Society* 81:2–10.

———. 1993. "Refractions of the Field at Home: American Representations of Hindu Holy Men in the Nineteenth and Twentieth Centuries." *Cultural Anthropology* 8 (4):476–509.

———. 1986. "Birds on a Branch: Girlfriends and Wedding Songs in Kangra." *Ethos* 14:47–75.

Nash, Dennison, and Valene L. Smith. 1991. "Anthropology and Tourism." *Annals of Tourism Research* 18 (1):12–25.

Nathan, Debbie. 1991. *Women and Other Aliens: Essays from the U.S.-Mexican Border.* El Paso, Tex.: Cinco Puntos Press.

Nietzsche, Friedrich. 1989. "On the Genealogy of Morals." In Friedrich Nietzsche, *On the Genealogy of Morals and Ecce Homo,* 13–163. Trans. Walter Kaufman and R. J. Hillongdale. New York: Vintage Books.

O'Hanlon, Roslind. 1988. "Recovering the Subject: Subaltern Studies and Histories of Resistance in Colonial South Asia." *Modern Asian Studies* 22 (1):189–224.

Omi, Michael, and Howard Winant. 1986. *Racial Formations in the United States: From the 1960s to the 1980s.* New York: Routledge.

Ong, Aihwa. 1987. *Spirits of Resistance and Capitalist Discipline: Factory Women in Malaysia.* Albany: State University of New York Press.

Orsi, Robert. 1992. "The Religious Boundaries of an Inbetween People: Street Feste and the Problem of the Dark-Skinned Other in Italian Harlem, 1920–1990." *American Quarterly* 44 (3):313–47.

Ortner, Sherry. 1991. "Reading America: Preliminary Notes on Class and Culture." In Richard Fox, ed., *Recapturing Anthropology,* 163–90. Santa Fe: School for American Research.

———. 1984. "Theory in Anthropology Since the Sixties." *Comparative Studies of Society and History* 26 (1):126–66.

Paredes, Américo. 1971. *With a Pistol in His Hand: A Border Ballad and Its Hero.* Austin: University of Texas Press.

Park, Steve. 1991. Interview. September 8.

Parker, Andrew, Mary Russo, Doris Sommer, and Patricia Yaeger, eds. 1992. *Nationalisms and Sexualities.* New York: Routledge.

Parry, Benita. 1987. "Problems in Current Theories of Colonial Discourse." *Oxford Literary Review* 9 (1–2):27–58.

Parry, Jonathan. 1979. *Caste and Kinship in Kangra.* London: Routledge and Kegan Paul.

Partington, Paul G. 1977. *W.E.B. Du Bois: A Bibliography of His Published Writings.* Whittier, Calif.: Penn Lithographics.

Peres, Yohanan. 1977. *Ethnic Relations in Israel.* Tel Aviv: Tel Aviv University Publishing and Sifrayat Hapo'alim Press (in Hebrew).

Pfohl, Stephen, and Avery Gordon. 1987. "Criminological Displacements: A Sociological Deconstruction." In Arthur Kroker and Marilouise Kroker, eds., *Body Invaders: Panic Sex in America,* 227–54. New York: St. Martin's Press.

Picard, Michel. 1992. *Bali: Tourisme culturel et culture touristique.* Paris: Harmattan.

———. 1990. "'Cultural Tourism' in Bali: Cultural Performances as Tourist Attractions." *Indonesia* 49:37–74.

Piore, M. J., and C. F. Sabel. 1984. *The Second Industrial Divide: Possibilities for Prosperity.* New York: Basic Books.

Polman, Dick. 1989. "After a Killer Eludes Jail, a 'Cultural Defense' Is on Trial." *Philadelphia Inquirer* (July 2):1A.

Pratt, Mary Louise. 1985. "Scratches on the Face of the Country: Or, What Mr. Barrows Saw in the Land of the Bushmen." *"Race," Writing, and Difference.* Spec. iss. *Critical Inquiry* 12 (Autumn):119–43.

Pratt, Minnie Bruce. 1984. "Identity: Skin Blood Heart." In Ellie Bukin et al., eds., *Yours in Struggle: Three Feminist Perspectives on Anti-Semitism and Racism,* 11–63. Brooklyn, N.Y.: Long Haul Press.

Radner, Joan N., and Susan S. Lanser. 1987. "The Feminist Voice: Strategies of Coding in Folklore and Literature." *Journal of American Folklore* 100:412–25.

Rafael, Vincente. 1993. "The Cultures of Area Studies in the U.S." Paper given at conference "Beyond Orientalism?" University of California at Santa Cruz, November 12.

Raheja, Gloria. 1994. "Women's Speech Genres: Kinship and Contradiction." In Nita Kumar, ed., *Women as Subjects.* Charlottesville: University Press of Virginia.

Raheja, Gloria, and Ann Grodzins Gold. 1994. *Listen to the Heron's Words.* Berkeley: University of California Press.

Ramanujan, A. K. 1991. "The Flowering Tree: A Woman's Tale." Unpublished manuscript.

Randhawa, Mohinder Singh. 1963. *Kangra: Kala, lok te geet*. Delhi: Attarchand Kapurchand.

Rao, Narayana. 1991. "A Ramayana of Their Own: Women's Oral Tradition in Telugu." In Paula Richman, ed., *Many Ramayanas: Diversity of a Narrative Tradition in South Asia*, 114–36. Berkeley: University of California Press.

Reed, Adolph. 1992. "Du Bois's 'Double-Consciousness': Race and Gender in Progressive Era American Thought." *Studies in American Political Development* 6 (Spring):93–139.

Renteln, Alison Dundes. 1993. "A Justification of the Cultural Defense as Partial Excuse." *Southern California Review of Law* 2 (2):437–526.

Retamar, Roberto Fernandez. 1989. "Caliban: Notes Towards a Discussion of Culture in Our America." In Roberto Fernandez Retamar, *Caliban and Other Essays*, 3–45. Trans. Lynne Garofola, David Arthur McMurray, and Roberto Marquez. Minneapolis: University of Minnesota Press.

Rhode, Deborah. 1989. *Justice and Gender: Sex Discrimination and the Law*. Cambridge, Mass.: Harvard University Press.

Riding, Alan. 1992. "Parisians on Graffiti: Is it Vandalism or Art?" *New York Times* (February 6):A6.

———. 1991. "Europe's Growing Debate over Whom to Let Inside." *New York Times* (December 1):E2.

———. 1990. "A Surge of Racism in France Brings a Search for Answers." *New York Times* (May 27):I-1, I-16.

Rieff, David. 1991. *Los Angeles: Capital of the Third World*. New York: Simon and Schuster.

Rimonte, Nilda. 1991. "A Question of Culture: Cultural Approval of Violence Against Women in the Pacific-Asian Community and the Cultural Defense." *Stanford Law Review* 43 (6):1311–27.

Roberts, Hugh. 1994. "Algeria Between Eradicators and Conciliators." *Middle East Report* 24 (4):24–27.

Roediger, David R. 1991. *The Wages of Whiteness: Race and the Making of the American Working Class*. London: Verso Press.

Rogoff, Irit. 1994. "Daughters of Sunshine: Diasporic Impulses and Gendered Indentities." In Sigrid Weigel, ed., *Judische Kultur und Weiblichkeit in der Moderne*. Hamburg: Bohlau Verlag (in German).

Rooney, Ellen. 1990. "Discipline and Vanish: Feminism, the Resistance to Theory, and the Politics of Cultural Studies." *Differences* 2 (3):14–28.

Rosaldo, Michele. 1980. "The Use and Abuse of Anthropology: Reflections on Feminism and Cross Cultural Understanding." *Signs* 5 (3):389–417.

Rosaldo, Renato. 1989. *Culture and Truth: The Remaking of Social Analysis*. Boston: Beacon Press.

———. 1988. "Ideology, Place, and People Without Culture." *Cultural Anthropology* 3 (1):77–87.

Rosen, Lawrence. 1991. "The Integrity of Cultures." *American Behavioral Scientist* 34 (5):594–617.

Rosen, Miriam. 1990. "On Rai." *Artforum* (September):22–23.

Rosenfeld, Henri. 1964. "From Peasantry to Wage Labor and Residual Peasantry: The Transformation of an Arab Village." In R. Manners, ed., *Process and Pattern in Culture,* 211–34. Chicago: Aldine.

Rouse, Roger. 1991. "Mexican Migration and the Social Space of Post-Modernism." *Diaspora* 1 (1):8–23.

Rubin, Gayle. 1975. "The Traffic in Women: Notes on the Political Economy of Sex." In Rayna R. Reiter, ed., *Toward an Anthropology of Women,* 157–210. New York: Monthly Review Press.

Rushdie, Salman. 1991. *Imaginary Homelands: Essays and Criticism 1982–1991.* London: Viking.

———. 1989. *The Satanic Verses.* New York: Viking.

———. 1982. "The New Empire Within Britain." *New Society* 62, no. 1047 (Dec. 9):417–21.

Rutherford, Jonathan. 1990. "A Place Called Home: Identity and the Cultural Politics of Difference." In Jonathan Rutherford, ed., *Identity: Community, Culture, Difference,* 9–27. London: Lawrence and Wishart.

Safran, William. 1986. "Islamization in Western Europe: Political Consequences and Historical Parallels." *Annals of the American Academy of Political and Social Science* 485:98–112.

Said, Edward. 1986a. "Intellectuals in the Post-Colonial World." *Salmagundi* 70 (1):54–64.

———. 1986b. "Orientalism Reconsidered." In Francis Barker et al., eds., *Literature, Politics, and Theory: Papers from the Essex Conference 1976–84,* 211–29. London: Methuen.

———. 1983a. "The World, the Text, and the Critic." In Edward Said, *The World, the Text, and the Critic,* 31–53. Cambridge, Mass.: Harvard University Press.

———. 1983b. "Traveling Theory." In Edward Said, *The World, the Text, and the Critic,* 226–47. Cambridge, Mass.: Harvard University Press.

———. 1978. *Orientalism.* New York: Vintage.

Saldívar-Hull, Sonia. 1991. "Feminism on the Border: From Gender Politics to Geopolitics." In Héctor Calderón and José D. Saldívar, eds., *Criticism in the Borderlands: Studies in Chicano Literature, Culture, and Ideology,* 203–20. Durham, N.C.: Duke University Press.

Sams, Julia P. 1986. "The Availability of the 'Cultural Defense' as an Excuse for Criminal Behavior." *Georgia Journal of International and Comparative Law* 16 (Spring):335–54.

Sandoval, Chela. 1991. "U.S. Third World Feminism: The Theory and Method of Oppositional Consciousness in the Postmodern World." *Genders* 10:1–24.

Sangari, Kumkum, and Sudesh Vaid, eds. 1989. *Recasting Women.* New Delhi: Kali for Women.

Sarris, Greg. 1992. "Telling Dreams and Keeping Secrets: The Bole Maru as American Indian Religious Resistance." *American Indian Culture and Research Journal* 16 (1) (Spring):71–85.

Sassen, Saskia. 1993. "Rethinking Immigration." *Lusitania* 5:97–102.

———. 1991. *The Global City: New York, London, Tokyo.* Princeton: Princeton University Press.

———. 1982. "Recomposition and Peripheralization at the Core." *Contemporary Marxism* 5 (Summer):88–100.

Sayad, Abdelmalek, et al. 1991. *Migrance, histoire des migrations à Marseille.* Aix-en-Provence: Edisud.

Sayigh, Rosemary. 1979. *Palestinians: From Peasants to Revolutionaries.* London: Zed Press.

Schneider, David M. 1984. *A Critique of the Study of Kinship.* Ann Arbor: University of Michigan Press.

———. 1980. *American Kinship: A Cultural Account.* 2nd ed. Chicago: University of Chicago Press.

Segev, Tom. 1984. *1949—The First Israelis.* Jerusalem: Domino (in Hebrew).

"Seymour Hersh Sued over Book: Robert Maxwell, London Editor Deny Ties to Israeli Spy Network." 1991. *San Francisco Chronicle* (October 25): A12.

Shai, Eli. 1990. "Mothers, Sisters, and Step-Sons." Review Essay of *Alpayim* no. 2. *Kol Ha'ir* (in Hebrew).

Shammas, Anton. 1990. "Another Military Governor? Anton Shammas Replies to Reuven Snir's Article in *Alpayim.*" *Kol Ha'ir* (June 8) (in Hebrew).

———. 1986. *Arabesques.* Tel Aviv: Michaelmark Books and 'Am 'Oved (in Hebrew).

———. 1979. *No-Man's Land.* Tel Aviv: Hakibbutz Hame'uhad (in Hebrew).

Shamosh, Amnon. 1989. "Becoming an Israeli." Talk given at the Spinoza Institute of Jerusalem for the conference "Who Is an Israeli?—Israelis Viewing Themselves." Jerusalem, October 20.

———. 1974. *My Sister the Bride.* Ramat Gan: Massada (in Hebrew).

Sharma, Ursula. 1980. *Women, Work and Property in Northwest India.* London: Tavistock.

Sharpe, Jennifer. 1993. *Allegories of Empire: The Figure of Woman in the Colonial Text.* Minneapolis: University of Minnesota Press.

———. 1991. "The Unspeakable Limits of Rape: Colonial Violence and Counter-Insurgency." *Genders* 10:25–46.

———. 1989. "Figures of Colonial Resistance." *Modern Fiction Studies* 35 (1):137–55.

Sherman, Spencer. 1986. "When Cultures Collide." *California Lawyer* 6 (1):33ff.

Sherzer, Joel. 1976. "Play Languages: Implications for (Socio) Linguistics." In Barbara Kirshenblatt-Gimblett, ed., *Speech Play,* 19–36. Philadelphia: University of Pennsylvania Press.

Sheybani, Malek-Mithra. 1987. "Cultural Defense: One Person's Culture Is Another's Crime." *Loyola of Los Angeles International and Comparative Law Journal* 9 (3):751–83.

Shiblak, Abbas. 1986. *The Lure of Zion.* London: Al-Saqi.

Shohat, Ella. 1992. "Notes on the 'Post-Colonial.'" *Social Text* 31/32:99–113.

———. 1990. "Master Narrative/Counter Readings: The Politics of Israeli Cinema." In R. Sklar and C. Musser, eds., *Resisting Images: Essays on Cinema and History,* 251–78. Philadelphia: Temple University Press.

———. 1989. *Israeli Cinema: East/West and the Politics of Representation.* Austin: University of Texas Press.

———. 1988. "Sephardism in Israel: Zionism from the Standpoint of Its Jewish Victims." *Social Text* 19/20:1–35.

Shokeid, Moshe. 1971. *The Dual Heritage: Immigrants from the Atlas Mountains in an Israeli Village.* Manchester: Manchester University Press.

Singer, Daniel. 1991. "Le Pen's Pals—Blood and Soil." *Nation* (December 23):814–16.

———. 1988. "In the Heart of Le Pen Country." *Nation* (June 18):845, 861–64.

Smith, Barbara. 1983. *Home Girls.* New York: Kitchen Table Press.

Smith, Neil. 1984. *Uneven Development: Nature, Capital and the Production of Space.* Cambridge, Mass.: Basil Blackwell.

Smith, Raymond T. 1988. *Kinship and Class in the West Indies: A Genealogical Study of Jamaica and Guyana.* Cambridge: Cambridge University Press.

Smith, Valene L., ed. 1989. *Hosts and Guests: The Anthropology of Tourism.* 2nd ed. Philadelphia: University of Pennsylvania Press.

Smith, Valerie. 1989. "Black Feminist Theory and the Representation of the 'Other.'" In Cheryl A. Wall, ed., *Changing Our Own Words: Essays on Criticism, Theory, and Writing by Black Women,* 38–57. New Brunswick, N.J.: Rutgers University Press.

Snir, Reuven. 1990a. "'One of His Wounds': Palestinian–Arab Literature in Israel. *Alpayim* 2:244–68 (in Hebrew).

———. 1990b. "He Climbed a Tree: Reuven Snir Replies to Hanna Hever's Response." *Kol Ha'ir* (June 15) (in Hebrew).

———. 1990c. "A Robbed Kossak: Reuven Snir Replies to Anton Shammas." *Kol Ha'ir* (June 15) (in Hebrew).

Spillars, Hortense. 1991a. "Introduction: Who Cuts the Border? Some Readings on 'America.'" In Hortense Spillars, ed., *Comparative American Identities: Race, Sex, and Nationality in the Modern Text,* 1–25. New York: Routledge.

———. 1991b. "Moving on Down the Line: Variations on the African-American Sermon." In Dominick LaCapra, ed., *The Bounds of Race: Perspectives on Hegemony and Resistance,* 39–71. Ithaca, N.Y., Cornell University Press.

Spivak, Gayatri Chakravorty. 1990a. "Interview (with Walter Adamson)." In Russell Ferguson et al., eds., *Discourses: Conversations in Postmodern Art and Culture,* 105–12. New York: New Museum of Contemporary Art/MIT Press.

———. 1990b. *The Postcolonial Critic.* New York: Routledge.

———. 1988a. "Can the Subaltern Speak?" In Cary Nelson and Lawrence Grossberg, eds., *Marxism and the Interpretation of Culture,* 271–313. Urbana: University of Illinois Press.

———. 1988b. "Subaltern Studies: Deconstructing Historiography." In Ranajit Guha and Gayatri Spivak, eds., *Selected Subaltern Studies,* 3–32. New York: Oxford University Press.

———. 1987. "Subaltern Studies: Deconstructing Historiography." In Gayatri C. Spivak, *In Other Worlds: Essays in Cultural Politics,* 215–19. New York: Methuen.

———. 1985. "The Rani of Sirmur." In Francis Barker et al., eds., *Europe and Its Others,* vol. 1, 128–51. Colchester: University of Essex Press.

Spivak, Gayatri Chakravorty, and Ellen Rooney. 1989. "In a Word." *Differences* 1 (Summer):124–56 (interview).

Stepto, Robert B. 1979. "The Quest of the Weary Traveler: W.E.B. Du Bois's *The Souls of Black Folk*." In Robert B. Stepto, *From Behind the Veil: A Study of Afro-American Narrative*, 52–91. Urbana: University of Illinois Press.

Stoler, Ann Laura. 1991. "Carnal Knowledge and Imperial Power: Gender, Race and Morality in Colonial Asia." In Michela DiLeonardo, ed., *Gender at the Crossroads of Knowledge: Feminist Anthropology in the Postmodern Era*, 51–101. Berkeley: University of California Press.

Stora, Benjamin. 1992. "L'Intégrisme islamique en France: Entre fantasmes et réalité." In Pierre-André Taguieff, ed., *Face au racisme*, vol. 2, 216–22. Paris: Editions La Découverte.

Swirski, Shlomo. 1982. *Campus, Society, and State*. Haifa: Mifras (in Hebrew).

———. 1981. *Orientals and Ashkenazim in Israel*. Haifa: Mahbarot Lemehkar Ulevikoret (in Hebrew).

Swissa, Albert. 1991. "Bound to Each Other." *Kol Ha'ir* (August 16): 50–52 (in Hebrew).

———. 1990. *The Bound*. Tel Aviv: Hakibbutz Hame'uhad (in Hebrew).

Taguieff, Pierre-André, ed. 1991–1992. *Face au racisme*. 2 vols. Paris: Editions La Découverte.

Talha, Larbi. 1991. "La Main-d'oeuvre émigrée en mutation." In Camille Lacoste and Yves Lacoste, eds., *L'Etat du Maghreb*, 497–500. Paris: Editions La Découverte.

Tan, Amy. 1989. *The Joy Luck Club*. New York: G. P. Putnam.

Taussig, Michael. 1993. *Mimesis and Alterity: A Particular History of the Senses*. New York: Routledge.

———. 1987. *Shamanism, Colonialism, and the Wild Man: A Study in Terror and Healing*. Chicago: University of Chicago Press.

Tawadros, Gilane. 1989. "Beyond the Boundary: The Work of Three Black Women Artists in Britain." *Third Text* 8/9:121–50.

Tharu, Susie, and K. Lalita. 1991. *Women Writing in India: 600 B.C. to the Present*. New York: Feminist Press.

Thompson, Mark. 1985. "The Cultural Defense." *Student Lawyer* 14 (1):24–29.

Torstrick, Rebecca L. 1993. "Raising and Rupturing Boundaries: The Politics of Identity in Acre, Israel." Ph.D. diss., Department of Anthropology, Washington University, St. Louis.

Tourancheau, Patricia. 1991. " 'Assistance sécurité': Epinglée par police." *Libération* (March 30–31):19.

Trawick, Margaret. 1991. "Wandering Lost: A Landless Laborer's Sense of Place and Self." In A. Appadurai, F. Korom, and M. Mills, eds., *Gender, Genre and Power in South Asian Expressive Traditions*, 224–66. Philadelphia: University of Pennsylvania Press.

Trinh, T. Minh-ha. 1991. *When the Moon Waxes Red*. New York: Routledge.

———. 1990. "Not You/Like You: Post-Colonial Women and the Interlocking Questions of Identity and Difference." In Gloria Anzaldúa, ed., *Making Face, Making Soul/Haciendo Caras*, 371–75. San Francisco: Aunt Lute Foundation.

———. 1989. *Woman, Native, Other: Writing Postcoloniality and Feminism*. Bloomington: Indiana University Press.

Turner, Frederick Jackson. 1963. *The Significance of the Frontier in American History*. Ed. Harold P. Simonson. New York: Frederick Ungar.

Turner, Victor, and Edward M. Bruner, eds. 1986. *The Anthropology of Experience.* Urbana: University of Illinois Press.

Uno, Kathleen S. (in press). *Motherhood, Childhood, and State in Early Twentieth Century Japan.* Honolulu: University of Hawaii Press.

———. 1991. "Women and Changes in the Household Division of Labor." In Gail Bernstein, ed., *Recreating Japanese Women, 1600–1945,* 17–41. Berkeley: University of California Press.

Urla, Jacqueline. 1993. "Contesting Modernities: Language Standardization and the Production of an Ancient/Modern Basque Culture." *Critique of Anthropology* 13(2):101–18.

Urry, John. 1990. *The Tourist Gaze: Leisure and Travel in Contemporary Societies.* London: Sage.

Vickers, Adrian. 1989. *Bali: A Paradise Created.* Berkeley: Periplus Editions.

Videau, André. 1991. "À la recherche de la culture immigrée." *Hommes et migrations* 1144 (June):35–39.

Virolle-Souibès, Marie. 1993. "Le Raï de Cheikha Rimitti." *Mediterraneans* 4:103–15.

———. 1989. "Le raï entre résistances et récupération." *Revue d'études du monde musulman et méditerranéen* 51:47–62.

———. 1988a. "Le ray, côté femmes: Entre alchimie de la douleur et spleen sans idéal, quelques fragments de discours hédonique." *Peuples méditerranéens* 44–45:193–220.

———. 1988b. "Ce que chanter erray veut dire: Prelude à d'autres couplets." *Cahiers de littérature orale* 23:177–208.

Viswesvaran, Kamala. 1994. *Fictions of Feminist Ethnography.* Minneapolis: University of Minnesota Press.

Vivier, Jean-Pierre. 1991a. "Culture hip-hop et politique de la ville." *Hommes et migrations* 1147 (October):35–44.

———. 1991b. *Culture hip-hop et politique de la ville.* Paris: Centre d'Etudes et d'Actions Sociales de Paris.

———. 1991c. *"Bandes de zoulous" et culture hip-hop: Revue de presse (mai 1990–mars 1991).* Paris: Centre d'Etudes et d'Actions Sociales de Paris.

———. 1991d. *"Malaises" des jeunes et politique de la ville: Revue de presse (octobre 1990–août 1991).* Paris: Centre d'Etudes et d'Actions Sociales de Paris.

Volpp, Leti. 1994. "(Mis)identifying Culture: Asian Women and the 'Cultural Defense.'" *Harvard Women's Law Journal* 17:57–101.

Vyathit, Gautam. 1980. *Dholru: Himachal ki lok gathae.* Palampur: Sheela Prakashan.

———. 1973. *Kangri lok geet.* Palampur: Sheela Prakashan.

Wallace, A. F. C. 1970. *The Death and Rebirth of the Seneca.* New York: Knopf.

Weedon, Chris. 1987. *Feminist Practice and Poststructuralist Theory.* London: Basil Blackwell.

Weingrod, Alex. 1965. *Israel: Group Relations in a New Society.* London: Pall Mall.

West, Cornel. 1988. "Marxism and the Specificity of Afro-American Oppression." In Cary Nelson and Lawrence Grossberg, eds., *Marxism and the Interpretation of Culture,* 17–33. Urbana: University of Illinois Press.

———. 1987. "Race and Social Theory: Towards a Genealogical Materialist Analysis." In Michael Davis et al., eds., *American Year Left Yearbook* 2:74–90. London: Verso Press.

———. 1982. "A Genealogy of Modern Racism." In Cornel West, *Prophesy Deliverance! An Afro-American Revolutionary Christianity,* 47–65. Philadelphia: Westminster Press.

Wideman, John Edgar. 1986. Introduction. In W.E.B. Du Bois, *The Souls of Black Folk,* xi–xvi. New York: Library of America.

Wieviorka, Michel. 1992. *La France raciste.* Paris: Editions du Seuil.

Williams, Patricia. 1991. *The Alchemy of Race and Rights: Diary of a Law Professor.* Cambridge, Mass.: Harvard University Press.

Williams, Patrick and Laura Chrisman. 1994. *Colonial Discourse and Post-Colonial Theory: A Reader.* New York: Columbia University Press.

Williams, Raymond. 1991. "Base and Superstructure in Marxist Cultural Theory." In Chandra Mukerji and Michael Schudson, eds., *Rethinking Popular Culture,* 407–23. Berkeley: University of California Press.

———. 1977. *Marxism and Literature.* Oxford: Oxford University Press.

Willis, Paul. 1977. *Learning to Labor.* New York: Columbia University Press.

WOMAD (World of Music and Dance). 1990. Festival program. Toronto, August.

Women Against Fundamentalism. 1989. Press statement, March 9. *Feminist Review* 33 (Winter):110.

Woo, Deborah. 1989. "*The People* v. *Fumiko Kimura:* But Which People?" *International Journal of the Sociology of Law* 17:403–28.

Worsley, Peter. 1968. *The Trumpet Shall Sound: A Study of "Cargo" Cults in Melanesia.* New York: Schocken.

Yamada, Mitsuye. 1976. *Camp Notes.* San Lorenzo, Calif.: Shameless Hussy Press.

Yemini, Ben-Dror. 1986. *Political Punch.* Haifa: Mifras (in Hebrew).

Young, Robert. 1990. *White Mythologies: Writing History and the West.* New York: Routledge.

Yúdice, George. 1992. "We Are Not the World." *Social Text* 31/32:202–16.

Zavella, Patricia. 1987. "The Problematic Relationship of Feminism and Chicana Studies." Paper delivered at the Conference on Women: Culture, Conflict, and Consensus. University of California, Los Angeles, February 21.

INDEX

Smadar Lavie is Associate Professor of Anthropology and Critical Theory at the University of California, Davis. She is the author of *Poetics of Military Occupation* and coeditor of *Creativity/Anthropology*. She is currently working on a book about Third World (Palestinian and Mizrahim) Israeli writers.

Ted Swedenburg is Assistant Professor of Anthropology at the American University in Cairo and the author of *Memories of Revolt: The 1936–1939 Rebellion and the Palestinian National Past*. He is currently studying how diasporic, ethnic, and national identities are articulated through various genres of Arab-Islamic musics.

Norma Alarcón is Associate Professor of Ethnic, Chicano, and Women's Studies at the University of California, Berkeley. She is the author of a book on the Mexican writer Rosario Castellanos and of numerous essays on Chicana feminist discourse. She is the translator into Spanish of the well-known book *This Bridge Called My Back*.

Edward M. Bruner is Professor Emeritus of Anthropology and Professor Emeritus of Criticism and Interpretive Theory at the University of Illinois, Urbana. He has published numerous articles in professional journals and his edited volumes include *Art, Ritual, and Society in Indonesia* (with Judith Becker), *Text, Play, and Story: The Construction and Reconstruction of Self and Society*, and *The Anthropology of Experience* (with Victor W. Turner). He is a past president of the American Ethnological Society and the Society for Humanistic Anthropology. He is currently working on a comparative study of tourist performances.

Nahum D. Chandler is Assistant Professor in the Department of English at Duke University. In addition to his work on W.E.B. Du Bois, he writes on the history of scholarship on African Americans in the United States.

Ruth Frankenberg is Associate Professor of American Studies at the University of California, Davis. She is author of *White Women, Race Matters: The Social Construction of Whiteness*, and editor of *Local Whitenesses, Localizing Whiteness.*

Joan Gross is Associate Professor of Anthropology at Oregon State University, where she teaches courses on linguistic anthropology and popular culture. She is working on a manuscript on heteroglossia and mimesis in the puppet theater of Liège, Belgium.

Dorinne Kondo is MacArthur Associate Professor of Women's Studies and Anthropology at Pomona College. She is the author of *Crafting Selves: Power, Gender, and Discourses of Identity* and the forthcoming *About Face: Fashion, Theater, (Counter) Orientalism*. An aspiring playwright, Kondo was a dramaturge for the world premier of Anna Deavere Smith's play *Twilight: Los Angeles 1992* at the Mark Taper Forum in Los Angeles and was represented as a character in the version of *Twilight* that played at the New York Shakespeare Festival and on Broadway.

Kristin Koptiuch is Assistant Professor of Anthropology at Arizona State University West in Phoenix. She is a recovering Middle East area-studies specialist, now pursuing transnational studies in culture and political economy, especially assessing the effects of the third-worlding of the United States on urban culture and social space.

Lata Mani teaches Women's Studies at the University of California, Davis. Her work in Indian historiography and feminist and cultural theory includes the following: "Cultural Theory, Colonial Texts: Reading Eyewitness Accounts of Widow Burning," in L. Grossberg, C. Nelson, and P. Treichler, eds., *Cultural Studies;* "Multiple Mediations: Feminist Scholarship in the Age of Multi-National Reception," *Feminist Review* 35 (July 1990); and "Contentious Traditions: The Debate on Sati in Colonial India," *Cultural Critique* 7 (Fall 1987).

David McMurray teaches part-time at Oregon State University. He is writing a book on the impact on the northeastern Moroccan city of Nador of labor migration to Europe.

Kirin Narayan is Associate Professor of Anthropology and South Asian Studies at the University of Wisconsin, Madison. She is author of *Storytellers, Saints, and Scoundrels: Folk Narrative in Hindu Religious Teaching, Love, Stars and All That* (a novel), and a forthcoming book on women's folktales in Kangra.

Greg Sarris is currently Professor of English at the University of California, Los Angeles, and the former elected chairman of the Coast Miwok Tribe. He is the author of *Keeping Slug Woman Alive: Essays Toward a Holistic Approach to American Indian Texts, Mabel McKay Weaving the Dream, Grand Avenue,* and the editor of *The Sound of Rattles and Clappers: An Anthology of California Indian Writing.* Currently, his novel *Grand Avenue* is being made into a three-hour miniseries for HBO. He has written the teleplay and is executive producer of the movie.